The Early Life of William Wordsworth

The Early Life
of
William Wordsworth
1770–1798

A Study of *The Prelude*

EMILE LEGOUIS

NEW INTRODUCTION BY NICHOLAS ROE

Libris

Libris, 10 Burghley Road, London NW5 1UE

First published as
La Jeunesse de William Wordsworth
by G. Masson, Paris, 1896

This translation by J.W. Matthews first published
by J.M. Dent, 1897
Second edition, with additional Appendix, 1921
This edition first published 1988
New Introduction © Nicholas Roe, 1988

British Library Cataloguing in Publication Data:

Legouis, Emile
The early life of William Wordsworth,
1770–1798: a study of The Prelude by Emile Legouis.
1. Poetry in English. Wordsworth, William,
1770–1850 – Biographies
I. Title
821'.7

ISBN 1–870352–01–7 (paperback)
ISBN 1–870352–30–0 (hardback)

Designed and produced by Cinamon and Kitzinger, London
Typeset by Wyvern Typesetting Limited, Bristol
Printed and bound in Great Britain by
Redwood Burn Limited, Trowbridge, Wiltshire

Contents

BOOK I
Childhood, Youth and Education

BOOK II
The French Revolution. Moral Crisis

BOOK III
The Stages of Recovery

BOOK IV
Harmony Restored

New Introduction

Emile Legouis' *Early Life of William Wordsworth* was the first genuine critical biography of the poet to appear after Wordsworth's death in 1850. It was originally published as *La Jeunesse de William Wordsworth* (G. Masson, Paris, 1896), and was translated into English the following year. A century later the book retains the freshness essential to good biography, and an authority that establishes Legouis as the first modern scholar of Wordsworth. Looking back, his work stands as the example for a range of subsequent critics, editors, and biographers of Wordsworth, most obviously so in having treated Wordsworth's formative years up to 1798 and in taking *The Prelude* as the source for an understanding of Wordsworth's life and writing. The republication of Legouis' second 1921 edition of the *Early Life* in the present volume is welcome for giving readers renewed access to this seminal study of Wordsworth.

Before Legouis published his *Early Life* there had been three notable biographies of Wordsworth. The earliest was Christopher Wordsworth's two-volume *Memoirs of William Wordsworth* in 1851. An imposing memorial, his account was nevertheless selective in its consideration for Wordsworth's surviving family, and emphasised Wordsworth's life at Grasmere and Rydal after 1800. 'His life had not been a stirring one,' writes Christopher Wordsworth: 'It had been passed, for the most part, amid natural scenes of quiet beauty.'[1]* The *Memoirs* accordingly play down Wordsworth's turbulent years in France and London between 1792 and 1795. Wordsworth's involvement with Annette Vallon, which had not been public knowledge in the poet's lifetime, was understandably suppressed in the *Memoirs* and did not emerge until discovered by George McLean Harper in 1916; the relationship was not fully

* See notes on p. xxxvii.

elucidated until Legouis published *William Wordsworth and Annette Vallon* in 1922. Rather more surprising is Christopher Wordsworth's silence upon Wordsworth's allegiance to William Godwin and *Political Justice*. He passes over the time Wordsworth spent in London between February and August 1795, when he was meeting Godwin regularly. Instead, Wordsworth speeds directly from Windy Brow to Racedown Lodge thanks to the 'providential' legacy from Raisley Calvert.

Of course this is to criticise the *Memoirs* in the light of later scholarship and, particularly, for failing to treat matters which were to preoccupy Legouis in his *Early Life*. More immediately, however, the *Memoirs* formed a precedent for F. W. H. Myers's brief life of Wordsworth in John Morley's 'English Men of Letters' series. This appeared in 1880 and, as Myers admitted, was 'for the most part' drawn from Christopher Wordsworth's existing narrative.[2] William Knight was the first to enlarge upon this account, in his massive three volume *Life of William Wordsworth* published in 1889. Knight drew together a variety of hitherto unpublished material (poems; letters; Dorothy's *Journals*) and presented his *Life* as a 'quarry' of facts upon which 'future critics may work'. Unfortunately, however, Knight was frequently inaccurate in transcribing from manuscripts and in establishing significant dates in Wordsworth's life. Since his intention was to offer 'facts, and leave commentary alone', these weaknesses are not compensated by any insights Knight himself might have offered by way of a gloss upon his 'plain unvarnished tale'.[3] But Knight's reticence effectively left the field open for Emile Legouis' *Early Life of William Wordsworth* which broke new ground in tracing Wordsworth's emergence as a poet by means of a critical study of *The Prelude* and other early poems, particularly *An Evening Walk* and *Descriptive Sketches*. Where Christopher Wordsworth, Myers, and Knight had agreed that Wordsworth's '*Life*' is written in his WORKS' and refrained from further comment, Legouis was the first to attempt a sustained analysis of the relation between the two. In doing so, he brought about a fundamental shift in the critical perception of Wordsworth's writing, orienting it upon *The Prelude* rather than *The*

Excursion and upon the earlier, not the later, years of his life. Critical approaches to the poetry have of course varied since Legouis' day, and not everyone would agree with his involvement of biography with literary criticism. But the bearings of Legouis' work have endured.

Writing in 1930, Ernest De Selincourt acknowledged his own debt when he claimed that 'Legouis was the first to realise the paramount importance of *The Prelude*, to view his subject in the true perspective, and to throw the emphasis where it should be thrown'.[4] Before the *Early Life*, the status of *The Prelude* had been relatively obscured. There were a number of reasons for this. One was Wordsworth's unwillingness to publish the poem in his own lifetime, so that only his family and a few friends – among them Coleridge, Hazlitt, Lamb, De Quincey – were aware of its existence. Because of this delay, when *The Prelude* eventually appeared in July 1850 it was overshadowed by Tennyson's contemporary popularity. Matthew Arnold pointed out in the preface to his *Poems of Wordsworth* that 'Mr Tennyson drew to himself, and away from Wordsworth, the poetry-reading public, and the new generations'.[5] In his preface Arnold argues for Wordsworth's greatness, although his anthology was compiled from Wordsworth's shorter poems and neglected *The Prelude* except for four brief extracts. As De Selincourt was aware, Legouis' work on *The Prelude* effectively rescued the poem for the twentieth century, and was the precedent for his own parallel 1805 and 1850 texts of the poem as published in 1926. On that occasion *The Times Literary Supplement* acknowledged Legouis' example by asserting that *The Prelude* had only 'come into its own' with his *Jeunesse de William Wordsworth*.[6] De Selincourt's texts of *The Prelude* have in turn formed the basis for numerous subsequent editions and studies of the poem, up to the Norton Critical Edition of 1979 which presented the original two-part *Prelude* of 1799 alongside the extended later versions of 1805 and 1850. The relative merits of the three texts of *The Prelude* are the subject of considerable scholarly debate at present, and Legouis only had access to *The Prelude* as published in 1850.[7] Nevertheless the recent presentation of the 1799 text of the poem and, more generally, the reproduction of manuscript versions of Wordsworth's early poetry in the Cornell Wordsworth Series reflect Legouis' influence in 'throwing the emphasis' of his own scholarship upon the formative period of the poet's life.

Appropriately, then, Legouis begins his book in the marvellous springtime of 1798, and explores the genesis of *The Recluse* and *The Prelude* as a response to widespread disappointment at the failure of the French Revolution. His opening pages provide a concise description of the crisis in Britain at this moment. The British response to the Revolution had been divided since the appearance of Burke's *Reflections on the Revolution in France* in November 1790; during the following years this division had hardened with the outbreak of war, and the Terror in France. But by the winter of 1797–1798 an impasse had been reached. As France threatened military expansion throughout Europe, the friends of liberty and their conservative opponents in Britain found what Legouis terms 'a mutual and silent acquiescence in pessimism' (p. 3).[8] William Pitt's government and its supporters were alarmed at the prospect of a French invasion, and their fears were compounded by anxiety that the invader might 'find a thousand English hands outstretched in welcome, acclamation, and support' (p. 1). On the other hand the friends of liberty, who as Legouis rightly says had forgiven even 'the bloodiest days of the Terror' and hitherto would have welcomed a French intervention in Britain, were now finally dismayed by the 'overwhelming intelligence' of French aggression in Switzerland, 'the first refuge of liberty'. 'Nowhere in Europe,' Legouis says, 'was there a corner left in which it was possible to prolong that dream of regeneration and of happiness on earth, which for eight years had been so fearlessly pursued in face of the most cruel disillusion' (p. 2).

Legouis' account of this critical period has since been complemented – though not bettered – by only one other writer. In his essay 'Disenchantment or Default?', E. P. Thompson argues that Wordsworth's creativity in the spring of 1798 emerged from the vortex of the French Revolution. 'The creative impulse,' he says, 'came out of the heart of this conflict':

> There is a tension between a boundless aspiration – for liberty, reason, *égalité*, perfectibility – and a peculiarly harsh and unregenerate reality. So long as that tension persists, the creative impulse can be felt. But once the tension slackens, the creative impulse fails also.[9]

For Thompson Wordsworth's revolutionary experience and his poetry are continuous. His argument has not, I think, been seriously challenged by those who would present Wordsworth's creativity after 1798 as a function of political reaction to become – in Marilyn Butler's words – 'the poet of counter-revolution'. Butler argues that from 1796 onwards Wordsworth's poetry celebrates 'the Burkean conservative ideology', and that *The Borderers* reveals this incipient conservatism in Marmaduke's lament for Idonea, who

> was made an orphan
> By One who would have died a thousand times,
> To shield her from a moment's harm.

Butler shows that this is an echo of Burke's description of Marie-Antoinette in the *Reflections*, and she is right to present *The Borderers* as 'a stylized account of the French Revolution'. Her political argument collapses, though, because it is based upon a quotation from the play as published by Wordsworth in 1842. The echo from Burke is absent in the earliest surviving text of *The Borderers*, which can be dated to 1797–9; it represents a later revision, and is not evidence of Wordsworth's 'conservative ideology' in 1796.[10] E. P. Thompson's account of Wordsworth's position in 1797–8 is persuasive because he avoids reducing the complex interaction of politics and poetry to inaccurate and unhelpful clichés about 'counter-revolution' and 'conservatism'. But Thompson's thesis was not original. It derives from, and echoes, Legouis' recognition that political tension in spring 1798 gave impetus to Wordsworth's earliest plan for *The Recluse*.

'In the very heart of this crisis,' Legouis writes at the start of his *Early Life*, on the 11th March 1798, a young Englishman, but a short time earlier one of the most fervent reformers, now living poor and unknown in a lonely nook in Somerset, was writing to a friend . . . (p. 4).

– and he goes on to quote from Wordsworth's letter to James Losh:

I have been tolerably industrious within the last few weeks. I have written 706 lines of a poem which I hope to make of considerable utility. Its title will be, The Recluse, or Views of Nature, Man, and Society.[11]

Legouis says that Wordsworth identified the 'utility' of *The Recluse* in consoling 'a disheartened and sceptical generation' at a time when the friends of liberty had been silenced by repression, gone underground, or left for exile abroad – as Wordsworth and Coleridge were themselves to do in September 1798. But the confidence of Wordsworth's letter to Losh was short-lived. Wordsworth's doubts about his ability to fulfil his public calling as poet of *The Recluse* gave issue to the introspective and memorial poetry that began to flow during the winter of 1798–1799, while Wordsworth and Dorothy were isolated at Goslar in Germany. This poetry forms the earliest drafts of *The Prelude*, and it shows Wordsworth returning upon his own past to justify his election as poet of *The Recluse*.

Wordsworth's preoccupation with his childhood at this moment in 1798–1799 is the starting point for Legouis' *Early Life*, and it explains his decision to make *The Prelude*, never before 'an object of serious study', the focus for his book. Unlike previous biographers of Wordsworth, his intention is to offer a critical analysis of the poem in the light of Wordsworth's other poems and his correspondence, and by 'a suitable account of its relations to history' (p. 11). Legouis' method is empirical and determinist in establishing the relation of poetry to historical moment, and these are qualities that have been challenged in the deconstructive and theoretical criticisms of recent years. Nevertheless, as this reprint of the *Early Life* goes to press, one element in contemporary Wordsworth scholarship seeks a reconciliation of textual theory with a renewed interest in the social and political context of the poetry. Literary history is being revived in the guise of 'New Historicism', one strategy of which is to explore textual silence or 'erasure' as evidence of ideological pressures at work on the poet. So, for Kenneth Johnston, Wordsworth subdues troubling 'human, social implications' present in the landscape of the Wye valley to preserve his meditative hymn to nature as the 'soul/Of all [his] moral being' in *Tintern Abbey*: as a 'powerfully *de*politicized' poem *Tintern Abbey* is 'by that token, a uniquely political one'.[12] Marjorie Levinson elaborates Johnston's argument by claiming that an 'extreme disinterest' in social or political themes in poems written after 1798 indicates Wordsworth's 'resumption of those problematic themes at the level of image and metaphysics, precisely because they were deadlocked at a practical level'.[13] But she is making heavy weather of a point already made by Thompson in 'Disenchantment or Default?' and by Legouis in his discussion of the origin of *The Recluse*. Although Legouis may lack some of the fashionable terminology of 'New Historicism', his intention in the *Early Life* was in fact to deconstruct *The Prelude* in its social, political and intellectual context. Few biographers or critics of Wordsworth have shown a clearer grasp of the poet's place in his own time than Emile Legouis.

The *Early Life* is divided into four parts, each of which correspond to a substantial section of the 1850 *Prelude*. The first, 'Childhood, Youth and Education' treats Wordsworth's life up to the end of his time at Cambridge in 1791 (*Prelude*, Books 1 to 6). The second explores Wordsworth's experiences in France, 1791–2, his enthusiasm for the Revolution, and the connection between Godwin and Wordsworth's 'moral crisis' (*Prelude*, Books 9 to 11). 'The Stages of Recovery' comprise the third part of the *Early Life*, which includes Wordsworth's relationship with Dorothy and Coleridge at Racedown and Alfoxden, and the final part – 'Harmony Restored' – presents Wordsworth's achieved identity as a poet in 1798 (*Prelude*, Books 12 to 14). So the shape of the whole book is circular, like that of *The Prelude*, and concludes on the threshold of *The*

Recluse which Legouis had discussed in his introduction.

Following *The Prelude*, Legouis presents Wordsworth's early childhood at Cockermouth as that of a 'favoured being'. His sources for this period, besides *The Prelude*, were limited to Christopher Wordsworth's family history in his *Memoirs* and the 'Autobiographical Memoranda' dictated by Wordsworth in 1847. His account is largely anecdotal as a result, but he does emphasise the significance of the death of Wordsworth's mother. It was 'the signal for the dispersion of the family' and Wordsworth's departure for Hawkshead school in 1779 (p. 27).[14] Looking ahead, Legouis mentions Wordsworth's effort to revive 'the faded image of his mother' in his poetry, and he shows how in *The Prelude* the child's bond to its mother is a pattern for its relation to nature in later years. This territory has subsequently provided a rich source for a Freudian interpretation of the poetry in which, to quote Richard Onorato, nature becomes a 'mother-substitute' for the growing child.[15] Legouis falls short of an oedipal reading of *The Prelude*; a compensating aspect, though, is his discussion of how Wordsworth's ideas of childhood and nature relate to and differ from those of Rousseau. He gives a brisk résumé of Rousseau's popularity in late eighteenth-century England, demonstrating how inevitable it was that Wordsworth should have 'imbibed' his ideas about childhood and nature. But he also goes on to show that Rousseau's idea of childish vulnerability is at odds with Wordsworth's faith in the strength of 'simple childhood' (pp. 37, 55–67).

Legouis traces Wordsworth's 'independence of soul' to his years at Hawkshead Grammar School, and particularly to the freedom allowed him to roam the countryside outside school hours. He gives a short account of the school's history and of the village, both of which have since been explored in detail by T. W. Thompson in *Wordsworth's Hawkshead*.[16] But his principal concern is with Wordsworth's earliest spots of time in *The Prelude*, which he dates to this period of Wordsworth's life: that is, the raven's-nesting and bird-snaring spots; the boat-stealing episode; the drowned man of Esthwaite Lake. In such

moments, of course, Wordsworth recognised the sources of his
power as a poet, and it is in this sense that one should understand
Legouis' claim that Wordsworth was 'never . . . more truly a
poet than at Hawkshead' (p. 54). All the same, he does date
Wordsworth's consciousness of his own poetic calling unseason-
ably early. He mentions Wordsworth's schoolboy verse, but not
his most ambitious poem of this time, *The Vale of Esthwaite*. A
few pages later he remarks upon Wordsworth's unwillingness to
compete for poetry prizes at Cambridge University, but
Legouis' explanation of this is rather too generous. 'Wordsworth', he suggests,

> was even thus early unwilling to write verses to order. He had already
> too lofty an idea of the poet's art, and too deep a feeling for poetry, to
> regard it as a mere educational exercise (pp. 87–8).

He concludes that 'no vocation, except that of a poet, had
recommended itself [to Wordsworth] during his residence at the
University'.

Legouis' belief in Wordsworth's early sense of a poetic
vocation was doubtless underlined by his own detailed work on
An Evening Walk and *Descriptive Sketches*. His account of
Wordsworth's use of the language and poetic techniques of
earlier writers in these two poems has not been surpassed.
Moreover, he suggests that Wordsworth's later awareness of
faults in these poems explains his effort to 'reform' poetic
language in the Prefaces to *Lyrical Ballads*. 'Little given . . . to
self-criticism,' Legouis adds, '[Wordsworth] will throw the
whole responsibility for his errors upon his predecessors (pp.
146–7)'. This is an intriguing idea, not least because it develops
Harold Bloom's theory in *The Anxiety of Influence* that
Wordsworth's dominant anxiety as a 'strong' poet was his
relation to Milton. Legouis' reading of Wordsworth's emergence as a poet in *An Evening Walk* and *Descriptive Sketches*
extends the burden of priority to a whole range of seventeenth
and eighteenth century precursors besides Milton.

Yet, given Legouis' contention that *An Evening Walk* and
Descriptive Sketches are 'the earliest form in which Words-

worth's poetical genius found expression' (p. 121), the period to which one can date Wordsworth's vocation remains in doubt. Whatever Wordsworth thought of his future career while at Hawkshead and at Cambridge, becoming a poet was not at the front of his mind. His letters from this time right up until his move to Racedown in September 1795 reveal a marked uncertainty as to his future life. His letters to William Mathews in 1791, for example, refer successively to his 'indolence', his unwillingness to 'vegetate on a paltry curacy', and to his 'idleness'.[17] His reluctance to enter the church, law, army, or to become a private tutor encouraged him to visit France in 1791–1792 by way of postponing an awkward decision. As Legouis acknowledges, 'none of Wordsworth's biographers have laid sufficient stress upon the waywardness he displayed at this period of his life' (pp. 163–4). Recently, however, Kenneth Johnston has argued that Wordsworth's preoccupation with the frustration of his own 'talents' may be the key to identifying his authorship of essays on this theme in the radical journal *The Philanthropist* published by Daniel Eaton in 1795–6.[18] Whether or not this was the case, Wordsworth's 'waywardness' and lack of vocational direction was certainly one condition for his involvement in the revolutionary movement in France and his possible role as an 'active partisan' of that cause in Paris and in London.

The bicentenary of the storming of the Bastille, 1789–1989, is already generating a renewed interest in the impact of the French Revolution upon English Literature. As a Frenchman, Legouis was especially well qualified to write about Wordsworth's revolutionary experience, and this aspect of the *Early Life* was of particular interest to him as well as being of critical relevance now. He argues that Wordsworth's trip to France and the Alps in summer 1790 was significant imaginatively and politically. It introduced him to a sublime mountain landscape, the effect of which was that

> From this time forward there arose, in the back-ground . . . of his thought, forms of more majestic grandeur than those of Helvellyn. His imagination dilated that it might embrace a horizon wider and more fascinating than those of Hawkshead and Grasmere (p. 118).

In tracing the Wordsworthian sublime to his 1790 tour of the Alps, Legouis is vindicated by the Simplon Pass section of *Prelude*, Book Six. There, Wordsworth recognises the expansive power remarked by Legouis as the prerogative of his own imagination. Furthermore, when Wordsworth wrote these apocalyptic lines in 1804, he concluded his hymn to the imagination with a metaphoric reference to an army at war:

> Our destiny, our nature, and our home,
> Is with infinitude – and only there;
> With hope it is, hope that can never die,
> Effort, and expectation, and desire,
> And something evermore about to be.
> The mind beneath such banners militant
> Thinks not of spoils or trophies, nor of aught
> That may attest its prowess, blest in thoughts
> That are their own perfection and reward . . .
>   (1805 text, VI. 538–546)

In these lines Wordsworth's imagination has assumed the crusade of the French armies he had seen at Blois in 1792. Common to both is 'effort, and expectation, and desire' for a redeemed existence, although by 1804 the 'spoils and trophies' of revolutionary victory have been discarded by the self-sufficient power of the poet's mind.

As Legouis shows, Wordsworth's vacation in the Alps was encouraged by the writings of earlier tourists such as Horace Walpole, Thomas Gray, Rousseau, and Ramond de Carbonnières (pp. 112–14).[19] It was also his first opportunity to see the French Revolution for himself. 'A new sentiment awoke within him; one destined shortly to transform both his life and his poetry,' Legouis says: 'He became enamoured of France and of the Revolution. (p. 118) While not yet a 'passionate adherent' of the cause in summer 1790, Wordsworth's latent sympathy was to develop during his months in London after quitting Cambridge in January 1791. Although this was not his first visit to London, it was to this springtime that Wordsworth returned in *Prelude*, Book Seven ('Residence in London') as the period of his shaping experience of city life. Legouis contrasts Wordsworth's treatment of London in his poetry with the Juvenalian satire of Swift, Gay, and Johnson. But he underestimates Cowper's portrayal of London in Book Three of *The Task*, when he claims that Wordsworth was

> the first . . . to attempt to render in verse worthy of the theme, and without satirical design, the grandeur of London and the intensity of its life (p. 170).

This is much too solemn. Book Seven of *The Prelude* contains some fine instances of Wordsworth's satirical vein, in the 'strain/transcendent' of the young parliamentary orator, and of his sense of humour in listing 'the invisible girl' among the sights at Bartholomew Fair. When William Hazlitt recalled his visit to Alfoxden in May 1798 he mentioned the 'worn pressure of thought' upon Wordsworth's forehead. But he also recollected Wordsworth's 'convulsive inclination to laughter', and this is a part of his character that has too often been obscured since.[20] Writing to William Mathews in August 1791, Wordsworth mentions his lack of familiarity with 'modern literature' except for *Tristram Shandy*.[21] Perhaps he thought Tristram's inconsequential narrative appropriate for a period when his own life lacked immediate direction, but Wordsworth's poems do sometimes reveal a sly Shandean wit, for example in the protracted delay of a 'tale' in *Simon Lee*. However, Legouis says that in spring 1791 the 'shock' needful to rouse Wordsworth 'was at hand', and the evidence for this appears in some of Wordsworth's other reading at this moment.

Besides *Tristram Shandy*, it is certain that he had also recently been scanning 'the master pamphlets of the day', namely Burke's *Reflections*, Paine's *Rights of Man* and other contributions to the pamphlet war about the French Revolution. These pamphlets were all recent, controversial, and available on the bookstalls while Wordsworth was in London after January 1791.[22] Furthermore, Legouis points out that at this time Wordsworth may well have heard Edmund Burke fomenting the debate about France in speeches at the House of Commons (pp. 177–8). Like Coleridge, Wordsworth 'retained a deep impression of Burke' that later emerged in the panegyric to his eloquence in Book Seven of the 1850 *Prelude*. Legouis also suggests that Wordsworth's poetry did much to 'popularize Burke's political and social theories' throughout his life, a hint that has recently been followed-up in James Chandler's study of Wordsworth's creative debt to Burke.[23] It should be emphasised, though, that while Wordsworth may have been impressed by the speeches be heard in the House of Commons in 1791, his political sympathies were with the Revolution as presented in Tom Paine's *Rights of Man*; that is, as 'a renovation of the natural order of things' rather than the 'systematic ruin' described by Burke. In this way the debate about France in pamphlets and speeches encouraged Wordsworth's interest while clarifying his own political position. It also provides a further explanation for Wordsworth's decision to return to France at the end of the year.

During 1792 the Revolution provided Wordsworth with a transcendent cause that united all the potential careers he had left England to avoid: soldier, priest, journalist, and tutor. Legouis says that the 'inward revolution' by which Wordsworth 'became a patriot' took place at Blois, and was a product of his friendship with the republican soldier Michel Beaupuy (p. 195). Legouis' biography *Le Général Michel Beaupuy* was published in 1891. It has not been translated into English, which is unfortunate since it contains much that is relevant to Wordsworth's revolutionary experience – particularly its military context. In *Prelude*, Book Nine Wordsworth remembers how the sight of soldiers,

> Even files of strangers merely, seen but once,
> And for a moment, men from far with sound
> Of music, martial tunes, and banners spread
> (IX. 275–7)

– had convinced him that the Revolution was a 'cause/Good'. 'These are the feelings of a patriot,' Legouis comments (p. 201). One might also add that in this moment can be found the germ of Wordsworth's calling as a poet, and, specifically, his missionary purpose as poet of *The Recluse*. For Beaupuy and Wordsworth the patriot army was not simply defending the Revolution from European reaction; it had 'no object so narrow as the deliverance of a single nation', but was intent upon the liberation of the whole world (p. 208). 'Beaupuy in Wordsworth's eyes was the ideal at once of a warrior and of a citizen,' Legouis says, and he provided Wordsworth with a model for his own identity as a 'soldier-philosopher' (p. 212). In discussions together they planned a 'philosophic war/Led by philosophers', and their scheme finds an equivalent in Blake's vision of human regeneration as Urthona rises 'to form the golden armour of science/For intellectual war' at the conclusion of *The Four Zoas*. Six years later, in March 1798, Wordsworth was to identify the philosophic 'utility' of *The Recluse* with the fraternising vision of One Life in which – as Coleridge writes in *Religious Musings* – the whole of creation participates as 'Parts and proportions of one wondrous whole'. For Wordsworth the One Life transfigured revolutionary idealism in a universal democracy of creation, and simultaneously permitted the internalisation of benevolent action as a personal communion of 'intensest love'. In this way the 'philosophic war' Wordsworth had planned with Beaupuy in 1792 was sustained in the redemptive scheme of *The Recluse* in 1798 and, for that matter, as long as Wordsworth cherished the hope of writing his philosophic poem.

But how did Wordsworth conceive his role in the 'philosophic war' while at Blois in summer 1792, and at Paris the following autumn? Christopher Wordsworth hints in his *Memoirs* that Wordsworth had been 'intimately connected' with the Brissotins at Paris, and that he would probably have 'fallen a victim' to the Jacobins had he stayed in the city after December 1792.[24] Following the *Memoirs*, Legouis also claims that Wordsworth 'would doubtless have associated with the Girondists' in making a 'common cause' against Robespierre (p. 220). He may have been acquainted with Brissot, leader of the Gironde. He certainly knew the revolutionary journalist Gorsas and, given this contact, one can plausibly conjecture that Wordsworth would have fought his 'philosophic war' in the Paris *journeaux* – but that his purpose would now have been to save the Revolution from the extreme policies of the Jacobins.

At the end of his life Wordsworth told Carlyle that he had seen Gorsas executed at Paris in October 1793.[25] This mysterious third trip to France has not been verified, so far as I know, and Legouis does not mention it at all. On the other hand Gorsas is a likely inspiration for Wordsworth's shadowy career as a pamphleteer and journalist between 1792 and 1795. Having left Paris in December 1792, Wordsworth made straight for London. Legouis is surely right when he says that Wordsworth's inability to participate in the Revolution in Paris meant that 'he was impatient to take up arms in England on behalf of progress' (p. 221). But in *The Prelude* Wordsworth remained silent about his activities in London, and Legouis' account of 'Wordsworth as a Republican in England' is reconstructed from a number of other sources.

In many respects this is one of the most perceptive sections of the *Early Life*. We do know that early in 1793 Wordsworth was living in London and writing his pamphlet *Letter to the Bishop of Llandaff*, subtitled 'By a Republican'. Legouis gives a detailed reading of this pamphlet, and places it in the contemporary political context (pp. 221–38). He shows how political division in England had sharpened during Wordsworth's year away. The London Corresponding Society had been founded by Thomas Hardy in January 1792, and its practical campaign for reform developed over the following year. In the autumn of 1792, a number of these societies sent addresses to the National Convention congratulating it on recent French victories, and looking forward to a republic in Britain. Legouis points out that Wordsworth may have heard these addresses read out in Paris, but that after his return he found that they had served to encourage 'a rigorous reaction' against French sympathisers and reformists (p. 224). But Legouis overestimates the effect of political reaction early in 1793 when he says: 'The ranks of those who had at first been ardent supporters of the Revolution had daily grown thinner, and now became almost entirely empty (p.

225).' Wordsworth's own comment on the morale of the friends
of liberty at this time appears in his *Letter to the Bishop of
Llandaff*, where he says:

> The friends of liberty congratulate themselves upon the odium
> under which they are at present labouring; as the causes which have
> produced it have obliged so many of her false adherents to disclaim
> with officious earnestness any desire to promote her interest; nor are
> they disheartened by the diminution which their body is supposed
> already to have sustained.[26]

Wordsworth's immediate target was of course Richard Watson,
Bishop of Llandaff, one of liberty's 'false adherents' who had
taken fright at the execution of Louis XVI and published a
reactionary appendix to his 'Sermon to the Stewards of the
Westminster Dispensary' on 30 January 1793. Hitherto, Watson
had taken liberal views on reform and toleration, and his
recantation at this moment is a symptom of widespread panic
and unease. But as Wordsworth says, the true friends of liberty
had been undeterred by the September Massacres, the execution of Louis, and the trial of Paine in London on 18 December
1792. In her edition of *The Papers of the London Corresponding
Society* Mary Thale points out that despite government
sponsored opposition in the 'Association for the Preservation of
Liberty and Property against Republicans and Levellers', the
London Corresponding Society 'maintained [its] membership'
during 1793.[27]

So: given the available information, where is Wordsworth
likely to have been found in London during the early spring of
1793? If one takes his *Letter to the Bishop* and reads it against
Legouis' account of the political climate at this moment, it is
possible to make an informed guess. By presenting himself as 'a
republican' and identifying with the friends of liberty, Wordsworth clearly allied himself with the citizens in the London
Corresponding Society who were coordinating 'the general call
for a parliamentary reform'. There is no evidence that he
actually joined the society at this time, although after his return
to London in February 1795 he was much in company with its

leaders and spokesmen, some of whom he knew personally. He was certainly moving in similar circles in 1793. When Wordsworth arranged for the publication of *An Evening Walk* and *Descriptive Sketches* in January of that year, he took his poems to the dissenting bookseller Joseph Johnson in St Paul's Churchyard. At this time, and as Legouis says, Johnson's shop was a regular meeting place for intellectual radicals and reformists (p. 264). Here Wordsworth could have met assorted citizens such as John Horne Tooke, William Godwin, Thomas Holcroft, George Dyer, Mary Wollstonecraft, the brilliant young barrister Felix Vaughan, as well as old Cambridge friends such as James Losh and John Tweddell who were involved with reformist politics in London.

If this profile of Wordsworth in 1793 is correct, it explains his decision not to publish his *Letter to the Bishop of Llandaff*, as well as his subsequent reticence in *The Prelude*. Johnson is likely to have cautioned Wordsworth that his defence of Louis' execution in the pamphlet was too outspoken; shortly afterwards, in May 1793, Coleridge's hero William Frend was prosecuted for expressing identical opinions in *Peace and Union*, and banished from Cambridge University. But Wordsworth's unforthcoming recollection of this period in *The Prelude* is not so easily unravelled. It was not the result of apostasy, a deliberate refusal to own his former republican self. As E. P. Thompson says, 'when aspiration is actively denied, we are at the edge of apostasy, and apostasy is a moral failure, and an imaginative failure'.[28]

The whole of Legouis' book demonstrates that the poet of *The Prelude* is emphatically in touch with the aspirations of the revolutionary decade, albeit in a translated form. This is why it is a travesty to present Wordsworth as a poet of 'counter revolution' at any time while he still anticipated work on *The Recluse*. Wordsworth's silence about his connection with the reform movement derives from his sense of having failed those former associates in London, precisely by not making progress with that larger project. It was these men and women that Coleridge had in mind when he entreated Wordsworth to write a poem, in blank verse, addressed to those, who, in consequence of the complete failure of the French Revolution, have thrown up all hopes of the amelioration of mankind, and are sinking into an almost epicurean selfishness, disguising the same under the soft titles of domestic attachment and contempt for visionary *philosophes*. It would do great good, and might form a part of 'The Recluse'.[29]

While Wordsworth took stock of his qualifications for writing *The Recluse* in *The Prelude*, those despondent friends of liberty were still awaiting the poem that would sustain the 'philosophic war' to which they had been committed in former years. Wordsworth could approach the sources of his own calling in *The Prelude* – Beaupuy, the patriot armies, his thoughts of a 'common cause' with France – but he could not treat the readers of *The Recluse* as described by Coleridge without confronting the failure of his ministry to date. Hence the absence of any reference to his former associates among the friends of liberty in London, although that silence serves to amplify his self-dedication as poet of *The Recluse* at the end of *The Prelude*:

> Prophets of Nature, we to them will speak
> A lasting inspiration . . .
>
> (XIV, 446–7)

In the course of the revolutionary decade, Wordsworth's sense of his own calling evolved in response to successive moments of political and philosophical crisis. In this development Wordsworth's *Letter to the Bishop of Llandaff* is his manifesto as a republican and as a reformist, and it represents the sum of his experiences in France in 1792. It is also Wordsworth's first attack upon the government's 'infatuated' policy of war with France, and as such it is the threshold to the years of political and social protest when Wordsworth found intellectual guidance from William Godwin and *Political Justice*. Legouis was the first to treat Wordsworth's response to Godwin in any depth, and he argues that Wordsworth's own account of this period in *The Prelude* 'becomes almost an inward history of his generation' (p. 253).

For Wordsworth, as for many of his contemporaries, the

attraction of Godwin was that he offered an immaculate scheme for human perfectibility at a time when war, the Terror, and the British repression contradicted former hopes and expectations. In *The Prelude* Wordsworth specifies the outbreak of war in February 1793 as the first moment of crisis and disappointment. Legouis interprets this as a conflict between Wordsworth's patriotic feeling for his homeland, and the alternative loyalty of his 'love of humanity' which was rooted in France (p. 232). 'It was patriotism, in this painful struggle, that had to accept defeat,' Legouis says, and he goes on to show how, 'even in 1804', Wordsworth had not forgiven Pitt for 'this grievous crisis';

> Oh, much have they to account for, who could tear
> By violence at one decisive rent
> From the best youth in England their dear pride,
> Their joy, in England.
> (1805 text, x. 275–278)

Many other friends of liberty shared Wordsworth's anguish in 1793, and this disenchantment with the British government explains their unwillingness to blame Robespierre for the Terror which began in October of that year. In 1795 Coleridge was to argue that Pitt had forced Robespierre to adopt extreme policies in order to maintain the French war effort; 'Who, my Brethren! was the cause of this guilt, if not HE, who supplied the occasion and the motive?' And in the following year John Thelwall made a last vindication of France in his pamphlet *The Rights of Nature*:

> Notwithstanding the many adventitious horrors which have clouded the revolution, I regarded it as a great and glorious effort for the emancipation and moral improvement of the human race.[30]

Thelwall's experience of imprisonment, intimidation and assault by agents of the British government inclined him to accuse Pitt of introducing his own system of terror – but without the moral justification that Robespierre could claim. To establish Wordsworth's response to the Terror between 1793 and 1795 one should take bearings from John Thelwall, and Legouis' account agrees with this pattern almost exactly.[31]

'For [Wordsworth] there was a kind of fearful poetry in the Terror,' Legouis says: 'He felt "daring sympathies with power"' (pp. 244–5). During 1793 and 1794 the Terror encouraged Wordsworth to reconsider his idea of revolution and his political position in Britain. Like Thelwall, he was prepared to justify Robespierre's Terror as 'a chastisement for the crimes of the past', and an expedience forced by the British policy of war; 'it did not destroy his confidence in happier days to come', Legouis concludes (p. 244). On 8 June 1794 Wordsworth announced to William Mathews that he recoiled 'from the bare idea of a revolution'. While deploring 'the miserable situation of the French', though, his immediate purpose was to prevent the 'dreadful event' of civil violence in Britain which the government's policies of war and repression appeared certain to provoke.[32] However, if one turns to Books Ten and Eleven of *The Prelude*, Wordsworth has played down this domestic context and magnified Robespierre into 'the evil genius of revolution incarnate', as Legouis puts it (p. 245). Legouis suggests that Wordsworth's identification of Robespierre with Satan in *Paradise Lost* was the result of 'an ever-growing hatred of the Terrorists'. But the matter was more complicated than this, and derived from Wordsworth's own sense of implication in the Terror. By presenting Robespierre as Satan, Wordsworth sublimated his own responsibility for the bloodshed as a partisan of the revolutionary cause since 1792. Furthermore, by focusing all blame upon Robespierre and his followers, Wordsworth decoyed attention from his own failure to act decisively in Paris in 1792 so as to prevent the deterioration of the Revolution into violence.

At the time of Robespierre's execution in July 1794, Wordsworth was projecting a political journal, *The Philanthropist*, which would popularise William Godwin's ideas in *Political Justice* so as to achieve a peaceful reform 'and establish freedom with tranquillity'.[33] Legouis argues that, given Wordsworth's contact with Joseph Johnson and his intellectual friends, he must have been familiar with *Political Justice* 'from the date of its appearance' in February 1793 (p. 264). The effect of the war with France and the Terror was to consolidate his admiration for Godwin's abstract theories, but at the cost of his own 'natural feelings'. Legouis describes this hardening of Wordsworth's heart particularly well:

> the farther men seemed to him from truth and happiness, the farther he withdrew from the real world to bury himself in that of abstract thought, where the irony of events could no longer exasperate by its inconsistency with theory, nor an illogical reality confront the logical mind with its discrepancies and incoherence (p. 259).

He goes on to explain how the timely appearance of *Political Justice*, and the unhappy course of events in France thereafter, combined to make Godwin the 'intellectual master of all the young Jacobins of his country' (p. 260). But the effect of *Political Justice* on those young Jacobins has been misunderstood, and Wordsworth's account in *The Prelude* is partially responsible for this. In 1805 *Prelude*, Book Ten (Book Eleven in 1850) Wordsworth recalls that *Political Justice* encouraged him to withdraw from political affairs into abstract philosophy. Legouis follows this account in his *Early Life*, and he also claims that Godwin tried 'to reform the world from the seclusion of his study' (p. 263). On the contrary, Godwin was one of the most visibly active figures in metropolitan politics from the beginning of the French Revolution. When Wordsworth met Godwin at William Frend's house in London on 27 February 1795, they were in company with some of the most prominent and outspoken radicals of the day, including George Dyer, Thomas Holcroft, and William Frend himself. It may have been on this occasion that *The Philanthropist* as published by Daniel Eaton was initiated, with Wordsworth supplying the journal's title and contributing as an editor.[34] Godwin gave Wordsworth intellectual guidance between 1793 and 1795, as *The Prelude* recalls, but that is only half of the story. He also offered Wordsworth another chance to participate in the events of the day as an 'active partisan', specifically by using Godwin's philosophy to counter the threat of revolutionary violence in Britain. Wordsworth's 'moral crisis' arose when he recognised that a deadly abstraction was common to Godwin's philosophy and Robespierre's politics, and that by popularising *Political Justice* he might encourage the violence he sought to prevent. But that realisation was fruitful in another direction because it prompted Wordsworth to write *The Borderers*, and Legouis' discussion of this process marks the first serious criticism of Wordsworth's play.

'It was the Terror,' Legouis says,

> which gave birth to Wordsworth's tragedy. It is the work of a Godwinian, who, having at first seen only the grandeur of his master's system, is horror-struck when he suddenly perceives its consequences (p. 270).

Legouis' point is that Godwin's denial of human feeling and kinship in favour of an abstract concept of the 'general good' might be used to justify 'wholesale executions . . . in the name of public welfare' like those decreed in Paris during 1793–4 (p. 270). This recognition, Legouis says, was the starting point for Wordsworth's creation of the philosopher-murderer Oswald (Rivers) in *The Borderers*. He shows how Oswald differs from Iago in his systematic justification of murder, and establishes important similarities between *The Borderers* and Ann Radcliffe's *Romance of the Forest* as a further source for Wordsworth's play besides *Political Justice* (pp. 271–2). Robert Osborn's recent work for the Cornell Edition of *The Borderers* underlines Wordsworth's debt to *The Romance of the Forest*, and explores other sources for the play in *Caleb Williams* and *Paradise Lost*.[35] Osborn demonstrates the literary context of Wordsworth's play with great effectiveness; his work has been influential in deflecting critical attention away from *Political Justice*, and in concentrating upon the immediate dates and circumstances of Wordsworth's work on *The Borderers*. Legouis may now appear relatively limited in reading the play as an attack upon Godwin's philosophy. But his comments are still valuable for allowing one to see the play against a broad perspective of Wordsworth's political and intellectual development in the 1790s. In particular, Legouis claims that *The Borderers* 'purged' Wordsworth of the pessimistic view of human nature he had derived from Godwin, and assisted the process of self-restoration which would make him a great poet (p. 278).

The third section of the *Early Life* comprises the 'stages of [Wordsworth's] recovery' at Racedown in Dorset, and the benign influence of Dorothy and Coleridge at this time. At the outset, however, Legouis turns back to review Wordsworth's life between 1792 and 1795, and emphasises his isolation from his family and from Dorothy in particular. Because of Wordsworth's republican sympathies and his 'inexcusable idleness, his uncles and guardians left him to himself'. For personal and political reasons, Legouis argues, Wordsworth was attracted by 'a secluded life quite apart from his hostile family, and beyond the pale of a society with which he had no sympathy' (p. 281). In spring 1794 Wordsworth shared a brief but 'delightful interval' with Dorothy at Windy Brow above Keswick. After six months in London between February and August 1795, Wordsworth moved via Bristol to live with Dorothy at Racedown Lodge in Dorset. They were to stay here until June 1797, when they left for Alfoxden, and they never lived apart again for any great length of time.

Legouis uses Dorothy's letters and journals, as well as descriptions of her by Coleridge and De Quincey, to suggest her 'intense and distinct' personality. He is particularly concerned to present Dorothy as Wordsworth's literary mentor, watching over his writing from the earliest years, and he points to her constructive criticism of *An Evening Walk* and *Descriptive Sketches* as evidence of this (pp. 295–6). But despite Dorothy's anxiety that Wordsworth might be distracted by politics and 'miss his way' as a poet, *The Prelude* indicates that Wordsworth's own awareness of his poetic calling did not emerge until they were living together at Racedown:

> She, in the midst of all, preserved me still
> A Poet, made me seek beneath that name,
> And that alone, my office upon earth . . .
>
> (XI. 345–347)

Dorothy's presence reminded Wordsworth of his 'true self' by 'recovering his early capacity for delight and admiration' of nature. Legouis quotes extensively from Dorothy's Alfoxden Journal to show how her powers of observation and description countered Godwin's 'abstract thought', and returned Wordsworth to 'the ready wonder of his own youth' in which he would eventually recognise the source of his creative power (p. 297–304). For Legouis, therefore, Dorothy's influence was essential to Wordsworth's later development as poet of *The Prelude*. Furthermore, he argues that Wordsworth's recovery of his 'true self' was accompanied by a renewed power 'of seeing and loving humanity as it is'; 'by observation of the poor', Legouis says, 'Wordsworth restores one by one the feelings of which ideal man has been stripped by Godwin' (pp. 304, 312). The 'ideal man' promised by revolutionary change and by *Political Justice* gave place to 'man as he is' represented by the inhabitants of the countryside around Racedown and Alfoxden. And that rediscovery of humanity provided Wordsworth with the subjects for some of his ballads written at Alfoxden in spring 1798.

Legouis reads Wordsworth's *Lyrical Ballads* – like *The Borderers* – as a critique of Godwin and *Political Justice*. *Simon Lee* vindicates gratitude against Godwin's strictures; *The Last of the Flock* presents the shepherd's property as 'a vigorous instinct closely interwoven with the noblest feelings', not one of Godwin's 'vices'. Similarly, *The Idiot Boy* and *The Mad Mother* articulate 'the pathos of unreasoning affection' as a reply to the arid rationalism of *Political Justice*. Finally, Wordsworth's poems about children, *We are Seven* and *Anecdote for Fathers*, reject the Godwinian intellect in favour of the instinctive wisdom of childhood (pp. 309–15). While Legouis dates the 'most acute stage' of Wordsworth's 'moral crisis' to his residence at Racedown, his discussion of these poems shows a creative continuity in Wordsworth between 1795 and 1798 that is focused in the poet's changing relation to Godwin. More recent criticism of Wordsworth's *Lyrical Ballads* has turned away from Godwin to emphasise the diversity of these poems; their complex relation to literary tradition; and their role in Wordsworth's creative dialogue with Coleridge.

Robert Mayo's article 'The Contemporaneity of the *Lyrical Ballads*' (1954) did much to initiate this trend by arguing that Wordsworth's style and subject matter were not innovative when viewed in the literary context of the 1790s.[36] His work has lately been answered by at least three notable studies of Wordsworth's ballads, the earliest of which was Stephen Parrish's *Art of the Lyrical Ballads* (1973). Parrish acknowledged Mayo's 'abundant and persuasive evidence', but proceeded to show that Wordsworth's ballads were indeed innovative and that his radical genius was one aspect of his poetic and critical incompatibility with Coleridge.[37] Three years later Mary Jacobus explored Wordsworth's challenge to, and assimilation of tradition in *Tradition and Experiment in Wordsworth's 'Lyrical Ballads' 1798* (1976). Most recently, in *Coleridge, Wordsworth, and the Language of Allusion* (1986), Lucy Newlyn has used patterns of echo and allusion in both poets' work to establish their poetic relationship and 'the extent to which disparities mould their creative exchange'. Newlyn's first chapters trace the poets' earliest mutual awareness between 1793 and 1795 and she touches, inevitably, upon their relations to William Godwin. Similarly, Mary Jacobus's study had opened with an examination of 'The Godwinian Background' to *Lyrical Ballads* with reference to *Caleb Williams*, *The Borderers*, and *Lines Left upon a Seat in a Yew-Tree*.[38] For both Newlyn and Jacobus, Godwin forms only part of a more complex understanding of Wordsworth's creativity and his relation to Coleridge, but Godwin's place is of central importance nonetheless. Despite changing critical interests, Legouis' work retains a pioneering relevance for the most up-to-date criticism of Wordsworth, in his analysis of Godwin's influence and by tracing Wordsworth's developing relationship with Coleridge after their first meeting at Bristol in 1795.

Dorothy's effect upon Wordsworth had been to put him back in touch with nature, humanity, and his 'true self', although without offering 'any common bond of unity' from which he could form 'a comprehensive philosophy of his own' (p. 318). 'It was Coleridge,' Legouis says, 'who provided, or rather assisted [Wordsworth] to find, the one thing still needful to make him the poet he finally became, namely, a philosophy (p. 319).' Legouis acknowledges Coleridge as Wordsworth's philosophic guide, but he also emphasises the disparities between the two poets: in their childhood and upbringing; in their respective characters; and in their intellectual lives. 'Like Wordsworth, Coleridge was . . . a republican, a poet, and a philosopher,' Legouis writes, but he goes on: 'Yet beneath these surface resemblances, how deep and lasting were the differences!' Those 'radical differences' between the two poets preoccupied Coleridge in *Biographia Literaria*, and represent an important focus of contemporary critical debate in recent work by Stephen Parrish, Richard Gravil, Lucy Newlyn, and Thomas McFarland.[39] While recognising Wordsworth as the dominant personality and poet, Legouis also describes the nature of Coleridge's philosophical influence upon Wordsworth particularly clearly:

> Love as the law of the world, God as the soul of the universe, intuition preferred to analysis and reasoning for the discovery of truth, visible things considered as symbols of reality, all beings, including animals and flowers, regarded as 'Monads of the infinite Mind' – these, for Wordsworth, were all new and wonderful conceptions (p. 331).

Legouis rightly says that Coleridge gave Wordsworth 'the idea of a mighty synthesis', but he misleadingly suggests that it dates from the poets' first encounter at Bristol in late August or September 1795. On that occasion, Wordsworth most likely read Coleridge *Salisbury Plain* (which Legouis knew only in its later form as *Guilt and Sorrow*), and the poem confirmed Coleridge's earlier recognition of Wordsworth's powers in *Descriptive Sketches*. But Legouis is probably mistaken when he suggests that Coleridge responded by reading Wordsworth *Religious Musings*, and he wrongly implies that this initiated Coleridge's philosophic influence upon Wordsworth (p. 329). Wordsworth certainly admired passages from Coleridge's poem, and he may have read the extract published as 'The Present State of Society' in the second issue of Coleridge's *Watchman*, 9 March 1796. But he does not appear to have read the whole of *Religious Musings* until it appeared in Coleridge's *Poems on Various Subjects* in April 1796.

Between 1795 and 1797, Wordsworth and Coleridge shared political sympathies and literary ambitions. They knew each other's work, and had a number of friends in common.[40] It was on this basis that they met in June 1797, when Coleridge visited Racedown, and it is to this moment that their poetic and philosophic interaction can be dated. Legouis summarises the effect of this exchange concisely:

> After meeting one another on a more familiar footing at Racedown, the two young men felt that each was necessary to the other, and found it impossible any longer to live apart. On the 3rd of July the Wordsworths returned the visit of Coleridge, and on the 13th took up their residence in the country-house of Alfoxden, a couple of miles from Nether Stowey, where he was living. From this time a daily intercourse was established between them, and upon each its influence was continuous and profound (p. 357).[41]

In describing the Wordsworths' move to Alfoxden, Legouis arrives at the period of poetic creativity and political isolation that he had previously discussed in his introduction. Here, though, he introduces some of the other individuals who formed part of their community at Stowey. Besides Tom Poole, who had assisted Coleridge and Wordsworth to settle at Stowey, the company at various times included George Burnett, who had joined Southey's and Coleridge's scheme for Pantisocracy in 1794; Charles Lloyd, recently a pupil of Coleridge's; Charles Lamb, who visited in July 1797; and Citizen John Thelwall, political lecturer and poet, who arrived at Stowey on 17 July, shortly after Lamb's departure (pp. 359–368). 'For all of them,' Legouis says, 'the issue between happiness and despondency hung in doubt (p. 360).' It was finally resolved in the winter of 1797–8, when France invaded Switzerland. 'To the English friends of France, the blow was fatal,' Legouis says. Coleridge responded by writing his poems of political retraction *France, an Ode* and, in April 1798, *Fears in Solitude*. Wordsworth's thoughts on this occasion are not known, but Legouis argues that it encouraged his poetic creativity in spring 1798 as well as his earliest idea of *The Recluse* (pp. 378–380). In returning to this decisive moment, Legouis is now able to show how Wordsworth's exploration of his own childhood in *The Prelude* represents the culmination of his revolutionary experience in more recent years:

> He had believed in the Revolution, had believed in his own reason, because both alike had at first given promise of felicity for all mankind. And it was still in search of some assurance of happiness that he turned once more to nature. At last he recognised the principle of his existence; it was joy (p. 382).

With that recognition, too, came Wordsworth's realisation that the sources of joy lay in his own childhood and early youth: 'The idea of *The Prelude* was springing up within him, and before many months had elapsed the first fragments of it were written' (p. 382). In showing how *The Prelude* came to be written, Legouis also explains why the philosophic poem projected in *The Recluse* could never be completed. As originally conceived by Wordsworth in March 1798, *The Recluse* was intended to sustain the hope of 'felicity for all mankind' after the failure of France. But, as Legouis explains so well, Wordsworth's 'assurance of happiness' lay in the self-sufficing power of his own mind in relation to nature and to his own past. It was not, in the end, systematically explicable as a philosophy. In the fourth and final section of the *Early Life*, however, Legouis offers an assessment of the grounds for Wordsworth's achieved 'optimism' in 1798 and afterwards.

In looking back over Wordsworth's life, Legouis shows how easy it would have been for Wordsworth to 'miss his way' as a poet during his early years. Wordsworth achieved his identity as a writer in 1798 by 'a vigorous reaction of his nature' against the circumstances of his life since the death of his parents. For Legouis it is 'thoroughly characteristic' of Wordsworth to begin *The Recluse* 'just at the time when the invasion of Switzerland was ruining the last hopes which he had staked on the behaviour of France' (p. 386). His point is that Wordsworth's claim to be a poet of human consolation was based upon a profound awareness of 'how greatly men stood in need of consolation', which he had gained through his own recent experience (p. 389). Wordsworth – like Coleridge and others of their generation – was disenchanted with the prophets of abstract perfection, 'the philosophers and false professors' of revolutionary change and *Political Justice*. Wordsworth's distinct originality, though, was to combine 'feeling, instinct, intuition, and imagination' in poetry that is genuinely in touch with life (p. 401). To support this thesis, Legouis gives a detailed reading of *Peter Bell* to show how nature and imagination work to produce Peter's 'terror and remorse' and, in the end, his moral restoration.

However, it was the presence of Coleridge, above all, that sharpened Wordsworth's awareness of his own poetic identity. This came about not by collaboration but as a product of Wordsworth's 'conflict with Coleridge's preference for the fantastic' in *The Ancient Mariner* and *The Wanderings of Cain*. Legouis shows Wordsworth's response to this conflict in his Prologue to *Peter Bell*, 'a farewell, not unmingled with irony, to their schemes for writing supernatural poems together' (p. 429). 'Conscious of having renounced illusion in order to perceive that which is,' Legouis concludes, 'and of having found that which is to be not only magnificent but moral, he is able to proclaim the good news to mankind in all sincerity (p. 467).'

After Legouis' death in October 1937, Ernest De Selincourt regretted that he had never written a sequel to the *Early Life*, 'if not to the end of [Wordsworth's] career, at least to include a full consideration of his greatest masterpieces'.[42] The concluding pages of the *Early Life* give a 'key to the interpretation of the even greater poetry which was to follow', as De Selincourt says, and in the 1914 edition of *The Cambridge History of English Literature* Legouis wrote about some of Wordsworth's later poems. However, when he was preparing the *Early Life* for republication in 1921 his interests had once again returned to Wordsworth's earlier life, and to Wordsworth's newly discovered relationship with Annette Vallon in particular. In the second appendix to the 1921 edition (pp. 477–80 below) he gave details of Harper's findings, listed some corrections of the *Early Life*, and announced his own forthcoming study *William Wordsworth and Annette Vallon*. But Legouis' realisation that Wordsworth had deliberately omitted this relationship from *The Prelude* eroded his confidence in his own critical method, which assumed that the poem is a reliable guide to the poet's life. In his introduction to the *Early Life* Legouis had announced *The Prelude* as 'a firm and harmonious unity', a 'perfect intelligibility', only to discover that 'there *was* self-mutilation in Wordsworth's case':

> As a poet he was, at least from an artistic point of view, reticent to a fault, maimed his autobiographical recollections and presented to the public a partial, incomplete, and, to a certain extent, enfeebled, image of his life and feelings (p. 480).

Legouis idealised *The Prelude* as autobiography, and perhaps it was inevitable that he should have been disillusioned sooner or later. He was evidently disenchanted when he recognised the unreliability of *The Prelude*, but that realisation also anticipates the more wary, sceptical criticism of the poem in recent times. His response is, in fact, a measure of the 'sound perspective, subtle and penetrative appreciation, and sane judgment' that De Selincourt found in all Legouis' critical writings. Fifty years after Legouis' death, his *Early Life of William Wordsworth* remains indispensible to an understanding of Wordsworth's life and work. It has proved a fertile resource for the best criticism of Wordsworth over the last century, and it will surely continue to do so for many years to come.

NICHOLAS ROE

Notes

1. Christopher Wordsworth, *Memoirs of William Wordsworth* (2 vols, London, 1851), i. 2. Cited in future here as *Memoirs*.

2. F. W. H. Myers, *Wordsworth* (London, 1880), p. 2.

3. William Knight, *The Life of William Wordsworth* (3 vols, Edinburgh, 1889), i. x, 4. Cited in future here as Knight. Legouis used Knight as a source for his own study, and reproduced several of Knight's errors listed below.

4. Ernest De Selincourt, 'Émile Legouis and Wordsworth', in 'Hommage à Émile Legouis', *Études Anglaises* (1938), 259. Cited in future here as 'Émile Legouis and Wordsworth'. The issue of *Études Anglaises* contains five commemorative articles about Legouis, and a detailed list of his publications between 1882 and 1938.

5. *Poems of Wordsworth*, edited by Matthew Arnold (London, 1879), vi.

6. See *The Times Literary Supplement*, 29 April 1926, 309.

7. See 'The Great Prelude Debate', *The Wordsworth Circle*, 17 (Winter 1986). Throughout the *Early Life* Legouis quotes from the 1850 text of *The Prelude*, and I have followed his precedent in this introduction except for two instances where the 1805 text provides a more accurate indication of Wordsworth's position in 1804–5 than the poem as published in 1850.

8. Page references to the *Early Life* in this introduction will all be cited in the text.

9. E. P. Thompson, 'Disenchantment or Default? A Lay Sermon', in *Power and Consciousness*, C. C. O'Brien and W. D. Vanech (eds) (New York and London, 1969), 152. Cited in future as Thompson.

10. Marilyn Butler, *Romantics, Rebels, and Reactionaries, English Literature and its Background, 1760–1830* (Oxford, 1981), 64–5.

11. Legouis, following Knight, i. 148, misquotes Wordsworth's letter to Losh. The passage should read:

> I have been tolerably industrious within the last few weeks. I have written 1300 lines of a poem which I hope to make of considerable utility; its title will be *The Recluse or views of Nature, Man, and Society.*

See *The Letters of William and Dorothy Wordsworth*, edited by E. De Selincourt, second edn, *The Early Years 1787–1805*, revised by C. L. Shaver (Oxford, 1967), 214. Cited in future as EY.

On pp. 344–54 Legouis quotes 'The Ruined Cottage' as an extract from *The Excursion* (1814). Despite being misled by Knight, he reconstructs an early textual history for 'The Ruined Cottage' between 1795–7, and rightly implies that in March 1798 Wordsworth regarded it as part of *The Recluse*. For a recent confirmation of Legouis' conjectures, based on manuscript evidence not available to him, see Jonathan Wordsworth, *The Borders of Vision* (Oxford, 1982), 352.

12. See Kenneth Johnston, 'The Politics of "Tintern Abbey"', *The Wordsworth Circle*, 14 (Winter 1983), 6–14.

13. Marjorie Levinson, *Wordsworth's Great Period Poems* (Cambridge 1986), 5.

14. Legouis, following *Memoirs*, i. 36, mistakenly has 1778 as the date of Wordsworth's entry to Hawkshead school.

15. Richard Onorato, '*The Prelude*: Metaphors of Beginning and Where they Lead', reproduced in William Wordsworth, *The Prelude, 1799, 1805, 1850*, J. Wordsworth, M. H. Abrams, S. Gill (eds) (Norton Critical Edition, New York and London, 1979), 623.

16. T. W. Thompson, *Wordsworth's Hawkshead* (Oxford, 1970).

17. See EY, 49, 59, 62.

18. Kenneth Johnston, 'Philanthropy or Treason? Wordsworth as "Active Partisan"', *Studies in Romanticism*, 25 (1986), 371–409. Cited in future here as Johnston.

19. For Wordsworth's debt to Ramond, see Appendix One, pp. 475–7 below.

20. See 'My First Acquaintance with Poets', *The Complete Works of William Hazlitt*, edited by P. P. Howe (21 vols, London, 1930–34), xvii. 118.

21. EY, 56.

22. See Nicholas Roe, 'Citizen Wordsworth', *The Wordsworth Circle*, 14 (Winter 1983), 21–30.

23. James Chandler, *Wordsworth's Second Nature* (Chicago and London, 1984).

24. *Memoirs*, i. 76–7.

25. *Reminiscences by Thomas Carlyle*, edited by J. A. Froude (2 vols, London, 1881), ii. 335.

26. *The Prose Works of William Wordsworth*, W. J. B. Owen and J. W. Smyser (eds) (3 vols, Oxford, 1974), i. 49.

27. *Selections from the Papers of the London Corresponding Society, 1792–1799*, edited by Mary Thale (Cambridge, 1983), xvii.

28. Thompson, 152–3.

29. *The Collected Letters of Samuel Taylor Coleridge*, edited by E. L. Griggs (6 vols, Oxford, 1956–71), i. 527.

30. S. T. Coleridge, 'On the Present War', *Lectures 1795 on Politics and Religion*, L. Patton and P. Mann (eds) (Bollingen Collected Coleridge, Princeton, 1971), 74. John Thelwall, *The Rights of Nature, Against the Usurpations of Establishments* (London, 1796), 46–7.

31. For John Thelwall on Robespierre see *The Tribune* (3 vols, London, 1795), i. 254, and Nicholas Roe, 'Imagining Robespierre', in *Coleridge's Imagination*, R. Gravil, L. Newlyn, N. Roe (eds) (Cambridge, 1985), 165–8. This volume is cited in future here as CI.

32. EY, 124.

33. EY, 124.

34. Johnston, 379–80.

35. See the introduction to William Wordsworth, *The Borderers*, edited by R. Osborn (Cornell Wordsworth Series, Ithaca and London, 1982); and Robert Osborn, 'Meaningful Obscurity: The Antecedents and Character of Rivers', in *Bicentenary Wordsworth Studies*, edited by J. Wordsworth (Ithaca and London, 1970), 393–424.

36. Robert Mayo, 'The Contemporaneity of the *Lyrical Ballads*', *PMLA*, 69 (1954), 486–522.

37. Stephen Parrish, *The Art of the Lyrical Ballads* (Cambridge, Mass., 1973), 80.

38. Mary Jacobus, *Tradition and Experiment in Wordsworth's Lyrical Ballads, 1798* (Oxford, 1976), 15–37. Lucy Newlyn, *Coleridge, Wordsworth,*

and the Language of Allusion (Oxford, 1986), 5–10, cited in future here as Newlyn.

39. See Stephen Parrish, 'Coleridge's lyrical ballads', and Richard Gravil, 'Imagining Wordsworth: 1797 – 1807 – 1817', in CI, 102–116 and 129–142. See also '"Radical Difference": Wordsworth and Coleridge in 1802' in Newlyn, 87–116, and Thomas McFarland, 'The Symbiosis of Coleridge and Wordsworth' in *Romanticism and the Forms of Ruin* (Princeton, 1981).

40. For Wordsworth's and Coleridge's first meetings see Newlyn, 3–16, and Robert Woof, 'Wordsworth and Coleridge: Some Early Matters' in *Bicentenary Wordsworth Studies*, 76–91. For the political context of their early friendship, see Chapter Seven of my *Wordsworth and Coleridge. The Radical Years* (Oxford, 1988).

41. Legouis' dating of the Wordsworths' move to Alfoxden follows Knight, i. 114. Mark Reed, *Wordsworth, The Chronology of the Early Years, 1770–1799* (Cambridge, Mass., 1967), 199–201, gives details of the move, and favours 16 July 1797 as the date of their residence at Alfoxden.

42. 'Émile Legouis and Wordsworth', 263. Jonathan Wordsworth's *Borders of Vision* (Oxford, 1982) is in many ways a sequel to Legouis' *Early Life*: 'it centres . . . on the years of *Prelude* composition, 1798–1805, and . . . [it has] . . . rather the same shape as the full length 1805 version of the poem', as Jonathan Wordsworth says in his preface.

The Early Life of William Wordsworth

Gratefully dedicated
to
Professor Alexandre Beljame
University of Paris

Author's Preface

WHEN I was applied to for the right of translating this critical biography into English, I felt greatly honoured and not a little perplexed. My work had been written chiefly with an eye to the requirements of French readers, to very few of whom Wordsworth is more than a name : hence it contains an abundance of quotations from the poet, and also some statements and observations which may appear trite to such of his countrymen as are familiar with his writings and those of his critics. On the other hand I felt that the study was here and there wanting in those finer touches which could not well have been presented to readers unacquainted with the English language and poetry. Such apprehensions would have induced me to recast the work throughout, had not some eminent English critics expressed the opinion that, besides any novelty that the general plan and certain especial parts of the book might possess, the very fact of its being distinctly French in its aim would not render it the less acceptable to English admirers of Wordsworth. The contemplated reconstruction has therefore been limited to thorough revision, and a few changes, chiefly additions, made by myself. Such other fears as I might entertain have been much lessened by the care of the translator, more favoured than myself in that he has been able to retain the original words of the quotations.

Author's Preface

It is my very pleasant duty to express my thanks to Mr Ernest Hartley Coleridge for his kindness in imparting to me some valuable information before its appearance in his recently-issued collection of the letters of Coleridge ; and to Mr Thomas Hutchinson of Dublin, who, no less untiring than obliging, has allowed me to draw upon the stores of his perhaps unrivalled knowledge of all matters relating to Wordsworth's life and poetry.

ÉMILE LEGOUIS.

LYON, *27th December* 1896.

Introduction

I

SELDOM had general uneasiness and moral disorder been so justifiable in England, rarely had the signs of their existence been so unequivocal, as during the winter of 1797-1798. By the peace of Campo-Formio, England was left in solitary opposition to the revolutionary government of France, which had compelled all its other enemies one by one to lay down their arms. Still in possession of her supremacy at sea, she had, nevertheless, as yet won no naval victory which so enhanced her prestige as to console her pride for defeats upon the Continent, none sufficiently decisive to convince her that she had an impregnable rampart in the waters which girdled her shores. So formidable had been the recent outbreaks of disaffection in her fleets, that scarcely even could she place reliance upon them. Ireland, shaking off her bondage, was meanwhile summoning the foreigner, and a scheme of invasion appeared to be ripening in France. There was not a point on the coasts of Britain but felt itself threatened. Worse still, those Englishmen, by far the more numerous party, who had at heart not only the success of their country's arms, but also the preservation of her time-honoured institutions, were asking one another with painful anxiety whether an invader, who landed on that British soil which had been so long free from desecration, would not find a thousand English hands outstretched in welcome, acclamation, and support. Well aware that the fascinations of revolution were strong enough to have destroyed the patriotism of an unknown number of their fellow-countrymen, they detected spies and traitors wherever they turned their restless glance. But a few months had elapsed since the death of Burke, and already they recognised the truth of those prophecies which, until his last hour, he had not

ceased to repeat ; already they perceived that he at any rate
had accurately gauged the mighty strength of the subversive spirit against which his eloquent voice had strenuously
urged a new crusade. No longer was it a question of
crushing that spirit abroad ; fortunate indeed would they
be, if they could prevent its spread and victory at home.

Still more painful, at the same period, were the reflections
of those Englishmen who were well disposed towards
France. With unshaken fortitude they had supported the
new Republic in the face of insult and suspicion, of enmity
from their friends and persecution from their rulers.
They had forgiven it the bloodiest days of the Terror,
and the lingering fury of that hurricane after which the
most indulgent survey could reveal nothing but wreckage
without a single token of solid reconstruction. Only
yesterday they would have desired its triumph over
England, and some were prematurely enthusiastic at the
thought of an invasion which, in their opinion, was amply
warranted by the attitude of their country. France made
no movement but in self-defence ; in protecting herself
she protected the cause of human progress ; she took up
arms in defence of future peace. She made war to put
an end for ever to all wars of ambition and self-interest.
But now overwhelming intelligence reached them: the
armies of the Directory, during a time of continental
peace, had invaded Switzerland,—that country which, of
all the nations of Europe, should have been most sacred,
on account of its weakness, and from the fact that for
centuries it had been throughout the world the first
refuge of liberty. The young Republic showed itself no
less the ruthless aggressor than the monarchs who had
formed a league for the spoliation of Poland. Nowhere
in Europe was there a corner left in which it was possible
to prolong that dream of regeneration and of happiness
on earth, which for eight years had been so fearlessly
pursued in face of the most cruel disillusion. Those gloomy
objections to their theories which had already presented
themselves again and again to the minds of the most eager
reformers, only to be immediately thrust out of sight,
now arose once more, victorious and irresistible. Man,

they concluded, is after all not good by nature. It is not in his power to submit himself to the guidance of reason. There is nothing in common between man as he is and that being free alike from prejudice and from error, ready to be enlightened by the invincible logic of justice, whose glowing image philosophers have drawn with such delight. And reason, which has been so grossly deceived in its estimate of its own power, and has so completely misconceived the nature of the evil reality which it aspired to transform, is now seen to be condemned by the very experiment which it has been permitted to make.

Thus, between the two parties :—the Conservatives on the one hand, whose opinion from the outset has been that an imperfect state of society, woven out of good and evil, is all that man in his imperfection deserves; who have greeted with a smile of sarcastic incredulity the promise of another golden age and the regeneration of mankind; who, as the sky grows darker, and the hour of destruction seems near at hand, become more and more rooted in their distrust;—and, on the other hand, the reformers or revolutionists who persist in believing society as it is to be no longer tolerable, but who are losing hope of establishing in its place a better order of things—between these two parties we find a mutual and silent acquiescence in pessimism. Man is by nature perverse and unreasonable; life at best a poor possession; evil rooted in the very depths of human nature, and ineradicable save with that existence of which it forms a vital part; progress impossible, or so slow and inconsiderable that the contemplation of it brings no delight. The millennium of our dreams is the idlest of fancies. Minds imbued with religion, or those who are driven by such reflections to seek its consolation, can at least transfer to another life the glorious hopes of which the earthly realization has been foretold. For the remainder there is no refuge but in scepticism. The less scrupulous, in order to secure for themselves the better portion of the spoils of a foolish and miserable race, will, for the future, only think of using for their own ends the melancholy wisdom they have so dearly purchased. The more honest will take refuge in selfishness, and, while they may perhaps extend that principle so far as to include love towards their family or their country, they will refuse henceforth to bestow their faith and affection on a wider circle, and will expend nothing but sarcasm on the simple-minded "visionaries" who still can talk of infinite and universal perfectibility.[1]

In the very heart of this crisis, on the 11th March 1798, a young Englishman, but a short time earlier one of the most fervent reformers, now living poor and unknown in a lonely nook in Somerset, was writing to a friend :[2]

"I have been tolerably industrious within the last few weeks. I have written 706 lines of a poem which I hope to make of considerable utility. Its title will be, The Recluse, or Views of Nature, Man, and Society."

The utility alluded to consists in restoring gladness to the heart of man. The poet's object is precisely that which every one seems ready to abandon as an idle dream : it is the recovery of happiness. He designs to increase the joys of life, and, though not denying the existence of its sorrows, to transform them into peace. He preaches no political or social reform. Whether the existing forms of society endure, or are destroyed, is for him at this time a matter of secondary importance. Nor does he speak in the name of any religion. He does not, as Chateaubriand already dreams of doing, offer to souls in search of pious emotion the solemn dogmas and the touching ceremonial of Christianity. He concerns himself with earthly happiness

---

[1] *Prelude*, ii. 432-441. These verses are almost a literal transcription of the following passage of a letter from Coleridge to Wordsworth in the summer of 1799: "My dear friend, I do entreat you go on with *The Recluse*, and I wish you would write a poem, in blank verse, addressed to those who, in consequence of the complete failure of the French Revolution, have thrown up all hopes of the amelioration of mankind, and are sinking into an almost epicurean selfishness, disguising the same under the soft titles of domestic attachment and contempt for visionary *philosophes*. It would do great good, and might form a part of *The Recluse*. . . ." (Memoirs of W. W. by C. Wordsworth, Vol. I. p. 139).

[2] Letter to James Losh, *The Life of W. Wordsworth*, by W. Knight, Vol. I. p. 148 (3 vols., Edinburgh, 1889).

alone. From creeds and forms of worship, from national constitutions and legal codes, it may, according to circumstances, derive faint assistance, or meet with feeble opposition. But its deepest source is elsewhere ; in the very centre of man's nature, in his senses and his heart. The one thing of true importance is the cultivation of the feelings, which, in the individual, may be, and ought to be, developed so as to be capable of the greatest possible amount of enjoyment. Already, in this world of pain, there are privileged beings whose eyes behold with quiet rapture the splendours of nature, whose ears detect her harmonies, whose hearts are thrilled spontaneously and with delight by all tender and lofty emotion.

> Why is this glorious creature to be found
> One only in ten thousand ? What one is,
> Why may not millions be ? What bars are thrown
> By Nature in the way of such a hope ?
> Our animal appetites and daily wants,
> Are these obstructions insurmountable ?
> If not, then others vanish into air.[1]

When every man shall possess the poet's eye, the poet's ear, the poet's heart, that millennium, so fondly looked for in other paths of progress, will have been reached indeed. A distant end, no doubt, but one towards which every step is a delight, and for which men can strive, both individually and in unison, free from rivalry or wrath. In those very feelings which proud reason but lately despised and resolved to crush, lies the true worth of man ; in those senses which that same reason regarded with suspicion or disgust, refusing to see in them anything beyond the evidence of his animal nature, lies man's true glory. The object of every sensation is nature, and sensation, as it becomes purer and more susceptible, will wonder the more at " the immenseness of the good and fair "[2] displayed before it.

The poet himself, conscious, from his own experience,

---

[1] *The Prelude*, xiii. 87-93.
[2] Coleridge, *Ode to Dejection*, 1st text, last stanza. Coleridge applies the words to Wordsworth.

of the wreck of all the lofty dreams of his generation, and having succeeded, by aid of his sentient nature, in recovering peace and joy of soul, resolves to impart to mankind the lessons he has learnt. The strong pleasures aroused within him by passing glimpses of nature's beauties or wonders shall be gathered like the flowers of a garland, and distributed among men as varied specimens of the delights this world can afford, the most sublime of which nevertheless defy alike description and communication. Every gathered flower shall have not only its peculiar charm, but also an added value by which that charm shall be surpassed. It shall stand at once for the token of infinite beauty, and for a testimony in behalf of the human being capable of perceiving that beauty.

Above all, he recalls men's attention to the true and lasting worth of the possessions they have cast aside in their vain pursuit of a paradise attainable only in dreams. He brings to their remembrance the genuine titles to nobility which the race possesses, that substantial inheritance of silent effort and modest virtue which they so imprudently rejected when their gaze became fascinated by the vision of ideal man, that figment of reason living without stain in a world where adversity is unknown. Have they not acted as did those adventurers of old, who sold the land they had inherited, in order to sail towards the fabulous mines of Cipango? The fortunate island has not been discovered, but the old world endures yet, and is worth no less than before the hour of fever. Its value will be greater still, if man, delivered from his vain illusions, returns to it with more of understanding and of love.

Contempt for man as he is, contempt for the world of reality, such at bottom is the twofold source of the disease from which men are suffering. This contempt, born of pride and impotence, is the height of impiety, and those who indulge in it may be said to be justly punished by the despair in which it results. Nothing that this world contains is worthy of contempt; none who inhabits it has the right to despise.

> . . . He who feels contempt
> For any living thing, hath faculties
> Which he has never used ; . . . thought with him
> Is in its infancy.[1]

Contempt means ignorance.

> 'Tis Nature's law
> That none, the meanest of created things,
> Of forms created the most vile and brute,
> The dullest or most noxious, should exist
> Divorced from good—a spirit and pulse of good,
> A life and soul, to every mode of being
> Inseparably linked.[2]

If this is true of every created being, how much more of every human creature. Those lowly ones for whom hitherto the wise man has felt no sentiment but pity, of whom he has never thought without a sense of indignation at their degraded condition, to whom he has never spoken but to make them conscious by his very compassion of their insignificance and unworthiness—in order that such as these may be restored to their rights, it is useless to await the uncertain hour of the equal division of this world's false goods : wealth, shallow pleasures, adornments of the person, and intellectual gifts. We must recognise here and now their full value as they are. We must raise them in their own eyes and make them conscious of their usefulness, of the beauty and even of the brightness which may crown their simple life. Wretched and degraded as they are, they must be brought to feel that it is within their own power to shed a lustre round them in the cottage or the hovel in which they dwell.

And the proof that there is no occasion to despair of man's future will be all the more overwhelming, if we can determine the presence of the fundamental virtues and the moral perceptions in that class of men which is at once the most neglected and the most numerous. The proof

---

[1] *Lines left upon a seat in a yew-tree*, 52-55.
[2] *The old Cumberland Beggar*, 73-79.

that life is rich in pleasures will be the more impossible of refutation, if the joys of which the poet testifies are more accessible to all, more widely spread, less confined to particular seasons; if, unlike some rare plants, they require no journey to discover them, but blossom, like the daisy of the meadow, in familiar profusion beneath our feet. He, therefore, who would be the benefactor of his race, must be prepared both to point out those elements of the beautiful in man which are at once most essential and least understood, and to indicate those characteristics of the beautiful in nature, which are not only the most liable to be overlooked, but, at the same time, the most universal.

Such was the object of the great poem, designed to be of some " utility " to a disheartened and sceptical generation, the composition of which was occupying Wordsworth's mind at twenty-eight years of age. This poem, entitled *The Recluse*, was, indeed, never to be completed. But the existing portions of the vast Gothic cathedral[1] which Wordsworth had planned are of so imposing a character, that the chief of them, *The Excursion*, contains nine thousand lines, and *The Prelude*, which was designed merely as the ante-chapel, seven thousand. And these poems not only afford evidence of the huge proportions to which the whole work would have attained, but at the same time form each a harmonious and independent whole, embodying his teaching in its entirety, and therefore depriving us of all cause for the regret so commonly felt at the sight of an unfinished work of art. Further, the central idea of that teaching is repeated in a great number of shorter pieces, designed to be to the whole structure what " the little cells, oratories, and sepulchral recesses "[2] are to a church. And if, in these, its expression has less of imposing dignity than in the vast nave of the edifice, it has, nevertheless, more variety, and a charm less difficult to appreciate. These shorter poems are infinitely diverse in form: homely ballads recounting some scene of innocence and love, some flash of artless wisdom from child or simple-minded peasant; pastorals in which the poet adorns the stern

---

[1] Preface to *The Excursion.*   [2] *Ibid.*

reality of rural life only by bringing to light the eternal beauty of its setting; gems of description which reveal the happy spirit of some solitary spot shining through its garment of moss and foliage; odes in which a cherished idea hides its abstraction beneath a material form and becomes the living companion of mankind; sonnets enshrining a transient feeling

> from the bosom thrown,
> In perfect shape, whose beauty Time shall spare
> Though a breath made it.[1]

For fifty years it was Wordsworth's lot to labour with unflagging persistence to create in his fellow-men, and to keep alive within himself, the conviction that the present is not without cause for thankfulness, nor the future without grounds for hope. Destined, in the course of this unceasing warfare against the pessimism of his age, to take rank among the greatest poets of his country, his claim to that honour was to find its sanction in his possession of three essential gifts. The chief of these was the surpassing truth of his imagination. Mistrustful of the fancy which aspires to create a world of its own, familiar with the agonising sense of disillusion which is the termination of our brightest dreams, he closes his eyes to everything but reality, that he may distinguish therein that beauty which to-morrow will be no less fair than it was yesterday, and which, once perceived, remains a joy for evermore. Austerely stripped of all the ornamental equipment sanctified by poetic tradition, purified for the very purpose of this communion, his mind becomes a faithful mirror of the external world, the images of his poetry an embodiment of the eternal truth of nature. Severely pure in all their naked simplicity, they are redolent of its vigour and freshness. Nor is it in the work of Wordsworth alone that we must look for the effects of this directness of vision. It may be found in all contemporary English poetry, shamed, by his example, into casting aside the factitious adornments long soiled by conventional usage, rescued by him from the mere verbal imitation from which

[1] Sonnet, *Happy the Feeling*.

it was pining away, and restored to the exact yet reverent observation of living and inanimate nature.

With this imaginative gift Wordsworth united, in a less degree, that of expression. Wanting both in consistency and in flexibility ; awkward at times, from his very vigour ; at times also, in his scrupulous adherence to rigid accuracy, pushing explicitness to the very verge of platitude ; he excelled in the terse and austere delineation of moral emotion, and as an interpreter of some of the most obscure phenomena of sensation, has had no rival. He rendered almost palpable more than one sense-intuition, which, for want of clear and appropriate language, had previously remained unexpressed, or disregarded although universally experienced. To him, therefore, the poetical presentation of human psychology owes some of its most precious pages.

Lastly, if the wilder flights and more " liquid " tones of lyrical song were denied him, within him rang music appropriate to his intense meditation, the measured and stately march of epic strains. The halting prose of daily events, long moulded in his mind, more than once came forth with a full and solemn harmony, not unworthy to rank with that which formed the accompaniment to Milton's religious narrative of the origins of the world.

What Wordsworth desired to be, that he has succeeded in being—the benefactor of mankind. He has left poetry the richer for his poems, and nature more fair by his discovery of her charms.

II

What formative process had produced the man who, at twenty-eight, had conceived such an ambition, and possessed the genius necessary to its realization ? What had been his experience of the life within, as well as of the life without ? In a poem undertaken immediately he had arrived at a clear conception of his poetic mission, the most remarkable of all his writings for depth and originality, Wordsworth himself has given us the answer. It seemed to him that *The Recluse*, as yet scarcely sketched out, was receding before his gaze. The outlines of this poem on nature, man, and society were so vast that they eluded his grasp. Was he really capable of giving form to the matter of his conception? Had he not had too presumptuous a confidence in his powers? Were there within him the conditions necessary to the accomplishment of so pretentious a work? To answer these questions he would have to trace the path his mind had followed from its earliest beginnings, and thus it was that he came to compose *The Prelude*.

It is the object of the present writer to make a study of Wordsworth's youth in the light of this unique autobiographical poem. It is intended to give as complete an account of it as direct quotation, supplemented by analysis, can convey; to explain or amplify it, by means of all the obtainable evidence in the shape of Wordsworth's other poems, and his own and his friends' correspondence; to determine the allusions, and to assign to each particular fact its full importance by giving a suitable account of its relations to history; and, in conclusion, to analyse separately the principal features of the work of Wordsworth's maturity in a few chapters for which but little matter is furnished by *The Prelude*.

And in a work which keeps such an ideal in view, although it may seem to follow the original poem somewhat humbly, and to be confined within somewhat narrow limits,—rather indeed by reason of that humble fidelity and of those limitations,—something perhaps of novelty may be found. The many large works which have been devoted to Wordsworth's life and poems,—and there is scarcely an English critic of this century but has made a point of passing judgment upon the founder of modern English poetry,— have rather assumed the reader's knowledge of *The Prelude* than made that work an object of serious study. Can it be that the fact of a poem being written in his own language places the critic at some disadvantage—so far as the literary or historical appreciation of it is concerned? Is there not some risk that what is too easily accessible may have too slight a hold upon the attention? To judge from the notes, scanty and not seldom erroneous, appended to some editions of *The Prelude*, one would certainly think there is. For the same reason we have to observe, in almost every case, the omission of certain essential features, both in the portrait of the poet and in the account of his life; a partial neglect of his earlier verses, to the importance of which *The Prelude* nevertheless draws attention; and an absence of any adequate endeavour to analyse that moral crisis of his early manhood, without which the man in his maturity would never have been what he was. It is also to an imperfect recognition of the superior claims of *The Prelude* that we must attribute the common tendency to form a judgment of the whole of Wordsworth's moral and poetical work from the later specimens of his art, and to regard *The Excursion* as the masterpiece of the structure; a poem which, although of more imposing proportions, reveals some diminution of his early imaginative vigour and capacity for joy.

On the other hand, by publishing this partial biography in France, the writer lays himself open to a serious objection. It might appear the height of rashness to devote so detailed a study to the youth of a foreign poet, whose work has never been translated into French, and whose life, as a whole, has never been made the subject of a special work. It is true that Sainte Beuve felt for Wordsworth an admiration which led him to imitate some of his sonnets; that M. Schérer took a lively interest in his moral reflections, and M. Bourget and M. Gabriel Sarrazin in his subtle symbolism; that M. Angellier has recently pronounced a eulogy, remarkable for its penetration, upon the insight displayed in his interpretation of nature; and that various other tributes have been paid to him, the most curious, perhaps, by Maurice de Guérin and Hippolyte de la Morvonnais. It was the dream of these young Breton poets to bring about in the matter and form of French poetry a revolution similar to that which Wordsworth had accomplished in England. But all this sympathy and admiration, on the part of men differing so widely both in character and generation, cannot blind us to the fact that France is, of all countries, that one in which the poet's wish, an echo of that expressed by Milton, has been most completely realised :—

> Fit audience let me find, though few ! [1]

This being the case, the production of so detailed an account of a mere fragment of the life of an unknown man would be quite inexcusable, did not Wordsworth's youth, interpreted in the light of *The Prelude*, take shape as a firm and harmonious unity. Studied thus as a separate whole, it acquires an interest entirely its own, and a perfect intelligibility. It is not the minute examination of what is unknown that causes perplexity, it is rather the too rapid succession of unfamiliar thoughts and fresh facts, of which the origins have not been distinctly perceived, nor the elements fully analysed. Moreover *The Prelude* forms the necessary introduction to all work in the wider field, not only of Wordsworth's poetry as a whole, but also of modern English poetry in general. Until a more complete account of the man and his time is forthcoming, this study of Wordsworth's youth may perhaps find some justification, and, so far as it goes, may, it is hoped, be found complete in itself.

Although written between the ages of twenty-eight and thirty-five, that is to say, between 1799 and 1805, when Wordsworth's vigour and boldness were at their height, *The Prelude* was not published until 1850, after the death of its author. Not that he felt any doubt as to the value of his work, which Coleridge, to whose judgment alone Wordsworth occasionally deferred, greeted, after a first perusal, with an enthusiastic pæan. But he hesitated to lay before the public a poem which dealt at such length with his own experience, until this apparent self-glorification should have been justified by the completion of *The Recluse*.

No autobiography, however, is so free from the taint of vanity as *The Prelude*. There are no theatrical attitudes, no arrangements of drapery for the sake of effect. The

---

[1] *The Recluse*, 796. For a more detailed account of the relations of Wordsworth to French poetry and criticism of the xixth century, see an able essay by Joseph Texte, *Revue des Deux Mondes*, 15th July 1896.

poet takes no pains to give statuesque beauty to his gestures, or dramatic sequence to his actions. Wordsworth
had too much pride—if the word may be used to denote
justifiable self-confidence—to be vain. He felt, he knew,
that he was a great poet, and did not disguise the fact.
He was unconscious of any obligation to wrap himself in
the detestable cloak of false modesty. Moreover he was
writing *The Prelude* primarily for himself, and in the
second place for Coleridge, "the brother of his soul."
He desired to convince himself of the reality of his poetic
mission and of the justice of the high hopes placed in him
by his friend. He aimed not at self-glorification, but at
self-knowledge. *The Prelude* is less a narrative than a
study of origins, less the history of a man than the philosophy of a mind. What Wordsworth seeks above all to
discover is "the origin and progress of his own powers"; [1]
and as this investigation invariably penetrates the veil of
external characteristics proper to the individual, in order
to arrive at those feelings which are essential to him as
man, far from being egotistic, it becomes broadly human.
This penetration, indeed, renders it almost impersonal.
We feel that the poet chooses himself for hero simply
because he can fathom no other soul so deeply, because
there is no other from which he could derive so many
fresh and indubitable truths.

Not, however, that Wordsworth has said, or pretended
to say, everything concerning himself. He has left neither
"Confessions" nor "Confidences." It is doubtful whether
he had any reasons for addressing the world in an undertone like Lamartine, or for shouting to it the painful avowals
of a Rousseau. But, however this may be, he thought it
proper to make a selection from among the events of his
own clear and tranquil life. Out of the darkness of the
past he has brought to light those elements alone which,
in his opinion, had effectually contributed to the development of his genius. The poet of man's moral nature
would confer immortality only on the nobler and more
wholesome parts of his being. Before we follow in his
footsteps we must be prepared to find our path confined

---

[1] Preface to *The Excursion*.

to the uplands; however minutely we explore the districts
we pass through, we shall never lose sight of the loftiest
peaks. Scrupulously truthful, Wordsworth is also intentionally incomplete. One caution only need be added, and
this he has himself expressed in a striking piece of imagery.
Looking back from the distance of his thirtieth year upon
his earliest infancy, summoning out of the past the recollections of days now so far distant, could he help fearing
that he might unconsciously encumber the simplicity of
original impressions with the weight of reflections which
came long afterwards ?

> As one who hangs down-bending from the side
> Of a slow-moving boat, upon the breast
> Of a still water, solacing himself
> With such discoveries as his eye can make
> Beneath him in the bottom of the deep,
> Sees many beauteous sights—weeds, fishes, flowers,
> Grots, pebbles, roots of trees, and fancies more,
> Yet often is perplexed and cannot part
> The shadow from the substance, rocks and sky,
> Mountains and clouds, reflected in the depth
> Of the clear flood, from things which there abide
> In their true dwelling; now is crossed by gleam
> Of his own image, by a sunbeam now,
> And wavering motions sent he knows not whence,
> Impediments that make his task more sweet ;
> Such pleasant office have we long pursued
> Incumbent o'er the surface of past time
> With like success.[1]

While it is well to take note of this admission, we may
nevertheless count ourselves fortunate in owing our knowledge of Wordsworth's childhood to the only man who
could describe it with certainty. Even when the biographer
has been a contemporary of his hero, nay, even when they
have been brought up together, there is no part of his
task more difficult, or more liable to lead him astray, than
that of determining without assistance the circumstances
that have influenced the growth of his hero's imagination.
What has the appearance of an important event to those

[1] *The Prelude*, iv. 256-273.

around him, often passes unnoticed by the child, while a detail imperceptible to others, the existence of which no member even of the same family has suspected, has sometimes occasioned one of those mysterious impulses which gives a permanent bent and direction to the youthful mind. We shall find that Wordsworth's memory, taking little note of the events commonly held important in a life-history, retained many others which none of those around him could have observed.

Some of these recollections may at first appear odd or trifling, but to thrust them aside without further investigation would be to expose ourselves to the danger of losing the most subtle and original passages. And a further disadvantage would be that by refusing, on account of its length, to follow the track beaten out by the poet in search of his deepest and most personal convictions, we should run the risk of being unable to find any other path which would lead to them. We should run the risk, in short, of entirely failing to understand the philosophy, and at the same time the poetry, of the poet-philosopher. The truth is that his philosophy finds its tap-root, as his poetry its fairest foliage, in his recollections of childhood. Amidst the chorus of poets, which, from the day when Rousseau first proclaimed the immaculate conception of the Child, has not ceased to address the young idol in hymns of devout praise, the voice of Wordsworth is heard, deeper, more sustained, more fervent than them all. The child, above all the child Wordsworth, has been the source and inspiration of his most enthusiastic strains. He lived with his eyes habitually turned towards his past. Arrived at man's estate, he felt himself filled with such reverence for the little being, whom, as he looked back towards the dawn of his life, he saw already so far off, that he invested him at last with something of a divine character, by attributing to him a celestial origin and superhuman powers:

> Thou, whose exterior semblance dost belie
> Thy Soul's immensity;
> Thou best Philosopher! . . .
> Mighty Prophet! Seer blest! [1]

---

[1] *Ode on intimations of Immortality from recollections of early Childhood,* 108-114.

Always so intent upon the mysterious, Wordsworth never came nearer to piercing its darkness than when questioning

> Those shadowy recollections,
>   Which, be they what they may,
> Are yet the fountain-light of all our day,
> Are yet a master-light of all our seeing;
>   Uphold us, cherish us, and have power to make
> Our noisy years seem moments in the being
> Of the eternal Silence.[1]

If he looked back " so fondly to the walks of childhood," it was that there his soul still clearly discerned

> The dear memorial footsteps unimpaired
> Of her own native vigour.[2]

He loved to explore that

> isthmus, which our spirits cross
> In progress from their native continent
> To earth and human life.[3]

far more than that wide and vaguely defined region in which the years of our maturity glide by. If in this life man can discover any indication of his destiny, it seemed to Wordsworth that it must be by attempting to recall the instinctive tendency of his earliest footsteps. Doubtless therefore he would have taken exception to any narrative of his life which did not linger fondly around his cradle. He would not have understood how any one could pretend to give an account of the talent of the man, without first making a detailed study of its germs as manifested in the child who is " the father of the man."[4]

---

[1] *Ode on intimations of Immortality from recollections of early Childhood*, 153-159.
[2] *Excursion*, ix. 36-40.   [3] *Prelude*, v. 536-538.   [4] *The Rainbow*, 7.

BOOK I

Childhood, Youth and Education

CHAPTER I

Cockermouth (1770-1778)

On the father's side, Wordsworth was descended from a long line of yeomen, or farming proprietors, who had settled in the south of Yorkshire before the Norman Conquest. They were people of some importance in their parish of Penistone, and their names occur over and over again in its deeds. His maternal ancestors included an eminent man, Richard Crackanthorpe, "one of the ablest and most learned divines in the most erudite age of English theology, the reign of James I."[1] Beyond these facts we know little or nothing of the poet's forefathers, but those interested in symbolism will doubtless find an instance of it in these antecedents of a man who was destined so to weld together nature and theology, as to form from them the most complete and most orthodox scheme of natural religion.

Little is known even of Wordsworth's own parents. His father, a man of intelligence and energy, was an attorney-at-law, resident at Cockermouth, in Cumberland. In 1766 he was also appointed steward of the manor and forest of Ennerdale, by Sir James Lowther, afterwards Earl of Lonsdale. In the same year he married Anne Cookson, the daughter of a Penrith mercer. Husband and wife were both very young, the former twenty-five, the latter nineteen. Of this marriage five children were born in eight years, the second of them being William Wordsworth, born on the 7th of April 1770.

The little town of Cockermouth, where he first saw the light, has to-day little claim to consideration from a poetic standpoint, beyond that of having given him birth.

[1] Christopher Wordsworth, *Memoirs of William Wordsworth* (2 vols., London, 1851), ch. IV.

Divested for the moment, by an effort of imagination, from the manufactories which have increased there so rapidly since the close of the last century, it still seems to us, standing as it does at one of the approaches to the beautiful lake-district, like the joyless guardian of that English paradise of whose far-off peaks it can obtain but a glimpse in fair weather. The Derwent, it is true, flows through the town, but it is not here that it merits the epithet "fairest of all rivers."[1] Were it not that a few patches of greensward and a running stream contain for a child all the elements of supreme delight, it might be suspected that here Wordsworth, who declares himself "much favoured in his birthplace,"[2] became for the first time guilty of one of those sins of optimism, of which he was afterwards to commit so many.

The house formerly occupied by the Wordsworth family is still in existence. A square building of rather considerable size, somewhat cold in appearance, it derives from the humbler dwellings around it something of a manorial air. Situated in the principal street of Cockermouth, it opens at the back upon a terrace-like garden, which reaches as far as the Derwent. It is to this terrace, and to the meadows of which it commands a prospect, that the poet is first carried in imagination, as he seeks within the past the germs of his love for nature.

> The fairest of all rivers loved
> To blend his murmurs with my nurse's song,
> And, from his alder shades and rocky falls,
> And from his fords and shallows, sent a voice
> That flowed along my dreams.

"Thou didst," he exclaims further

> O Derwent! winding among grassy holms
> Where I was looking on, a babe in arms,
> Make ceaseless music that composed my thoughts
> To more than infant softness, giving me
> Amid the fretful dwellings of mankind
> A foretaste, a dim earnest, of the calm
> That Nature breathes among the hills and groves.[3]

---

[1] *Prelude*, i. 270.   [2] *Ibid.* 303.   [3] *The Prelude*, i. 269-281.

As soon as the child is able to run alone, the door is open to him, and, free to play and frolic as he pleases, he seeks at once the companionship of his favourite river :

> Oh, many a time have I, a five years' child,
> In a small mill-race severed from his stream,
> Made one long bathing of a summer's day ;
> Basked in the sun, and plunged and basked again
> Alternate, all a summer's day, or scoured
> The sandy fields, leaping through flowery groves
> Of yellow ragwort ; or when rock and hill,
> The woods and distant Skiddaw's lofty height,
> Were bronzed with deepest radiance, stood alone
> Beneath the sky, as if I had been born
> On Indian plains, and from my mother's hut
> Had run abroad in wantonness, to sport,
> A naked savage, in the thunder shower.[1]

Left thus to himself, the child experiences, on more than one occasion, the dread of the mysterious and unseen ; that influence which, in Goethe's opinion, should be allowed free exercise during the growth of the imagination. At times Wordsworth went to play in the green courts of Cockermouth Castle, near which he dwelt. There, after boldly climbing to pluck the flowers which waved around the shattered stronghold, he once happened to enter the dungeon of the keep, where he became " a prey to soul-appalling darkness." Thus was it that his young thoughts were made "acquainted with the grave." [2]

Not always, however, were the amusements of the child so solitary, or so wild in character. William had an elder brother, and two others younger than himself. But his especial companion was his sister Dorothy, who, twenty months his junior, shed, even over the sports of his childhood, that gracious influence so precious to him in later years. Gifted with a sensibility always exquisitely alert, always strung to the highest pitch, the child was already able to give her brother eyes and ears, " and humble cares, and delicate fears." When, during an excursion to White-haven, she heard for the first time the sound of the sea,

---

[1] *The Prelude*, i. 288-300.   [2] *Address from the Spirit of Cockermouth Castle.*

she burst into tears.[1] She was well adapted to awaken in her brother's less tender heart the sentiment of love. Together they went to look at the blue eggs in the sparrow's nest, so closely ensconced amidst the thick leafage of rose and privet against the terrace-wall :

> She looked at it and seemed to fear it;
> Dreading, tho' wishing, to be near it:
> Such heart was in her, being then
> A little Prattler among men.[2]

Together they chased the butterflies; he, like a true hunter, rushing upon the prey, while she " feared to brush the dust from off its wings." [3]

Doubtless William too was capable of these transports of tender emotion, but his disposition retained more of impetuosity and strength. He was a true boy, and none of the gentlest. From his earliest childhood he breathed

> Among wild appetites and blind desires,
> Motions of savage instinct his delight
> And exaltation.

Nothing so fascinated him as dangerous feats. Already he sought

> Deep pools, tall trees, black chasms, and dizzy crags,
> And tottering towers; he loved to stand and read
> Their looks forbidding, read and disobey,
> Sometimes in act, and evermore in thought.[4]

The same fearless disposition drove him to set at defiance such of his relations as had no hold on his affections. Before he had completed his eighth year he was stubborn, wayward and intractable. His unmanageable temper became particularly manifest at Penrith, on the occasion of a long visit to his mother's relations. The Cooksons seem to have been narrow and unyielding people, suspicious and harsh in their treatment of children, whom they did not hesitate to address with reproach and insult. One day, when an undeserved indignity had been put upon him, William went up to the attic with the firm intention of

---

[1] *Evening Voluntaries*, vi., Prefatory note.   [2] *The Sparrow's Nest.*
[3] *To a Butterfly.*   [4] *The Recluse*, 723-734.

killing himself with one of the foils which he knew to be kept there. He took down the weapon, but his courage failed him.[1]

At times he actually provoked punishment. On one occasion when, with his elder brother Richard, he was whipping tops in the drawing-room, the walls of which were hung round with family pictures, he cried : " Dare you strike your whip through that old lady's petticoat ? " " No," replied Richard. " Then here goes ! " And he struck his lash through the hooped petticoat of his venerable ancestress. Doubtless, Wordsworth tells us, he was properly punished, but, possibly from some want of judgment in punishments inflicted, he had become hardened to all chastisement, and was rather proud of it than otherwise.[2] We find his mother informing a friend of hers that the only one of her five children whose future caused her any anxiety was William. He will be remarkable, she added, either for good or for evil.[3]

Mrs Wordsworth did not survive to see her fears proved groundless. She died when her son was only eight years old. Too young to retain more than a vague recollection of her, he nevertheless remembered her pinning a nosegay to his breast before sending him to church to say the catechism :

> O lost too early for the frequent tear,
> And ill requited by this heart-felt sigh ! [4]

Not in such fashion alone, however, did he requite her to whom he owed the happiness of his infancy, and who, as the first to foresee his genius, had awakened his gratitude. To his father, whom he was not to lose until six years later, Wordsworth has not devoted a single line ;—indeed, the Father, the earliest visible presentation of right judgment, occupies but an inconspicuous place in poetry, especially in that of our own days. It is the faded image

---

[1] *Autobiographical Memoranda, dictated by Wordsworth* at Rydal Mount, November 1847. (The Prose Works of William Wordsworth, edited by the Rev. Alexander Grosart, London, 1876, Vol. III., pp. 219-224.)
[2] *Ibid.*
[3] *Ibid.* And see *H. C. Robinson's Diary*, 2 Feb. 1836.
[4] *Ecclesiastical Sonnets*, iii. 22.

of his mother, for him the personification of intuitive wisdom, that he has striven to revive. He has filled in her shadowy figure by means of knowledge acquired later; and partly by aid of memory, partly by conjecture, has sketched a gracious portrait of the homely guide to whom he owed his early education, and who allowed his young imagination to develop itself in freedom.

> She, not falsely taught,
> Fetching her goodness rather from times past,
> Than shaping novelties for times to come,
> Had no presumption, no such jealousy,
> Nor did by habit of her thoughts mistrust
> Our nature, but had virtual faith that He
> Who fills the mother's breast with innocent milk,
> Doth also for our nobler part provide,
> Under His great correction and control,
> As innocent instincts, and as innocent food;
> Or draws for minds that are left free to trust
> In the simplicities of opening life
> Sweet honey out of spurned or dreaded weeds.
> This was her creed, and therefore she was pure
> From anxious fear of error or mishap,
> And evil, overweeningly so called;
> Was not puffed up by false unnatural hopes,
> Nor selfish with unnecessary cares,
> Nor with impatience from the season asked
> More than its timely produce; rather loved
> The hours for what they are, than from regard
> Glanced on their promises in restless pride.[1]
> Such was she—not from faculties more strong
> Than others have, but from the times, perhaps,
> And spot in which she lived, and through a grace
> Of modest meekness, simple-mindedness,
> A heart that found benignity and hope,
> Being itself benign.[2]

Mrs Wordsworth had not however neglected the

---

[1] Mrs Wordsworth thought, with Julie, that "La Nature veut que les enfans soient des enfans avant que d'être hommes. Si nous voulons pervertir cet ordre, nous produirons des fruits précoces, qui n'auront ni maturité ni saveur, et ne tarderont pas à se corrompre; nous aurons de jeunes docteurs et de vieux enfans. . . ." *Nouvelle Héloïse*, Part V., letter 3.

[2] *The Prelude*, v. 267-293.

education of her son. She had been his first teacher,
giving him instruction in reading, while his father made
him learn by heart passages from Shakspeare, Milton
and Spenser. The death of a mother who had been
"the heart and hinge" of five youthful intelligences was
the signal for the dispersion of the family. The two
elder children required a more advanced course of instruction than could be obtained in the small schools of Cockermouth and Penrith. Their father, who, after the death
of his wife, never recovered his usual cheerfulness, was
unable by himself to manage his business, and at the same
time to attend to the education of his children. Accordingly, in 1778, William and his brother Richard were
dispatched to Hawkshead Grammar School.

CHAPTER II

Hawkshead (1778-1787)

I

IN almost every case the impression left by their school-days on the minds of modern French poets is one of gloom and irritation. The commencement of school life has marked for them the beginning of a period of useless annoyance and joyless constraint. "It took some time" (says Chateaubriand, who became a pupil in the grammar-school at Dol in the year in which Wordsworth went to Hawkshead) "for an owl like me to get accustomed to the cage of a school, and to time his flight by the sound of a bell." [1] The first thought of Lamartine, when, after leading the joyous life of a shepherd lad in the neighbourhood of Milly, he is sent at eleven years of age to a boarding-school at Lyon, and finds himself unable to endure the two-fold loss of his mother's fondness and his free roaming life in the open air, is how to escape from the hateful prison. [2] Victor Hugo, in the midst of his gay and careless existence in the garden at Feuillantines—where, unknown to himself, the first flowers of poesy were springing up within him—finding his abounding happiness in danger from the approaches made by the principal "of some grammar-school or other," congratulates himself on having been rescued for the time being by his mother's wisdom and affection. [3] For him too, however, confinement was to come ; and he has freely execrated in verse that period of seclusion at Cordier's boarding-school, which, at the instance of his father, broke in upon the happy romance of his early education. Alfred de Vigny, seeking, in his manhood, for the causes of his melancholy disposition, finds them partly in "the cold

[1] *Memoires d'outre-tombe.* [2] *Confidences,* book vi. [3] *Rayons et Ombres,* xix.

grammar-school where countless sufferings and countless
miseries used to prey upon his heart."[1]   Victor de
Laprade, looking back, in old age, towards his youth,
affirms that he always preserved " the most horrible
recollections "[2] of the grammar - school at Lyon, and
is convinced that he might have been a great poet
if he had herded cattle until he was eighteen years old,
instead of growing pale within four walls.[3] We find
the same ill-feeling expressed by Théophile Gautier,[4] the
same painful impression on the part of M. Sully-Prud-
homme.[5] Brizeux, almost alone among French poets of
the present century, regrets the time when he was a
schoolboy ; but his life at Arzanno bore no resemblance
to that at a *lycée*.

Nor is this the mere petulant caprice of dispositions
impatient of all control. It would be impossible to
deny the sincerity of these unanimous protestations, and
presumptuous to condemn them, without further investigation, as frivolous or unreasonable. The same objection
underlies all these different manifestations of anger and
vexation. French poets are agreed in attacking a system,
which, in their opinion, is regardless of the needs of the
body and the feelings, cultivates the reasoning faculty at
the expense of the others, and destroys or maims the imagination. The system of school-education, as forced upon
them, seemed hostile to their most precious gifts. They felt
compelled to defend those gifts against it. What they
received from it appeared contemptible at the price of
their lost happiness and liberty. Yet, precisely because
he was of a similar nature, and gifted with the same
instincts, Wordsworth has described the time he spent
at Hawkshead as the happiest and most fruitful period
of his life. The difference lies not between the men,
but between the institutions. When we pass from France
to England the picture changes. Not, indeed, that all
English writers are agreed in praising unreservedly the

---

[1] Letter to Brizeux, 2 August 1831.
[2] *L'Education libérale*, p. 77 (Paris, 1873).   [3] *Ibid.*, p. 288.
[4] Maxime du Camp, *Théophile Gautier*, pp. 13-19.
[5] *Les Solitudes*, Première solitude.

schools of their country. Its private seminaries, especially, have been made the object of the bitterest satire; and the public schools have not escaped abuse. Some writers, Cowper for instance,[1] have loudly denounced their immorality. Others, far more numerous, have, with Shelley,[2] protested against the brutality of scholars and masters. Yet, of those who received their education at an English public-school, none (except, now and then, Coleridge)[3] has called them either dull or gloomy.[4] The recollection of the free and joyous years of school-life, on the contrary, universally awakens the deepest gratitude and the most passionate enthusiasm. It is pretty generally known that the discipline in English schools is much more liberal than in our own, a difference which has been greatly widened in this century, since the introduction of military discipline into our *lycées* by Napoleon. But Frenchmen will hardly learn without surprise the extent of liberty that was permitted, towards the close of the eighteenth century, in a small grammar-school in the North of England, preserved, by the fact of its insignificance, and of its thoroughly rural situation, from the worst vices of which larger and more famous institutions have been accused.

II

Very modest in appearance was the school in which Wordsworth became a pupil. A small building, standing

---

[1] *Tirocinium* (1784). Here Cowper, with the assistance of Rousseau and of his own recollections, amplifies the judgment pronounced by Fielding's "Parson Adams": "Public schools are the nurseries of all vice and immorality." (*Joseph Andrews*, iii. 5.)

[2] Prelude to *Laon and Cythna*.

[3] Particularly as Charles Lamb represents him : ˉ*Christ's Hospital five and thirty years ago* (1820). In his own name Lamb had spoken most affectionately of the same school. *Recollections of Christ's Hospital* (1819).

[4] In the *Edinburgh Review* of August 1810, schools are indeed described as "scenes of present misery," but the article is so vague that the author seems to have had no experience of the schools which he condemns. He only dwells upon the favourite ideas of Rousseau. In the reply which was made to him, on the other hand (*The Pamphleteer*, August 1814), his opponent speaks of his own school with no less detail and enthusiasm than Wordsworth of his.

beneath the church and adjoining the village graveyard, it was scarcely to be distinguished from the cottages around it. One of the many grammar-schools which sprang up simultaneously in England in the sixteenth century, under the combined influence of the religious reformation and the revival of learning, it was already venerable. Here, in accordance with the statutes of its founder, Sandys, Archbishop of York, free instruction was given to the children of the district. The school was chiefly attended by farmers' sons, who were destined for the church, and brought with them the rough and brutal manners of their home-life.[1] A head-master and an usher constituted the entire staff; they taught Latin, and the elements of Greek and Mathematics. During the winter the hours of attendance were from seven in the morning till eleven, and from one till four in the afternoon. In summer-time the school opened an hour earlier and closed an hour later. These limits included the time devoted to study, as well as that spent in class, so that the boys left the school each day free from cares and duties, at liberty to pick up the thread of home-life, or at any rate of a life closely similar to it. They lodged in the village with old cottage-dames, who often treated them as their own children, and after dividing among their boarders their frugal fare—more than the lads wished they " knew the blessing then of vigorous hunger "—[2] left them free to ramble where they would, to play about the village square or wander off on more distant expeditions.

Although Wordsworth readily acknowledged that he might have found elsewhere " a fatter soil of arts and letters,"[3] we are not to suppose that education was neglected at Hawkshead. Towards the close of the eighteenth century this school was reputed one of the best establishments in the North, and we might mention the names of more than one of its *alumni* who afterwards attained the highest distinction at College. Yet the poet's gratitude is not for the instruction he received, but for the free and natural life which he led at Hawkshead. It was

---

[1] Prefatory note to *The Excursion*.   [2] *The Prelude*, ii. 78-81.
[3] *Ibid.*, v. 408-410

not his fate to breathe that unnatural atmosphere in which most boys pass their school-life. Even within the bounds of the establishment, teachers and pupils were on a footing of the most unusual familiarity. The masters not only directed the scholars in their studies, nor merely companionized them in their games; occasionally they became also their friends, so far as to throw off the professional mask which disguised their characters, and even at times to confide to the elder boys their manly joys and sorrows. This is evident from those of Wordsworth's poems in which he blends with the characteristics of a personage of his own creation the living recollections which he retained of his masters. Nothing can bear less resemblance than Wordsworth's *Matthew* to the rustic pedagogue, that solemn pedant crammed with dog-Latin, who up to that time had only found a place in satire. Wordsworth has divested him of all the professional characteristics sanctioned by convention, and has described him as an old man easy of approach, blending gaiety with sadness, and shedding the light of a cheerful and benevolent disposition alike over the stately halls and rude cottages of the neighbourhood.[1]

Wordsworth and he would talk with open heart together, although the one was not yet sixteen years of age, while the other was sixty-two. The old man with " hair of glittering grey," who would sing idle songs of his own composition, was no stranger to " fun and madness," [2] and at times would become the gayest of the gay. But

> when the secret cup
> Of still and serious thought went round,
> It seemed as if he drank it up—
> He felt with spirit so profound.[3]

Even in the midst of his fits of glee a sigh would betray his hidden grief. A floating cloud, "the very brother" of one seen years before,[4] the gurgling of a stream heard in former

---

[1] *Address to the Scholars of the Village School of . . .*
[2] *Matthew.*   [3] *Ibid.*   [4] *The two April Mornings.*

days, would remind him of the past. He grows old in
solitude; yet when the school-boy offers to take the place
of his lost children, he presses the lad's hand and replies
" That cannot be." Then, but a few moments later, he
takes up his song again, light-hearted as a bird.[1]

Although, in his sketch of this character, Wordsworth
aimed at poetic rather than literal truth, he admits having
derived several of its lineaments from William Taylor,
his favourite teacher, who acted as headmaster of the
school during the last four years which the boy spent
there, and died some months before he left. Taylor,
whose death occurred in his prime, is certainly not the
exact original of *Matthew*. But a similar close bond of
affection seems to have attached him to Wordsworth.
When, on his death-bed, he summoned the older scholars
to his room, and bade them farewell with his solemn
blessing, Wordsworth, who was among the number, kissed
the dying man's cheek, undertook to announce to the
younger boys the death of their master, and carried away
a lasting recollection of his homely precepts. Himself
imbued with the love of nature [2] Taylor was perhaps the
first to detect and stimulate it in Wordsworth, as he was
certainly the first to encourage his early efforts in poetry.
Thus when eight years later the poet, no longer a stripling, paid a visit to Taylor's grave, the tears came into his
eyes as in fancy he once more heard the voice and saw the
countenance of his master. He felt that in him, if he were
still alive, his poetry would find an indulgent critic,
and that one at whose bidding his first lines had been
laboriously composed, would welcome with delight the
realization of his hopes. [3]

But it was not within the college alone that the schoolboy's affectionate nature contrived to find satisfaction, and
his feelings their first opportunity of culture. No barriers
shut off the school from the world outside it, and the
child was in constant contact with human life. He lived
among the village people, as a little village lad, loving
some, interested in the occupations of others, at home

[1] *The Fountain.*   [2] *Address to the Scholars of the Village School of* . . .
[3] *The Prelude,* x. 532-552.

with all. In the first place there was old Anne Tyson,
" so kind and motherly," [1] with whom he lodged. The
habit of taking in scholars to board had engendered in her
none of that harshness and indifference which arise from
the methodical performance of a duty. Devoid of every
trace of conventionality and affectation, treating her
lodgers as her own family, she became known to them
not only in her daily performance of a compulsory task,
but in all the detail of her humble life. She concealed
from them neither the cares nor the joys which visited her
roof, and told them many a story of those who lived, or
had lived, in the neighbourhood. [2]

Wordsworth could not leave his lodging without catch-
ing sight at once of other well-known figures ; sometimes
of peasants, sometimes of pedlars or tramps who visited
the village in the course of their regular round ; faces
seen so often that, many years later, their impression
remained graven on his recollection in the minutest
detail. There was old Daniel, so old that he had relapsed
into second childhood, and had ceased to be stirred by
any passion save avarice. Every morning, one of the first
in the village to rise, he would set out, holding the hand
of his little three-year-old grandson. By mutual consent
they used to steal everything they came across in their
walk ; the shavings fallen from the carpenter's plane, the
sods of turf piled on a cart. The dull expressionless eyes
of the old man, who set the example to the child, would
assume meanwhile a look of cunning ; but their offence
was really no sin, for the child only half knew what he
was doing, and old Daniel did not know at all. Every
one was aware of their pilferings, yet neither rich nor
poor sought to restrain them. Every face, as they passed,
broke into smiles. For Daniel had a daughter at home
who was always ready to repair the wrong he had done,
and to restore its value, if need were, three-fold. [3] Even
the schoolboy found, in the daily walk of these two

---

[1] *Prelude,* iv. 28.

[2] For instance, of the Jacobite and the Hanoverian (*Excursion,* vi. 404-
521), see prefatory note to *The Excursion* ; and also of the mother of
Benoni " the child of sorrow " (prefatory note to *Peter Bell*).

[3] *The Two Thieves.*

creatures, food for pity and reflection. "No book could have so early taught me to think of the changes to which human life is subject"; and while looking at old Daniel, "I could not but say to myself—we may, one of us, I or the happiest of my playmates, live to become still more the object of pity than this old man, this half-doting pilferer!"[1]

Then there was the old beggar who, in the course of his round, would knock, on a regular day, at the doors of certain houses where he received alms. So old, so feeble that he excites the pity of all;

> So helpless in appearance, that for him
> The sauntering Horseman throws not with a slack
> And careless hand his alms upon the ground,
> But stops,—that he may safely lodge the coin
> Within the old Man's hat; nor quits him so,
> But still, when he has given his horse the rein,
> Watches the aged Beggar with a look
> Sidelong, and half-reverted. She who tends
> The toll-gate, when in summer at her door
> She turns her wheel, if on the road she sees
> The aged Beggar coming, quits her work,
> And lifts the latch for him that he may pass.
> The post-boy, when his rattling wheels o'ertake
> The aged Beggar in the woody lane,
> Shouts to him from behind; and, if thus warned
> The old man does not change his course, the boy
> Turns with less noisy wheels to the roadside,
> And passes gently by, without a curse
> Upon his lips or anger at his heart.

The school-boy observed with jealous care the softening, helpful influence exercised by this poor creature, to all appearance so useless, on the parsimonious hearts of the villagers. He marked the almsdeeds of a neighbour, poor herself, as every Friday brought the old beggar to her door.

> She from her store of meal
> Takes one unsparing handful for the scrip
> Of this old Mendicant, and, from her door
> Returning with exhilarated heart,
> Sits by her fire, and builds her hope in heaven.

[1] *The Two Thieves*, prefatory note.

Wordsworth comes very near attributing to the vagrant the birth of his own genius.

Some there are,

By their good works exalted, lofty minds,
And meditative, authors of delight
And happiness, which to the end of time
Will live, and spread, and kindle : even such minds
In childhood, from this solitary Being,
Or from like wanderer, haply have received
(A thing more precious far than all that books
Or the solicitudes of love can do !)
That first mild touch of sympathy and thought,
In which they found their kindred with a world
Where want and sorrow were.[1]

These characters however were merely passers by, known only by sight. With others Wordsworth formed curious and even close acquaintanceships ; as, for instance, with the pedlar who lived from time to time at Hawkshead, and could tell stories, which the boy loved to elicit, of his wandering life and of what he had seen and noted. He is, to some extent, the original of the pedlar in *The Excursion*.[2]

He loved me ; from a swarm of rosy boys
Singled out me, as he in sport would say,
For my grave looks, too thoughtful for my years.
As I grew up, it was my best delight
To be his chosen comrade. Many a time,
On holidays, we rambled through the woods :
We sate—we walked ; he pleased me with report
Of things which he had seen ; and often touched
Abstrusest matter, reasonings of the mind
Turned inward ; or at my request would sing
Old songs, the product of his native hills ;
A skilful distribution of sweet sounds,
Feeding the soul, and eagerly imbibed
As cool refreshing water, by the care
Of the industrious husbandman, diffused
Through a parched meadow-ground, in time of drought.
Still deeper welcome found his pure discourse :
How precious when in riper days I learned

---

[1] *The Old Cumberland Beggar.*   [2] *The Excursion*, prefatory note.

> To weigh with care his words, and to rejoice
> In the plain presence of his dignity ! [1]

The mild discipline of the school permitted of the strangest and most varied intercourse. Thus Wordsworth tells us that one day he followed an angler up to the source of the Duddon beyond the hills, and after fishing with him all day under a pelting rain, was carried home on his back, worn out with fatigue.[2] On another occasion he made the acquaintance of an Irish lad employed by a strolling mountebank, and took him to see a favourite spot on the borders of Esthwaite Water. He wished to enjoy his chance companion's pleasure in the prospect, nor was he deceived in his expectation.[3]

III

The pupils at Hawkshead seem to have enjoyed in the matter of reading the same liberty as was allowed them in their acquaintanceships, and Wordsworth affirms that he derived no less pleasure from his excursions in the world of books than from his friendships formed in chance encounters on the Cumberland roads. If we may believe him, the development of his intellectual powers was due principally to his private reading, and not to the regular tasks which were prescribed for him. On this point he is frankly at variance with Rousseau, although he agrees, or seems to agree, with him in all other respects on the subject of education. Rousseau looked upon reading as " the plague of childhood," and condemned all the works read by the young in his day as unintelligible or immoral, absurd or fantastic.[5] Accordingly, after the success of *Emile*, and in spite of Rousseau himself, there sprang up a new literature for children designed to combine amusement with moral teaching and general instruction. Under

---

[1] *The Excursion*, i. 52-76.   [2] *The River Duddon*, prefatory note.
[3] *The Yew-tree Seat*, prefatory note.   [4] *Emile*, book ii.
[5] On this point Rousseau agrees with Lord Chesterfield, the law-giver of artificial education, who excluded the novels of the last two centuries, and also the "ravings and extravagancies" of the Arabian story-tellers. Letter to his son, No. 184, 5 Feb. 1750.

the thin disguise of a slender thread of narrative it conveyed, often very unskilfully, some simple moral lesson or some chapter in natural science. Weisse in Germany, Berquin in France, and Thomas Day,[1] Mrs Trimmer[2] and Mrs Barbauld[3] in England were beginning to enrich the young with their sapient and improving works just at the time when Wordsworth entered Hawkshead grammar-school.

The poet congratulates himself on having come into the world early enough and having been brought up in a district so secluded as to escape reading of this kind. But we may say more. He "pours out thanks with uplifted heart" when he reflects how he has been preserved from a pest "that might have dried him up body and soul."[4] He rejoices that instead of these books he has read the artless and diverting fables which make the child forget himself; the legendary exploits of Robin Hood, the wonderful adventures of Jack the Giant Killer or of Fortunatus, the owner of the magic cap.[5] One of his favourite books was the *Thousand and One Nights*. He had read some scanty extracts from them at Cockermouth, in "a little, yellow, canvas-covered book," a priceless treasure in his eyes. When he learnt from his schoolfellows that this volume was "but a block hewn from a mighty quarry" he could scarcely contain himself for joy. On the spot he entered into partnership with another boy as poor as himself, and the two agreed to lay aside all their pocket-money in order, some day, to purchase the four big volumes which contained the Arabian tales complete. For several months they adhered to their compact in spite of all temptations. But their firmness failed at last, and they never possessed the coveted work.[6]

---

[1] The first part of *Sandford and Merton* appeared in 1783, the second in 1789.

[2] Mrs. Trimmer (1741-1810) wrote a multitude of educational works, principally religious ones.

[3] Her *Early Lessons* appeared in 1775. Between 1792 and 1795 appeared the *Evenings at Home*, which she wrote in collaboration with her brother, Dr John Aikin. Miss Edgeworth continued the movement in her *Practical Education* (1798) and her *Moral Tales* (1801).

[4] *The Prelude*, v. 225-229.   [5] *Ibid.*, 341-346.   [6] *Ibid.*, v. 460-476.

The poet's gratitude overflows at the recollection of these fairy-books, which seem to him more appropriate than any others to the special genius of childhood. He blesses the " dreamers," the " forgers of daring tales," whom philosophy treats as drivelling dotards. Is it not just that strange elastic faculty which they alone possess that is so eminently adapted to the expansive energy of the little being who, newly arrived on earth, is as yet ignorant of the narrow limits of his capacities, who has not yet become resigned to human weakness, who has not yet bowed his head beneath the yoke of custom, whose unbroken spirit is still full of boundless hope? Their wonderful stories satisfy within us those " dumb yearnings, hidden appetites " which " *must* have their food." [1] These imaginative works become the child's true friends. They turn his desires into fruition, his dreams into reality. Time and space become their slaves; for them " the elements are potter's clay." [2]   Instead of clipping the child's wings to prevent him from soaring into that free air which is his true dwelling-place, they lay bare before him, if but for a moment, the vast plains of that wide firmament where the laws of matter are unknown.

What contempt, therefore, what wrath he pours forth upon the presumption of those who pretend to train the child by meting out to him the joys of imagination, marking out in advance the limits of his reading, making a selection of his books and of the chapters within the books. " Oh! where had been the Man, the Poet where," he says to Coleridge,

> Where had we been, we two, beloved Friend! [3]
> If in the season of unperilous choice,

---

[1] *The Prelude*, v, 506-507.   [2] *Ibid.*, v, 531.

[3] There is something in this which seems to contradict the general import of Wordsworth's teaching,—his vindication of the beauty of the real world as distinguished from the land of dreams and fancy. It may perhaps be ascribed to the influence of Coleridge, as well as to Wordsworth's remembrance of his early delight in fairy tales. In 1797 Coleridge anticipated Wordsworth by attributing the origin of his best intellectual gifts to the fairy-tales he had read. " I know no other way," he wrote, " of giving the mind a love of the Great and the Whole. Those who have been led to the same truths step by step, through the constant testi-

In lieu of wandering, as we did, through vales
Rich with indigenous produce, open ground
Of Fancy, happy pastures ranged at will,
We had been followed, hourly watched, and noosed,
Each in his several melancholy walk
Stringed like a poor man's heifer at its feed,
Led through the lanes in forlorn servitude ;
Or rather like a stallèd ox debarred
From touch of growing grass, that may not taste
A flower till it have yielded up its sweets
A prelibation to the mower's scythe.[1]

The liberty of reading enjoyed by Wordsworth was by no means confined to fairy-tales. It extended, we must admit, to other works which English people of to-day would either expurgate or place under lock and key. From the very commencement of his school days [2] he read, at the college as well as at home during the holidays, the whole of Fielding, *Don Quixote*, *Gil Blas*, and all that he cared to read of Swift. *The Travels of Gulliver* and *The Tale of a Tub* delighted him above everything else.

Though destined afterwards to become so thoroughly independent of books, he was at that time passionately fond of reading. He loved it with an almost guilty love ; a love so strong that it provoked the stings of conscience. When, on coming home for his first vacation, he discovered again the rich store of volumes he had left there, he was beside himself with delight. " How often," he says,

> though a soft west wind
> Ruffled the waters to the angler's wish,
> For a whole day together, have I lain

mony of their senses, seem to me to want a sense which I possess. They contemplate nothing but *parts*, and all *parts* are necessarily little. And the universe to them is but a mass of *little things*." Letter to Thomas Poole, 16 October 1797. *Letters of S. T. Coleridge*, edited by E. H. Coleridge, London, 1895, vol. i. p. 12.

Charles Lamb followed up with spirit the attacks of Coleridge upon profitable reading for children. (Letter to Coleridge, Oct. 23, 1802). " Mrs Barbauld's stuff has banished all the old classics of the nursery . . . Think what you would have been now, if, instead of being fed with tales and old wives' fables in childhood, you had been crammed with geography and natural history."

[1] *The Prelude*, v. 232-245.   [2] *Autobiographical Memoranda*, op. cit.

Down by thy side, O Derwent! murmuring stream,
On the hot stones, and in the glaring sun,
And there have read, devouring as I read,
Defrauding the day's glory, desperate!
Till with a sudden bound of smart reproach,
Such as an idler deals with in his shame,
I to the sport betook myself again.[1]

Strange, this compunction on deserting his sport! It was the pleasures of the body, not the exercises of the mind, which the lad was thus ashamed to neglect. In truth he had already a dim perception that the best and most powerful agent in his training was nature. The principal part in his education was played neither by his masters nor by his books, but by his open-air life, his games with his companions, his expeditions in the country around Hawkshead. The chief interest of his existence as a school-boy lay not in his intellectual labours but in his physical recreations. We shall see what these were, and, in the first place, the scene amidst which they beguiled the passing hour.

IV

Hawkshead is an old market-town, its narrow, winding alleys paved with broad blue flagstones. Above it the spirit of the past seems to hover; it remains benumbed, as it were, with age, amidst the villages, scattered about the lake-district, which seem to grow daily newer and more gay; one of those ancient spots where life seems at a standstill, and old customs and old dwellings are sheltered from the wind of fashion and of progress. Archbishop Sandys, if he were to see it again to-day, after an interval of three centuries, would recognise it without difficulty. The surrounding country, peaceful rather than sublime, intensifies this impression of repose. The little lake of Esthwaite, rather more than half a mile further south, is bordered with smooth green pastures, the hills around it being of very moderate elevation. But

1 *The Prelude*, v. 477-490.

at short distances, in all directions, there is a profusion of the most varied and picturesque scenery. To the east, three miles from Hawkshead, stretches the great sheet of Windermere, the largest of the English lakes, situated on the borders of Lancashire and Westmoreland. Six miles to the north lie the lovely little meres of Grasmere and Rydal, in the neighbourhood of the poet's future home. Beyond them are the lofty summits of Fairfield and Helvellyn, visible from Hawkshead. Nearer still, to the west, on the shores of Coniston lake, rise the peaks of Coniston Old Man and Wetherlam. And, lastly, a day's ride will bring one to the sandy shores of Morecambe bay, or to the Irish sea.

These beauties, which would have been a dead letter for boarders rigorously confined, lay spread before Wordsworth and his companions as a banquet on which they might feast at their pleasure. Doubtless the need of companionship often kept them in the market place around the mass of rock which was the centre of their games, and on which, in the open air, an old dame used to spread such dainties as were within their slender means.[1] Often, too, on winter evenings, they delighted to assemble in one of the houses in the village, and to play at cards while the wind roared outside.[2] But their diversions did not stop there. No bound was set to their expeditions; there were no fixed times, other than class-hours, for going out and coming in. Early morning, broad daylight, and evening shed around them in turn their poetic charm. Sometimes, on a sunny afternoon, they would climb a hill to fly a kite, which rose among the fleecy clouds and tugged at its rein like an impetuous courser; sometimes they would launch it from the meadows below, to see it breast the wind and then fall headlong, hurled from aloft by a squall.[3] In autumn a troop of them would set out to gather the harvest of hedgerow and wood. In summer, often, with rod and line they sought the rocks and pools shut out from every star, or the bends of mountain-streams.[4] Or else, if it were spring time, they would

---

[1] *The Prelude*, ii. 33-46.
[2] *Ibid.*, i. 499-513.
[3] *Ibid.*, i. 491-498.
[4] *Ibid.*, i. 483-490.

scale the mountain precipices to rob the ravens' nests.
Then Wordsworth would experience the keen delight of
dangerous enterprise.

> Oh! when I have hung
> Above the raven's nest, by knots of grass
> And half-inch fissures in the slippery rock
> But ill sustained and almost (so it seemed)
> Suspended by the blast that blew amain,
> Shouldering the naked crag, oh, at that time
> While on the perilous ridge I hung alone,
> With what strange utterance did the loud dry wind
> Blow through my ear! the sky seemed not a sky
> Of earth—and with what motion moved the clouds! [1]

But it is in his solitary adventures most of all that
Wordsworth feels himself influenced by obscure yet
powerful agencies. How many of them he has comme-
morated—those precious moments in which Nature works
on the mind by fear, astonishment, or the sense of beauty!
The first sentiment to affect his young imagination is fear,
that vague and mysterious emotion, which, when inspired
by nature, derives from her both beauty and dignity.

See him as in wintertime he ranges the mountain slopes
setting springes for birds. He is scarcely ten years old.
During half the night he runs anxiously from snare to
snare to see whether any birds have been caught. Moon
and stars are shining above him, and it seems to him, in
his loneliness, that he troubles the peace which dwells
among them. Sometimes it befalls that he gives way to
temptation, and secures for himself a bird caught in a
trap belonging to another; and when the deed is done he
hears among the solitary hills low breathings, as it were,
coming after him, sounds of 'undistinguishable motion,'
steps scarcely less silent than the turf they tread. [2]

Every transgression is visited by a mysterious and
inevitable compunction. One summer evening the boy
unlooses a boat which is not his own, and pulls vigorously
out upon Esthwaite lake. But, as he rows onward,
remorse for his stealthy deed mingles itself with his

[1] *The Prelude*, i. 326-339.   [2] *Ibid.*, i. 306-325.

pleasure.　To guide his course he fixes his view on the highest point of a low craggy ridge.　Suddenly

> from behind that craggy steep, till then
> The horizon's bound, a huge peak, black and huge,
> As if with voluntary power instinct
> Upreared its head.

As the lad rows steadily onwards the fearful shape towers up higher and higher between him and the stars, and like a living thing strides rapidly after him.　In terror he turns his boat, crosses the meadows, and gains his dwelling once more.　But for many days after witnessing this spectacle his brain is beset with a dim and undetermined sense of unknown modes of being.　A cloud of darkness hangs over his thoughts; he forgets the dear familiar spots, the graceful forms of the trees, the flowers, the sky, the greenness of the fields; and huge phantoms that do not live like living men move slowly through his mind by day and become a trouble to his dreams.[1]

Nature provides her own defence against his attacks upon her, in the pity which she inspires and the remorse which she excites within him.　One day the schoolboy leaves his lodging, and wallet on shoulder and nutting-crook in hand seeks a grove of hazels.　He finds at last one as yet unvisited.　No withered leaves droop mournfully from its branches; the hazels stand erect, untouched, loaded with tempting fruit.　For a time the lad remains motionless, his heart oppressed with delight, and relishes in anticipation the banquet within his reach.　Then, in leisurely security, he stretches himself beneath the trees, gradually captivated by the peculiar charm of the spot where violets bloom and fade unseen and a fairy waterbrook murmurs on perpetually.　Rising at last, however, completely possessed by the lust of plunder, he ruthlessly drags down the branches, and the beautiful, secluded grove patiently yields up its quiet life.　His ravages ended, his wallet filled to overflowing, he turns to go; but as he does so his glance is arrested by the scene of devastation, and the

[1] *The Prelude*, i. 357-400.

sight of the deep shades, an hour ago unbroken, but now rent by the intruding light of heaven, fills him with secret pain.[1]

Nothing can be at once more subtle and more universal than these impressions. Though Wordsworth has been the only one to express them, it is impossible to conceive an age or a clime in which they have not been felt. They are so elementary that it seems as if only in the childhood of humanity could they have been experienced with such intensity and interpreted with so much freshness. Such must have been the impressions which inspired the creators of myths, the earliest members of the human race. It is some avenging deity, invisible but distinctly heard, whose steps pursue the school-boy after his transgression; some wrathful Titan who in the form of that living crag terrifies him by the suddenness of its apparition; some dryad that haunts the hazel-grove, her fair form which is maimed by his brutality, her life which he destroys, her sanctuary which he lays in ruins. Nay, Wordsworth's sensations are anterior even to the myths which have arisen from such sensations, and by explaining them and substituting for the obscurity of their origin the familiar forms of beings almost human, have little by little altered their form and destroyed their vividness, until at last the invented fable has overpowered the vague sense of dread. We must go back further still, beyond the age when the earth was peopled by gods and demons made in the likeness of men, to the time when the mountain itself had a conscious life all the more fearful because it was quite unknown, and when in place of the dryad there was " a spirit in the woods."[2] Wordsworth's childish hallucinations are perhaps more nearly akin to those of the superstitious savage who trembles amidst the weird forms assumed by natural objects.[3] According to the primitive moral philosophy to which it gives rise, Nature conceals by day a multitude

---

[1] *Nutting.*   [2] *Nutting.*
[3] *Cf.* Jean Lahor, *l' Illusion* (Lemerre 1893):—
    Certains soirs, en errant dans les forêts natales,
    Je ressens dans ma chair les frissons d'autrefois,
    Quand la nuit grandissant les formes végétales,
    Sauvage, halluciné, je rampais sous les bois.

of terrible beings who come forth at night to punish evil-doers. The earliest remorse of childhood, in the infancy of humanity as in that of individual man, is accompanied by, and even confounded with, physical terrors.

But not all Wordsworth's sensations conveyed at this time the same clear moral teaching. Often they were merely mysterious suggestions of ideas or visual impressions never to be forgotten. Such for example is the celebrated skating scene on Esthwaite lake. School-time is over at sunset, and shod with steel the boys amuse themselves upon the ice, repeating their usual games in changing groups. The precipices echo around them, the leafless trees and ice-bound crags tinkle like iron, while the distant mountains mingle with the joyous tumult an alien sound of melancholy, the stars sparkle clearly in the east, and in the west the orange light of evening dies away. Often, at such times, Wordsworth forsakes the uproar for a silent bay, or glides off far from the noisy crowd to cleave the flying image of a star which gleams ever before him as he skims the ice. Often too, as he flies before the wind, while the black and gloomy shores sweep rapidly past him in the darkness, he leans backwards on his heels and comes to a standstill,—and the solitary cliffs go spinning onwards before him, as if the earth's diurnal motion had become visible. Behind him, too, they march, ever more and more slowly, in solemn procession, as he stands gazing until all resumes again the tranquillity of a dreamless sleep. [1]

The depressing effect of some of the spectacles presented to him by nature received an occasional corrective from his study of imaginative literature. Instead of aggravating

---

[1] *The Prelude*, i. 425-463. A fine skating-scene occurs also in the *Confidences* of Lamartine (bk. v. 5), though it is altogether different from that described by Wordsworth. And the difference is very characteristic of the two poets, whose genius presents more than one analogy, and whose youth was passed in much the same manner. What Wordsworth especially enjoys is some sudden strangeness in the aspect of his surroundings; what pleases Lamartine is the beauty of his own form and movements; "Se sentir emporté avec la rapidité de la flèche et avec les gracieuses ondulations de l'oiseau dans l'air, sur une surface plane, brillante, sonore et perfide; s'imprimer à soi-même, par un simple balancement du corps, et, pour ainsi dire, par le seul gouvernail de la volonté, toutes les courbes, toutes les inflex-

his fears, as is the case with most children, his reading allayed the dread which nature inspired in him, by detaching it from the objects of the external world and mingling with it a beauty derived from itself. During the first week of his residence at Hawkshead, Wordsworth was roaming in the open fields which thrust out their green peninsulas into Esthwaite lake. Twilight was at hand, but he could make out upon the opposite shore a heap of clothes apparently left there by a bather. Soon the still lake grew dark with shadows, and every sound was hushed, save when

> a fish upleaping snapped
> The breathless stillness.

The next day, those unclaimed garments told a tale which drew an anxious crowd to the lake side, some remaining on the bank to watch with passive expectation, others taking a boat and leaning over its side to sound the water with grappling-irons and long poles.

> At last, the dead man, 'mid that beauteous scene
> Of trees and hills and water, bolt upright
> Rose, with his ghastly face, a spectre shape
> Of terror.

Young as he was, however, the lad felt " no soul-debasing fear," for his

> inner eye had seen
> Such sights before, among the shining streams
> Of faery land, the forest of romance.
> Their spirit hallowed the sad spectacle
> With decoration of ideal grace ;
> A dignity, a smoothness, like the works
> Of Grecian art and purest poesy.[1]

ions de la barque sur la mer ou de l'aigle planant dans le bleu du ciel c'était pour moi et ce serait encore, si je ne respectais pas mes années, une telle ivresse des sens et un si voluptueux étourdissement de la pensée que je n'y puis songer sans émotion."

Wordsworth also prided himself on his proficiency as a skater, but if we may believe the malicious de Quincey he skated as gracefully as a duck disports itself on dry land.

[1] *The Prelude*, v. 426-459.

During the earlier part of his school-life it is not Wordsworth who seeks Nature; it is rather Nature who, at
certain hours in the midst of his sport, thrusts herself upon
him. Even thus early he perceives "gleams like the
flashing of a shield;"—

> the earth
> And common face of Nature spake to me
> Rememberable things.[1]

But it is his games alone that really absorb him. He
gives himself up unreservedly to the delight of exercising
his healthy body, and wearying out his robust limbs.
What delights him is the pure gratification of his senses,
the unconscious pleasure derived from organic sensation.
He is never happier than when he reaches home

> Feverish with weary joints and beating mind.[2]

If perchance in his wanderings Nature manifests herself
or speaks to him, he is alarmed and rendered uneasy as
if within the presence of an unfamiliar being. Only very
gradually does he come to take delight in being with her,
and to prefer among his pleasures those which have her
beauty for their background. He discovers then how she
restrains his impetuosity in sport, and how her pervading
charm almost surpasses the intoxication of his amusements.

On half holidays the boys would set off for Windermere
lake, to indulge in a boat-race on its broad surface. Sometimes the goal would be an island ringing with the ceaseless
music of melodious birds, sometimes a sister-isle where
lilies of the valley bloomed beneath the shade of oaks, or
else a third where might still be seen the ruins of a chapel
dedicated to Our Lady. In such contests disappointment,
pain and jealousy could have no place; victors and van-
quished stretched themselves in the shade, equally happy
and contented, the pride of strength was subdued, and
the vanity of superior skill forgotten. Thus Wordsworth
received his first lessons in self-distrust and modesty, and
learned to feel, perhaps too much, the self-sufficing power
of Solitude.[3]

Or again they cross the same lake to play and drink in

---

[1] *The Prelude*, i. 585-8.   [2] *Ibid.*, ii. 18.   [3] *Ibid.*, ii. 54-77

a smart tavern at Bowness where their bursts of glee make
the hills around them ring.   Then, before nightfall, they
return at their leisure over the shadowy lake, touch at a
small islet, and row gently off again, leaving behind them
one of their number, the minstrel of the troop, who plays
his flute upon the rock.   "Oh, then" says Wordsworth,

> the calm
> And dead still water lay upon my mind
> Even with a weight of pleasure, and the sky,
> Never before so beautiful, sank down
> Into my heart, and held me like a dream ! [1]

When their purses were full, there were riding
excursions as far as Furness Abbey.   There, in the roofless nave of the old ruin, where he had sought shelter
from the rain, Wordsworth heard one day a wren singing
so sweetly in the darkness that, in spite of the water which
dripped from the streaming ivy, he would fain have made
his dwelling place there and have lived for ever in that
spot to hear such music.   Thence the young riders gallop
back to Hawkshead, with the moonlight gleaming brightly
about them ; and when the horses slacken speed to climb a
steep hill-side, or while their hoofs thunder on the level sand
and the sea throws back the moon-beams, Wordsworth feels
a spirit of peace shed abroad on the evening air.[2]

Thus the recollection of nature in her awful or gentle
aspects, her grand or tender moods, becomes for him
inseparable from the joys which he has tasted in her
presence.   But while the vulgar pleasure fades quickly
from his memory, the scenes which were a witness of it
remain imprinted in their essential lineaments on his mind,
and daily visible before his eyes.[3]   Then there springs up
within him an affection born of gratitude.   "I loved the
sun," he says, because

> I had seen him lay
> His beauty on the morning hills, had seen
> The western mountain touch his setting orb,
> In many a thoughtless hour, when, from excess
> Of happiness, my blood appeared to flow

---

[1] *The Prelude*, ii. 138-174.   [2] *Ibid.*, ii. 115-137.   [3] *Ibid.*, i. 597-602.

For its own pleasure, and I breathed with joy.
And, from like feelings, humble though intense,
To patriotic and domestic love
Analogous, the moon to me was dear;
For I could dream away my purposes,
Standing to gaze upon her while she hung
Midway between the hills, as if she knew
No other region, but belonged to thee,
Yea, appertained by a peculiar right
To thee and thy grey huts, thou one dear Vale! [1]

Finally, towards the close of his life at Hawkshead, when he is seventeen years old, gratitude yields to pure love, a feeling thenceforth strong enough to dispense with the support which has hitherto contributed to its maintenance and growth. The additional attraction of games is no longer required in order to draw him towards nature; the pleasures he has known at her side are not needed in order to arouse his love. [2] He enters into direct communion with her; he dedicates to her the adoration of a devoted fervent heart; yet, even before the object of his worship, he retains the independence of his soul. In her presence, it will be seen, he finds himself not crushed, but exalted.

V

Hitherto Wordsworth has revealed himself to us merely as absorbed in passive contemplation of nature's forms and in silent attention to her voices. We are now to learn from him something of the active and creative faculties of his mind. He has told us how he had been moulded and fashioned by nature ; he will be seen moulding and fashioning her in his turn.

If he seems to have been backward in alluding to the active side of his being, it is not because he believes it to have originated at a late stage of his development, but rather because he was slow to become conscious of it. It existed in him, as it exists in each of us, from early

[1] *The Prelude*, ii. 175-197.   [2] *Ibid.*, ii. 198-203.

childhood. The slender frame of the nursling cradled in
his mother's arms is not merely the plaything, but is also
in measure the source, of the gravitation which binds it to
the universe ; the pebble thrown by the child's tiny hand
attracts to itself the earth's enormous mass and puts innumerable worlds into imperceptible motion.   Similarly
his little soul lives and exercises its powers within the
bosom of the universal soul.   Among the mysterious
threads which connect it with the universe there are some
which proceed from itself, and have been woven out of
its own substance. His sensibility, that "great birth-
right of our being," is already creative as well as
receptive. From the moment when the child has held,
"by intercourse of touch," "mute dialogues with his
mother's heart," there flows from both of them "a virtue
which irradiates and exalts" the objects around them.
Seen through the atmosphere of love which enfolds the
mother as she bears the child in her arms, those objects
are refracted and transformed. The flower to which the
infant points, with a hand as yet too feeble to pluck it, is
beautified in his eyes by a love "drawn from love's purest
earthly fount." "Shades of pity cast" by the tenderness
of the mother's heart "fall around him upon aught that
bears unsightly marks of violence or harm." [1]

When the danger of his first experience of solitude was
over, when he was separated from his mother that he
might learn to walk alone, and might grope his own way
to a knowledge of the visible world, Wordsworth preserved unimpaired that capacity for love which transforms
and sanctifies, that "first poetic spirit of our human life," [2]
which in the majority of men so soon grows faint or
disappears. The props of his affection were removed

> And yet the building stood, as if sustained
> By its own spirit. [3]

To the vitality of these gifts in him he owed his burning
desire to learn, and his keen delight in discovering, every
day something fresh in a world where all was so dear to

[1] *The Prelude*, ii. 232-265.   [2] *Ibid.*, ii. 261.   [3] *Ibid.*, ii. 265-281.

him. From the same source, too, he derived a vigilant eye and an ear ever ready to grasp the secrets of nature and of man. The sublime and radiant visions of his imagination are due to the beauty and intensity with which he himself infused external nature.[1] The keenness of his sensibility imparted to objects the power of creating impressions so clear in outline and so vivid in colour, that their image became imprinted on his mind like reality itself; hence he afterwards finds it difficult to distinguish that image from the objects actually presented to his senses. [2]

Never, in the slightest degree, does his soul lose consciousness of itself, or feel its separate personality absorbed in the universe. His individuality is, on the contrary, so irreducible, and so intense, that its warmth seems to melt within itself, as in a central crucible, the solid matter of the world. The Hawkshead schoolboy has at times a sense of the dissolution of the material world, of

> Fallings from us, vanishings;
> Blank misgivings of a Creature
> Moving about in worlds not realised.[3]

" I was often unable," he says, " to think of external things as having external existence, and I communed with all that I saw as something not apart from, but inherent in, my own immaterial nature. Many times while going to school have I grasped at a wall or tree to recall myself from this abyss of idealism to the reality." [4]

Yet, far from shunning these states of ecstasy, it happens, at times, that he actually induces them. Raising the latch of his cottage-door early in the morning, before a single chimney in the village has begun to smoke, he goes to sit alone in the woods on an abrupt eminence, whence he watches the first gleams of the dawn, across the solitude of the slumbering valley.

---

[1] *The Prelude*, ii. 281-329.
[2] *The Excursion*, i. 136-9. The Wanderer's education is an epitome of that of Wordsworth, with a few variations.
[3] *Ode on Intimations of Immortality*. st. ix.
[4] *Ibid.*, prefatory note.

> Oft in these moments such a holy calm
> Would overspread my soul, that bodily eyes
> Were utterly forgotten, and what I saw
> Appeared like something in myself, a dream,
> A prospect in the mind.[1]

When he awakes from these trances in which the world
becomes a part of his consciousness and nothing more;
when he recovers the idea of a real universe apart from
himself, his personality remains none the less supreme
and all-powerful. But it no longer merely absorbs, it
overflows. He takes his own nature for the universal
type, and imposes on all other beings the law of his own
being. He conceives everything in his own image.
Since joy fills his own life he transfers his "own enjoyments to inorganic natures." He sees "blessings spread
around him like a sea." Intensely sensible of his own
existence, he cannot but feel

> the sentiment of Being spread
> O'er all that moves and all that seemeth still,
> O'er all that leaps and runs, and shouts and sings,
> Or beats the gladsome air; o'er all that glides
> Beneath the wave, yea, in the wave itself,
> And mighty depth of waters.[2]

This faculty of endowing the visible world with life
and warmth and colour is no other, if we are to believe
him, than the very essence of poetic genius. Henceforth
he possesses the creative imagination.

> A plastic power
> Abode with me; a forming hand, at times
> Rebellious, acting in a devious mood;
> A local spirit of his own, at war
> With general tendency, but, for the most,
> Subservient strictly to external things
> With which it communed. An auxiliar light
> Came from my mind, which on the setting sun
> Bestowed new splendour; . . . . . .
> . . . . . and the midnight storm
> Grew darker in the presence of mine eye.[3]

[1] *The Prelude*, ii. 339-352.   [2] *Ibid.*, ii. 376-418.   [3] *Ibid.*, ii. 362-374.

Never was he more truly a poet than at Hawkshead. If the few verses he composed there bear the marks of a schoolboy's hand, this is because they did not spring immediately from the very sources of his being—because he had not, at that time, become conscious of his own power and originality. Life at Hawkshead was for him a "seed-time"; years must pass before the crop could appear. But his imagination, though destined to remain long ill-employed or not employed at all, was henceforth present within him, vigorous and ample. Not in vain had he been witness of "Presence of Nature in the sky and on the earth"; not in vain caught glimpses of the "Souls of lonely places."[1] The first portion of his moral and poetic training was ended, and as he reflects how and from whom he had received it, he overflows with gratitude to his supreme and all-powerful teacher.

> Wisdom and Spirit of the universe!
> Thou Soul that art the eternity of thought,
> That givest to forms and images a breath
> And everlasting motion, not in vain
> By day or star-light thus from my first dawn
> Of childhood didst thou intertwine for me
> The passions that build up our human soul;
> Not with the mean and vulgar works of man,
> But with high objects, with enduring things—
> With life and nature—purifying thus
> The elements of feeling and of thought,
> And sanctifying, by such discipline,
> Both pain and fear, until we recognise
> A grandeur in the beatings of the heart."[2]

VI

One can scarcely receive the lessons of the divine instructress without conceiving some contempt for those of man. It is natural, therefore, that Wordsworth, who

---

[1] *The Prelude*, i. 464-6.   [2] *Ibid.*, i. 401-414.

derived all his ideas on education from recollections of
his own training, should appear indifferent or hostile to
those new systems, of which so many were invented and
put into practice by his contemporaries.   But with
Rousseau, who, though he had initiated those reforms,
had proposed to re-instate nature as guardian of the child
in place of man, we should expect to find him in entire
agreement.   Was it not Rousseau who had laid down
most of those principles which were practically applied
at Hawkshead?   Had he not said that "the greatest,
the most important, the most useful rule of all education
is not to gain time, but to lose it?"[1]   Had he not
maintained that a child's time is well spent only when he is
happy, when he is "leaping, playing and running about
the whole day long?"[2]   In spite of his dislike to public
schools Rousseau would surely have been delighted, if
he had paid a visit to Hawkshead during his travels in
England in 1766, to see, playing about him on every hand,
troops of living Emiles, less learned than robust.

Wordsworth never acknowledges the extent to which
he had imbibed Rousseau's doctrines.   But, intentionally
or otherwise, he makes it clear that he is steeped in Rousseau.   What else indeed could we expect?   *Émile* was
at that time on every one's lips, and England, like the
continent, was full of it.   In the interval of four years,
between 1763 and 1767, it was four times translated into
English.   Rousseaumania, in England as elsewhere,
manifested itself not only in the production of works such
as Cowper's *Tirocinium*, inspired by or written in imitation
of *Émile*, but also in the practical application of its theories,
attended by the most curious eccentricities.   Thomas Day
(1748-1789), the author of *Sandford and Merton*, who
proclaimed Rousseau "the first of human-kind," endeavoured to regulate his life in every respect in conformity with the principles of his master, and, further,
actually compelled the lady he married to make the Sophie
of the philosopher her model.[3]   In 1771, his friend,
Richard Edgeworth, the father of the celebrated authoress,

[1] *Emile*, book ii.   [2] *Ibid.*
[3] See *Dictionary of National Biography*, article on Thomas Day.

visited Rousseau and presented to him his son, a child of six. This boy, who had been brought up in strict accordance with the principles of *Emile*, developed into an ideal young savage, brave and generous, and endowed with marvellous strength and agility.   But as he was quite destitute of the idea of obedience he soon became absolutely unmanageable, obstinately refusing to do what he did not like, in other words, to undertake any work whatever.   James Beattie, the poet, in 1773, in order to inculcate a knowledge of God in his son's mind, sowed some cress-seed in the form of the initial letters of the child's name, with the object of eliciting from him the conclusion that such a combination of lines could not be the work of chance.   It was Beattie's intention, by means of this object lesson, to disprove one of Rousseau's characteristic ideas ; but the influence of the Genevan philosopher is clearly revealed n the very form of the attempted refutation.[1]

Such was the influence of Rousseau on those who had already reached manhood when *Emile* appeared.   Wordsworth belongs to the following generation, which offered several examples of the result of the new education.   One, at least, of these was among Wordsworth's friends.   Robert Southey's aunt, who had undertaken his education, had bought a copy of *Emile* in order to employ the new and excellent method.[2]   In consequence of this, at twenty years of age Southey's head was "full of Rousseau,"[3] he became a republican and "pantisocrat," he sacrificed both propriety and position to a love-match, and the imprudent lady who had trained him was compelled to turn him out of doors.   Enthusiastic disciples of Rousseau surrounded Wordsworth on every side.   It is true that most of them, such as Charles Lamb,[4] Charles Lloyd,[5] and William Hazlitt expend their love and admiration principally upon the *Confessions* and *La Nouvelle Héloïse*.   But

---

[1] *The Poetical Works of James Beattie*.   Aldine Poets.   Memoir of J. B., pp. lxvi.-lxix.
[2] Edward Dowden, *Robert Southey*, p. 6, English Men of Letters.
[3] *Ibid.*, p. 26.
[4] Letter from Lamb to Coleridge, 8 November 1796.
[5] Charles Lloyd, by de Quincey.   *The Collected Works of Thomas de Quincey*, edited by David Masson, 1889, Vol. ii. pp. 388-390.

what a marked preference for *Emile* is shewn by Thomas
Poole, the active and intelligent Somerset farmer! " I have
never," he writes (April 2, 1796) " felt any delights in
reading English literature comparable to those which I
have experienced in reading French. *L'Émile* de Rousseau,
for example—what a book is there! ' *Comme il pense et
comme il fait penser*,' as has been well said." [1]   And William
Godwin, the philosopher, who afterwards became for
a time Wordsworth's intellectual master, summed up
the opinion of many minds when he declared that,
though teeming with absurd notions, " *Émile* is upon
the whole to be regarded as the principal reservoir
of philosophic truth as yet existing in the world." [2]

But even were we unaware how completely Wordsworth
was surrounded by disciples and admirers of Jean-Jacques,
his works would reveal to us the extent of the influence
exercised upon him by the Genevan philosopher; [3] an
influence more powerful, perhaps, than any other to which
he was subjected, all the more profound because, instead
of manifesting itself in any particular portion of his work
or at any special period of his life, it permeates the whole.
Nevertheless, it is in his opposition to what Wordsworth
conceives to be the errors of Rousseau, that this very
influence is manifested.   If Wordsworth is inevitably
agreed with him as to first principles, he differs from
nearly all his conclusions.   Like Rousseau he is convinced of the child's innate moral excellence, of the beneficent tendency of his natural instincts, of the dangers
that attend the continual interference of man, as vitiated
by society, with the natural purity and uprightness of his
disposition.   But Rousseau, disturbed by the recollection
of his own precocious waywardness, yields the child his
trust with one hand, only to take it away with the other.
In order to maintain him in his original integrity, he con-
siders it necessary to surround him with a network of
precautions suggested by the most fastidious mistrust; in

[1] Mrs Sandford, *Thomas Poole and his Friends*, 2 vols., 1888, Vol. i. p. 167.
[2] Inquiry into Political Justice, 1793, Vol. ii. pp. 503-504.
[3] The *Émile* (edition in 2 vols., Frankfort, 1782) and the *Confessions*
(edition in 2 vols., 1782) are included in his scanty store of books.

order to protect him from the evil influence of mankind, he feels obliged to place near him some one whose presence is as continuous as it is invisible, whose influence is as persistent as it is imperceptible. Convinced beforehand that he will give way if he lives the customary life of mankind and shares in its conflicting interests, he conceives the idea of transporting him to a utopia where beings and objects exist for no other purpose than that of his instruction.

With such fears and suspicions Wordsworth has no sympathy. He ridicules Rousseau's precautions as equally useless and impracticable. For him the child's innate excellence is no abstract virtue realizable only in an ideal state of existence, no fragile crystal to be broken at the slightest touch.

> Our childhood sits,
> Our simple childhood, sits upon a throne
> That hath more power than all the elements.[1]

It is not enough to assert its innocence, and to compare it to a spotless vessel unpolluted by a single stain. Of what use would be this passive purity, at the mercy of the least grain of dust from without ? The moral nature of the child is an active power in a real world, transforming into good the mingled elements of which that world consists. It is a happy adaptation to the universe, imparting to man an initial impetus in his journey along the path which leads most surely to the noblest end of human life. Let not man, who does not know the route the child will have to follow, pretend to smooth that path by removing the stones which he supposes will cause the child to stumble. In attempting to preserve him from obstacles, he runs the risk of placing them directly in his path. Let not man regret a lost state of nature in which the child's faculties enjoyed full freedom of action, for the truly natural state is simply that at which man, under the guidance of his natural instincts, has arrived in every age, nor could any state of things be more artificial and more entirely due to

[1] *The Prelude*, v. 508-510.

human, as distinct from natural, agency than a return to savage life in the midst of civilisation.

Instead, therefore, of setting up to be educational reformers, men should pursue that treatment of the child which the progressive wisdom of the ages has evolved. If its formation has been but slow, the fact is a practical guarantee of its excellence and of its divine origin. That which is new, on the contrary, however speciously disguised under the name of nature, is of questionable utility, and untrustworthy because of human origin. What, for example, was the outcome of the educational revolution advocated by Rousseau? That the theorists of the latter part of the eighteenth century; starting, like Rousseau, from the ideas of love and respect for childhood, became unconsciously the instruments of a blind and relentless tyranny. So zealously did they study and analyse the nature of the child, that they deceived themselves into believing that they understood it completely, and could tell with infallible certainty the treatment that was adapted to it.

> These mighty workmen of our later age,
> Who, with a broad highway, have over-bridged
> The froward chaos of futurity,
> Tamed to their bidding; they who have the skill
> To manage books, and things, and make them act
> On infant minds as surely as the sun
> Deals with a flower; the keepers of our time,
> The guides and wardens of our faculties,
> Sages who in their prescience would control
> All accidents, and to the very road
> Which they have fashioned would confine us down
> Like engines; when will their presumption learn
> That in the unreasoning progress of the world
> A wiser spirit is at work for us,
> A better eye than theirs, most prodigal
> Of blessings, and most studious of our good,
> Even in what seem our most unfruitful hours?[1]

To prove that there are some circumstances which they can neither foresee nor control, Wordsworth confronts

[1] *The Prelude*, v. 347-363.

them with a lesson, singularly impressive and unusual, by which Nature influenced the imagination of one of his comrades :

> There was a Boy [1] : ye knew him well, ye cliffs
> And islands of Winander !—many a time
> At evening, when the earliest stars began
> To move along the edges of the hills,
> Rising or setting, would he stand alone
> Beneath the trees or by the glimmering lake,
> And there, with fingers interwoven, both hands
> Pressed closely palm to palm, and to his mouth
> Uplifted, he, as through an instrument,
> Blew mimic hootings to the silent owls,
> That they might answer him ; and they would shout
> Across the watery vale, and shout again,
> Responsive to his call, with quivering peals,
> And long halloos and screams, and echoes loud,
> Redoubled and redoubled, concourse wild
> Of jocund din ; and, when a lengthened pause
> Of silence came and baffled his best skill,
> Then sometimes, in that silence while he hung
> Listening, a gentle shock of mild surprise
> Has carried far into his heart the voice
> Of mountain torrents ; or the visible scene
> Would enter unawares into his mind,
> With all its solemn imagery, its rocks,
> Its woods, and that uncertain heaven, received
> Into the bosom of the steady lake.

Doubtless a rare and subtle impression, this ; and one which the authorities attacked by Wordsworth must have ridiculed as an odd and trivial caprice, valueless but for the beauty and dignity with which it is clothed by the poet's imagination.   Such as it is, however, Wordsworth has not chosen it without intention.   Fully conscious himself of having been moulded by a multitude of similar delicate sensations, which would be considered no less strange and exceptional, he desires to prove that the soul of childhood is a mystery to man, that man's knowledge of it is insignificant in comparison with his ignorance of it, and that in

[1] *The Prelude*, v. 364-388.

the face of such ignorance it becomes his duty to abstain
from interference with its development. He is led, in fact,
to deny almost entirely man's right to authority over the
child. He is

> convinced at heart
> How little those formalities, to which
> With overweening trust alone we give
> The name of Education, have to do
> With real feeling and just sense. [1]

The running stream in which he loves to find an image
of human life was a symbol well adapted to confirm him
in the principle of non-interference. While the philosophers of the eighteenth century held it lawful to imprint
as many facts and as many of their own ideas as possible
on that white page to which they compared the mind of
infancy, Wordsworth, who looked upon childhood as the
source of the river of life, feared to discover therein
evidence too clear of the handiwork of man, just as
he would have mourned over any attempt to straighten
the windings of the Duddon or the Derwent. Because
yonder spring, which gushes from the mountain side,
offends your taste for the rectilinear by the vagaries of
its course, or startles your cautious prudence by an impetuous leap, you would control it, and render it smooth
and navigable from its very source. Well and good; yet
beware lest, once confined to an inflexible course, it no
longer wears its old capricious beauty. Avoid, above all,
the loss of a single drop of its precious water, a loss you
can never make good, whereby you impair its very life,
and rob it of a portion of itself. It will enter with less of
impetuous energy on its long journey across the plains
which await it at the foot of its native mountain, its once
rapid current will sooner become sluggish and then stag-
nant, the stream itself will more quickly dry up and
disappear.

The sight of the youthful prodigies turned out by
officious modern education was not calculated to modify
Wordsworth's opinions. By dint of patience man can no
doubt succeed in producing a little wonder who has all

[1] *The Prelude*, xiii. 168-172.

the outward marks of learning, virtue, and wisdom ; but
what can be more insufferable or more deplorable than
this sham master-piece, this child who, instead of being
the embryo, is the epitome of the adult ?

> Full early trained to worship seemliness,
> This model of a child is never known
> To mix in quarrels ; that were far beneath
> Its dignity ; with gifts he bubbles o'er
> As generous as a fountain ; selfishness
> May not come near him, nor the little throng
> Of flitting pleasures tempt him from his path ;
> The wandering beggars propagate his name,[1]
> Dumb creatures find him tender as a nun,
> And natural or supernatural fear,
> Unless it leap upon him in a dream,
> Touches him not.   To enhance the wonder, see
> How arch his notices, how nice his sense
> Of the ridiculous ; not blind is he
> To the broad follies of the licensed world,
> Yet innocent himself withal, though shrewd,
> And can read lectures upon innocence ;
> A miracle of scientific lore,[2]
> Ships he can guide across the pathless sea,
> And tell you all their cunning ; he can read

[1] It was Locke's opinion that the child should be incited to liberality.
Rousseau had already protested against this doctrine : " L'aumône est une
action d'homme qui connaît la valeur de ce qu'il donne et le besoin que
son semblable en a.   L'enfant qui ne connait rien de cela, ne peut avoir
aucun mérite à donner ; il donne sans charité, sans bienfaisance."
Émile, book ii.

[2] In a similar manner Coleridge ridicules the little prodigies of his day,
as captious as they are precocious.   He insists on the necessity of developing the child's faculty of admiration, and also (wherein he differs from
Wordsworth) that of memory.   [*Biographia Literaria*, ch. i.] The youthful
sage is frequently made a subject of criticism at this period.   See, among
others, Chateaubriand (*Mélanges littéraires*.   Article on De Bonald's Primitive Legislation, December 1802).   Chateaubriand is anxious to see those
little naturalists well whipped who define man as "a mammiferous animal
having four extremities, two of which terminate in hands."   And as the
type is still to be found, so also are the protests.   Pierre Loti, whose
recollections of childhood bear a marked resemblance to those of Wordsworth, speaks with contempt of " ces petits Parisiens de douze ou treize ans
élevés par les méthodes les plus perfectionnées et les plus modernes, qui déjà
déclament, pérorent, ont des idées en politique." (*Le Roman d'un Enfant*,
par. lxiii.)   But the keenest piece of satire occurs in Dickens's novel, *Hard
Times*.

The inside of the earth, and spell the stars;
He knows the policies of foreign lands;
Can string you names of districts, cities, towns,
The whole world over, tight as beads of dew
Upon a gossamer thread; he sifts, he weighs;
All things are put to question; he must live
Knowing that he grows wiser every day
Or else not live at all, and seeing too
Each little drop of wisdom as it falls
Into the dimpling cistern of his heart:
For this unnatural growth the trainer blame,
Pity the tree.—Poor human vanity,
Wert thou extinguished, little would be left
Which he could truly love; but how escape?
For, ever as a thought of purer birth
Rises to lead him toward a better clime,
Some intermeddler still is on the watch
To drive him back, and pound him, like a stray,
Within the pinfold of his own conceit.
Meanwhile old grandame earth is grieved to find
The playthings, which her love designed for him,
Unthought of: in their woodland beds the flowers
Weep, and the river sides are all forlorn.[1]

Wordsworth does not need to describe an ideal child, produced by an imaginary education, as a counterpart to this portrait of the little pattern of the day, coloured as it is by the indignation of the poet and kindled here and there by a touch of satire. In opposition to Rousseau's adversaries or false disciples, who would repress every outburst of childish glee, and would stifle the imaginative faculty in its birth, it is unnecessary for Wordsworth to invent in full detail a fantastic educational paradise. He is not obliged, like Bernardin de Saint Pierre, to erect "Schools of the Fatherland," to be provided with an extensive park containing the trees and shrubs peculiar to the country, planted in the unstudied arrangement of nature; where no "clamorous bells would be used to announce the different tasks, but rather the sound of flutes, hautboys and bagpipes," where all instruction would be conveyed by means of poetry and

[1] *The Prelude*, v. 298-340.

music; and where, in order to instil ideas of God and
virtue, "the daisies in the grass, and the fruits which
hang from the trees within their domain, would supply the
children with their first lessons in theology, and form the
occasion of their early efforts in self-control and obedience."[1]

Such fanciful pastorals are in Wordsworth's view entirely useless. Nor is he in any way concerned to force
the growth of genius in accordance with the suggestion
of one of his countrymen, who recommended "that the
new Émile should be led to traverse mountain, torrent
and precipice; to lose himself in the silence of forest
solitudes; to take his stand on the lava of the volcano,
listen to its thunder and watch its eruption; to make his
home on board a vessel which should bear him from the
frozen deserts of the North to the burning climate of the
tropics; to feast his eyes, in short, on every sublime or
marvellous spectacle that Nature can present."[2]

Wordsworth has recourse to no such device. Genius
should spring to life, happiness should find its home in the
youthful heart, unaided by human wisdom. Of man he
asks merely that joyousness shall be allowed to display itself,
the imagination be permitted to thrive, without hindrance.
Everything produced by artifice seems to him evil; he
claims for the child the privileges of his failings; he
would have him restless and disorderly rather than a
model of behaviour, selfish instead of prematurely
generous. Wordsworth is neither feverishly impatient
nor immoderately sanguine. He desires to see no better

---

[1] Bernardin de St Pierre, *Études de la Nature*, xiv., De l'Education. The
Études were published in 1784.
[2] Thus is the work described in Roucher's *Mois* (Paris, 1779, Vol. i.
p. 35, note). Roucher had not read the book but had heard of it, and
he renders the title in French by *Moyens de donner du génie*. It is most
characteristic of the period that while at first he treated the whole matter
with ridicule, he adds that "it no longer appeared preposterous when
the author's system had been explained to him." The reference is to
Martinus Scriblerus, B. I. ch. ii.

But the most amusing result of a want of understanding in reading *Émile*
is beyond dispute to be found in the *Elève de la Nature*, of Gaspard Guillard
de Beaurieu (1763). To counteract the effects of artificial education,
Beaurieu, who is incredibly serious, sentimental and declamatory, imprisons
his hero in a cage until he is twenty years old, and then lets him loose,
stark naked on a desert island.

type of schoolboy than that to which he himself and his companions at Hawkshead belonged.

> A race of real children ; not too wise,
> Too learned, or too good ; but wanton, fresh,
> And bandied up and down by love and hate ;
> Not unresentful where self-justified ;
> Fierce, moody, patient, venturous, modest, shy ;
> Mad at their sports like withered leaves in winds ;
> Though doing wrong and suffering, and full oft
> Bending beneath our life's mysterious weight[1]
> Of pain, and doubt, and fear, yet yielding not
> In happiness to the happiest upon earth.[2]

Wordsworth does not mourn over the elements of evil which found their way into Hawkshead school ; on the contrary he almost rejoices over them, as affording him, at a very early age, an opportunity of studying the passions and intricate by-paths of human nature. A fine field of observation had presented itself to him, compelled, as he was,

> In hardy independence, to stand up
> Amid conflicting interests, and the shock
> Of various tempers ; to endure and note
> What was not understood, though known to be ;
> Among the mysteries of love and hate,
> Honour and shame, looking to right and left,

[1] Rousseau's idea : " J'ai pensé que la partie la plus essentielle de l'éducation d'un enfant, celle dont il n'est jamais question dans les éducations les plus soignées, c'est de lui bien faire sentir sa misère, sa faiblesse, sa dépendance et le pesant joug de la nécessité que la nature impose à l'homme." (*Nouvelle Héloïse*, 5th part, letter 3).

[2] *The Prelude*, v. 411-420. Here again we find a resemblance to Rousseau's portrait of boyhood at Geneva : "On était plus grossier de mon temps. Les enfants rustiquement élevés n'avaient point de teint à conserver et ne craignaient point les injures de l'air auxquelles ils s'étaient aguerris de bonne heure. . . . Timides et modestes devant les gens âgés, ils étaient hardis, fiers, querelleurs entre eux ; ils n'avaient point de frisure a conserver ; ils se défiaient à la lutte, à la course, aux coups ; ils se battaient à bon escient, se blessaient quelquefois, et puis s'embrassaient en pleurant. Ils revenaient au logis suants, essouflés, déchirés ; c'étaient de vrais polissons ; mais ces polissons ont fait des hommes qui ont dans le coeur du zèle pour servir la Patrie et du sang à verser pour elle." (*Lettre sur les Spectacles*, edit. Léon Fontaine, § 192.)

> Unchecked by innocence too delicate,
> And moral notions too intolerant,
> Sympathies too contracted.

Hence the transition to life amongst men became easy, for he had learned very early to separate

> the two natures,
> The one that feels, the other that observes.[1]

Thus at Hawkshead, everything, including evil, was for the best. The sturdy schoolboy loved everything at his school, even the blows he gave and received. It is impossible that Hawkshead alone can have been free from the brutality then universal in English schools, yet Wordsworth says not a word in protest. The vigorous and hardy mountaineer retains no poignant recollections of outrages such as shocked the delicate sensibilities of Cowper and Shelley. He does not censure this evil, for it has caused him no suffering. As he looks back across the years to his life at Hawkshead, his only visions are those of happy hours spent amid scenes of beauty. His only memories are "of pleasures lying upon the unfolding intellect plenteously as morning dew-drops,—of knowledge inhaled insensibly like the fragrance,—of dispositions stealing into the spirit like music from unknown quarters,—of images uncalled for and rising up like exhalations, . . . of nature as a teacher of truth through joy and through gladness, and as a creatress of the faculties by a process of smoothness and delight." [2]

It was no halo of romance, due to distance merely, which clothed these memories with beauty. Wordsworth's attachment to Hawkshead had found utterance, even on the eve of quitting it, in a genuine premonition that the evening of his life would be spent amid the scenes which had witnessed its dawn. As he took his farewell of the familiar spot, a vision of singular accuracy revealed to him the entire course of his existence. On the western shore

---

[1] *The Prelude*, xiv. 329-347.
[2] Answer to the letter of Mathetes, *Wordsworth's Prose Works*, vol. i, p. 318.

of Coniston Lake a grove of sycamores used to extend its
branches over the borders of the mere

> With length of shade so thick that whoso glides
> Along the line of low roofed water, moves
> As in a cloister.

One evening, as Wordsworth and his companions rested
on their oars beneath the trees, and

> watched the golden beams of light
> Flung from the setting sun, as they reposed
> In silent beauty on the naked ridge
> Of a high eastern hill,

his thoughts flowed " in a pure stream of words fresh
from the heart " :[1]

> Dear native regions, I foretell,
> From what I feel at this farewell,
> That, wheresoe'er my steps may tend,
> And whensoe'er my course shall end,
> If in that hour a single tie
> Survive of local sympathy,
> My soul will cast the backward view,
> The longing look alone on you.

> Thus, while the Sun prepared for rest
> Hath gained the precincts of the west,
> Though his departing radiance fail
> To illuminate the hollow vale,
> A lingering light he fondly throws
> On the dear hills where first he rose.[2]

---

[1] *The Prelude*, viii. 459-476.

[2] The text here given is that of 1815. The date of composition is stated
by Wordsworth to be 1786, but he must have retouched it for publication.
The seventh and eighth lines are apparently imitated from Bowles'
sonnet *On entering Switzerland* (1789, lines 10 and 11) :

> And soon a longing look, like me they cast
> Back on the mountains of the morning past.

CHAPTER III

Cambridge (1787-1791)

I

ONE day, just before the commencement of the Christmas
holidays in 1783, Wordsworth, feverish at the prospect of
departure, had climbed a great mass of rock which stood
at the junction of two roads, and commanded a distant
view of both. Here, " scout-like," he stationed himself,
watching impatiently for the horses which were to be
sent by his father to fetch him and his brothers, and
might come by either of the two roads. The day was
tempestuous, dark, and wild. Seated upon the grass,
at a spot where a bare wall afforded him a meagre shelter,
the schoolboy had no companion save a solitary sheep on
his right hand, while to his left stood a blasted hawthorn.
Long he remained there, gazing intently before him, till
his eyes grew weary with peering into space whenever the
parting mist gave him an occasional glimpse of wood and
plain below.

Ten days later, during the vacation to which he had
looked forward so eagerly, the lad, with his three brothers,
followed their parent's lifeless form to the grave. With
superstitious simplicity he concluded that his affliction was
sent as a punishment for his impatience, and however
trivial its cause might be, the repentance with which he
"bowed low to God, Who thus corrected" his desires,
was both deep and sincere. So strong was the impression,
that often in later days he recalled the stormy night and
wild landscape, the scene of his guilty impatience, that he
might " drink, as at a fountain," from the recollection.
Often, too, from that time forward, the mere sound of the
wind, as it stirred the leaves or whistled around the house,

was sufficient to fill him with a deep emotion capable of beguiling " thoughts over busy in the course they took." [1]

The serious consequences which the death of their father seemed likely to entail upon Wordsworth and his brothers were probably at first concealed from him by this singular remorse and by his childish grief.   Although the father had been in a fair way of attaining wealth and reputation, he left his children in a precarious position. Almost the whole of his fortune was in the hands of his patron, Sir James Lowther, who had compelled his steward to entrust him with £5000.   Sir James, afterwards Earl of Lonsdale, has been described by De Quincey [2] as a potentate proud of his rank, his vast estates, and his authority as lord-lieutenant, and eccentric to the verge of madness.   A thorough feudal chief, it was his delight to convince himself of his power and to demonstrate it to others by frequent violations of both law and justice.   At one period of his life he refused to pay any of his creditors ; some, because they were his neighbours and he knew them to be knaves; others because they lived so far off that he really could not find out what they were. It was for some such reason as this that he refused during the remainder of his life to discharge his debt to the children of his steward.   An action was brought in their name, but when the case came before the court at Carlisle, Lord Lonsdale had retained every counsel on the circuit, and appeared in court with a hundred witnesses.   The judge ordered the case to stand over, and the Wordsworth family did not recover their property until after Lord Lonsdale's death, nearly twenty years later.   The remainder of their father's fortune was almost entirely spent in futile proceedings against the debtor.[3]   Their guardians had the greatest difficulty in raising the sum required to enable Wordsworth and his

---

[1] *The Prelude*, xii. 287-335.
[2] De Quincey, op. cit., vol. ii., pp. 252-255.
[3] Letter from Wordsworth to Sir George Beaumont, Feb. 20th, 1805 (W. Knight, *Life of Wordsworth*, i. p. 98) and "Report of the Commissioners of Inquiry into Bankruptcy and Insolvency" (*ibid.*, ii. pp. 38-39). See also letter of Dorothy Wordsworth, Dec. 7th, 1792 (*ibid.*, i. p. 52).

brothers to complete their studies at Hawkshead, where Wordsworth, who was thirteen and a half years old when his father died, remained until 1787. But a time of trial, which the holidays, spent during the last three years at Penrith, must have led him to anticipate, awaited him on leaving school. It has been mentioned that his mother's parents were stern, and wanting in natural affection. Dorothy Wordsworth, who lived with them, and was obliged to render assistance in their shop, unbosoms herself in her letters to one of her friends, and makes endless complaints of their harshness and narrow-mindedness. The incessant lectures of her grandmother upon the duty of being sedate and docile stifled her lively imagination and chilled the impulsive warmth of her affections. Her letters remind one of the sufferings of Aurora Leigh under her aunt's cold and mechanical guardianship. The maiden of the " wild eyes " felt keenly the loss of her open-air life, and was miserable on sunny week days because she could only go out on Sunday. No doubt she presented a somewhat forbidding countenance to the Cooksons' customers, who constantly interrupted her when she wanted to read the books which her brother William had lent her. She was very fond of the Iliad, but she could only snatch the time to read it in secret, and to study French, by doing the work of two hours in one. She had no joys but in the affection of her four brothers ; her only happy days were those which saw them all united under one roof. They too, however, had to suffer from the harshness and ill-will of their relations, who frequently called them liars, and left them exposed to the worst kind of mortification, the insults of servants. The eldest seems to have been of a more pliant and submissive disposition, but the others would gather around their sister and shed tears of the bitterest sorrow over the melancholy lot which the death of their parents had brought upon them.[1]

But the loss of their fortune, while it caused them many hardships at the threshold of life, compelled them to make sure of a livelihood as early as possible. Deprived of their

[1] W. Knight, *Life of Wordsworth*. See the letters of Dorothy Wordsworth on pp. 35-36 and 47-49, vol. i.

inheritance by an act of high-handed injustice, they could scarcely have entered life under more unfavourable auspices; yet this did not prevent any of them from reaching a position of honour or of fame. The eldest, who followed his father's profession, went to London, and in spite of very moderate abilities became a prosperous solicitor. John Wordsworth, the third son, chose a sea-faring career, and entering the eastern mercantile service, embarked on a large vessel of which he ultimately became the captain. The fourth son, Christopher, still a school-boy at Hawkshead, was already giving evidence of a tractable intelligence united with perseverance. He had a brilliant career as a student at Cambridge, where he after-wards became a professor, and finally rose to be Master of Trinity, one of the principal colleges of his University.

Of the four sons, William alone gave his guardians any trouble or cause for anxiety. Though his genius was as yet unsuspected by others and even by himself, he ex-hibited remarkable qualities of mind. But he was im-patient of advice, self-confident, and unable to apply himself to any prescribed employment. He was quite unconscious of what is called a vocation. Inspired, no doubt, by the example of his father and his elder brother, he seemed inclined to study law, but the violent headaches to which he was subject made him shrink from an entirely sedentary occupation.[1] Finally his uncles decided to give him a University training, as a necessary preliminary to the bar, the teaching profession, or holy orders. In October 1787, therefore, he set out for Cambridge, in order to enter St John's College as an under-graduate. His age was then seventeen years and a half.

II

The young student entered Cambridge during one of the least brilliant epochs in the history of the old University. It was then in the very last stage of intellectual languor.

[1] Letter of Dorothy Wordsworth, 1787 (W. Knight, *Life of Wordsworth*, i. p. 48).

During the years immediately preceding the violent excitement of the French Revolution, its atmosphere was heavy and drowsy, as if at the approach of a tempest. Classical scholarship had not been represented by a single man of mark since the death of the learned Richard Bentley in 1742, and Porson, the eminent Greek scholar, by whom it was revived, did not receive his appointment as professor until 1793. To tell the truth, learning was not in high repute at Cambridge, which was more especially the stronghold of Anglicanism and the nursery of the clergy.[1]

It was natural that the theologians, who had taught or written at Cambridge during the eighteenth century, should devote all their efforts to the protection of the rising generation of clergy from the dangerous influences which, in an age of great freedom and audacity of thought, might reach them from every corner of Europe. Men such as Conyers Middleton, and, later, Paley, John Hay, and Richard Watson,[2] expended the whole vigour of their intellect in devising an antidote to the poison disseminated by deists such as Toland and Collins, or by foes more formidable still—the French Encyclopædists, and David Hume the Scotchman. The cause of religion had sometimes to suffer from the zeal of its defenders. Faithful followers of Locke,[3] firmly convinced of the efficacy of their logic, they claimed to demonstrate the authenticity of the sacred writings, the possibility of miracles, and the

---

[1] Dr Watson, the Bishop of Llandaff, derived an income of £1000 a year from the Royal Chair of Divinity, of which he was merely the nominal occupant. Porson received only £40 a year as professor of Greek.

[2] Conyers Middleton (1683-1750), head librarian at the University, did not lecture, but published a number of controversial pamphlets. Paley, the author of the *Evidences of Christianity* (1794), still a classic at Cambridge, lectured in philosophy from 1767 to 1775. John Hay occupied the Norrisian chair of theology from 1780 to 1794. On Watson, see the preceding note, and the present work, book ii., ch. iii. Mr Leslie Stephen's excellent work, *English Thought in the Eighteenth Century* (2 vols., London, 1881) may be consulted in reference to each of these theologians.

[3] Locke seems to have been held in particular esteem at St John's College, where Wordsworth entered as a student. A correspondent of the *Gentleman's Magazine* (Jan. 1793), whilst admitting the excessive attention paid to mathematics at Cambridge, makes an exception in favour of St John's, "where, also, there is a proper respect paid to the sagacious Locke and the profound Butler."

truth of the mysteries of Christianity in just the same way
as one demonstrates a theorem in geometry. The course
of their argument occasionally raised such dangerous
questions that one of their number, Middleton, was even
suspected of being an adversary of religion in the disguise
of a friend. Sound reasoners within their own limited
sphere, they neither could, nor would, follow out their
reasoning to its logical conclusion. As rigid logicians
they could admit no high-road to belief save through the
understanding; of that through the heart they were
entirely ignorant. Communicating with the students only
through the medium of college tutors, who transmitted
the doctrines of the professors in stereotyped formulæ
which were faithfully reproduced by their pupils during
examination, the Cambridge philosophers exerted but
a faint and far-off influence on the students of their time.
Religion was thus in a state of spiritless stagnation. The
ethical system was one of self-interest expressed in the
crudest possible manner. Its maxims were derived from
Paley, who assigns as a motive for right action that God
is stronger than we are, and that He can condemn us to
eternal punishment if we do wrong.[1] Doubtless there
were some signs of a turn of the tide. Priestley, the
Unitarian, was making strenuous efforts to convert the
members of the Anglican University to his own opinions
by means of numerous pamphlets, and in 1787 succeeded
in winning over one of the Fellows, William Frend by
name. But among the students themselves the spirit
of free discussion was not destined to awake until 1792,
when the French Revolution had shaken the hitherto
peaceful soil of the old University to its very depths.
At that time, however, Wordsworth was no longer in
residence.[2]

---

[1] J. S. Mill, article on Coleridge, *Westminster Review*, 1840, p. 283.
[2] Frend became a Unitarian in 1787, and published in the following
year "An address to the Inhabitants of Cambridge and its neighbourhood
to turn from the false Worship of Three Persons to the Worship of the One
True God." In 1788 he was removed from his post as tutor. When
brought to trial in 1793 for the publication of another revolutionary work,
entitled *Peace and Union*, a great number of students, including Coleridge,
became his adherents.

The supreme object of the University was to train for the Anglican priesthood men capable of meeting the enemies of the Church with concise and closely-marshalled arguments; and this was to be accomplished by the ingenious method of making the exact sciences the predominant and almost exclusive subject of study. Mathematics were in high repute, while polite literature and historical science were neglected. The mathematical tripos, or principal competitive examination, was instituted in 1747, the classical tripos not until 1824. Newton was, in fact, the god of Cambridge, and his *Principia* its Bible. His statue, carved by Roubillac for Trinity Chapel, was that of the local divinity. The University was prostrate before its idol. The consequence was that a thorough spirit of revolt against the course of study and against the examinations was provoked among such students as had definitely literary tastes, but cared little for geometry and algebra. Thomas Gray, who spent nearly the whole of his life at Cambridge, and was passionately fond of polite literature, never forgave his University for her neglect of his favourite study, nor for the miseries he endured in attempting to learn mathematics. "Surely," he wrote when a student, "it was of this place now Cambridge, but formerly known by the name of Babylon, that the prophet spake when he said: 'The wild beasts of the desert shall dwell there, and their houses shall be full of doleful creatures, and owls shall build there, and satyrs shall dance there; their forts and towers shall be a den for ever, a joy of wild asses.' "[1]

Somewhat later in life Gray settled at Cambridge as a resident, but did not alter the opinion he had formed of his University as a student. In 1742 he wrote in her honour a *Hymn to Ignorance*, the "soft, salutary Power" "whose influence breath'd from high augments the native darkness of the sky." The details of his life, passed almost entirely in one or other of the Cambridge colleges, together with the correspondence which he maintained from 1742 until his death in 1771, reveal an atmosphere of petty rivalry, and a society composed of characters eccentric

[1] Letter to Richard West, Dec. 1736.

though by no means original, pedants whose learning was entirely barren, and easy-going idlers who took every advantage of their peaceful and privileged existence.[1]

And if the melancholy Gray may be suspected of exaggerating his grievances, the same cannot be said of another student, who echoed his complaints nearly a century later. If throughout the length and breadth of English literature there has been a mind exceptionally adapted to shine in University studies and examinations, it is that of Macaulay. But Macaulay, unable to conquer his repugnance to mathematics, was contemptuously called a reader of romances because he was addicted to the study of poetry and history, and, finding no means of attaining a high position in the examinations most in repute, keenly regretted his inability to exchange the Cam for the Isis, Cambridge with its science for Oxford with its letters.[2] Such was the stern mental discipline to which Wordsworth was subjected, and against which he was no less rebellious than Gray who preceded, and Macaulay who followed, him.

We are not, however, to suppose that the intellectual labours of the students, such as they were, constituted the most important part of their college life. The members of the University had no intellectual life in common. There were no courses of lectures which the members of all colleges alike were expected to attend, but merely practical lessons in the individual colleges. Separated for the purpose of work, the students were only united for that of amusement. There were doubtless those among them who applied themselves industriously, in order to obtain honours in the examinations as a means to securing professorships or the best appointments in the church.

---

[1] The *Gentleman's Magazine* (April and May 1774, December 1792, January, February and July 1793) contains a heated controversy between past students of Cambridge University, some protesting against the excessive attention paid to mathematics, others defending the accredited method of education.

[2] Letter to his mother in 1818, *Life and Letters of Lord Macaulay*, by Trevelyan, ch. ii. De Quincey said that "a sufficient basis of mathematics and a robust though common-place intellect" were all that was required to ensure success at Cambridge.

The majority, however, were either already well off or destitute of ambition, and therefore gave all their time to the amusements traditional at the University, their superiors, even, at times inciting them to do so. Thus the Fellows of St John's encouraged Wilberforce in idleness, " because, forsooth, he was a talented young man of fortune, and did not need to work to earn his bread." [1] There were as yet no organised contests of strength or skill, and for want of some such counter-attraction the students led a very loose life. Gray, who himself became a victim of their coarse tricks, being of a peaceable and timid disposition, was secretly horrified to see them place " women upon their heads in the streets at noon-day, break open shops, game in the coffee-houses on Sundays," [2] though, in so doing, they merely followed the example of those in authority. " The Tuns Tavern at Cambridge was the scene of nightly orgies, in which professors and fellows set an example of roistering to the youth of the University. Heavy bills were run up at inns and coffee-houses, which were afterwards repudiated with effrontery. The breaking of windows and riots in public parts of the town were indulged in to such an extent," about the middle of the eighteenth century, " as to make Cambridge almost intolerable." [3] In 1748, when the Duke of Newcastle was appointed Chancellor, everyone was intoxicated on the evening of his installation. " I make no exceptions," says Gray, " from the Chancellour to Blew-coat," that is to say, the Chancellor's servant. [4]

It is true that the same duke, with the assistance of the bishops, afterwards endeavoured to restore order, and that he imposed new regulations for the maintenance of discipline, which were adopted by the Senate of the University in 1750. This somewhat checked the excesses of the students, but did not put a stop to them. Wordsworth acknowledges that " the manners of the young men were

---

[1] *Social Life at the English Universities in the Eighteenth Century,* compiled by Christopher Wordsworth, 1874, p. 99.
[2] Letter to Thomas Wharton, 1747.
[3] E. W. Gosse, *Gray* (English Men of Letters), p. 90.
[4] Letter to Thomas Wharton, 8th August 1749.

very frantic and dissolute" in his time.[1]   Nor were these
manners peculiar to Cambridge : Oxford in this respect
was not a whit behind her rival.   In 1785, again, we find
Cowper accounting for the deterioration of his country
by the decline of discipline in the Universities, where he
could see none but " gamesters, jockeys, brothellers impure,
spendthrifts and booted sportsmen."[2]   He considered that
the youths who had passed through these hot-beds of corruption could learn nothing more of vice from the outside
world.   It filled him with amazement and admiration to
learn that his brother had remained undefiled at Oxford,
and had left it without losing his innocence.   Similarly
Coleridge, who went to Cambridge just as Wordsworth
was quitting it, says in 1817, that " to those who remember
the state of our public schools and universities some twenty
years past, it will appear no ordinary praise in any man to
have passed from innocence into virtue, not only free from
all vicious habit, but unstained by one act of intemperance,
or the degradations akin to intemperance."[3]   Finally we
may adduce the gloomy forebodings of a correspondent
of the *Gentleman's Magazine* in January 1798.   " When I
recollect the estimation in which our Universities were once
deservedly held, and mark their present debasement ; more
especially when I anticipate the dreadful state of licentious
insanity to which they are so visibly accelerating,—my
blood curdles in my veins and my whole soul quivers with
apprehension."

Such was the dismal yet uproarious atmosphere to which
the Hawkshead scholar found himself suddenly transported ;
a schoolboy with all the shyness of his mountain childhood
still upon him, ignorant of any pleasures but those which
an open-air life could yield, and incapable alike of any
enthusiasm for studies which seemed to him destitute of
loftiness and of poetry, and of surrendering his will to
masters in whom he could discover neither greatness of
mind nor nobility of soul.

[1] Letter to De Quincey, 29th July 1804. *De Quincey Memorials*, edited by
Alexander Japp, 1891, vol. i. p. 124.
[2] *The Task*, Time-Piece, 751-752
[3] Coleridge, *Biographia literaria*, ch. ii.

III

In the depths of his remote county Wordsworth had
naturally formed a very lofty conception and a most brilliant
picture of the University of Cambridge; and accordingly,
in spite of the gloom of an autumn morning, and the leaden
clouds which seemed to weigh heavily upon a wide level
country, he was thrilled with delight when from the coach
he caught sight of the towers of King's College Chapel
rising above a dark mass of trees. His gaze became riveted
upon the first student he discovered, dressed in the orthodox
gown and tasselled cap, and hurrying along by himself as
if pressed for time or eager for air and exercise. He could
not take his eyes from him until he was left an arrow's
flight behind. The town, as they drew near, seemed to
Wordsworth to draw him to itself with the strength of
an eddy. The coach passed beneath the castle, allowed
him, as it crossed Magdalene Bridge, a momentary glimpse
of the Cam, and drew up before the celebrated Hoop
Inn.

Scarcely had he alighted when he found himself
surrounded by the familiar faces of old schoolfellows,
mere acquaintances at Hawkshead, who, in this unfamiliar place, appeared like friends; simple schoolboys
then, but now full of importance. Questions, directions,
warnings and advice flowed in upon him as he passed
along; and he had the impression, on this first proud
and happy day, of being a man of business and expense,
as he went from shop to shop about his own affairs.
Among the motley crowd of townspeople and members
of the university, students and doctors, gowns severely
plain or gorgeous, through street and cloister, college-
court and chapel, he wandered "with loose and careless
mind." He was the Dreamer, his surroundings were the
Dream. He paid a visit to his prospective tutor, then
hastened to a tailor's shop, and presently came out
splendidly attired, as if by the touch of a magic wand.
He wore silk stockings; his powdered hair resembled a

tree whitened by hoar-frost;[1] he had bought a sumptuous
dressing gown, and other signs of manhood destined to
supply the lack of beard.[2]   His purchases concluded, he
returned to his college.

St John's was not one of the finest buildings in Cambridge; its principal claim to admiration lay in its great
library, which was more worthy of a University than
of a simple college, and contained a collection of French
works, chiefly historical, the gift of Matthew Prior the
poet, who had been a student there.   But some compensation for its want of architectural beauty was afforded
by its splendid avenues of tall elms, which ran along the
river and skirted the neighbouring meadows.[3]

Wordsworth took up his abode in the room assigned
to him, which looked out from an obscure nook upon
the first of the three Gothic courts of the college.
Exactly underneath him was the kitchen, from which
a ceaseless hum arose, as busy, if not so musical, as the
sound of bees, and mingled with the sharp commands
and scolding tones of the servants.   Close by was the loud-
toned organ of Trinity College, and its loquacious clock
which never failed, day or night, to chime the quarters,
nor to tell the hours twice over, with a male and female
voice.   And from his pillow, by moonlight or starlight,
he could see the porch of Trinity chapel,

> where the statue stood
> Of Newton with his prism and silent face,
> The marble index of a mind for ever
> Voyaging through strange seas of thought, alone.[4]

The succeeding weeks, beguiled by invitations, and

---

[1] Powdering the hair did not go out of fashion until 1795.   Its cessation
was due to the Revolution.

[2] *The Prelude*, iii. 18-42.

[3] *A concise and accurate description of the University, Town and Country of
Cambridge* (Cambridge, 1790?).

[4] *The Prelude*, iii. 46-64.   These beautiful lines on Newton seem to be
inspired by the equally happy lines of Thomson:
> "The noiseless tide of time all bearing down
> To vast eternity's unbounded sea,
> Where the green islands of the happy shine,
> He stemmed alone."   (*Death of Isaac Newton*).

suppers with wine and fruit, closely resembled the day of
his arrival, and were devoted to acquiring the tone and
manners of the place.   Yet, from the very first, in spite
of the attraction of these unaccustomed pleasures, he
had an obscure feeling that he was, and would remain,
a stranger at Cambridge.   He felt that he " was not for
that hour nor for that place," that there he would find
no use for the " holy powers " with which he had been
endowed when he entered it.   Thus, when the first
glamour of college life had worn off, he would frequently quit his companions, and leaving the town
behind, would wander alone about the surrounding plain.
And though the neighbourhood of Cambridge offered
neither the prospect nor the awe-inspiring voices of his
native mountains, the very bareness of his new surroundings led him to detect that universal beauty which is
bestowed by nature as a recompense on the spots to which
she has been least generous, and is discernible in the
every-day appearance of earth and sky ; of

> Earth nowhere unembellished by some trace
> Of that first Paradise whence man was driven ;
> And sky, whose beauty and bounty are expressed
> By the proud name she bears —the name of Heaven.

Thus he experienced at Cambridge the same intuitions
as at Hawkshead ; here, too, he attributed life and
feeling

> To every natural form, rock, fruit, or flower,
> Even the loose stones that cover the highway.
> .   .   .   .
> .   .   .   Whate'er of Terror or of Love,
> Or Beauty, Nature's daily face put on
> From transitory passion, unto this
> I was as sensitive as waters are
> To the sky's influence.   .   .   .
> Unknown, unthought of, yet I was most rich—
> I had a world about me—'twas my own ;
> I made it, for it only lived to me.[1]

[1] *The Prelude*, iii. 75-142.

If, however, by look or gesture he betrayed the visions which haunted him, they were set down to madness. Finding no one to whom he might confide them, he was compelled to keep them to himself. But though within his mind there were caverns which the sun could never penetrate, at the same time it did not lack

> leafy arbours where the light
> Might enter in at will.[1]

Greatly as he enjoyed solitude, his sociable disposition would not allow him to shun his fellow-students. If a troop of young fellows drew near he was naturally attracted towards it, for his heart loved companionship, and idleness, and joy. How could he behold unmoved

> So many happy youths, so wide and fair
> A congregation in its budding-time
> Of health, and hope, and beauty, all at once
> So many divers samples from the growth
> Of life's sweet season,   .   .   .
> That miscellaneous garland of wild flowers
> Decking the matron temples of a place
> So famous through the world ? [2]

Comrades, friends, mere associates of a day, were all alike welcome, or those of them at any rate who devoted themselves more willingly to pleasure than to study. Obliged to choose between the indolent and the industrious, he preferred the former, and spent his days in frivolity and amusement. They filled the morning with idle chat, and then sauntered about the streets and avenues. They

> Read lazily in trivial books, went forth
> To gallop through the country in blind zeal
> Of senseless horsemanship, or on the breast
> Of Cam sailed boisterously, and let the stars
> Come forth, perhaps without one quiet thought.[3]

In this easy-going fashion Wordsworth spent whole months, not in scandalous or disorderly proceedings, but

---

[1] *The Prelude*, iii. 234-246.   [2] *Ibid.*, iii. 218-225.   [3] *Ibid.*, iii. 246-255.

in vague and loose indifference, and the satisfaction of easily attainable desires. Nature did not supply the place of the forgotten idea of duty ; memory was languid and lethargic ; his heart was wrapped in the heavy slumber of summer noon-tide. His shallow existence might be compared

> To a floating island, an amphibious spot
> Unsound, of spongy texture, yet withal
> Not wanting a fair face of water-weeds
> And pleasant flowers.[1]

There was nothing in his environment to shame him out of his indolence, or to inspire him with the resolution necessary to energetic effort. Slowly and insensibly, during a year of this existence, his "nature's outward coat" became changed.[2] If his attention was once more to be concentrated upon himself, and his taste for super-ficiæl pastimes replaced by devotion to meditation, such a result could only be produced by the stay he made at Hawkshead during his first Long Vacation.

The two remaining years of his life at Cambridge were therefore less frivolous than the first. The boisterous amusements which had at first allured him no longer had their old charm. He led a more solitary life, opening his heart to the gentle influence of melancholy, and loving

> A pensive sky, sad days, and piping winds,
> The twilight more than dawn, autumn than spring.[3]

He became conscious of his poetic genius, and occupied himself in putting the finishing touches to a certain de-scription of *An Evening Walk* in the lake-district, which had been sketched out at Hawkshead. He grew bold enough to hope that he might leave behind him some monument "which pure hearts should reverence."[4] Grad-ually the instinctive humility which he had hitherto felt at the mere mention of authorship, or at the sight of a printed book, faded away. The reverential awe with which great names among the poets had impressed him

---

[1] *The Prelude*, iii. 321-336.　　[2] *Ibid.*, iii. 205-6.
[3] *Ibid.*, vi. 174-5.　　[4] *Ibid.*, vi. 56-7.

gave way to a desire to follow in their footsteps, and to the delight of feeling that there was something in common between himself and them.

During the winter Wordsworth would linger in the college garden later than anyone else, leaving it only when the inexorable nine o'clock bell drove him to his room.

> Lofty elms,
> Inviting shades of opportune recess,
> Bestowed composure on a neighbourhood
> Unpeaceful in itself.   A single tree
> With sinuous trunk, boughs exquisitely wreathed,
> Grew there ; an ash which Winter for himself
> Decked as in pride, and with outlandish grace :
> Up from the ground, and almost to the top,
> The trunk and every master branch were green
> With clustering ivy, and the lightsome twigs
> And outer spray profusely tipped with seeds
> That hung in yellow tassels, while the air
> Stirred them, not voiceless.   Often have I stood
> Foot-bound uplooking at this lovely tree
> Beneath a frosty moon.   .   .   .
> .   .   .   Scarcely Spenser's self
> Could have more tranquil visions in his youth,
> Or could more bright appearances create
> Of human forms with superhuman powers,
> Than I beheld loitering on calm clear nights
> Alone, beneath this fairy work of earth.[1]

Thus, in delightful reverie, many an hour was wiled away. Study, with Wordsworth, occupied only a secondary position, and he himself explains to us why it was that he did not fall in with the methods of work then current at his University.

IV

" For I," says Wordsworth,

> bred up 'mid Nature's luxuries,
> Was a spoiled child, and, rambling like the wind,
> As I had done in daily intercourse

[1] *The Prelude*, vi. 73-94.

With those crystalline rivers, solemn heights,
And mountains, ranging like a fowl of the air,
I was ill-tutored for captivity ;
To quit my pleasure, and, from month to month,
Take up a station calmly on the perch
Of sedentary peace.[1]

Unusual as it may appear, in exchanging the life of a schoolboy for that of a student, in passing from boyhood to early manhood, he had exchanged a liberty which was all but absolute for comparative restraint. He found the discipline of the University, easy and even lax as it was, more burdensome than the homely rule of Hawkshead Grammar School.   Every evening at nine o'clock the gates of St John's College were bolted, whereas Anne Tyson's Cottage was only closed by an easily-raised latch.   He could no longer indulge in those nocturnal rambles and early morning walks of which he was so fond.

Then, too, his rural pleasures had been so keen that little room remained in his heart for the peaceful charms of study, all that was left being taken up quickly by the only books for which he had any inclination, those on literature and history. He read much and eagerly, consulting his own taste and paying no attention to the course prescribed at the University. While he did not neglect the dead languages, it was the modern ones that really excited his interest, although these did not command much respect at that time. He learnt something of French and Spanish, and for Italian he conceived a genuine and lasting passion. His master, Agostino Isola, whom Thomas Gray, twenty years earlier, had chosen as his deputy, and with whom he had delighted to read the Italian poets, took pride in the progress of his new pupil.[2] Wordsworth's zeal for these studies, which were then almost against the rules, unfortunately deprived him, as his sister informs us, " of the power of chaining his

[1] *The Prelude,* iii. 351-359.
[2] *Autobiographical Memoranda,* and see *Gray,* by E. Gosse (English Men of Letters), p. 181.

attention to others discordant to his feelings."[1] He had
no pleasure in

> the Lecturer's room
> All studded round, as thick as chairs could stand,
> With loyal students faithful to their books,
> Half-and-half idlers, hardy recusants,
> And honest dunces.

He concerned himself very little about the

> important days,
> Examinations, when the man was weighed
> As in a balance,

and was free, except on very rare occasions, from the
extravagant hopes, the tremulous agitation, the small
jealousies, and the fears, legitimate as they might be, of
those who sought academic distinction.[2] He could not
indeed have taken a place among such disputants without
conquering his growing dislike to mathematics. Possessed
on his arrival at Cambridge of some advantage over the
freshmen of his year, he very soon fell into the habit of
neglecting those branches of knowledge which there took
precedence of all others, and were absolutely indispensable
to any sort of success.   He "never opens a mathematical
book," his sister tells us[3]; but, to balance this neglect,
he found a pleasure in detecting the hidden poetry of the
sciences in which he had advanced "no farther than the
threshold."

> There I found
> Both elevation and composed delight :
> With Indian awe and wonder, ignorance pleased
> With its own struggles, did I meditate
> On the relation those abstractions bear
> To Nature's laws, and by what process led,
> Those immaterial agents bowed their heads
> Duly to serve the mind of earth-born man ;
> From star to star, from kindred sphere to sphere,
> From system on to system without end.

[1] Letter of Dorothy Wordsworth.   Knight, *Life of Wordsworth*, i. p. 79.
[2] *The Prelude*, iii. 64-74.
[3] Letter of Dorothy, 26th June 1791 (W. Knight, *Life of Wordsworth*,
i. p. 57).

More frequently the same source yielded him a deep and
quiet pleasure, a consciousness of an eternal and universal
power, and an invincible faith. "There," he continues,

> I recognised
> A type, for finite natures, of the one
> Supreme Existence, the surpassing life
> Which—to the boundaries of space and time,
> Of melancholy space and doleful time,
> Superior, and incapable of change,
> Nor touched by welterings of passion—is,
> And hath the name of, God. Transcendent peace
> And silence did await upon these thoughts
> That were a frequent comfort to my youth.[1]

Consequently, instead of learning formulæ, he was so
sadly misguided as to conceive an enthusiasm, without
a nearer acquaintance with the science, for "that clear
synthesis built up aloft so gracefully," and to seek therein
a refuge from the images by which his mind was beset,
or a stimulus to vague and daring speculations. It was
quite open to him, it appears, to take up other branches of
study in place of the abstract sciences. But he did not
care for the "timid course" of the scholastic study of the
period; he would

> have wished
> To see the river flow with ampler range
> And freer pace.[2]

Above all he was distressed at the jealous passions
excited in the generous heart of youth by competitive
examinations. Only twice had he himself experienced
that spirit of rivalry which so soon degenerates into envy.
On the first occasion he had tripped up his brother in
a foot race in which he saw that he was getting the worst
of it. The second occurred during his residence at
Cambridge, when he became jealous of a fellow-student
who surpassed him in the only subject of study on which
he prided himself—that of Italian. "It is a horrible

---

[1] *The Prelude*, vi. 115-141.   [2] *Ibid.* iii. 493-496.

feeling," he said later.[1]   " My own case," he wrote to his nephew, Charles Wordsworth, on March 12th 1846, " is, I am aware, a peculiar one in many ways ; but I can sincerely affirm that I am not indebted to emulation for my attainments, whatever they be.   I have from my youth down to this date cultivated the habit of valuing knowledge for its own sake and for the good that may come, and ought to come, out of it—the unmixed, pure good."[2]

No prize, in his opinion, could be any compensation for the harm done by these unwholesome contests.   He was not attracted by those whose minds were filled with the feverish suspicion due to rivalry ; he preferred those of an easier temper, who were not constantly worrying themselves about the result of an examination, but would devote a little of their time to friendship.

He lost, in consequence, all chance of obtaining a fellow-ship at St John's College, and with it the fixed income for the time being which the post brought with it, as well as the prospect of obtaining a profitable appointment in the future.   He did not even attempt to make himself con-spicuous by any of those poetical compositions by means of which the students at English Universities often manage. to attract the notice of their professors.   He wrote no Latin verses for a prize or medal, and took equally little advantage of his opportunities for writing English verse. The master of his college died very soon after Words-worth's arrival at Cambridge, and his coffin having been placed, according to the custom of the time, in the hall of the college, several of the students fastened copies of Latin or English verses to the pall which covered it. Doctor Cookson, Wordsworth's uncle by the mother's side, was annoyed to find that none of these productions was the work of his poetical nephew, who had thus lost a fair opportunity of distinguishing himself.   But Words-worth, who had been practically unacquainted with the deceased master, and felt no regret at his death, was even

[1] Mrs Davy's note, 7th April 1846. Knight, *Life of Wordsworth*, iii. pp. 459-460.
[2] Charles Wordsworth, *Annals of My Early Life* (1806-1846), 1891.

thus early unwilling to write verses to order.[1] He had already too lofty an idea of the poet's art, and too deep a feeling for poetry, to regard it as a mere educational exercise.

If the abilities or the character of any one of his teachers had made any deep impression upon him, Wordsworth's refractory spirit might have been subdued. But such was not the case. Those responsible for instruction or discipline—the *Dons*, or high functionaries of the University—seemed to him much less worthy of respect than the shepherds whom he had met on his native mountains. This perhaps is the only piece of irreverent mockery in which he agrees with Byron, who, twenty years later, made the acquaintance of the same eccentric characters, or their successors, and pronounced them

> Vain as their honours, heavy as their ale,
> Sad as their wit, and tedious as their tale.[2]

They did nothing for Wordsworth beyond sharpening his sense of the ridiculous by their whimsical idiosyncrasies, and even in that respect it must be admitted that they did not benefit him much. The only recollection he retained of them was of their eccentric habits. At a more mature age they occasionally recurred to his mind, as phantoms "of texture midway between life and books."[3]

Wordsworth has not thrown the whole responsibility for his comparative idleness upon them, for he insists that the fault was principally his own, and reproaches himself for his disobedience to his relations, the pride and selfishness of his rebellious spirit, and his "spurious virtue" of independence, which was in reality nothing but cowardice; but nevertheless he took pleasure in picturing to himself a University "whose studious aspect" would immediately have conquered all his opposition, and would at once have compelled him to pay to science, to polite letters, and to learning the same homage which he had paid to Nature. His description of this ideal Univer-

---

[1] *Autobiographical Memoranda*, Prose Works, iii, p. 221.
[2] Thoughts suggested by a College Examination, *Hours of Idleness*.
[3] *The Prelude*, iii. 534-578.

sity is quite a satire upon the Cambridge of the eighteenth century; Cambridge, where, he says,

> Mine eyes were crossed by butterflies, ears vexed
> By chattering popinjays; the inner heart
> Seemed trivial, and the impresses without
> Of a too gaudy region.[1]

The University of his dreams—that which he expected to find when he left Hawkshead—would of course be no gloomy abode. The shade of its ancient trees would often echo with joyous song. Yet in its general aspect it would appear to be the habitation of sober reflection, a domain in which thoughtful youth might wander in quietness, where

> A healthy sound simplicity should reign,
> A seemly plainness, name it what you will,
> Republican or pious.[2]

The majesty of its groves and edifices would be matched by a corresponding dignity in the inner world of mind. Youths would be influenced by powerful incentives to the loftiest morality. The sociable tendency natural to their age would not be allowed to squander itself on frivolous pleasures, but trained instead to minister to such fair and noble deeds as its inherent enthusiasm might perform with love. The heart of the student would be solemnly and religiously impressed with a conviction of the power which knowledge can confer, when it is sought with sincerity and prized for its own sake.[3]

Futile and hypocritical ceremonies would be replaced by the worship of truth. Wordsworth raises an indignant protest against the severe regulations by which it was sought to enforce attendance at morning and evening prayers in the college chapels. Discipline, so easy in other respects, was on this point quite inflexible. Only a few years had passed since the discontinuance of the special form of punishment known as the *stang*, whereby those who failed to attend chapel were compelled to ride upon a triangular colt-staff,

---

[1] *The Prelude*, iii. 441-446.   [2] *Ibid.*, iii. 395-398.   [3] *Ibid.*, iii. 378-392.

like soldiers in disgrace during the early days of the **French**
army.[1] This penalty had fallen into disuse, but other severe
forms of punishment had taken its place.

Hence there sprang up among the students a thoroughly
irreligious spirit disguised under an outward show of piety.
" Was ever known," exclaims Wordsworth,

> The witless shepherd who persists to drive
> A flock that thirsts not to a pool disliked?
> A weight must surely hang on days begun
> And ended with such mockery.   Be wise,
> Ye Presidents and Deans, and, till the spirit
> Of ancient times revive, and youth be trained
> At home in pious service, to your bells
> Give seasonable rest, for 'tis a sound
> Hollow as ever vexed the tranquil air;
> And your officious doings bring disgrace
> On the plain steeples of our English Church,
> Whose worship, 'mid remotest village trees,
> Suffers for this.   Even Science, too, at hand
> In daily sight of this irreverence,
> Is smitten thence with an unnatural taint,
> Loses her just authority, falls beneath
> Collateral suspicion, else unknown.[1]

But if Wordsworth found little to satisfy him in the present,
the planning of an ideal University was not the only refuge
for his mind.   The monuments of Cambridge displayed on
every hand the marks of a past which he could contemplate with satisfaction.   How glorious a part in the English
Renaissance had been played by his own college of St
John's, of which Nash said in 1589: " Yet was not
knowledge fullie confirmed in hir Monarchie amongst vs,
till that most famous and fortunate Nurse of all learning,
Saint *Johns* in *Cambridge*, that at that time was as an Vniuer-
sitie within it selfe; . . . hauing more candles light in it,
euerie Winter Morning, before fowre of the clocke, than the
fowre of clocke bell gaue stroakes; till Shee (I saie) . . .
sent from her fruitefull wombe, sufficient Schollers, both

---

[1] *Social Life*, etc., op. cit.   The *stang* was not discontinued until 1770, or
thereabouts.
[2] *The Prelude*, iii. 398-422.

to support her owne weale, as also to supplie all other inferiour foundations defects." [1]

Wordsworth therefore calls to mind the sterner days of the middle ages and of the Revival of Learning, when those who dwelt within the walls of Cambridge led a studious and abstemious life ; when, cooped and crowded in forlorn and naked chambers, they pored with eagerness over their ponderous tomes,

> Like caterpillars eating out their way
> In silence, or with keen devouring noise
> Not to be tracked or fathered.

He regrets the time when princes, piously trained to love a frugal diet, patient labour and plain attire, rose to shiver at matins and sought their rest at curfew ; when Learning, sounding her trumpet throughout Christendom like a stranger come from far, roused alike the peasant and the king ; when humble scholars left their native village for some distant University on which they had set their minds, and bearing their ponderous folios in their hands, begged their way as they journeyed onwards ; and when illustrious men, such as Bucer, Erasmus or Melancthon, enamoured of truth but oppressed by poverty, would read by moonlight at the door or window of their cell, for want of the means to purchase a taper. [2]

V

Keenly as he regretted the glories of the past, Wordsworth was not without a suspicion that his regret rested on an illusion due to distance. He has declared moreover that in spite of all drawbacks his residence at Cambridge was upon the whole a fortunate privilege, little as the University was adapted to his needs. Preserved by his healthy nature from the most dangerous temptations, he

---

[1] From a letter of *Thomas Nash*, which stands as the preface to Robert Greene's romance, *Menaphon* (*Arber's English Scholar's library*), p. ii.

[2] *The Prelude*, iii. 447-478.

did not contract the prevailing habits of excess, and thus acquired at Cambridge the certainty of his moral soundness.

Further, although his imagination remained dormant during his University career, it did not fall into absolute lethargy. The stately memories from which the English Universities derive their greatness and their glory left a deep impression on his mind. Through Cambridge had passed in turn poets so illustrious as Spenser, Marlowe, Milton, Dryden, Gray, and (it was supposed) Chaucer. Thomas Otway and Matthew Prior, among others, had been educated at St John's, the college in which Wordsworth was a student. He could not tread without emotion soil where the " grass had yielded to the steps of generations of illustrious men." Not always heedlessly could he cross the threshold of gateways through which they had passed, sleep where they had slept, and wake where they had awakened ; not without reflexion could he " range that inclosure old," that garden which had witnessed the unfolding of lofty intellects. Through proximity these great men became endeared to him ; the traditions handed down concerning them lent them a closer kinship to humanity.

He used to read the amorous tales of Chaucer in the hawthorn shade near Trompington Mill, celebrated in one of the *Canterbury Tales*.[1]

> And that gentle Bard,
> Chosen by the Muses for their Page of State—
> Sweet Spenser, moving through his clouded heaven
> With the moon's beauty and the moon's soft pace,
> I called him Brother, Englishman, and Friend !
> Yea, our blind Poet, who, in his later day,
> Stood almost single ; uttering odious truth—
> Darkness before, and danger's voice behind,
> Soul awful—if the earth has ever lodged
> An awful soul—I seemed to see him here
> Familiarly, and in his scholar's dress
> Bounding before me, yet a stripling youth—
> A boy, no better, with his rosy cheeks

[1] *The Reve's Tale.*

Angelical, keen eye, courageous look,
And conscious step of purity and pride.

One of Wordsworth's friends had the very room in Christ's
College which Milton had occupied. Wordsworth con-
fesses that one evening, in joyous company, the libations
he poured out to the memory of the temperate poet were
so copious that their fumes mounted to his brain, and
caused his first and only experience of intoxication. The
bell of St John's chapel had ceased to ring for evening
prayers, so that he was obliged to fly at his utmost speed
through the streets, huddle on his surplice in haste, and
shoulder his way through the crowd of simple townspeople crowded beneath the organ, lest he should arrive
disgracefully late for the ceremony he was compelled to
attend.

If he deems it fortunate that the memories of students
famous in the past exercised so happy an influence upon
him, he congratulates himself no less upon the experience,
gained at the University, of a world distinct in itself,
intermediate between that which is dreamed of by the
boy and that which is to be inhabited by the man. Therein he saw, on a smaller scale, a copy of the virtues and the
vices with which he would shortly be brought in contact,
and thus witnessed, before entering the arena of life, a
mock contest or kind of tournament, where blows, if
never mortal, were hardly dealt.[1]

In short, although he evinces no such enthusiastic gratitude towards Cambridge as that with which Hawkshead
had inspired him, he recognised that his residence there
had not been without its beneficial effect upon his intelligence. There he had roamed—

As through a wide museum from whose stores
A casual rarity is singled out
And has its brief perusal, then gives way

---

[1] *The Prelude*, iii. 579-584. Fielding makes Joseph Andrews say (Book
iii. ch. v.) : " Great schools are little societies, where a boy of any observation may see in epitome what he will afterwards find in the world at
large."

To others, all supplanted in their turn;
Till 'mid this crowded neighbourhood of things
That are by nature most unneighbourly,
The head turns round and cannot right itself;
And though an aching and a barren sense
Of gay confusion still be uppermost,
With few wise longings and but little love,
Yet to the memory something cleaves at last,
Whence profit may be drawn in times to come.[1]

[1] *The Prelude*, iii. 616-629.

CHAPTER IV

College Vacations

I

CAMBRIDGE did not demand of Wordsworth three years of unbroken exile from nature, nor deprive him of all communication with her. The effect of college life, which, all things considered, was artificial and repugnant to the instincts of his genius, was opposed and counteracted by the influence of his vacations.

The summer holidays of 1788 saw him once more at Hawkshead, unable to resist the attraction of the village in which the brightest days of his boyhood had been passed. Bereft, also, of home and parents, and separated from his brothers and his sister, it was only here, beneath the motherly roof of old Anne Tyson, that he could find some approach to family life. So deep and lasting were the impressions he received during his stay, that its most trifling events remained faithfully graven on his memory. After a year's absence from Hawkshead he seemed to see the place more clearly, or with other eyes, than heretofore. Familiar objects acquired for him a new meaning; the impression they now made upon him was almost as fresh as at first, while they derived an additional charm from early memories.

The noon-day sun shone brightly when he reached the edge of a bare upland and saw once more at his feet the waters of Windermere, its islands, its promontories, and its gleaming bays.

> A universe of Nature's fairest forms
> Proudly revealed with instantaneous burst,
> Magnificent, and beautiful, and gay.[1]

[1] *The Prelude*, iv. 9-11.

Down the hill he bounded, shouting loudly for the old ferryman, whose well-known skiff bore him across the lake. An hour's rapid walking brought him at last in sight of Hawkshead Church, standing white upon its hill,

> like a throned lady sending out
> A gracious look all over her domain.[1]

Scarcely had he crossed the cottage threshold when his old landlady gave him a joyful yet tender welcome, "perusing" him with motherly pride. He too was glad to see once more the aged dame, who, childless herself, was regarded by the scholars she had nourished with little less than filial love, and with her "innocent and busy stir of narrow cares," had nevertheless her "little daily growth of calm enjoyments." Proudly she accompanied him, and would even (quite needlessly) show him the way when he expressed a wish to look over the house once more—the rooms, the court, and the garden. Willingly, nay gladly, he on his part submitted to be led. Again he visited

> The famous brook, who, soon as he was boxed
> Within the garden, found himself at once,
> As if by trick insidious and unkind,
> Stripped of his voice and left to dimple down
> (Without an effort and without a will)
> A channel paved by man's officious care ;

a brief and gentle bondage in which Wordsworth could see an emblem of the pre-arranged and uniform course of his own life at Cambridge.[2] Then, still accompanied by the good woman, he passed beyond the premises, hailing the neighbours encountered by the way, and exchanging distant greetings with the labourers working in the fields. In presence of the old schoolfellows whom he met he had at first a feeling of constraint, for his fashionable clothes inspired him with a certain pride, not unmingled with shame ; yet he was none the less delighted to take his place at table with them as heretofore. But the keenest joy of all came when he lay down in the lowly bed where

---

[1] *The Prelude*, iv. 21-23.   [2] *Ibid.* iv. 50-64.

he had heard the wind roaring and the rain lashing the window panes, where, so often, he

> Had lain awake on summer nights to watch
> The moon in splendour couched among the leaves
> Of a tall ash, that near [the] cottage stood ;
> Had watched her with fixed eyes while to and fro
> In the dark summit of the waving tree
> She rocked with every impulse of the breeze.[1]

The delightful expeditions he had made in the neighbourhood of Hawkshead came back to his mind in all their freshness "like a returning Spring."[2] A terrier dog had often accompanied the boyish poet in his solitary walks, and with this companion he determined as soon as possible to make the circuit of the little lake of Esthwaite. The sun was setting when he started, and the evening air was cold, and raw, and windy; but his heart was overflowing with a serene and boundless happiness which no gloomy skies could dispel. Perhaps they even added to the charm of the landscape, " as a face we love is sweetest then, when sorrow damps it," or rather, when our own heart is full.[3] Gently laying aside her veil his soul stripped herself bare, as if in the presence of her God. It seemed to him, as he walked onward, that consolation came to him although he had felt no sorrow, strength when he had been unconscious of weakness, healing although he had known no ailment. Grasping the balance, he weighed his soul with an unfaltering hand. In this abstracted state he was scarcely aware of the scenes around him, yet nevertheless he felt within him the swellings of hope, and had a glimmering apprehension of the strength and permanence of the soul, of its creative and informing power, and its capacity to dissolve with its own warmth the icy crust which, during long slumber, may gather around it. Nor was he without more tender thoughts ; thoughts of love, of innocence, of leisure, and of pastoral quiet, accompanied by visions of a peaceful or glorious end, won by his own endurance. Full of dreams like these he

[1] *The Prelude*, iv. 85-92.   [2] *Ibid.*, iv. 136-7.   [3] *Ibid.*, iv. 146-147.

seated himself in a wood alone, and continued his reverie.

> The slopes
> And heights meanwhile were slowly overspread
> With darkness, and before a rippling breeze
> The long lake lengthened out its hoary line,
> And in the sheltered coppice where I sate,
> Around me from among the hazel leaves,
> Now here, now there, moved by the straggling wind,
> Came ever and anon a breath-like sound,
> Quick as the pantings of the faithful dog,
> The off and on companion of my walk;
> And such, at times, believing them to be,
> I turned my head to look if he were there;
> Then into solemn thought I passed once more.[1]

As the days slipped by he became conscious of a new interest in the life of the peasants. The peaceful village filled him with surprise; he found it

> Changed like a garden in the heat of spring
> After an eight days' absence.[2]

In this narrow vale, where each was known to all, he could not feel indifferent when he observed the leafy bower, and sunny nook where an old man had been wont to sit alone, now vacant; children, once pale-cheeked and carried in their mothers' arms, now rosy prattlers running with tottering steps to the feet of a happy grandmother; and well-grown girls whose beauty with all its promise had fled to deck the cheek of some slighted playmate.

After his absence, too, he found his eyes no longer blindfolded by familiarity. Hitherto he had considered all he saw as universal and necessary; it had not yet occurred to him to study the thoughts and acts of the simple folk among whom he had lived and grown. But he returned from Cambridge with a new capacity for judging and comparing, and ready to smile at local customs. He saw the woodman in the forest, the shepherd on the mountain, with a different eye. He noticed now

[1] *The Prelude*, iv. 178-190.   [2] *Ibid.*, iv. 195-196.

for the first time—he had seen it a hundred times before
without observing it—how old Anne Tyson equipped
herself "in monumental trim" to go to church, with

> Short velvet cloak, (her bonnet of the like),
> A mantle such as Spanish Cavaliers
> Wore in old times. Her smooth domestic life,
> Affectionate without disquietude,
> Her talk, her business, pleased me ; and no less
> Her clear though shallow stream of piety
> That ran on Sabbath days a fresher course ;
> With thoughts unfelt till now I saw her read
> Her Bible on hot Sunday afternoons,
> And loved the book, when she had dropped asleep
> And made of it a pillow for her head.[1]

During the same holidays he began to feel for natural
objects, the trees and brooks, the hills and stars, a tender
affection similar to that inspired by human beings. Hitherto
these objects had been for him the personal riches, the
absolute possession, of his own being. He had loved
them as an angel, "if he were to dwell on earth, might
love in individual happiness."[2] Now, his affection
became tinged with sadness, as he thought of their
changes for better or worse. The vague intimations of
mortality and dissolution of which he had once been
dimly aware in presence of those objects had commonly
been gloomy and austere in character; they had preserved some remnant of the undefined dread of his
early childhood. Now he found them tempered, and,
as it were, softened, by the thought of universal change.

If, however, during Wordsworth's absence and residence at Cambridge, his intellect and feelings had undergone development in certain directions, he had also
acquired a hundred frivolous notions, a taste for dress,
feasts, dancing, and public revelry. He was fond
of these pleasures for their own sake, still more because
they were the new badge of manhood and independence; hence they all conspired to turn him aside
from nature, and to quench the enthusiasm he had known

---

[1] *The Prelude*, iv. 218-230.   [2] *Ibid.*, iv. 236-238.

in the days of his wild boyhood and freedom from worldly thoughts. His elegant garments, like a tunic of Nessus, imprisoned his limbs and preyed upon his vitality. From the common diversions which allured him he might indeed gain some knowledge of character and of life, but this, after all, was of trifling value in comparison with the benefits which he might have derived from study or from books. Far better would it have been had he exalted his mind by solitary reading, and strengthened his intense desires through peaceful meditation. The vain pursuits of this period of his life would have caused him deeper remorse, had not the memory of one particular hour risen up in protest against such regret. He had passed a night in dancing and amusement at a farm among the hills, yielding himself unreservedly to the pleasures of the dance, and feeling now and then, for the " frank-hearted maids of rocky Cumberland, slight shocks of young love-liking,"

> Whose transient pleasure mounted to the head
> And tingled through the veins.[1]

The morning cock had crowed before he started homeward, and from the footpath, which wound through humble copse and open field, he could see the sky kindling in the east.

> Magnificent
> The morning rose, in memorable pomp,
> Glorious as e'er I had beheld—in front,
> The sea lay laughing at a distance ; near,
> The solid mountains shone, bright as the clouds,
> Grain-tinctured, drenched in empyrean light ;
> And in the meadows and the lower grounds
> Was all the sweetness of a common dawn—
> Dews, vapours, and the melody of birds,
> And labourers going forth to till the fields.[2]

His heart was full to the brim; he made no vows, but vows were then made for him; a bond was given, unknown to him, that he should be, " else sinning greatly,

---

[1] *The Prelude*, iv. 317-319.   [2] *Ibid.*, iv. 323-332.

a consecrated spirit." And as he went on his way he was filled with a "thankful blessedness," destined for many years to linger in his memory.

Nor was this the only warning which at that time came, as he believed, from above, to induce him to reflect on the vanity of the life he was leading. His mind was not so far transformed by frivolity that it was no longer capable of reflection. Rather was it the centre of thoughts both grave and gay, both deep and superficial, which occupied the same habitation in peace and harmony. And by reason of this it was always capable of recovering its innate power, of again becoming conscious of its true and lofty destiny, whenever for a moment the incentives to idle pleasure relaxed their sway. Solitude, that "benign" and "gracious" power, is especially favourable to reflection when the world has kept us too long divided from our better selves ;

> Most potent when impressed upon the mind
> With an appropriate human centre—hermit,
> Deep in the bosom of the wilderness ;
> Votary (in vast cathedral, where no foot
> Is treading, where no other face is seen)
> Kneeling at prayers ; or watchman on the top
> Of lighthouse, beaten by Atlantic waves.

Even so it sometimes happens that the soul of solitude takes bodily form before our eyes upon the public road, at the hour when it is deserted for the night, and lies wrapped in deeper quiet than that of pathless wastes.[1]

Such a chance encounter, at once disturbing and regenerative, with the soul of solitude, came to Wordsworth towards the close of his vacation. Autumn had come, bringing its round of rowing and sailing matches on the spacious surface of Windermere, followed by banquets and merry-making. The night was far advanced as Wordsworth returned from one of these gatherings, overwrought by a whole day of frivolous and fatiguing amusement. The white road which he followed climbed a hill-side, and glittered like a river in the moonlight.

---

[1] *The Prelude*, iv. 354-370.

Everything was at rest; not a living creature could be discerned on earth or in the air; not a sound broke the silence of the night save the peaceful murmur of a running brook. Suddenly, at a sharp turn of the road, a strange form appeared, so near at hand that Wordsworth stepped aside into the shade of a thick hawthorn in order to observe it unseen. It was a man, of lofty stature, stiff and lank, with long arms and pallid hands. In the moonlight his mouth looked like that of a spectre; he was standing, yet he leaned against a tall mile-stone; his dress was the faded uniform of a soldier. There he stood, alone, without a dog, and without a stick to support him. Presently low mutterings fell from his lips, sounds expressive of bodily or mental suffering. Yet his figure retained its stiff, commanding attitude; his shadow lay motionless at his feet. Wordsworth's cowardice caused him some self-reproach as he watched the stranger from his hiding-place, and, making up his mind at last, he approached and hailed him. Rising slowly from the stone against which he leant, the man raised his thin arm to his head to return Wordsworth's salutation, and then resumed his former posture. When the young man enquired his story, the veteran was neither slow nor eager to reply. Unmoved, in a quiet, uncomplaining voice, and with a mild yet dignified air of indifference, he told in a few plain words a soldier's tale: how he had seen service in the islands of the tropics, whence he had arrived scarcely three weeks earlier; how he had been dismissed on landing and was now travelling on foot towards his native home. Moved with pity, Wordsworth asked the soldier to accompany him. The man stooped to pick up an oaken staff which was lying in the grass, and followed him with a weak and cautious step, yet apparently without pain. The student could scarcely conceal his astonishment at seeing the ghostly figure moving on at his side, nor refrain from asking questions about the wars and battles in which the soldier had taken part, so anxious was he to learn the impression they had made upon him. The man answered calmly and concisely, and might even have appeared solemn and sublime, had it not been for an air of absent-mindedness

distinctive of one who knows too well the importance
of what he relates, but feels it no longer. Their conversation therefore soon came to an end, and the two companions passed without a word through a dark and silent
wood. Then Wordsworth knocked at the door of a
cottage, and commended the soldier to the charitable care
of the country people, as a poor traveller, belated and ill.
He entreated him not to remain longer upon the road in the
open air, but to solicit at farm-houses the shelter and
assistance which his condition required. The soldier
replied, with the same ghastly yet gentle look—" My
trust is in the God of heaven, and in the eye of him who
passes me." The cottage door opened, once more the
soldier raised his hand in salutation of his guide, and
thanked him in a faltering tone which betrayed a reviving
interest in life. Wordsworth lingered near the door until
the man had disappeared behind it, " Then sought with
quiet heart his distant home."[1]

Striking, from the circumstances both of time and
of place under which it occurred, was this unexpected
meeting with a man whose thoughts were weaned from
the cares of life and fixed upon death, for whom war
and glory were no longer anything but hollow-sounding
words. It was in fact an experience calculated to recall a
mind occupied, as Wordsworth's then was, with frivolity
to matters of higher and lasting interest. Folly, at such
moments, shrank "from the frown of fleeting Time";[2]
once more he felt the solid foundations of his nature.
His holidays altered, though they did not transform him.
He had returned to poetry, and had sketched out the
Evening Walk. On leaving Hawkshead for Cambridge, he
felt neither regret nor sadness, yet he bore away within
him some serious thoughts which rendered him, during
his second year of college life, less eager for boisterous
amusements, and gave him a keener relish for work and
solitary musing.

[1] *The Prelude*, iv. 370-469.   [2] *Ibid.*, iv. 348-349.

II

A year later, during the vacation of 1789, he set his face
again towards the lake district, breaking his journey in
order to visit those spots in Yorkshire and Derbyshire
which were celebrated for their natural or architectural
beauty.   He explored the banks of the Dove—that
picturesque tributary of the Trent—

> whose blue current works its way
> Between romantic Dovedale's spiry rocks; [1]

and pried curiously into the hidden nooks of the district in
which he was born.   Not Hawkshead, however, but
Penrith, was this time his destination; Penrith, where
" a joy above all joys " awaited him, in the presence of
his only sister, from whom he had been separated so long
" that she seemed a gift then first bestowed." [2]   The
varied banks of Emont, and the tall trees upon its margin
which surround Brougham's " monastic castle," saw them
side by side.   More than once they climbed together the
dark windings of the mansion's ruined stair-case, crept,
not without trembling, along a crumbling wall, and looked
forth, from the opening of some Gothic window, upon a
far-stretching landscape beautified by the light of morning
or purple evening; together, with no less delight, they
lay upon the crown of some turret, and while the noon-
day heat hung heavily upon the plains, caught the faintest
whisper which the passing breeze awoke among the tufts
of grass and flowering hare-bells. [2]

And often Wordsworth's sister was accompanied by
a friend, a maiden whom he had known in his childhood
when they learned to spell in the same little school at Penrith.
This was Mary Hutchinson, of the same age as himself, whom
thirteen years later he was to wed.   His love had its commencement in their intercourse during this holiday-time,
when " her exulting outside look of youth," through which

[1] *The Prelude*, vi. 192-193.   [2] *Ibid.*, vi. 195-203.
[3] *Ibid.*, vi., 203-224.

shone the serenity of her soul, first endeared her to him.[1]
New splendour decked for him the neighbourhood of
Penrith, the narrow lanes bordered with eglantine, the
crags and shady woods with which he had become familiar
in childhood. The earlier feelings reinforced the new.
The scenes once transfigured by his first joys and fears
were those best adapted to the walks of a lover ; for
impressions, however they may differ in character, mutually
strengthen one another, and the soul of youth is more
responsive to love amid scenes where formerly it responded
to joy or innocent fear.

Of the hills which surround Penrith there was one which
was associated with a very lively recollection of childish
terror. Once, in the days when his inexperienced hand
could scarcely hold a bridle, he had started for a ride on
horseback with an old servant of his father's as guide,
from whom, by chance, he soon became separated. Alarmed
at being left alone he dismounted, and leading his horse
down the rough and stony moor, reached a hollow where a
murderer had once been hung in iron chains. The gibbet-
mast had fallen from decay, the bones and irons had entirely disappeared, but close by, at the time when the
execution took place, some unknown hand had carved the
murderer's name. Ever since then the characters had
remained fresh and visible, for every year the grass which
threatened to cover them was cleared away by local superstition. In a furtive glance the boy caught sight of these
letters, and fled in terror.[2] Reascending the bare moor,
he beheld a naked pool that lay at the foot of the hills, the
beacon on one of their summits, and near at hand a girl,
who bore a pitcher on her head, and found great difficulty
in walking against the wind. "It was," he says,

> An ordinary sight ; but I should need
> Colours and words that are unknown to man,
> To paint the visionary dreariness
> Which, while I looked all round for my lost guide,
> Invested moorland waste, and naked pool,

[1] *The Prelude*, vi. 224-227.
[2] May not Hugo have had these lines in his mind when he described
Gwymplaine's childish terror before the gallows? (*L'homme qui rit.*)

> The beacon crowning the lone eminence,
> The female and her garments vexed and tossed
> By the strong wind.

Yet now chance brought him daily to the spot which had once appeared so melancholy ; as he saw it with the loved one at his side the golden gleam of youth, the spirit of pleasure, descended upon it, and the place became dearer still from the recollection of his former fears.[1]

Thus his second vacation, like the first, drew closer the bonds between the present and the past. Not only did it sow within him the first seeds of love ; it developed at the same time those of brotherly affection and of attachment to the region of his birth. To his sister Dorothy he dedicated *An Evening Walk*, which was completed at this time. But these feelings, henceforth vigorous within him and capable of growth, were not yet, happily, so engrossing as to curb his passion for distant travel and his desire to visit other places of which the very names excited his enthusiasm. His last long vacation, we shall find, was spent very far from the lake district, amidst scenes at once more famous and more sublime.

III

In 1790 Wordsworth came to a determination which seemed an unprecedented slight to the curriculum and traditions of the University. Instead of devoting his last recess to preparation for the approaching examinations and scholarships, he resolved to see the Alps. He had not cherished the idea of this tour without some feeling of remorse, and a fear that it would bring upon him the censure of his relations. " But," he tells us,

> Nature then was sovereign in my mind,
> And mighty forms, seizing a youthful fancy,
> Had given a charter to irregular hopes.[2]

---

[1] *The Prelude*, xii. 208-269, and vi. 230-236. Mr Knight, who fails to connect the two passages, places the scene in the neighbourhood of Cockermouth.

[2] *The Prelude*, vi. 333-336.

Even had the period been one of uneventful calm, he would doubtless have formed a similar project, but in 1790 the charms of Alpine scenery were re-inforced by an additional attraction :

> Europe at that time was thrilled with joy,
> France standing on the top of golden hours,
> And human nature seeming born again.[1]

A year had passed since

> To the wide world's astonishment, appeared
> A glorious opening, the unlooked-for dawn,
> That promised everlasting joy to France ! [2]

> The dread Bastille,
> With all the chambers in its horrid towers,
> Fell to the ground :—by violence overthrown
> Of indignation ; and with shouts that drowned
> The crash it made in falling ! From the wreck
> A golden palace rose, or seemed to rise,
> The appointed seat of equitable law
> And mild paternal sway.[3]

When the Bastille fell Wordsworth was on his way to join his sister at Penrith, and, in a distant county, probably felt little interest in an event of which he could not possibly conceive the importance. But on returning to Cambridge he had found the University thrilled by the first act of the French Revolution. From the memoirs of Linguet England had grown accustomed to regard the towers of the Bastille as the very symbol of continental despotism. Hence Cowper's famous apostrophe addressed to them in 1785 :

> There's not an English heart that would not leap
> To hear that ye were fall'n at last.[4]

Among many others, those in authority at Cambridge had expressed their sympathy at the news that the Bastille had fallen. The vice-chancellor had pronounced it " a subject

---

[1] *The Prelude*, vi. 339-341.   [2] *The Excursion*, ii. 210-213.
[3] *Ibid.*, iii. 709-716.   [4] *The Task*, book v. 389-390.

of triumph and congratulation." Wordsworth easily
became a convert to these sentiments, and the pleasure of
his journey was doubled by the fact that it made him
acquainted with a country which had swept away the
barriers to its liberty by so impetuous an onslaught.

He was accompanied by one of his fellow-students, like
himself an inhabitant of a mountainous district. Robert
Jones was a native of Wales, and had acquired in that
country the same passion for nature which the English
lakes had inspired in Wordsworth. An attractive combination of the careless and the serious, the gay and the
gloomy,[1] he knew when to laugh and when to be silent,
and was the very man to be an invaluable travelling companion for his friend. In order to cross a part of Europe
on foot, each was provided with a walking-stick, a few
necessaries done up in a pocket-handkerchief, and about
twenty pounds in his pocket. Thus equipped, and dressed
in a fashion which aroused the smiles of the villagers as
they passed, the two young fellows must have borne as
little resemblance as possible to the ostentatious tourists
of that day.

Landing at Calais on the eve of the Federation, they
noticed in this little town

> How bright a face is worn when joy of one
> Is joy for tens of millions.[2]

> A homeless sound of joy was in the sky :
> From hour to hour the antiquated Earth
> Beat like the heart of Man : songs, garlands, mirth,
> Banners and happy faces far and nigh.[3]

> The senselessness of joy was then sublime ! [4]

Through Ardres, where they spent the 14th of July,
Arras, which they entered at evening

> under windows bright
> With happy faces and with garlands hung,
> And through a rainbow-arch that spanned the street,
> Triumphal pomp for liberty confirmed,[5]

---

[1] *A Character.*   [2] *The Prelude*, vi. 347-349.
[3] Sonnet, *Jones, as from Calais.* . . .
[4] Sonnet, *Festivals have I seen.* . . .   [5] *The Prelude*, x. 493.

through Péronne and Soissons, they made their way south-
wards, finding everywhere the relics of the festival
withering where they had been left. Now following the
public road, now taking to the footpaths in order to
shorten their long journey, they found even in the remotest villages

> benevolence and blessedness
> Spread like a fragrance everywhere, when spring
> Hath left no corner of the land untouched.

Long this spirit of rejoicing kept them company, as they
paced onward league by league beneath the files of elms
which bordered the high roads and lulled the poet's
imaginative melancholy with the rustling of their leaves.

> More than once,
> Unhoused beneath the evening star we saw
> Dances of liberty, and, in late hours
> Of darkness, dances in the open air
> Deftly prolonged, though grey-haired lookers on
> Might waste their breath in chiding.

Walking rapidly they left behind them Château-Thierry
and Sézanne, followed the banks of the Seine almost to
its source, and at Châlon embarked upon the Saône which
glides so gently between "the vine-clad hills and pleasant
slopes of Burgundy." At Lyon the swift Rhone lent them
its "wings," on which they "cut a winding passage with
majestic ease" between its lofty rocks. And at Lyon on
the 31st of July they were joined on board by

> a merry crowd
> Of those emancipated, a blithe host
> Of travellers, chiefly delegates returning
> From the great spousals newly solemnized
> At their chief city, in the sight of Heaven.
> Like bees they swarmed, gaudy and gay as bees;
> Some vapoured in the unruliness of joy,
> And with their swords flourished as if to fight
> The saucy air.

In their society the two strangers,

> Guests welcome almost as the angels were
> To Abraham of old,

landed at Condrieu and partook of the evening meal.

> The supper done,[1]
> With flowing cups elate and happy thoughts
> We rose at signal given, and formed a ring
> And, hand in hand, danced round and round the board ;
> All hearts were open, every tongue was loud
> With amity and glee ; we bore a name
> Honoured in France, the name of Englishmen,
> And hospitably did they give us hail,
> As their forerunners in a glorious course ;
> And round and round the board we danced again.

At daybreak Wordsworth resumed his voyage in company with this enthusiastic band, in whom, although he does not give their names, it is easy to recognise the delegates sent from Marseilles to the Federation.

> The monastery bells
> Made a sweet jingling in our youthful ears ;
> The rapid river flowing without noise,
> And each uprising or receding spire
> Spake with a sense of peace, at intervals
> Touching the heart amid the boisterous crew
> By whom we were encompassed.[2]

At Saint-Vallier the two foreigners disembarked, and taking leave of these friends of a day, continued their journey on foot towards the mountains.

On the 3rd August they reached the convent of the Grande-Charteuse, where fifty years earlier their countryman, Thomas Gray, had given utterance in the presence of the mountains to the first notes of enthusiasm for Alpine scenery which had been sounded in English literature.[3] Expressing his admiration for the genius of St Bruno, who

---

[1] *The Prelude*, vi. 374-406. [2] *Ibid.*, vi. 407-414.
[3] Letter to Richard West, 16th November 1739. We say " the first notes of enthusiasm." Two descriptions had previously been given, one (which at a later time Wordsworth knew and admired) by Thomas Burnet, in his *Sacred Theory of the Earth*, the other, short and precise, by Thomson, in *Liberty*, Part iv. ll. 344-362. See the noteworthy volume, *James Thomson*, by Léon Morel (Paris 1895), pp. 534-6.

had chosen this sublime spot for his retreat, Gray
affirmed that if born in St Bruno's time he might himself
perhaps have been among his disciples. But when
Wordsworth reached it the retreat of St Bruno's followers was no longer inviolate. As he approached the
convent, he saw a riotous troop of men under arms
advancing in the same direction with hostile intentions.
They did not come, as was supposed by the young
Englishman, who did not speak French, to expel

> The blameless inmates, and belike subvert
> That frame of social being which so long
> Had bodied forth the ghostliness of things
> In silence visible and perpetual calm.[1]

As yet it was nothing more than a domiciliary visit,
followed perhaps by confiscation.[2] But it was enough
to break the charm of that infinite peace. Wordsworth
believed that he heard the voice of Nature raised in
protest from her Alpine throne to summon the instruments of desecration to stay their sacrilegious hands.
Though he did homage to the new liberty and to the
" mighty projects of the time," he nevertheless addressed a
silent petition to the revolutionary spirit, imploring it to
spare " these courts of mystery," where man exchanges
" life's treacherous vanities for penitential tears and
trembling hopes." He claims immunity for the monastery
on account of the soul-inspiring grandeur of the spot, for
the sake of its crags and torrents, its " forests unapproachable by death, that shall endure as long as man endures "[3]
to hope and fear.

---

[1] *The Prelude*, vi. 426-429.

[2] " En 1790, on fit trois fois l'inventaire de notre mobilier, et la troisième
fois avec la dernière rigneur. Tout fut noté et l'argenterie d'église fut em-
portée." (*La grande Chartreuse par un Chartreux*, Grenoble, 1881.) The
armed occupation did not take place until May 20th, 1792. Wordsworth
alludes to this occupation in his *Descriptive Sketches*, which were written in
that year. In this poem, composed in the height of his revolutionary
fervour, he expresses himself much more vehemently against the desecrators
than in *The Prelude*, which was written long afterwards. " Blasphemy the
shuddering fane alarms. . . . The cross with hideous laughter Demons
mock . . ." he writes in the *Sketches*.

[3] *The Prelude*, vi. 441-471.

On the following day, when the band of persecutors had left the convent, he wandered through the dim cloisters, which from their foundation till that hour had never echoed to the tread of unhallowed footsteps; and then, quitting the monastery, entered the deep shades of the wood of Vallombre. Raising his eyes, he beheld in the different quarters of the sky, as though placed on the mountain-crests by angelic hands, the crosses which had been spared by a thousand storms only to be threatened at last by the undiscriminating whirlwind of anti-fanaticism.[1]

After leaving the Grande-Chartreuse, Wordsworth and Jones made their way to Savoy, and spent six weeks in exploring the Alps and the Swiss and Italian lakes. The two vigorous lads " several times performed a journey of thirteen leagues over the most mountainous parts of Switzerland without any more weariness than if they had been walking an hour in the groves of Cambridge."[2]

> A march it was of military speed,
> And Earth did change her images and forms
> Before us, fast as clouds are changed in heaven.
> Day after day, up early and down late,
> From hill to vale we dropped, from vale to hill
> Mounted—from province on to province swept,
> Keen hunters in a chase of fourteen weeks,
> Eager as birds of prey, or as a ship
> Upon the stretch when winds are blowing fair.[3]

Their march was in fact so rapid that it did not enable Wordsworth to describe fully, and at the same time with freshness, the scenery of the Alps or the manners of their inhabitants. When, two years later, he sought to extol the wonders of Switzerland, he found his own impressions so disconnected that he was obliged to refer to the descriptions of less hurried observers.

The number and the daring of those who came to do homage to the Alps had increased to a remarkable extent

[1] *The Prelude*, vi. 472-489.
[2] Letter from Wordsworth to Dorothy, 6th September 1790.
[3] *The Prelude*, vi. 491-499.

since Horace Walpole and Thomas Gray crossed from
France to Italy by the pass of Mont Cenis in 1739. " Such
uncouth rocks and such uncomely inhabitants," exclaimed
the former, ". . . I hope I shall never see them again." [1]
Gray himself, who was passionately fond of picturesque
scenery, declared that "Mont Cenis . . . carries the
permission mountains have of being frightful rather too
far ; and its horrors were accompanied with too much
danger to give one time to reflect upon their beauties." [2]
Thirty years later appeared *La Nouvelle Héloïse*, with its
glorification of the province of Vaud and of the Valais,
and the enthusiasm propagated by Rousseau gave rise to the
mania for Alpine exploration. Rousseau himself, as Sainte-
Beuve expressed it, had scarcely got beyond the hills, but
those who succeeded him began to describe the upper
valleys, to explore the unknown glaciers, and to climb the
less accessible peaks. [3] Of these accounts those of Ramond
de Carbonnières, the future "painter of the Pyrenees,"
were at once the most accurate and the most poetical. [4]
Wordsworth was only able to make a hurried acquaintance
with the high Alps, but Ramond had explored them at his
leisure in 1777. " I have travelled," he says, " or rather
wandered, among the mountains, without keeping to any
settled route, my only companion a native of the region
we explored. Like him I was acquainted with the various
dialects spoken in those districts, and both of us were able
to sacrifice comfort to the object of our journey. We sought
hospitality in the most sequestered huts, and have lived as
equals with the shepherds whom we visited." [5] When

[1] Letter from Walpole to West, November 11, 1739 (*Walpole's Works*, iv.
p. 431).
[2] Letter from Gray to West, November 16, 1739.
[3] Saussure reached the summit of Mont Blanc in 1787.
[4] On Ramond, see the article of Sainte-Beuve in the *Causeries du Lundi*, x.
[5] *Lettres de M. William Coxe à M. W. Melmoth sur l'Etat politique, civil et
naturel de la Suisse, traduites de l'anglais et augmentées des observations faites dans le
même pays, par le traducteur*, Paris, 1788, vol. i., préface, p. vii.
The second edition of the translation was the one used by Wordsworth.
The first appeared in 1781. Wordsworth acknowledges in his notes some
of the instances in which he has been indebted to Ramond ; *e.g.* the
impressions felt on the mountain summit (*Descriptive Sketches*, original text,
375-389; and *Ramond*, i. p. 213 and p. 260, and ii. pp. 134-6) and the

writing his *Descriptive Sketches*, Wordsworth had the good fortune to be already familiar with Ramond's account, and became indebted to this poet and naturalist for a certain number of thoughts and feelings which he first expressed in the *Sketches*, and afterwards scattered over the work of his maturity.   It may have been through Ramond that he first became acquainted with Rousseau, the greatest of his predecessors, of whom Ramond was an enthusiastic admirer.

The influence of Rousseau and Ramond over him was so powerful at the time when he wrote his *Sketches*, that he actually put their ideas into his verses even when those ideas were at variance with his own impressions.   He wrote to his sister, during the journey, that his partiality for Switzerland led him to hope that the manners of its inhabitants were amiable, but that his intercourse with them had been practically confined to dealings with innkeepers who had been corrupted by perpetual association with strangers, and that for his part the opinion he had conceived of them was unfavourable, and very different from that which he had formed of the French or Italians.[1] Nevertheless, carried away by the enthusiasm of Rousseau and Ramond [2] for the natives of the Swiss mountains, he extolled them in his poem as the free and proud descendants of primitive man, the child of Nature who

> all superior but his God disdain'd,
> Walk'd none restraining, and by none restrain'd,
> Confess'd no law but what his reason taught,
> Did all he wish'd, and wish'd but what he ought.[3]

In *The Prelude* he was less ambitious, and at the same

tradition in Switzerland of a golden age (*D. S.*, 475-491, and *Ramond*, i. p. 280).

Other instances in which Wordsworth has borrowed from Ramond are as follows:—The Chamois-hunter (*D. S.*, 393-413, and *Ramond*, i. p. 301); the effect of the ranz des vaches on Swiss soldiers in a foreign land (*D. S.*, 622-631, and *Ramond*, ii. p. 55); sympathy for the pilgrims of Einsiedeln (*D. S.*, 654-675, and *Ramond*, i. p. 118).   Ramond had already given expression to this feeling in answer to the attacks of the protestant William Coxe.   Some of Wordsworth's imitations are given in an Appendix.

[1] Letter from Wordsworth to Dorothy, 6th September 1790.

[2] *Lettres de M. William Coxe*, op. cit., vol. ii, pp. 64-5.

[3] *Descriptive Sketches*, 520-535, original text.   *The Poetical Works of William Wordsworth*, edited by Edward Dowden, London, 1893, vol. vii.

time more original. He contented himself with recording
such of his recollections as had left the deepest impression
on his mind. He did not attempt to make hasty moral
generalizations, nor aspire to celebrate scenes chiefly because they were already famous. He simply recalled his
own spontaneous feelings. The moments of his journey
which he preserved from oblivion were those which had
left indelible traces on the development of his imagination,
and had impressed themselves on it with the significance
of symbols.

One such impression was his sense of disillusion when
from the Col de Balme he caught his first glimpse of
Mont Blanc,

> and grieved
> To have a soulless image on the eye
> That had usurped upon a living thought
> That never more could be.[1]

Another was the disappointment he experienced while
crossing the Simplon. When he was hoping to rise still
nearer to the clouds, a peasant informed him that he need
not ascend any higher, for the rest of the way was entirely
downhill; in short, "that he had crossed the Alps."[2]
In the loss of this illusion he saw a proof that

> Our destiny, our being's heart and home,
> Is with infinitude, and only there ;
> With hope it is, hope that can never die,
> Effort, and expectation, and desire,
> And something evermore about to be.[3]

In this manner, collecting and condensing in *The Prelude*
the descriptions of mountain scenery dispersed throughout
the *Sketches*, he fashioned out of these stray touches a
sublime picture of the pass by which he descended from
the Simplon into Italy.

> The brook and road
> Were fellow-travellers in this gloomy strait,
> And with them did we journey several hours
> At a slow pace. The immeasurable height

---

[1] *The Prelude*, vi. 525-528.   [2] *Ibid.*, vi. 562-591.   [3] *Ibid.*, vi. 604-608.

Of woods decaying, never to be decayed,
The stationary blasts of waterfalls,
And in the narrow rent at every turn
Winds thwarting winds, bewildered and forlorn,
The torrents shooting from the clear blue sky,[1]
The rocks that muttered close upon our ears,
Black drizzling crags that spake by the way-side
As if a voice were in them,[2] the sick sight
And giddy prospect of the raving stream,
The unfettered clouds and region of the Heavens,
Tumult and peace, the darkness and the light—
Were all like workings of one mind, the features
Of the same face, blossoms upon one tree ;
Characters of the great Apocalypse,
The types and symbols of Eternity,
Of first, and last, and midst, and without end.

While the descent from the Simplon remained Wordsworth's ideal of awe-inspiring grandeur, the image of the lake of Como dwelt in his mind as the ideal of perfect beauty. "Among the more awful scenes of the Alps," he writes, "I had not a thought of man, or a single created being ; my whole soul was turned to Him who produced the terrible majesty before me." But "at the lake of Como my mind ran through a thousand dreams of happiness, which might be enjoyed upon its banks."[3]

His most amorous lines are in praise of this lake, of the music which rises from its humblest cottages, of its

> chestnut woods, and garden plots
> Of Indian corn tended by dark-eyed maids ;
>
> .   .   .   .   .   .
>
> Its lofty steeps, and pathways roofed with vines,
> Winding from house to house, from town to town,
> Sole link that binds them to each other.[4]

[1] This line is taken word for word from the *Descriptive Sketches* (l. 130), where it is applied to the shores of Lake Como.
[2] An almost literal transcript from the *Descriptive Sketches*, 249-250—

> " Black, drizzling crags, that beaten by the din,
> Vibrate, as if a voice complain'd within."

These lines occur in the description of the valley of Skellenen.
[3] Letter to Dorothy Wordsworth, 6th September 1790.
[4] *The Prelude*, vi. 663-7.

Amidst these scenes he passed like a breeze or a ray of sunlight, without a moment's pause, yet they left their beauty with him and their serene harmony of colour and of form. Passive as they were, they wielded over him an influence as sweet and gracious

> As virtue is, or goodness; sweet as love,
> Or the remembrance of a generous deed,
> Or mildest visitations of pure thought;

as sweet indeed as blessedness.[1]

Not less lively was the recollection of a night which the two travellers spent in the open air, on the shores of the same lake. They were at Gravedona, and had gone to rest, but were awakened from their first sleep by the church clock, which struck the hours in an unusual manner. Deceived thereby, they rose by moonlight, under the impression that day was at hand, and hoping soon to see the sunrise gild the slumbering landscape. But having lost their way among immense woods, they were obliged to seat themselves upon a rock and wait for daylight.

> An open place it was, and overlooked,
> From high, the sullen water far beneath,
> On which a dull red image of the moon
> Lay bedded, changing oftentimes its form
> Like an uneasy snake. From hour to hour
> We sate and sate, wondering as if the night
> Had been ensnared by witchcraft. On the rock
> At last we stretched our weary limbs for sleep,
> But *could not* sleep, tormented by the stings
> Of insects, which with noise like that of noon
> Filled all the woods: the cry of unknown birds:
> The mountains more by blackness visible
> And their own size, than any outward light;
> The breathless wilderness of clouds; the clock
> That told, with unintelligible voice,
> The widely parted hours; the noise of streams,
> And sometimes rustling motions nigh at hand,
> That did not leave us free from personal fear;
> And, lastly, the withdrawing moon, that set
> Before us, while she still was high in heaven;—

[1] *The Prelude*, vi. 675-687.

These were our food ; and such a summer's night
Followed that pair of golden days that shed
On Como's Lake, and all that round it lay,
Their fairest, softest, happiest influence.[1]

The truly precious moments of Wordsworth's journey,
those which contributed to mould his imagination in its
permanent form, were such as these. Except when he
wrote the *Sketches*, he was not, and had no ambition to be,
the poet of the Alps. But when once he had seen them,
however hastily, there remained ever after in his mind a
lofty exaltation with which the lakes and mountains of his
own country alone could never have inspired him. From
this time forward there arose, in the back-ground, as it
were, of his thought, forms of more majestic grandeur
than those of Helvellyn. His imagination dilated that it
might embrace a horizon wider and more fascinating than
those of Hawkshead and of Grasmere.   And, lastly,
although he afterwards protested unceasingly against the
practice of comparing the scenery of one country with that
of another, his travels in Switzerland enabled him to
understand better the peculiar charm of Cumberland.

But the effect of his continental journey was not limited
to its beneficial influence upon his imagination. A new
sentiment awoke within him ; one destined shortly to transform both his life and his poetry. He became enamoured
of France and of the Revolution, two objects which at that
time it was difficult to keep separate either in thought or
in affection.

In a letter which he wrote to his sister during his tour,
he described the charming impression made on his mind by
the courtesy, the vivacity, and the gay good-humour of the
French nation ; the " politeness diffused through the lowest
ranks," he wrote, " had an air so engaging that you could
scarce attribute it to any other cause than real benevolence . . . We had also perpetual occasion to observe
that cheerfulness and sprightliness for which the French
have always been remarkable. But I must remind you that
we crossed at the time when the whole nation was mad

---

[1] *The Prelude*, vi. 691-726.

with joy in consequence of the revolution. It was a most interesting period to be in France; and we had many delightful scenes, where the interest of the picture was owing solely to this cause." [1]

He had found a reflexion as it were of this enthusiasm beyond the borders of France, and had understood that more was involved than a mere national reform. He "left the Swiss exulting in the fate of their near neighbours." [2] And when October came and he had sailed down the Rhine as far as Cologne, he passed through Belgium in order to take ship at Calais, and "crossed the Brabant armies on the fret for battle in the cause of Liberty." [3]

He was not as yet, it is true, himself a passionate adherent of that cause.

> A stripling, scarcely of the household then
> Of social life, I looked upon these things
> As from a distance; heard and saw, and felt,
> Was touched, but with no intimate concern;
>
> .   .   .   .
>
> I wanted not that joy, I did not need
> Such help; the ever-living universe,
> Turn where I might, was opening out its glories,
> And the independent spirit of pure youth
> Called forth, at every season, new delights
> Spread round my steps like sunshine o'er green fields. [4]

But his sympathy with the Revolution, however feeble it may have been in its infancy, existed even then, and was destined before two years had passed to develop into strong affection.

[1] Letter to Dorothy Wordsworth 6th September 1790.
[2] *The Prelude*, vi. 761-2.   [3] *Ibid.*, vi. 764-765.
[4] *Ibid.*, vi. 766-778.

CHAPTER V

Early Poems

I

BEFORE this love takes possession of him, and by its alternations of enthusiasm and despair transforms his mind and feelings, and sows within him the seeds of the poetical revolution which he is destined to effect, it may be well to turn our attention to various poems which were composed before this metamorphosis was accomplished. Though none of these productions is to be reckoned among his master-pieces, they have various claims upon our interest. From them we may learn what were the standards in accordance with which the youthful poet framed his first attempts. From their very faults we can estimate the efforts he must have made to mould himself into the poet he ultimately became. The tone of melancholy which they affect is to all appearances inconsistent with the sincere joyousness of *The Prelude*. In short, they indicate very clearly the limit of his imaginative and intellectual faculties before the decisive crisis, and show distinctly what were the qualifications he had already acquired, and those in which he was still deficient.

With the exception of two sonnets, and about a hundred lines written by direction at Hawkshead, the *Evening Walk* and the *Descriptive Sketches* are the only poems written in Wordsworth's youth of which we possess the original text.[1] The other pieces attributed by him to this period of his life were all subjected to revision before they were published, and modified to such an extent that they are scarcely to be recognised, as may easily be ascertained by a comparison of them with the genuine

---

[1] This text has been reprinted in Dowden's edition (vol. vii.), and is the one which has been used in the present chapter.

examples of his early work.[1]   Both the *Evening Walk*
and the *Sketches*, though not published until the beginning of 1793, belong as regards their spirit and their
subjects, and one of them at least as regards the style
of its composition, to his Cambridge days.   These two
poems are our only source of information as to the
earliest form in which Wordsworth's poetical genius
found expression.

It may be that the taste for what is simple and natural
is the least spontaneous of all, and implies the greatest
amount of reflexion and refinement.   It is certainly as
rare in the child as in the savage, both of whom exhibit
an instinctive preference for that which glitters and
sparkles.   Now no one, in early life, could have less
predilection for the simple verity than young Wordsworth; no one could be more fascinated by the fictitious
and the fantastic in poetry.   He has said that as a schoolboy he was so enthusiastic an admirer of Ovid's *Meta-
morphoses* that he was quite in a passion whenever he
found him placed below Virgil in works of criticism.[2]
The same propensity gave rise to a wilful fancy which
mastered him when he stammered out his earliest lines,
and delighted in distorting his impressions of reality.
His first love was for " pathetic fallacy," since then the
object of Mr Ruskin's scorn.

> From touch of this new power
> Nothing was safe : the elder-tree that grew
> Beside the well-known charnel-house had then
> A dismal look ; the yew-tree had its ghost,
> That took his station there for ornament :
>
> .   .   .   .   .
>
> Then, if a widow, staggering with the blow

[1] We may perhaps except the narrative of *The Female Vagrant,* which
although it was first published among the *Lyrical Ballads* in 1798, was
partly written about the same time as the *Evening Walk,* and contains
many traces of Wordsworth's early style.   On the other hand, the lines
written in anticipation of leaving Hawkshead school (*Dear native regions*),
the sonnet (*Calm is all nature*), and the lines composed near Richmond
(*How richly glows* . . .) are early poems only in respect of their subject
matter.

[2] *Ode to Lycoris,* prefatory note.

Of her distress, was known to have turned her steps
To the cold grave in which her husband slept,
One night, or haply more than one, through pain
Or half-insensate impotence of mind,
The fact was caught at greedily, and there
She must be visitant the whole year through,
Wetting the turf with never-ending tears.[1]

Instead of seeking to acquire a knowledge of truth he delighted in illusion.

A diamond light
(Whene'er the summer sun, declining, smote
A smooth rock wet with constant springs) was seen
Sparkling from out a copse-clad bank that rose
Fronting our cottage.   Oft beside the hearth
Seated, with open door, often and long
Upon this restless lustre have I gazed,
That made my fancy restless as itself.
'Twas now for me a burnished silver shield
Suspended over a knight's tomb, who lay
Inglorious, buried in the dusky wood :
An entrance now into some magic cave
Or palace built by fairies of the rock ;
Nor could I have been bribed to disenchant
The spectacle, by visiting the spot.[2]

Nevertheless, to hold this passion for the fictitious in check, Nature, the subject of his early descriptive poems, was ever before his eyes.   He could not always arbitrarily distort what he saw, nor feel it allowable, "like one in cities bred," to form indiscriminate combinations of things of which he knew nothing.[3]   If wilful fancy "engrafted far-fetched shapes on feelings bred by pure Imagination,"[4] if it led him astray by giving him false conceptions of human passions which as yet he could not fully understand, there was necessarily a limit to its power of misleading him.   The reality of nature obtruded itself so forcibly on its senses that he could not falsify as he pleased.   By dint of comparing nature as it is with its

---

[1] *The Prelude*, viii. 376-392.   [2] *Ibid.*, viii. 406-420.
[3] *Ibid.*, viii, 433.   [4] *Ibid.*, viii. 421-423.

appearance as depicted by the poets, he early became an acute critic of the sincere or conventional type. He quickly detected a false ring in the poems imposed upon the world under the name of Ossian, and is almost the only poet of his generation who shows no sign whatever of having imitated Macpherson. "From what I saw with my own eyes," he says of the latter's work, "I knew that the imagery was spurious. In Nature everything is distinct, yet nothing defined into absolute independent singleness." In Macpherson it is exactly the reverse; "everything (that is not stolen) is in this manner defined, insulated, dislocated, deadened,—yet nothing distinct."[1]

Since the matter of Wordsworth's poems was not a soil in which it could thrive, his love of artifice concentrated itself entirely upon form. It was only by a gradual process, in consequence of a slowly-reasoned conviction and by means of a strenuous effort of will, that he brought himself to write poetry which was sparingly ornamented, or, indeed, intentionally unadorned. And even then the part played by the will was not always sufficiently concealed to give a natural appearance to the simplicity. Such is the result of every violent reaction against a besetting sin. At twenty years of age, or thereabouts, Wordsworth wrote in a style which was perhaps more perverse and distorted than that of any other poet of his generation. With all his sincerity of imagination, and his desire to paint the nature which his ardent eyes have seen, he subjects both style and metre to the strongest torture in making them the vehicle of his actual sensations. And although these deformities may at times be set down to the awkwardness of a novice, they usually proceed from the ideal of poetic diction which young Wordsworth sets before him. Evidently it was not the most fantastic passages with which he was at first least satisfied.

That the state of literature and the prevailing standard of taste are to some extent responsible for the corrupt style of the *Evening Walk* and the *Sketches* admits of no doubt. Wordsworth's fondness for poetry dates from the

[1] *Poetry as a Study*, Prose Works, ii. p. 122.

years during which the art reached its lowest ebb in England. " Twice five years," he tells us,

> Or less I might have seen, when first my mind
> With conscious pleasure opened to the charm
> Of words in tuneful order, found them sweet
> For their own sakes, a passion, and a power ;
> And phrases pleased me chosen for delight,
> For pomp, or love.[1]

His father laid the foundations of this taste when he made him learn by heart long passages from Spenser, Shake-speare, and Milton. But like most schoolboys in every age, he was not at first greatly enamoured of these old masters. It has been well remarked by Coleridge that " the great works of past ages seem to a young man things of another race, in respect to which his faculties must remain passive and submiss, even as to the stars and mountains." [2] It is the productions of his contemporaries that stimulate him, and provoke his imitation.

It was so in Wordsworth's case. But the works of those who, for various reasons, are considered to have been his immediate predecessors in the same path, had not yet appeared when the Hawkshead schoolboy had already formed his early taste. The latest productions must have been slow to reach Hawkshead, and in all probability he left school before becoming acquainted with Crabbe's *Village* and William Blake's *Poetical Sketches* (1783), Cowper's *Task* (1785), and the first collection of poems published by Burns (1787). Not one of these poets was to exercise an appreciable influence upon him for some time to come ; not even Burns, " whose light," Words-worth nevertheless assures us, he " hailed when first it shone," and from whom he learnt in youth

> How verse may build a princely throne
> On humble truth.[3]

It certainly never occurred to him, either in his school days

---

[1] *The Prelude*, v. 553-558.   [2] Coleridge, *Biographia Literaria*, ch. i.
[3] *At the grave of Burns*, 31-36.

or later during his student life, that these poems, written
in dialect, whatever their sincerity and intensity of feeling,
could be regarded as models worthy of imitation. It was
the same with the poems of Burns as with Bishop Percy's
collection of old English ballads. This collection had been
in existence for many years, and was doubtless not unknown to Wordsworth in his boyhood, yet it did not
enter into his head to turn to these ballads in search of the
true style, simple and direct, until he had reached the
threshold of maturity ; up to that time he no more thought
of drawing inspiration from them than from the ditties of
his nurse.

Instead of these innovators, whose works were either
unknown to him or rejected by him as too unpretentious,
he therefore read such of the poets who belonged to the
middle of the eighteenth century as fell into his hands.
His first thrill of poetic delight came to him while reading
some pompous verses[1] by Elizabeth Carter, a writer of
the school of Pope and a friend of Johnson. Artless as it
was, his admiration of her stately and ponderous ode did
not disappear without leaving an effect behind it. The ear
for rhythm in poetry is developed more quickly than a
discerning taste in style, and quite independently of it.

---

[1] It was doubtless through a lapse of memory that Wordsworth referred
these verses to an *Ode to Spring*. Mrs Carter (1718-1806) only wrote three
odes at all corresponding to the description given by Wordsworth. These
are the *Ode to Melancholy* (1739), the *Ode to Wisdom* (1749), and the *Ode to
Miss Hall* (1749). The most popular of these pieces, the *Ode to Wisdom*,
which was quoted by Richardson in his novel of *Clarissa Harlowe*, contains
the two following stanzas, which will give an idea of Mrs Carter's style,
and of the rhythm of which the young poet was so fond :—

> The solitary Bird of Night
> Thro' the pale shades now wings his flight,
>   And quits the time-shook tow'r :
> Where, shelter'd from the blaze of day,
> In philosophic gloom he lay,
>   Beneath his ivy bow'r.
>
> With joy I hear the solemn sound,
> Which midnight echoes waft around,
>   And sighing gales repeat :
> Fav'rite of Pallas ! I attend,
> And faithful to thy summons bend,
>   At Wisdom's awful seat.

Wordsworth always retained a fondness for the rhythm of the six-lined stanza which charmed him in Mrs Carter's poem, and frequently employed it himself.[1] Surely this must have been one of the pieces which Wordsworth, in company with a chosen comrade, would recite in the open air among the hills, when the dawn was gilding their summits with yellow light.

> For the better part
> Of two delightful hours we strolled along
> By the still borders of the misty lake,
> Repeating favourite verses with one voice,
> Or conning more, as happy as the birds
> That round us chaunted.

If the objects of his love and admiration were very often false and extravagantly high-flown, " yet," he said—

> Yet was there surely then no vulgar power
> Working within us,—nothing less, in truth,
> Than that most noble attribute of man,
> Though yet untutored and inordinate,
> That wish for something loftier, more adorned,
> Than is the common aspect, daily garb,
> Of human life.[2]

But the literary training he had undergone at school, by recommending as models those among the poets of that age who paid the most attention to correctness of form, restrained him for some time from giving way to his partiality for an involved and singular style. A proof of this may be found in the verses which he wrote at the age of fifteen in honour of the second centenary of his school.[3] Ideas, composition, and everything else in this poem, belong of course to a recognised type. In accordance with the orthodox fashion, Wordsworth has a vision. The Genius of education rises before his imagination, and inspires him with a panegyric on the founder of the school, and on the Protestant religion which, under the guidance of philosophy, had dispersed the dark shades of monkish

---

[1] In *Ruth, Three years she grew, The Wishing gate*, etc.
[2] *The Prelude*, v., 558-583.   [3] Dowden's edition, vol. v., pp. 173-6.

superstition. To-day some of his solemn phrases raise a
smile. This is what he makes of the simple statement
that the school has been in existence for two centuries :

> And has the Sun his flaming chariot driven
> Two hundred times around the ring of heaven,
> Since Science first, with all her sacred train,
> Beneath yon roof began her heavenly reign? (ll. 1-4)

But, upon the whole, the language is for the most part
simple and the versification easy. As yet the schoolboy has
come into contact only with the purest models of classical
poetry. A few borrowed expressions betray the fact that
he has prepared himself for the work by reading Pope and
Goldsmith.

But if, instead of dealing with a prescribed subject, he
attempts to put his own personal thoughts into words, then
he finds a difficulty in expressing himself. When he
wishes to interpret the sensations he feels in the presence
of nature, he forsakes the poets who deal with moral
duties for those of the descriptive school. But before we
can understand the significance of this change in his ideal,
we must understand what were the two great currents of
English poetry in the eighteenth century, and acquire
some knowledge of their principal characteristics.

II

The more important of these, that from which the
poetry of this epoch derives both its most characteristic
feature and its name, is unquestionably the one which was
either formed or followed by Pope and Addison, Johnson
and Goldsmith. At the very time when Wordsworth
was reciting his earliest verses this movement was being continued in the didactic poems of Cowper (1782), and in the
works of two poets then famous, though now forgotten,
William Hayley, the friend of Cowper and the author of
the *Triumphs of Temper* (1781), and John Langhorne, the
author of *The Country Justice* (1774-1777), who, in point

of style, occupies an intermediate position between Goldsmith and Crabbe. The work of these poets, also, is
chiefly didactic or satirical. It aims principally at the
incisive or sententious expression of moral reflexions,
though occasionally it breaks away towards the descriptive
type. Samuel Johnson, who, about the same time, gave
it a definition in his *Lives of the Poets*, attributes its origin
to Dryden. It was Dryden who had discovered the
rhythm and the diction appropriate to it. The versification almost invariably employed by him and his followers
was founded on the " couplet," or distich of two rhymed
lines of ten syllables each. They used it where French
poets had been accustomed to use alexandrines rhyming
in pairs, but since the couplet, from its shortness and the
regular recurrence of its accent on every alternate syllable,
was more forcible and at the same time more monotonous than the alexandrine, it was admirably suited to the
expression of epigrams and sententious phrases. Every
couplet makes a distinct and harmonious whole, separates
each thought from the rest, and renders all equally prominent and almost entirely independent. By means of it
Pope was able to coin an extraordinary quantity of maxims
which are as symmetrical and as clearly cut as proverbs,
and have, in fact, become proverbial. Its self-completeness,
on the other hand, renders the couplet unsuited to the
breadth of the oratorical style, and to sustained movements
of thought on a more ample scale. It compels the periods
to break themselves up, and isolates each fragment. And
just as the couplet makes it difficult to sustain the breath
throughout a narrative or an argument, so too it refuses to
lend itself to description, and compels the writer to place
everything, both the striking features and subordinate
details of the picture, in the foreground ; while it transforms description, to which the blending of tones is
essential, into an enumeration of distinct and independent
objects. Wordsworth, who made use of the couplet in
his early descriptive poems, presents some signal illustra-
tions of this fault. Principally by reason of this error in
the selection of his instrument he incurs himself the
reproach he had justly made against Macpherson of being

disconnected, as the following lines from *An Evening Walk*
will prove :

> Their pannier'd train a groupe of potters goad,
> Winding from side to side up the steep road ;—
> The peasant from yon cliff of fearful edge
> Shot, down the headlong pathway darts his sledge ;—
> Bright beams the lonely mountain horse illume,
> Feeding 'mid purple heath, " green rings " and broom ;—
> While the sharp slope the slacken'd team confounds,
> Downward the pond'rous timber-wain resounds ;—
> Beside their sheltering cross of wall, the flock
> Feeds on in light, nor thinks of winter's shock ;—
> In foamy breaks the rill, with merry song,
> Dash'd down the rough rock, lightly leaps along ;—
> From lonesome chapel at the mountain's feet,
> Three humble bells their rustic chime repeat ;—
> Sounds from the water-side the hammer'd boat ;
> And blasted quarry thunders heard remote.   (109-125.)

This passage is a series of exact details, but not a
picture.   Accordingly, the couplet has found favour with
scarcely any among the true descriptive poets.   Introduced
by Chaucer, whose skill had imparted to it an ease and
flexibility which were soon lost by his successors,
adopted for a moment, but quickly abandoned, by the
poets of the Renaissance, and restored to credit by
Dryden, the couplet had been invented and brought to
perfection by witty poets, for use in poems wherein wit
was the predominant feature.   Except in works of this
nature, it does not appear to have been very freely adopted,
at any rate without being twisted and transformed to such
an extent as to be hardly recognisable, as for instance in
Keats' *Endymion* and Shelley's *Julian and Maddalo*.   When
sharply opposed antitheses, neat and symmetrical phrases,
and incisive touches ceased to be considered the highest
qualities in poetry, the couplet fell into neglect and even
contempt.   Byron was almost the only one of the great
poets who flourished during the early part of this century
to make use of the couplet in something like the form
given to it by Dryden and Pope ; and it is not rash to
assert that no English poet of his time had more wit than he.

But modern poets are not only indebted to Dryden for the couplet; they have also derived from him the first examples of correctness in style. This, at least, was the opinion announced by Samuel Johnson in 1777: "There was before the time of Dryden no poetical diction, no system of words at once refined from the grossness of domestic use, and free from the harshness of terms appropriated to particular arts. Those happy combinations of words which distinguish poetry from prose had been rarely attempted: we had few elegancies or flowers of speech."[1]

Such was Johnson's statement of the doctrine, afterwards so vigorously opposed by Wordsworth, that between the language of prose and that proper to poetry there is a sharp distinction. But of the two principles upon which he founds the doctrine, that which enjoins upon the poet the avoidance of technical or familiar terms, and that which accords him the right to invent a vocabulary of his own, the former alone was really precious to the critic. He would willingly have argued against the second, if he had perceived the consequences which might be deduced from it. His ideal was, in the main, that of Buffon: a noble style which employs none but general terms. And in practice he was so far from preserving a sharp distinction between the prose and poetic styles, that his own poetry and prose, alike pompous and abstract, very nearly merge into one another, and differ simply by the presence or absence of a regular rhythm. His decided preference for Pope and Dryden is due to their skill in reasoning clearly and correctly in verse. Any departure from custom, in the matter of grammar or vocabulary in poetry, irritates him and incurs his condemnation. In his critical work his prosaic good sense constantly protests against breaches of grammatical rules, the illegitimate use of obsolete or invented words, and elaborate tricks of style, no less than against the absurdities of the traditional language of the pastoral, and the custom of using figures of speech drawn from mythology. He was a severe (some would say a philistine) critic of the pindaric odes of Gray, the pedantry of those who copied Milton, and the

[1] *Life of Dryden.*

false simplicity of the imitators of Spenser. Thus, when Wordsworth indicts the style of eighteenth century poetry he will more than once be found in unconscious agreement with the famous critic of the classical school which he intends to attack.

For the writers who have intentionally corrupted ordinary language we must look elsewhere; namely, in the current of reaction against the poetry and the principles of those to whom we have just alluded. We must turn to the writings of the lyrical and descriptive poets, perhaps for the reason that of all styles the descriptive is that which is least easily satisfied with general terms. We must refer to Thomson, to Collins, to Gray, and to Warton, not to mention a great number of minor landscape-poets, now forgotten, from whom Wordsworth derived his first inspiration. Some of these, such as Lady Winchelsea and George Dyer,[1] were at a later date restored by him to their rightful share of reputation, on the ground of their exact observation of nature's beauties. But, generally speaking, the astounding faults of Wordsworth's early poems are derived from the errors, a hundred times exaggerated, which these writers committed. It is they, far more than Pope or Johnson, who have intentionally erected a barrier between the style of prose and that of poetry, and have endowed the latter with a distinct vocabulary and a special grammar and syntax. But they took as their model, not Dryden, but now Spenser and now Milton. They discarded the couplet for blank verse or for the eight-syllabled rhyming lines of Milton, for the Spenserian stanza, and for metres of their own invention. Wordsworth never perceived, or was never willing to acknowledge, that Spenser, whom he loves, and Milton, whom he calls his great predecessor, are precisely the two English poets whose wilfully arbitrary style constitutes a triumphant argument against the principle of the

---

[1] As regards Dyer, he had been anticipated by the Quaker poet John Scott of Amwell. See *Critical Essays on some of the Poems of several English Poets*, by John Scott; London, 1785. Scott was an inferior critic, and was justly derided by Lamb, but his *Essays*, which Wordsworth read while he was writing the *Evening Walk* (see the note on l. 173) give here and there a foretaste of Wordsworth's opinions. Is not Wordsworth the Quaker of literary criticism?

identity of prose and poetry. It has been justly observed that Spenser and Milton " wrote no language " in existence, in other words that they possessed each a mode of speech peculiar to himself; and it is these two poets, the one with the archaisms of his *Faerie Queene*, the other with the Latin expressions and constructions of his *Paradise Lost*, who, all things considered, are the conscious creators of the distinctive language of poetry. Now Milton and Spenser had created this language for their own use; with them it was original, and was exquisitely adapted to their ideas and to their subjects. Yet a great number of eighteenth century writers either imitated it or employed it just as it was, clothing their thought in this ready-made garb, instead of allowing their style to take its form from their own minds. What was creation by the masters became for the disciples something like a mechanical trick; for them the chief aim of poetry seemed to be the employment of a language which bore no resemblance to any existing form of speech. Wordsworth was not mistaken when he described Gray as " at the head of those who, by their reasonings, have attempted to widen the space of separation betwixt Prose and Metrical composition."[1] It was Gray who said that "the language of the age is never the language of poetry; except among the French, whose verse, where the thought or image does not support it, differs in nothing from prose. Our poetry, on the contrary, has a language peculiar to itself; to which almost every one that has written has added something by enriching it with foreign idioms and derivatives; nay, sometimes words of their own composition or invention."[2]

Gray decided that the poet is justified in using terms a century old, provided their antiquity has not rendered them unintelligible. He also carried these principles into practice, but with a delicate instinct which enabled him to avoid pitfalls and preserved him from excess. He made novel experiments in subtle and unusual combinations of words. Johnson, who felt for Gray's poetry the contempt

[1] *Preface to the Lyrical Ballads*, Prose Works, ii. 85.
[2] Letter to Richard West, 1742 (?). *The Works of Thomas Gray*, edited by Edmund Gosse, 1884, vol. ii. pp. 108-9.

which finical elaboration excites in a solid, matter-of-fact
mind, took a delight in pointing out his tricks of style.
He shows how he takes up and exaggerates a metaphor
already sufficiently daring. Dryden speaks of "honey
redolent of spring," Gray of "gales redolent of joy and
youth." Johnson ridicules the compound words Gray
forms in so arbitrary a fashion, such as "velvet-green,"
"many-twinkling," and takes exception to the cumbrous
splendour he obtains by means of mythological terms.[1]

Now the faults which Johnson discovers only here
and there in Gray, with a vision, moreover, stimulated
by animosity, are committed by Wordsworth in every
line of the poems he wrote in early life. He pushed the
dangerous theories of Gray to an extreme. Nowhere
are the peculiarities of the distinctively poetical style more
complacently displayed than in his early poems.

III

Every characteristic of his language tends to distinguish
it from that of ordinary speech. In the first place we
find archaisms in the form of certain words;[2] verbs now
neuter employed in an archaic sense as active;[3] irregular
suppression of the article;[4] violent suppression of an
auxiliary,[5] or of a verb;[6] employment of obsolete

---

[1] *Life of Thomas Gray.*
[2] *Broke* for *broken; unbroke* for *unbroken; ope* for *open; forgot* for *forgotten;
beat* for *beaten,* etc.
[3] *To gaze* for *gaze on;*

> . . . I gaze
> The ever-varying charms. (*Evening Walk*, 17-18.)

See also *ibid.*, 57 and 130.
To listen for *listen to :*

> List'ning the music (*E. W.*, 436).

Observe also the strained use, in an active sense, of *to course* (*E. W.*, 31),
to roam (*E. W.*, 219), *to rove* (*Descriptive Sketches*, 80).
[4] Th' unwearied glance of *woodman's* echo'd stroke (*E. W.*).
From *lonesome chapel* . . . (*E. W.*, 121).
Or *yell* in the deep woods of *lonely hound* (*E. W.*, 446).
Followed by *drowsy crow* of *midnight cock* (*D. S.*, 228).
[5] They not the trip of harmless milkmaid feel (*E. W.*, 226).
[6] Spur-clad his nervous feet, and firm his tread (*E. W.*, 131).

words,[1] or of words used in an obsolete sense, at times with a somewhat pedantic regard to etymology,[2] or of words exceedingly rare,[3] if not newly coined;[4] abnormal constructions, for instance, the imitation of the Latin ablative absolute, to which Milton was very partial;[5] misuse of the inversion which consists in making the subject follow the verb, by employing it without beginning the sentence by any of the adverbs that justify its use;[6] separation of relative and antecedent for the sake of elegance;[7] nouns in oblique cases placed before those which govern them, a construction which Wordsworth manages with especial awkwardness, and never entirely discards;[8] violent displacement of a direct complement, which is too short for the purpose, to make it precede the verb;[9] inversion of the direct pronominal object, with all the characteristics of one of Milton's Latin constructions;[10] various uncommon elliptical con-

---

[1] *To illume* for *illumine* (*D. S.*, 625 and 633); *wildering* for *bewildering* (*D. S.*, 204); *wildered* for *bewildered* (*E. W.*, 357 and 376).

[2] *Ruining* for *falling down* (*D. S.*, 203):
    And, ruining from the cliffs their deafening load
    Tumbles, the wildering thunder slips abroad.
Haply for *perhaps* (*D. S.*, 410); *hapless* for *unhappy* (*E. W.*, 239); *aspires* for *ascends;*
    In brighter rows her table-wealth aspires (*D. S.*, 732).

[3] *Viewless* for *invisible* (*E. W.*, 148; *D. S.*, 36, 92, 227, 548, 648); *moveless* for *motionless* (*E. W.*, 104, 206; *D. S.*, 266, etc.); *sombrous* for *dark* (*E. W.*, 72).

[4] *Unbreathing* Justice (*D. S.*, 787); *Th' unbreathing* Vale (*E. W.*, 356); *Unpathway'd* for *pathless* (*D. S.*, 285).

[5]   Some, hardly heard their chisel's clinking sound,
    Toil   .   .   .   .   .   (*E. W.*, 145).

[6]   Starts at the simplest sight th' unbidden tear (*E. W.*, 44).
    Blows not a Zephyr but it whispers joy (*D. S.*, 18).
See also *E. W.*, 70, 123, 230, 280, 365, 377, 428; and *D. S.*, 62, 65, 146-7, 217, 229, 287, 506, 555, 701.

[7]   Till, but the lonely *beacon*, all is fled,
    That tips with eve's last gleam his spiry head (*E. W.*, 189).

[8]   Of boys that bathe remote the faint uproar (*E. W.*, 321).
    . . . of tranquil joy a sober scene (*D. S.*, 268, and *ibid.*, 390-1 and 502).

[9]   Th' unwearied sweep of wood thy cliffs that scales (*D. S.*, 122).
    Loose hanging rocks the Day's blessed eye that hide (*D. S.*, 255).
    The ray the cot of morning trav'ling nigh (*E. W.*, 47).

[10]   *Me*, lured by hope her sorrows to remove,
    A heart that could not much itself approve,
    O'er Gallia's wastes of corn dejected led (*D. S.*, 45).

structions,[1] or odd inversions of different kinds;[2] adjectives arbitrarily made to do duty as adverbs;[3] substantives used as adjectives;[4] and compound words either very rare, or of the poet's own invention.[5]

These are not all, but they are the most important, of the liberties and peculiarities in the grammar of the *Evening Walk* and the *Descriptive Sketches*, and in themselves go a considerable way towards the adoption of a special form of language. But his infatuation for figures of speech contributes still further to stamp Wordsworth's early style with artificiality.

It is not a fear of using the simple and appropriate word that leads the young poet to depart from ordinary language. Thus he rarely makes use of periphrasis, and the few instances of it which his work affords are due, not to his timidity, but to his fancy for ornament; for instance, " the thundering tube "[6] for a gun, or " the short thunder "[7] for its report, conceits to which parallels

---

[1] For example, this twofold ellipse of *where* and of the article :
  Where scarce the foxglove peeps and thistle's beard,
  And desert stone-chat, all day long, is heard (*E. W.*, 94-95).
[2] For example :
  Where rocks and groves the power of water shakes
  In cataracts, or sleeps in quiet lakes (*D. S.*, 11-12).
Or, again, this unusual inversion of *where* :
  The vales where Death with Famine scowrs,
for " Where Death with Famine scowrs the vales " (*D. S.*, 794).
[3] . . . The pale-blue rocks *ceaseless* ring (*E. W.*, 149).
  The starting cliff *unfrequent* rends (*D. S.*, 377).
  . . . The landscape fades
  Erroneous wavering 'mid the twilight shades (*D. S.*, 689).
See also *E. W.*, *busy*, 167; *gradual*, 187; *unweary'd*, 214; *wistful*, 255, and *D. S.*, *portentous*, 74; *obtrusive*, 88; *inconstant*, 108; *unfailing*, 720.
[4] *Clarion* throat (*E. W.*, 137); *aegis* orb (*E. W.*, 153); *walnut* slopes and *citron* isles (*D. S.*, 177); *hermit* doors (*D. S.*, 299); *sabbath* region (*D. S.*, 432); *needle* peaks (*D. S.*, 558); *whirlwind* sound (*D. S.*, 581); *deluge* train (*D. S.*, 697); *orange* gales (*D. S.*, 718); *pilgrim* feet (*D. S.*, 720); *comet* blaze (*D. S.*, 775).
[5] Every writer, whether of prose or of poetry, has a right to form new compound words, and it is needless to point out any but those which are somewhat obscure, or demand some investigation if they are to be understood. For example: " *Hollow-parting* oar," *i.e.* forming a hollow in the water, as well as dividing it (*E. W.*, 439); " *Hollow-blustering* coast," *i.e.* sounding hollow beneath the sudden squall. Thomson had applied the same epithet to the wind (*Winter*, l. 987).
[6] *D. S.*, 66.   [7] *D.S.*, 753.

may be found either in Pope or in the French poet Delille.[1] Nearly all Wordsworth's poetical devices are traceable to a single source, in his arbitrary habit of attributing life to things or abstractions, and of investing inanimate objects or creations of the mind with a human form, human will, and human feelings ; a practice due, not, as in Shakespeare, to a spontaneous act of the imagination, but to intentional conformity to a theory of poetry.

This theory was being worked out, and was already achieving great success, in the works of a poet, who, though not indeed the greatest, was certainly the most dazzling, of those who flourished in the latter years of the eighteenth century. Erasmus Darwin enjoyed in England, about the same time and for similar reasons, a celebrity corresponding to that of Delille in France. Though entirely forgotten to-day, he so fascinated the gaze of his contemporaries that Coleridge, who, however, had little admiration for him, called him in 1802 " the first literary character in Europe." [2] With Darwin, poetry is a process of painting. " The poet writes principally to the eye." [3] Allegory and personification are to be commended, because they give visible form to abstract conceptions. The poet's function is decorative; his guiding principle is the adornment of nature. " Nature may be seen in the marketplace, or at the card-table ; but we expect something more than this in the play-house or picture-room. The farther the artist recedes from nature, the greater novelty he is likely to produce ; if he rises above nature he produces

---

[1] The following lines might be suggested as a riddle. They refer to the peasants of the Swiss mountains :—

> Content upon some simple annual feast,
> Remember'd half the year, and hop'd the rest,
> If dairy produce, from his inner hoard,
> Of thrice ten summers consecrate the board. (*D. S.*, 586-589.)

The solution is provided by Ramond (i. pp. 282-284), who describes the manner in which the Swiss make and preserve their cheeses, and states that he has eaten one sixty years old.

[2] *Letters of S. T. Coleridge*, edited by Ernest Coleridge, 1895, i. p. 215.

[3] Darwin has set forth his theory of the poet's art in the form of interludes which follow the cantos of his great poem, *The Botanical Garden*, in the edition of 1799. The second part of this poem, *The Loves of the Plants*, appeared in 1789, before the first part, which, under the title of *The Economy of Vegetation*, was published in 1792.

the sublime; and beauty is probably a selection and new combination of her most agreeable parts." "The Muses are young Ladies; we expect to see them dressed." It is true that Darwin added, "though not like some modern beauties, with so much gauze and feather that the Lady herself is the least part of her." In practice he made no such restriction. It is impossible to conceive nature depicted in more glaring colours than in his *Loves of the Plants*. By an easy metamorphosis all the members of the vegetable world acquire a human existence, and as if the possession of human feelings were not enough, they seem also to have assumed man's form and gestures.

> From giant oaks, that wave their branches dark,
> To the dwarf moss that clings upon their bark,
> What beaux and beauties crowd the gaudy groves,
> And woo and win their vegetable loves.
> How snowdrops cold, and blue-eyed harebells blend
> Their tender tears, as o'er the streams they bend;
> The love-sick violet, and the primrose pale,
> Bow their sweet heads, and whisper to the gale;
> With secret sighs the virgin lily droops,
> And jealous cowslips hang their tawny cups.
> How the young rose, in beauty's damask pride,
> Drinks the warm blushes of his bashful bride;
> With honeyed lips enamoured woodbines meet,
> Clasp with fond arms, and mix their kisses sweet.

Wordsworth had his period of infatuation for Darwin, and this will perhaps cause less surprise if we recollect that so restrained and so delicate a painter of nature as Cowper addressed some lines, expressive of his admiration, to the "sweet harmonist of Flora's court."[1] Wordsworth, at a later period, objected to Darwin as "an eye voluptuary," and was enabled by his "genius and natural robustness of understanding . . . to act foremost in dissipating these 'painted mists' that occasionally rise from the marshes at the foot of Parnassus;"[2] but

---

[1] *Lines addressed to Dr. Darwin* (1792).
[2] Coleridge, *Biographia Literaria*, ch. i. The allusion to Wordsworth is transparent.

at first he was among those who, for some years, extolled *The Botanic Garden* to the skies.   Darwin, in return for this compliment, was one of the first to admire the young man's poems.[1]   Wordsworth had won his approval by sharing his opinion that the material image is the whole secret of poetry.

Accordingly, instances of personification, which in Collins and Gray were already plentiful, swarm in the *Evening Walk* and in the *Descriptive Sketches*.   *Impatience*, " panting upward," climbs mountains;[2] obsequious *Grace* pursues the male swan upon the lake, while *tender Cares* and *domestic Loves* swim in pursuit of the female;[3] *Pain* has a sad family;[4] *Independence* is the child of *Disdain*;[5] *Hope* leans ceaselessly on *Pleasure's* funeral urn;[6] *Consumption*, " with cheeks o'erspread by smiles of baleful glow," passes through the villages of France on a pale horse;[7] " *Oppression* builds her thick-ribb'd tow'rs"; *Machination* flees "panting to the centre of her mines"; *Persecution* decks her bed (of torture) with ghastly smiles; *Ambition* piles up mountains, etc.[8]

For the same reason the transference of epithets is among the favourite practices of the young poet.   Mention is made, at different times, of " th' *unwearied* glance of woodman's echoed stroke";[9] of " the *talking* boat that moves with pensive sound";[10] of " the low warbled breath of *twilight* luce";[11] examples chosen, from among a hundred such, of the exchange of qualities between objects which has at times a happy effect, but is certainly too systematically practised.

He is, in fact, determined to present everything by means of an image.   When he wishes to state that in childhood he was naturally so cheerful that he had no need of the charms of melancholy, he will say :

[1] Christopher Wordsworth, *Social Life at the English Universities in the Eighteenth Century*, note written 5th November 1793.

[2] *E. W.*, 35.   [3] *E. W.*, 200 and 206-7.

[4] *D. S.*, 2 (taken from Pope, *Essay on Man*, ii. 110).

[5] *D. S.*, 323-4.   [6] *D. S.*, 518.

[7] *D. S.*, 788-791.   [8] *D. S.*, 792-804.   [9] *E. W.*, 107.

[10] *E. W.*, 319.   [11] *D. S.*, 749.

> Then did no ebb of chearfulness demand
> Sad tides of joy from Melancholy's hand.[1]

The poet's fancy becomes still more whimsical when he attributes human or animal characteristics, not to abstractions which he can endow with any form he pleases, but to objects or phenomena so familiar to us that our knowledge of their nature protests against such a travesty. The blood which flows from the wounded feet of the chamois-hunter is

> Lapp'd by the panting *tongue* of thirsty skies.[2]

The mountain-shadow creeps towards the crest of the hill "with *tortoise foot*."[3] "Silent stands th' admiring *vale*" (*i.e.* the villagers).[4] Frequently false pathos is mingled with these effects. An old man's lyre is itself not old but *aged*.[5] The Grande Chartreuse, hoary with snow, *weeps* "beneath his chill of mountain gloom."[6] And these constantly-recurring personifications extend even to the grammar. The neuter gender tends to disappear,[7] and the genitive case, commonly used only in reference to living beings, is curiously applied to words of every sort.[8]

Nevertheless it is the young poet's method of embellishment, which he afterwards attributed to the practice of composing Latin verses at school, that it is especially important to point out.[9] "I was," he said,

> . . . a better judge of thoughts than words,
> Misled in estimating words, not only
> By common inexperience of youth,
> But by the trade in classic niceties,

---

[1] *E. W.*, 21-22.

[2] *D. S.*, 397.

[3] *D. S.*, 105.

[4] *E. W.*, 188.

[5]   There, by the door, a hoary-headed sire
    Touch'd with his wither'd hand an aged lyre (*D. S.*, 170-171).

[6] *D. S.*, 54.

[7] *Beacon* (*E. W.*, 189); *steep* (*E. W.*, 156); *mountain* (*E. W.*, 336-9), etc., are masculine.

[8] For example, *the rivulet's feet* (*E. W.*, 76); *affection's ear* (*E. W.*, 51). *the valley's hay* (*D. S.*, 274); *the cheek's unquiet glow* (*D. S.*, 153); *the mountain forest's brow* (*D. S.*, 225).

[9] Coleridge *Biographia Literaria*, ch. i.

> The dangerous craft of culling term and phrase
> From languages that want the living voice
> To carry meaning to the natural heart;
> To tell us what is passion, what is truth,
> What reason, what simplicity and sense.[1]

In the poets with whose works he was acquainted he not only preferred the most far-fetched figures, but laboured at them until by some alteration he had rendered them much more singular still. In so doing, it is true, he merely inflicted upon his immediate predecessors the modifications which those who came before them had undergone at their hands. This proceeding may be constantly detected in Thomson, Collins, and Gray, who add their own touches to the lines of Milton, and in Pope, who performs a similar operation upon those of Dryden. But while Pope chiefly aims at refining the harsher lines, Wordsworth improves upon such as are already curious, at the risk of rendering them extravagant.

Lady Winchelsea said that children's tears are merely "April-drops,"[2] but Wordsworth, speaking of his own childhood, writes,

> When Transport kissed away my April tear.[3]

Thomson invoked inspiration from her "hermit seat" (*Summer*, l. 15), and Collins in a celebrated line said that Simplicity had a "hermit heart,"[4] but Wordsworth, to whom the epithet appears an ingenious one, boldly applies it to the waves of a solitary lake ("hermit waves"),[5] or to the door of a humble Swiss cottage hidden among the mountains ("hermit doors").[6]

Collins, again, who had a weakness for unusual epithets, wrote in his Oriental Eclogues,[7]

> The lily peace outshines the silver store,

and Wordsworth, who seems to covet the image, says that wherever liberty is not, there one may see "the lily of

---

[1] *The Prelude*, vi. 106-114.
[2] But April-drops our tears (*Life's Progress*).
[3] E. W., 29.   [4] *Ode to Simplicity*, 7.   [5] E. W., 219.
[6] D. S., 299.   [7] *Oriental Eclogues*, ii. 33.

domestic joy decay."[1] But elsewhere he goes farther, and seeks a more striking attribute for Peace. Meaning to describe a cabin concealed among trees, he inwardly recalls the ballad of the children lost in the forest, whose frozen forms were buried with leaves by a redbreast ; and, without in any way preparing the reader for the suggestion, writes

> The red-breast Peace had bury'd it in wood.[2]

Whereas Gray spoke of "the cock's shrill clarion,"[3] Wordsworth speaks of his "clarion throat."[4] Gray represented the Nile as brooding "o'er Egypt with his watery wing;"[5] Wordsworth pictures the waves of Liberty as brooding "the nations o'er with Nile-like wings."[6] Gray's famous lines

> *Full many a gem of purest ray serene,*
> The dark, unfathom'd caves of ocean bear ;
> *Full many a flower is born to blush unseen,*
> *And waste its sweetness on the desert air,*

become, with Wordsworth,

> fairy holms . . .
> Whose shades protect the hidden wave serene ;
> Whence fragrance scents the water's desert gale.[7]

Whereas Thomson spoke of God as "On the whirlwind's wing, . . . Riding sublime,"[8] Wordsworth says that

> Oh give, great God, to Freedom's waves to ride
> Sublime o'er Conquest, Avarice, and Pride.[9]

Pope calls the second son of William the Conqueror his "second hope"[10]; Wordsworth describes the eldest son of a poor vagrant as her "elder grief."[11] With Pope the repose of death is "the sabbath of the tomb" ; for Wordsworth the

---

[1] *D. S.*, 723.   [2] *D. S.*, 169.   [3] *Elegy*, 19.   [4] *E. W.*, 137.
[5] The last line of *The Alliance of Education and Government.*
[6] *D. S.*, 805.   [7] *E. W.*, 222-3.   [8] *Hymn*, 18-19.
[9] *D. S.*, 792-3.   [10] *Windsor Forest*, l. 81.
[11] *E. W.*, 263. *Cf.* Shakesp., *Errors*, I. i. 125, "my eldest care."

canton of Unterwalden, with its silent summits, is a "sabbath region." [1]

But the occasions on which Wordsworth has borrowed are so numerous that a special edition would be required to exhaust the list. Suffice it to say that, besides the poets already mentioned,[2] many others of the eighteenth century are laid under contribution by him, whether the fact is acknowledged in his notes, and by quotations marks, or not, such as Young,[3] Home,[4] Smollett,[5] Beattie.

---

[1] *D. S.*, 432.

[2] The following are further instances of imitation from the same poets:—

> O stretch thy reign, fair Peace, from shore to shore
> Till conquest cease, and slavery be no more. . . .
> (Pope's Windsor Forest, ll. 407-8)

The strain is closely reproduced at the end of *D. S.*,

> O give, great God, to Freedom's waves to ride (etc).

Thomson's glowworm, "a moving radiance" (*Summer*, l. 1684) has been copied in "small circles of green radiance" (made by the same insect), *E. W.*

Collins' "Spartan fife" (*Ode to Liberty*, l. 1) is repeated in *E. W.*, l. 331. His "mellow horn" (*Ode to the Passions*, l. 61) is awkwardly copied in *E. W.*, l. 234. "The folding star" (*To Evening*) reappears in *E. W.*, l. 302, etc.

Gray's "golden fire," *i.e.* the Sun (*Sonnet to West*) is used in *D. S.*, l. 33.

> "The simplest note that swells the gale" (*Ode to Vicissitude*, l. 50)

becomes in *D. S.*, l. 20,

> "He tastes the meanest note that swells the gale," etc. . . .

[3] Young's

> So break those glittering shadows, human joys,

becomes in *E. W.*,

> So vanish those fair Shadows, human joys.

It is well known that so late, even, as 1798 Wordsworth derived one of his most famous lines in *Tintern Abbey* from the same poet. Young had said (*Night*, vi.) that the eyes

> ". . . half create the wondrous world they see."

Wordsworth has turned it into

> All the mighty world
> Of eye, and ear—both what they half create,
> And half perceive.   (*Tint. Abbey*, 105-6.)

[4] For Home, see *Descriptive Sketches*, ll. 213-4, and note.

[5]   . . . "prepared
> The blessings he enjoys to guard" (*D. S.*, l. 535),

is transcribed from Smollett's *Ode to Leven Water*.

To these might be added two French names—Delille [1]
and Rosset,[2] the author of *L'Agriculture ou Les Géorgiques
Françaises*, the most awkwardly periphrastic of our descriptive poets. Of course, Wordsworth's imitations are
not strictly limited to eighteenth century bards; some
incrustations from Spenser,[3] Shakespeare,[4] and especially
Milton,[5] are to be discovered in his mosaic-work; he even
makes use of passages from the Bible,[6] which look very

[1] Delille's *Inscription en vers pour Moulin Joli* is praised in a note to *D. S.*,
l. 760. It is interesting to notice that the theme of one of Wordsworth's most
popular poems, *The Reverie of Poor Susan*, seems to have been inspired by
Delille's description of the feelings of the young savage Potaveri when he
saw in the King's garden at Paris an exotic tree brought from his native
isle. At this sight, says Delille,

> . . . Mille objets pleins de charmes,
> Ces beaux champs, ce beau ciel qui le virent heureux,
> Le fleuve qu'il fendait de ses bras vigoureux,
> La forêt dont ses traits perçaient l'hôte sauvage,
> Ces bananiers chargés et de fruits et d'ombrage,
> Et le toit paternel, et les bois d'alentour,
> Ces bois qui répondaient à ses doux chants d'amour,
> Il les croit voir encore, et son âme attendrie
> Du moins pour un instant retrouve sa patrie.
> > *Les Jardins*, Chant 2.

[2] Wordsworth, in his description of the cock (*E. W.*, ll. 224-233),
remembered the following lines in *L'Agriculture*, ch. vi. :—

> Que le Coq, de ses sœurs et l'époux et le Roi
> Toujours marche à leur tête et leur donne la loi . . .
> Une crête de pourpre orne son front royal;
> Son œil noir lance au loin de vives étincelles ; . . .
> De sanglants éperons ornent ses pieds nerveux ·
> Sa queue en se jouant du dos jusqu' à la crête,
> S'avance et se recourbe en ombrageant sa tête. . . .

[3] For Spenser, see *E. W.*, l. 333 and note.
[4] Shakespeare's "toys of desperation" (*Hamlet*, I. iv. 75) become "desperation's toys" (*D. S.*, 467).
[5] *Cf.* the "silver threads" of *Arcades*, l. 17, and "faint silvery threads"
(*E. W.*, 427); "wood-notes wild" of *l'Allegro*, and "wild-wood mountain
lutes" of *D. S.*, 509:— "I hear the far-off curfew sound . . . swinging
slow with sullen roar" of *Il Penseroso*, with

> The solemn curfew swinging long and deep (*E. W.*, 318).
> Swing on th' astounded ear its dull undying roar (*D. S.*, 779).

[6] *Cf.* "Or ever the silver cord be loosed, or the golden bowl be broken, or
the pitcher be broken at the fountain, or the wheel broken at the cistern"
(*Eccles.*, xii. 6). with,

> For hope's deserted well why wistful look?
> Choked is the pathway, and the pitcher broke (*E. W.*, 256).

and

strange in the form of his elaborate couplet. To contemporary poets he seems to owe very little; only a Scotch word to Burns, whom he names,[1] a touch to Langhorne,[2] more perhaps to Cowper's *Task*,[3] and most to Samuel Rogers' *Pleasures of Memory*,[4] of which he makes no mention.

> And thou! fair favoured region! which my soul
> Shall love, till Life has broke her golden bowl,
> Till Death's cold touch her cistern-wheel assail. . . . (*D. S.*, 741-2).

[1] Note to *E. W.*, l. 317.
[2] The description of the female beggar's husband in *E. W.*, 254,
> Asleep on Minden's charnel plain afar,

is a reminiscence of the well-known lines of Langhorne, which a very few years before had drawn tears from the eyes of Burns, who was told by Walter Scott, then a stripling, where the lines were to be found:

> Cold on Canadian hills or Minden plain,
> Perhaps that parent mourned her soldier slain (etc.).
> > *The Country Justice.*

[3] *Cf.* Cowper's *Task*, vi. 11,
> . . . It [the sound of village bells] opens all the cells
> Where Memory slept;

and *D. S.*, 626-7,
> Soft o'er the waters mournful measures swell,
> Unlocking bleeding Thought's " memorial cell."

Also *The Task*, v. 446-8,
> Tis liberty alone that gives the flower
> Of fleeting life its lustre and perfume.
> And we are weeds without it;

and *D. S.*, 724-5,
> While Freedom's farthest hamlets blessing share
> Found still beneath her smile, and only there.

[4] "Sober reason" (with quotation marks), *D. S.*, 56, may come from *The Pleasures of Memory*, part ii. (towards the end).
Cf. also Rogers, *P. of M.*, pt. i. l. 103,
> Up springs, at every step, to claim a tear,
> Some little friendship found and cherished here;

and *E. W.*, 43,
> While, Memory at my side, I wander here,
> Starts at the simplest sight th' unbidden tear.

Cf. also Rogers, *P. of M.* pt. ii. 165-6,
> Long have ye known Reflection's genial ray
> Gild the calm close of Valour's various day . . .
> Full on her [*i. e.* Memory's] tablet flings its living rays;

and *E. W.*, 39-40,

In order to give some idea of the style which results from the employment of these various devices, it will now be necessary to quote a few extracts. Taking leave of the young Italian girls whom he has seen on the shores of the lake of Como, Wordsworth describes them as follows :—

> Farewel ! those forms that, in thy noon-tide shade,
> Rest, near their little plots of wheaten glade ;
> Those steadfast eyes, that beating breasts inspire
> To throw the " sultry ray " of young Desire ;
> Those lips, whose tides of fragrance come, and go,
> Accordant to the cheek's unquiet glow ;
> Those shadowy breasts in love's soft light array'd,
> And rising, by the moon of passion sway'd.[1]

Detestable as are the last lines, they are even less offensive than those in which the poet leaves his characters, who are usually chosen from rustic life, to speak for themselves, and makes them use the same figures of speech. A beggar-woman, overtaken with her children, by a tempest on a lonely road, cries :

> Now ruthless Tempest launch thy deadliest dart !
> Fall fires—but let us perish heart to heart.[2]

The poet who would one day suggest that poetry should adopt the ordinary speech of peasants as its exclusive language, first put the following discourse into the mouth of a Swiss mountaineer, an old man

> whose venerable head
> Bloom'd with the snow-drops of Man's narrow bed [3]
> > (*i.e,* the tomb).

> With Hope Reflexion blends her social rays,
> To gild the total tablet of his days.

Again, *cf.* Rogers,

> What soften'd views thy [*i. e.* Memory's] magic glass reveals
> When o'er the landscape Time's meek twilight steals ;

and *E. W.*, 381-3,

> But o'er the sooth'd accordant heart we feel
> A sympathetic twilight slowly steal,
> And ever, as we fondly muse, we find
> The soft gloom deep'ning on the tranquil mind.

[1] *D. S.*, 148-156.   [2] *E. W.*, 291-2.   [3] *D. S.*, 594-5.

This is how he sets forth the miseries of life among the Alps, and the bitter penury which compels aged parents to send their children far from home to win their bread.

> Here Penury oft from misery's mount will guide
> Ev'n to the summer door his icy tide,
> And here the avalanche of Death destroy
> The little cottage of domestic Joy.
> But, ah! th' unwilling mind may more than trace
> The general sorrows of the human race :
> The churlish gales, that unremitting blow
> Cold from necessity's continual snow,
> To us the gentle groups of bliss deny
> That on the noon-day bank of leisure lie.
> Yet more ; the tyrant Genius, still at strife
> With all the tender Charities of life,
> When close and closer they begin to strain,
> No fond hand left to staunch th' unclosing vein,
> Tearing their bleeding ties leaves Age to groan
> On his wet bed, abandon'd and alone.
> For ever, fast as they of strength become
> To pay the filial debt, for food to roam,
> The father forc'd by Powers that only deign
> That solitary Man disturb their reign,
> From his bare nest amid the storms of heaven
> Drives, eagle-like, his sons as he was driven,
> His last dread pleasure ! watches to the plain—
> And never, eagle-like, beholds again.[1]

If we have insisted upon the faults of these early poems, it is by no means for the sake of earning a cheap pleasure by criticising youthful productions, but from a conviction that in them must be sought the explanation of the reform which Wordsworth endeavoured at a later period to accomplish. The excess of the faults teaches us to expect excess even in the reformation. Now that this investigation is concluded, a word will give the key to the future of Wordsworth's art. Disgusted with his youthful eccentricities, he will exclude at one stroke all poetic diction, and will refuse to preserve any mark but that of rhythm, whereby to distinguish poetry from prose. Little given, moreover, to self-criticism, he will throw the whole

[1] *D. S.*, 597-621.

responsibility for his errors upon his predecessors. It was therefore important to show that the faults he attacks, though to some extent they were those of the age, were especially his own. That which would invalidate this assertion still remains to be discovered. In other words, we have yet to meet with a poem of any value (leaving out of account the absurdities of the school known as *Della Cruscan*), in which may be found so large a proportion of fantastic conceits as are collected and crowded together in the twelve hundred lines published by Wordsworth in 1793.

IV

Nevertheless, in spite of their unwholesome style, these poems are, in their way, works of genius. The layer of affectation which encumbers them is broken in numberless places by pieces of exquisite imagery. At a period when the descriptive writers seemed to have exhausted the whole flora, the young poet made his appearance loaded with a profusion of freshly gathered blossoms. " More descriptive poetry ! " cried *The Monthly Review*, in an article on one of his early works ; " have we not yet enough ? Must eternal changes be rung on uplands and lowlands, and nodding forests, and brooding clouds, and cells, and dells, and dingles ? Yes ; more, and yet more ; so it is decreed." [1] The lake district alone had given rise to much picturesque writing before the appearance of the *Evening Walk*. So early as 1753 John Brown had described the beauties of the valley of Keswick in an enthusiastic letter, and since then he had extolled them in a fragment of verse with which Wordsworth was familiar.[2] Thomas Gray, in his diary of a tour in the lake district, had recorded, somewhat dryly, but with wonderful exactness, his observations of its most important scenes.[1] William Gilpin's description had appeared in 1789,[2] and Walker's in 1792,[3]

---

[1] *The Monthly Review*, article on the *Descriptive Sketches*, vol. xii. p. 216.

[2] He quotes it with commendation in his *Guide to the Lakes* (Prose Works, ii. 255). He imitates the line referring to the sound of the streams, "unheard till now and now scarce heard," in the *Evening Walk*: "The song of mountain streams unheard by day, now hardly heard " (*E. W.*, 433-4).

shortly before Wordsworth's poem. Accordingly the *Critical Review*, expressing its appreciation of the *Evening Walk*, said : "Our northern lakes have of late years attracted the attention of the public in a variety of ways. They have been visited by the idle, described by the curious, and delineated by the artist." Nevertheless, the author of the article rightly congratulated Wordsworth on having managed to acquire in that region "new and picturesque imagery," and "many touches . . . which would not disgrace our best descriptive poets."[4] We may say more. The *Evening Walk* is a compact collection of images mostly derived from personal observation. Never perhaps had any English poet paid such close and loving attention to the most insignificant sights and sounds of the country; not even Milton in his *L'Allegro* and *Il Penseroso*, which, if they had more of subtle human interest, were less accurate ; not Thomson, more vague if more majestic ; nor even Cowper, who, although his touch was more distinct, was too much given to moralising. Wordsworth always claimed for this poem the quality of sincere observation. "There is not an image in it," he wrote afterwards, "which I have not observed ; and now, in my seventy-third year, I recollect the time and place where most of them were noticed." And quoting the two lines,

> And, fronting the bright west, yon oak entwines
> Its darkening boughs and leaves, in stronger lines,[5]

he adds the characteristic remark : "This is feebly and imperfectly expressed, but I recollect distinctly the very

---

[1] *Journal in the Lakes* (1769). *Works of Thomas Gray*, edited by E. Gosse, vol. i. Wordsworth borrowed a few features from Gray ; *e.g.* Gray describes the meadows of Grasmere as "green as an emerald" (p. 265). *Cf. E. W.*, 10: "emerald meads."—"The solemne colouring of night" (Gray, p. 258) is reproduced in *E. W.*, 330.—"The thumping of huge hammers at an iron forge not far distant" (Gray, p. 270) is imitated in *E. W.*, 445: "The distant forge's swinging thump profound."

[2] *Tour in the mountains and lakes of Cumberland and Westmoreland*, by the Rev. William Gilpin, 178-179. Gilpin, a fellow-countryman of Wordsworth, was born near Carlisle.

[3] *Remarks made in a tour from London to the lakes of Westmoreland and Cumberland in the Summer of* 1791, by A. Walker, lecturer, 1792. These remarks had previously appeared in the *Whitehall Evening Post*.

[4] *The Critical Review*, vol. viii. p. 347.   [5] *E. W.*, 193-4.

spot where this first struck me. It was in the way between Hawkshead and Ambleside, and gave me extreme
pleasure. The moment was important in my poetical
history; for I date from it my consciousness of the infinite variety of natural appearances which had been
unnoticed by the poets of any age or country, so far as I
was acquainted with them; and I made a resolution to
supply, in some degree, the deficiency. I could not have
been at that time above fourteen years of age." [1] It is no
exaggeration to say that in his first poem, which was
drafted at school and completed at college, this pledge
was already redeemed. Its subject is the gradual transformation of a landscape seen successively in broad daylight, at sunset, by twilight, and at night. The description of the dead of night, which brings the *Evening Walk*
to a close, is marvellous in its terseness and accuracy.

> But now the clear-bright Moon her zenith gains,
> And rimy without speck extend the plains;
> The deepest dell the mountain's breast displays,
> Scare hides a shadow from her searching rays;
> From the dark-blue "faint silvery threads" divide
> The hills, while gleams below the azure tide;
> The scene is waken'd, yet its peace unbroke,
> By silver'd wreaths of quiet charcoal smoke,
> That, o'er the ruins of the fallen wood,
> Steal down the hills, and spread along the flood.
> The song of mountain streams unheard by day,
> Now hardly heard, beguiles my homeward way.
> All air is, as the sleeping water, still,
> List'ning th' aëreal music of the hill,
> Broke only by the slow clock tolling deep,
> Or shout that wakes the ferry-man from sleep,
> Soon follow'd by his hollow-parting oar,
> And echo'd hoof approaching the far shore;
> Sound of clos'd gate, across the water borne,
> Hurrying the feeding hare thro' rustling corn;
> The tremulous sob of the complaining owl;
> And at long intervals the mill-dog's howl;
> The distant forge's swinging thump profound;
> Or yell in the deep woods of lonely hound. [2]

[1] *E. W.*, prefatory note.   [2] *E. W.*, 423-446.

In the *Descriptive Sketches*, taken as a whole, though they are more ambitious and more powerful than the *Evening Walk*, there is more to displease. They carry obscurity, mannerism, and a hard and strained style, to extravagance. Hence, in part, the hostile reception accorded to this poem.[1] The *Critical Review*, which had been favourably disposed to the *Evening Walk*, united with the *Monthly Review* in disparaging the *Sketches*. It quite admitted the novelty of the subject. " The wild, romantic scenes of Switzerland," it says, " have not yet been celebrated by an English poet "[2] In fact, as we have shown, Wordsworth had on this occasion drawn his inspiration chiefly from a prose-writer, and a Frenchman. The only one of his fellow-countrymen to touch upon the subject in verse had been Goldsmith, who supposes himself seated on an imaginary mountain in Helvetia, and thence indulges in some mild moral reflexions concerning the various European countries which he pictures as stretched beneath him.[3] But Goldsmith pities the Swiss people, and is astonished to find them so attached to their country *in spite of* its rocks and snows ; he therefore left the subject perfectly fresh for the Alpine enthusiast, though, according to the *Critical Review*, Wordsworth failed to turn his opportunity to account. He had "caught few sparks from these glowing scenes."

One tribute of admiration, if he had known of it, would have consoled him for these attacks. A young student, who entered Cambridge when Wordsworth left it, detected in his poem a proof of the " emergence of an original poetic genius above the literary horizon." [4] It was the imaginative power of the poem, warring with its rebellious style, which attracted the admiration of Coleridge, who, at a later period, gave an accurate indication of its faults. He pointed out that in addition to an obscurity arising from imperfect control over the language, it was not free from those " phrases at once

---

[1] The other reason consists in the revolutionary hymn with which it ends. It appeared at the very moment when war was declared between France and England.

[2] *The Critical Review*, vol. viii. p. 472.   [3] *The Traveller* (1764).

[4] Coleridge, *Biographia Literaria*, ch. iv.

hackneyed and fantastic, which hold so distinguished a
place in the technique of ordinary poetry." "The language
was not only peculiar and strong, but at times knotty
and contorted, as by its own impatient strength." But
the deformity of the plant did not prevent him from
admiring its latent vigour. "In the form, style, and
manner of the whole poem, and in the structure of the
particular lines and periods, there is a harshness and
acerbity connected and combined with words and images
all aglow, which might recall those products of the
vegetable world, where gorgeous blossoms rise out of
the hard and thorny rind and shell within which the rich
fruit was elaborating." And the same critic has selected
from the *Sketches* an admirable passage in which he fancied
that he saw "an emblem of the poem itself and of the
author's genius as it was then displayed." It describes a
storm seen at sunset on the shores of the lake of Uri.

> 'Tis storm ; and hid in mist from hour to hour
> All day the floods a deeper murmur pour,
> And mournful sounds, as of a Spirit lost,
> Pipe wild along the hollow-blustering coast,
> 'Till the Sun walking on his western field
> Shakes from behind the clouds his flashing shield.
> Triumphant on the bosom of the storm,
> Glances the fire-clad eagle's wheeling form ;
> Eastward, in long perspective glittering, shine
> The wood-crown'd cliffs that o'er the lake recline ;
> Wide o'er the Alps a hundred streams unfold,
> At once to pillars turn'd that flame with gold ;
> Behind his sail the peasant strives to shun
> The west that burns like one dilated sun,
> Where in a mighty crucible expire
> The mountains, glowing hot, like coals of fire.[1]

The existence of the genius for description is indeed
amply proved by a score of lines like these. Against such
evidence, faults avail nothing. The splendour of Thomson,
without any of the somewhat hollow inflation which mars
his finest passages, was at last attained. There was,
however, even more of significant promise in the note

[1] *D. S.*, 332-347.

which Wordsworth appended to these lines. Therein, not only does his admiration of Nature burst forth unimpeded by the trammels of stiff poetic forms, but, what is more, a sane and grand poetic theory first finds its expression.

" I had once given to these sketches the title of Picturesque; but the Alps are insulted in applying to them that term. Whoever, in attempting to describe their sublime features, should confine himself to the cold rules of painting would give his reader but a very imperfect idea of those emotions which they have the irresistible power of communicating to the most impassive imaginations. The fact is, that controuling influence, which distinguishes the Alps from all other scenery, is derived from images which disdain the pencil. Had I wished to make a picture of this scene I had thrown much less light into it. But I consulted nature and my feelings. The ideas excited by the stormy sunset I am here describing owed their sublimity to that deluge of light, or rather of fire, in which nature had wrapped the immense forms around me ; any intrusion of shade, by destroying the unity of the impression, had necessarily diminished its grandeur."

But no extract can convey an idea of that which constitutes the real merit of these two early poems. They are wonderful anthologies, containing not only the most accurate touches of description observed by the student in the poetry of the past—a selection which he always submitted to the verification of his own senses—but also the countless images which his study of nature had suggested to him. To this collection of impressions he constantly resorted in manhood, without ever exhausting it.[1] Often he was content merely to illuminate them by the use of a simpler style, carrying along on the current of his thought what had originally been but a casual and isolated observa-

---

[1] Nor is Wordsworth the only poet who has made use of it. Tennyson also appears to have studied it to advantage. His beautiful line, descriptive of deer in *The Brook*,

> . . . . . In copse and fern
> Twinkled the innumerable ear and tail,

is a clever imitation of the *Evening Walk*, ll. 63-64.

> In the brown park, in flocks, the troubled deer,
> Shook the still-twinkling tail and glancing ear.

tion, heightening the effect of each by the subtle discovery of the human feeling enwrought with it, and, last but not least, indicating the deeply-rooted ties which must bind it to the hearts of all to whom true happiness is dear.

V

It would appear that so faithful an observer, who was already, moreover, capable of such masterly strokes, had merely to get rid of the dross which encumbered his style. But it was not his language alone that was tainted with affectation. Everything he wrote, which was not descriptive of nature, was either shallow or artificial. The triteness of his moral reflexions, and a certain forced or false note in the expression of his own feelings, stamped his poems as immature productions.

He followed the fashion, and sensibility was at that time in vogue. Virtuous tears had flowed without intermission since the days of Rousseau and Sterne. Mr Henry Morley finds fifty instances of an outburst of tears in Mackenzie's short novel, *The Man of Feeling* (1771), and he does not include the sobs. Weeping was then the infallible sign of virtue, and the favourite source of voluptuous feeling. And since poets love to distil their tears into that exquisite urn, the sonnet, this type of poem reappeared and multiplied during the latter half of the eighteenth century. It was restored to honour by Thomas Warton, and after him Charlotte Smith poured forth her woes in some *Elegiac Sonnets* which appeared in 1784, and, thanks to an unprecedented success, ran through eleven editions. Wordsworth's first poem of personal interest therefore took the form of a " Sonnet on seeing Miss Helen Maria Williams weep at a tale of Distress." [1]

> She wept.—Life's purple tide began to flow
> In languid streams through every thrilling vein ;
> Dim were my swimming eyes—my pulse beat slow,

[1] This sonnet was published in *The European Magazine* in 1787, when Miss Williams (1762-1827), who afterwards became an ardent supporter of the Revolution and the translator of *Paul et Virginie* (1796), had already earned a reputation as a poetess.

And my full heart was swell'd to dear delicious pain.[1]
Life left my loaded heart, and closing eye ;
A sigh recall'd the wanderer to my breast ;
Dear was the pause of life, and dear the sigh
That call'd the wanderer home, and home to rest.
That tear proclaims—in thee each virtue dwells,
And bright will shine in misery's midnight hour ;
As the soft star of dewy evening tells
What radiant fires were drown'd by day's malignant pow'r,
That only wait the darkness of the night
To cheer the wand'ring wretch with hospitable light.

But the sentiment which at that time held despotic sway over poetry was Melancholy, an alloy, in unknown proportions, of real sadness with that of literary convention. The imitators of Milton derived it from a common source in his *Penseroso*, with its preference for sweet thoughtfulness over effusive gaiety. Thomas Warton, in his *Pleasures of Melancholy*, written in 1747, and his brother Joseph, in various odes published in 1746, indulged in the pursuit of Milton's fascinating theme. Possibly Joseph Warton, who was a master at Winchester, implanted the germs of melancholy in the mind of his pupil William Bowles, whose *Fourteen Sonnets* appeared in 1789. These plaintive effusions exercised an influence upon Southey and Lovell, Lamb and Lloyd, at the outset of their careers, and were to Coleridge a revelation of true poetry ; that, namely, in which the poet describes his own feelings and, especially, his own griefs, since poetry of this character gave Coleridge " pleasure when perhaps nothing else could." [2]

Wordsworth, too, was acquainted with Bowles, and early became an admirer of his work. Having bought the precious volume while walking in London with his brother, the sailor, he read it as he went along, and, to his companion's great annoyance, lingered in a niche on London Bridge until he had finished it.[3] But Bowles did

[1] *Cf.* Thomson's *Sophonisba*, nuptial song, " dear delicious dart."
[2] Preface to *Poems on various subjects*, by S. T. Coleridge. London, 1796.
[3] This must have been in the autumn of 1791, before Wordsworth's departure for France. His brother John, who had been absent from England since 1789, had then just returned.

not exercise over him the same exclusive influence as over
Coleridge. Wordsworth contracted the cherished complaint principally from others ; from Collins and Gray,
but most of all from Beattie's *Minstrel*. With Collins it
was indefinite and unobtrusive, being half concealed in
the *Ode to Evening*, and plainly revealed only in a sweet
stanza of the *Ode to the Passions*.

> With eyes upraised, as one inspired,
> Pale Melancholy sat retired ;
> And, from her wild sequestered seat,
> In notes by distance made more sweet,
> Poured through the mellow horn her pensive soul.[1]

The first who had shown a disposition to regard the
poet as the necessary victim of melancholy had been Gray,
who was naturally a prey to dejection, and wrote all his
sincerest poems under the inspiration of sadness. The
poet of his *Elegy*, in other words himself, includes in his
carven epitaph the line " and Melancholy mark'd him for
her own."[2]

Nevertheless it was left for Beattie to proclaim frankly
the identity of poetry and melancholy, and to lay a ban
upon those unacquainted with so divine and delicious a
sentiment.

> Ah, what is mirth but turbulence unholy,
> When with the charm compared of heavenly melancholy ! . . .
> . . . Is there a heart that music cannot melt ?
> Alas ! how is that rugged heart forlorn ;
> Is there, who ne'er those mystic transports felt
> Of solitude and melancholy born ?
> He needs not woo the Muse ; he is her scorn.[3]

Wordsworth, who, at a later time, asserted, in opposition to Beattie, that poetry is identical with joy, bore

---

[1] Collins, *Ode to the Passions*, 58-61. "The mellow horn" is borrowed
from him by Wordsworth, somewhat awkwardly, in *E. W.*, 234.

[2] *Elegy*, 120.

[3] *The Minstrel*, i. st. lv. and lvi. It was Beattie's melancholy which led
Châteaubriand to devote a laudatory article to him in June 1801. *Essai
sur la littérature anglaise.*

much resemblance, as a lad, to Edwin in the *Minstrel*.
In this light he appeared to his sister,[1] and thus no doubt
he loved to regard himself. Melancholy casts its shadow
over his early compositions ; it emanates from him and
diffuses itself over nature, in which he delights to find its
chastened reflexion. Profoundly happy as he was in
youth, so that in manhood the mere recollection of those
blissful years would raise a blush for his momentary
bondage to dejection, he nevertheless expresses, in the
midst of his delight, no sentiments but those of grief or
pain.

The note of melancholy makes itself heard immediately
we meet with one of the genuine poems of his youth. It
is clearly audible in the following sonnet, which was
inspired by the recollection of a vacation passed in his
sister's society.

> Sweet was the walk along the narrow lane
> At noon, the bank and hedgerows all the way
> Shagged with wild pale green tufts of fragrant Hay,
> Caught by the hawthorns from the loaded Wain
> Which Age, with many a slow stoop, strove to gain :
> And Childhood, seeming still more busy, took
> His little rake with cunning sidelong look,
> Sauntering to pluck the strawberries wild unseen.
> *Now* too, on Melancholy's idle dreams
> Musing, the lone spot with my soul agrees
> Quiet and dark ; for through the thick-wove trees
> Scarce peeps the curious Star till solemn gleams
> The clouded Moon, and calls me forth to stray
> Through tall green silent woods and ruins grey.[2]

In the *Evening Walk* his sadness becomes more pro-

---

[1] Letter written by Dorothy Wordsworth, June 1793. Knight, *Life of
Wordsworth*, i. p. 82. Beattie is clearly imitated in *The Evening Walk*
Wordsworth praises the melodies of evening, just as Beattie celebrated
those of morning. He takes two descriptive touches from stanza xxxix
of Beattie's poem (first part):

Thro' rustling corn the hare astonish'd springs. . . .
Down the rough road the pond'rous waggon rings. . . .

These lines are transferred almost unchanged to the *Evening Walk* (442 and
116).

[2] Sonnet inserted in a letter from Dorothy Wordsworth, 6th May 1792.
There were others written at this time, which have not been preserved.

nounced. Though only in his twentieth year, the poet looks back with wistful regret to his happy childhood, to the days when melancholy's sombre charms were not needed to take the place of lost gaiety. "Hope, itself," he says, "was all I knew of pain."[1] Thus, when he finds himself once more among the scenes where he lately sported in unconscious innocence, the "unbidden tear" "starts at the simplest sight."[2] But he has no wish to dwell upon these vain griefs. He desires to prove by his descriptions of nature that some joys remain to him still.[3]

Nevertheless, it is in the *Descriptive Sketches* that his melancholy reaches its most acute stage. Indeed, it is despair, rather than melancholy, to which he gives expression. At times he reminds us of Bowles, roaming about the continent in vain search for a remedy for his heart-ache ; at other times of the poet of whom Shelley was to write in his *Alastor*, that

> . . . virgins, as unknown he past, have sighed
> And wasted for fond love of his wild eyes.[4]

In the hamlets through which Wordsworth passes,

> While unsuspended wheels the village dance,
> The maidens eye him with inquiring glance,
> Much wondering what sad stroke of crazing Care
> Or desperate Love could lead a wanderer there.[5]

And, in truth, it was in order to escape from the pangs of love that his "heart, that could not much itself approve," had led him to wander through France and Switzerland.[6]

> —Alas ! in every clime a flying ray
> Is all we have to cheer our wintry way,
> Condemn'd, in mists and tempests ever rife,
> To pant slow up the endless Alp of life.[7]

Sometimes he vainly tries to throw off his burden of sorrow :

> Gay lark of hope thy silent song resume !
> Fair smiling lights the purpled hills illume !

[1] *E. W.*, 32.   [2] *E. W.*, 44.   [3] *E. W.*, 49-50.
[4] *Alastor*, 62-63.   [5] *D. S.*, 41-44.
[6] *D.S.*, 45-47, and see also 192-198.   [7] *D. S.*, 590-3.

Soft gales and dews of life's delicious morn,
And thou! lost fragrance of the heart return!
Soon flies the little joy to man allow'd,
And tears before him travel like a cloud.
For come Diseases on, and Penury's rage,
Labour, and Pain, and Grief, and joyless Age,
And Conscience dogging close his bleeding way
Cries out, and leads her Spectres to their prey,
'Till Hope-deserted, long in vain his breath
Implores the dreadful untried sleep of Death.[1]

Beset by these gloomy thoughts, he envies the pilgrims of Einsiedeln, whose abounding faith brings them to seek, at the foot of the cross, healing for the ailments of body or of soul :

Without one hope her written griefs to blot,
Save in the land where all things are forgot,
My heart, alive to transports long unknown,
Half wishes your delusion were its own.[2]

And with a sigh the poem closes :

To-night, my friend, within this humble cot
Be the dead load of mortal ills forgot,
Renewing, when the rosy summits glow
At morn, our various journey, sad and slow.[3]

Is it *The Prelude* that errs in representing the Swiss tour as a triumphal march, or the *Sketches* which, instead of describing the young man as he was, present us with the picture of an imaginary hero of the melancholy type then in fashion ? We might be unable to answer the question, had we not a narrative of the tour actually written by Wordsworth during his journey. It consists of a letter to his sister, in which he gives an ingenuous description of his impressions as they arose. Now this letter is the first frank expression of the heartfelt joy and concentrated enthusiasm which afterwards became the principal characteristics of his poetry. The delights of a rapid journey through splendid scenery are conspicuous in every line. "I am in excellent health and spirits," he assures

---

[1] *D. S.*, 632-644. *Cf.* Gray's *Eton College.* [2] *D. S.*, 676-679.
[3] *D. S.*, 810-813.

his sister, " and have had no reason to complain of the contrary during our whole tour. My spirits have been kept
in a perpetual hurry of delight, by the almost uninterrupted succession of sublime and beautiful objects which
have passed before my eyes during the course of the
last month." Beside the lake of Como he formed "a
thousand dreams of happiness which might be enjoyed
upon its banks." He anticipates great pleasure, on his
return to Cambridge, from exulting over those of his
friends who had prophesied that he would meet with
insurmountable difficulties. " Everything, however, has
succeeded with us far beyond my most sanguine expectations. We have, it is true, met with little disasters
occasionally, but far from distressing, and they rather gave
us additional resolution and spirits." Only once does he
give utterance to a feeling of dejection; it arises at the
thought of quitting the Swiss mountains.[1]

Nor does it appear that sadness found its way into his
heart in the interval between his journey and the publication of his poem. In London he had "many pleasant
hours."[2] Writing to a Cambridge friend in the summer
of 1791, he advises him, not without a touch of raillery,
to make a tour in order to gild his "long Lapland night
of melancholy."[3] And in France he was to find little
time for indulgence in that languid mood which requires
leisure and tranquillity.

Must we then say that the young poet's dark humour
is entirely due to convention? Certainly not. He
is translating into the language of artificiality the first
vague unrest of his senses and feelings, not feigning
all the symptoms of a melancholy which he does not
feel. Who that examines his own heart can fail to
discover within it, even on one and the same day, the
materials both for a sorrowful and for a joyous poem?
But it is the most superficial feelings which are naturally
the first to spring forth. And since the prevailing taste

[1] Letter from Wordsworth to his sister, 6th September 1790. *Prose
Works*, iii. pp. 224-230.
[2] Letter to Mathews, 17th June 1791. Knight, *Life of Wordsworth*,
i. p. 58.
[3] Letter to Mathews, 3rd August 1791. *Ibid.*, i. p. 59.

always captivates at first even the more independent spirits, it is inevitable that a young man should conceal his most heartfelt aspirations if they conflict with this taste, that he should fear and even despise them, and should at first attach importance only to those which bring him into harmony with people around him because they are common to all.

So far as we have followed him, Wordsworth has drawn from the stores of his own consciousness no materials for his poems but the sensations he has felt in the presence of nature. As yet, neither his heart nor his intelligence have performed their functions with sufficient vigour to acquire the proud consciousness of their worth. His descriptions are already those of a master; his reflexions still those of a schoolboy. He expresses the thoughts of his generation rather than his own. He is a prey to vague depression because he is without any occupation which gives him pleasure; without an aim, without enthusiasm, moral or intellectual. No cause, no principle, has hitherto won his devotion; his mind has been satisfied with the indolent acceptance of current formulas; to man and to society he has paid only a half-conscious attention. The shock needful to arouse him was at hand. During his stay in London Wordsworth's transformation began to take shape. It will be continued and extended in the course of the year which he is about to pass in France during the days of the revolution.

BOOK II

The French Revolution. Moral Crisis

CHAPTER I

Residence in London

I

AFTER taking his B.A. degree, in January 1791, Wordsworth left Cambridge. His education completed, prudence demanded that he should accede to the wishes of his friends, and choose a career without delay. But no vocation, except that of the poet, had recommended itself to him during his residence at the University. The next five years he spent in procrastination, and in making specious excuses for his indecision both to others and to himself. He refused at first to enter the church because he was not old enough to be ordained[1]; then, when he had attained the requisite age, alleged his conscientious scruples. He definitely abandoned the law, conceived a vague idea of entering the army, thought of obtaining a post as tutor, and also of becoming a journalist. These faint inclinations for regular work were his only concessions to practical life. At heart he had but a single passion, the desire for travel. Had he been born poor he would have become a pedlar, he says, in order to satisfy it.[2] If he had been born rich he would have spent his fortune in wandering about the world. As he was neither the one nor the other, his only plan for the future was to gain time, in the vague hope that some lucky accident would sooner or later allow him to indulge his natural bent.

Apparently none of Wordsworth's biographers have laid sufficient stress upon the waywardness he displayed at

[1] Letter to Mathews, 23rd September 1791. Knight, *Life of Wordsworth*, i. p. 60.
[2] Introductory note to *The Excursion*.

this period of his life. It is so customary to regard him
as having been a model for poets in the matter of a regular
and dutiful life, that they pass over his refractory youth
without dwelling upon the obstinate refusal with which
he met every suggestion of practical wisdom. Wordsworth's vocation, like that of most other poets, made itself
known through revolt. He had, as others had, his hours,
his years of disobedience, obstinacy, and rash defiance of
fortune. Like them he was a cause of anxiety to those
around him; and by his relations was long regarded as
the stubborn and presumptuous young man who would
"turn out badly." His noble life of calm acquiescence in
the established order of things began by a long conflict
with the discipline which commonly has to be faced at the
outset of one's career. And it was his struggles with that
discipline, and the success with which those struggles met,
that enabled him to preserve his precious gifts of mind unimpaired. Such at any rate is the opinion which he often
and boldly avowed. It is the opinion which he expressed
in the prime of life in his finest pages of prose—those
contained in the letter to *Mathetes*.[1] John Wilson, a
student fresh from Oxford, destined to attain some reputation as a poet, and still more, under the pseudonym of
Christopher North, as a writer of prose, entreated Wordsworth to undertake the guidance of the young men of the
period, who, though well-intentioned, were full of anxiety
and perplexity. He asked him to show them a sure path
to what is good, and to protect them from the dangers of
error and self-delusion. Wordsworth replied to this invitation by refusing to undertake the office. He answers the
appeal for a Teacher by a declaration that the lad who is
attaining manhood no longer requires one, that each should
beat out his own path, and should count upon nothing but
his own energy and intelligence. Evidently he was looking back to his own youth, and to the time when he had
had to make a choice like that of Hercules, in "the ancient
fable of Prodicus." On the one hand is the *World*, who
discourses only "of ease, pleasure, freedom, and domestic
tranquillity; or, if she invite to labour, it is labour in the

---

[1] Written in 1809, *Prose Works*, vol. i. pp. 297-308.

busy and beaten track, with the assurance of the complacent regards of parents, friends . . ." On the other hand is *Intellectual Prowess*, who does not conceal from the young man " the impediments, the disappointments, the ignorance and prejudice which her follower will have to encounter, if devoted, when duty calls to active life; and if to contemplative, she lays nakedly before him a scheme of solitary and unremitting labour, a life of entire neglect perhaps, or assuredly a life exposed to scorn, insult, persecution, and hatred. . . ." " Of these two, each in this manner soliciting you to become her adherent, you doubt not which to prefer; but oh ! the thought of moment is not preference, but the degree of preference ; the passionate and pure choice, the inward sense of absolute and unchangeable devotion." How clearly opposed is this to the doctrine of submission readily inculcated by Wordsworth in his old age, and too frequently identified with his name, in spite of his assertion that he only acquired or retained his greatness through disregarding it. " Every age," he says, " hath abounded in instances of parents, kindred, and friends, who, by indirect influence of example, or by positive injunction and exhortation, have diverted or discouraged the youth, who, in the simplicity and purity of nature, had determined to follow his intellectual genius through good and through evil, and had devoted himself to knowledge, to the practice of virtue and the preservation of integrity, in slight of temporal rewards. Above all, have not the common duties and cares of common life at all times exposed men to injury from causes the action of which is the more fatal from being silent and unremitting, and which, wherever it was not jealously watched and steadily opposed, must have pressed upon and consumed the diviner spirit ? "

It is doubtless his own behaviour on leaving the University of which Wordsworth here gives us a transformed and exalted picture, and, since he is generalizing, he is entitled to do so. He discloses only the lofty and poetic reasons for his revolt against prudence and custom. Upon the whole, however, he was not undeserving of the praise he bestows on the young man whose proud and unruly disposition leads him to despise the ordinary comforts of life. It is well to keep before our eyes the idealized portrait of the youth, drawn by the man of mature years, that we may beware of judging the whole of Wordsworth's life by his timorous and mistrustful old age. In 1791 he felt like a paladin ready to reform the universe, and in the same light he regarded himself after an inverval of eighteen years. "I will compare . . . an aspiring youth, leaving the schools in which he has been disciplined, and preparing to bear a part in the concerns of the world, I will compare him in this season of eager admiration, to a newly invested knight appearing with his blank un-signalized shield, upon some day of solemn tournament, at the court of the Faery queen. . . . He does not himself immediately enter the lists as a combatant, but he looks round him with a beating heart, dazzled by the gorgeous pageantry, the banners, the impresses, the ladies of over-coming beauty, the persons of the knights, now first seen by him, the fame of whose actions is carried by the traveller, like merchandize, through the world, and re-sounded upon the harp of the minstrel."

The new "knight," having some money in hand, was in no haste to submit to an irksome bondage. No longer subject to university discipline, he determined to make the most of his complete independence, and "to pitch a vagrant tent among the unfenced regions of society."[1] It was in London that he took up his abode first of all, in the character of an idler who stations himself at the heart of the world of business and of pleasure in order to satisfy his curiosity, or as a visitor, eager for novel scenes, whose fancy is always on the watch.

II

The increasing extent of London, and the spectacle presented by its streets, which every day became busier and more numerous, had long impressed the imagination

[1] *The Prelude*, vii. 57-58.

of men of letters in England. Addison, to go no further back, had given noble expression to the feelings of patriotic pride aroused in him by the sight of the City. He felt elated when he saw in the neighbourhood of the Royal Exchange, "so rich an Assembly of Countrymen and Foreigners, consulting together upon the private Business of Mankind, and making this Metropolis a kind of Emporium for the whole Earth." The contemplation of this great centre of business gave him "an infinite variety of solid and substantial Entertainments." "As I am a great Lover of Mankind," he said, "my Heart naturally overflows with Pleasure at the sight of a prosperous and happy Multitude, insomuch that I cannot forbear expressing my Joy with Tears that have stolen down my Cheeks." He had also enjoyed comparing with one another the varied aspects presented by the different quarters of London, since he looked upon the "great City" "as an Aggregate of various Nations distinguished from each other by their respective Customs, Manners, and Interests." His journals give evidence that he contemplated all the incidents and all the manifestations of London life with a ceaseless and delighted curiosity.

Addison's example had been followed by the novelists of the eighteenth century. The tales of Defoe, Fielding and Smollett abound in detailed pictures of the different parts of the metropolis, with a manifest preference for disorderly houses and prisons. In *Humphrey Clinker*, the last of his novels, published in 1771, Smollett contrived to give the subject some freshness and dramatic interest by making the various members of a provincial family describe in turn the feelings aroused in them by a visit to London. First of all there is Matthew Bramble, the excellent but eccentric misanthrope, who is incensed at finding the capital changed into an "incongruous monster;" sneers at the absurd extreme to which luxury is carried, and tawdry glitter of Ranelagh and Vauxhall, the popular resorts of the fashionable world;[1] and declares himself bewildered by the perpetual hubbub, and poisoned by the tainted and adulterated viands

[1] *Humphrey Clinker*, letter of 29th May.

served on every table.[1]   Then his niece, Lydia Melford, dazzled by the splendours of the town, and intoxicated by the ceaseless bustle of the streets, exclaims in her enthusiasm that all one reads "of wealth and grandeur, in the Arabian Nights Entertainment, and the Persian Tales, concerning Bagdad, Diarbekir, Damascus, Ispahan and Samarkand, is here realised."[2]   And the servant Winifred Jenkins can only express her amazement by the multiplication of distorted words and unpronounceable blunders; for what with the racket and "hulliballoo" she feels her "poor Welsh brain . . . spinning like a top."[3]

But while prose-writers were thus grasping the salient features of the vast city, and observing, from a humorous or serious point of view, the imposing effect which it presented as a whole, poetry still lingered in the beaten track, and continued to vent its ill-humour upon London after the manner of the Latin poets who poured abuse upon Rome.   Juvenal's third satire had served as a model for a series of invectives against the capital, beginning with a direct imitation by Oldham in 1682, and continued in the *City Shower* of Swift, *Trivia, or the Art of Walking the Streets of London*, by John Gay, down to Samuel Johnson's *Satire on London*.   Johnson is the most pronounced type of the eighteenth century poets, who were for the most part inveterate townspeople, and would not have exchanged the shops of Fleet Street for all the delights of Arcadia. Faithful, nevertheless, to classical tradition, they held themselves bound to celebrate the charms of the country, and to heap execrations upon city life.   Johnson spent almost the whole of his life in London, and regarded any other abode as a place of exile.   His biographer represents him as constantly chanting the praises of London before his friends.   Johnson had great difficulty in tearing himself away from the city, and immediately he left it felt ill and low-spirited.   He said that in its smoky atmosphere he got rid of his dropsy.   London was his "element." For him it was "a heaven upon earth."   He perceived

---

[1] *Humphrey Clinker*, letter of 8th June.
[2] *Ibid.*, letter of 31st May.   [3] *Ibid.*, letter of 3rd June.

also what it was that constituted the true majesty of the place, and said in the pompous manner habitual with him :—" Sir, if you wish to have a just notion of the magnitude of this city, you must not be satisfied with seeing its great streets and squares, but must survey the innumerable little lanes and courts. It is not in the showy evolutions of buildings, but in the multiplicity of human habitations which are crowded together that the wonderful immensity of London consists."[1] Country life appeared to him suited to fools. " They who are content to live in the country are fit for the country." And in *Rasselas* he drew a sarcastic comparison between the peasant as he is—boorish, stupid, discontented and envious—and the imaginary shepherd of pastoral poetry. Such were the thoughts and words of Johnson as a man; such the opinions he expressed in his prose. But as a poet, 'he only thing he wrote concerning the town he loved wa. a satire, though this, it is true, was composed soon after he first came to reside there. Poetic tradition had required that he should attack what was dear to him, and extol that for which he cared nothing.

Up to that time the only poet whose work had reflected something of the grandeur of London, was the very one who had turned from it in horror as a hot-bed of vice and corruption. For Cowper, towns were the work of man, or, in other words, of the devil, while the country was created by God. He had succeeded in suggesting a powerful image of the dreadful city, which appeared to him, as Satan appeared to Milton, the majestic personification of evil. It was the seat of the arts, of eloquence, philosophy, and knowledge; the market of the earth; " the fairest capital of all the world."

> Babylon of old
> Not more the glory of the earth than she,
> A more accomplished world's chief glory now.

These utterances, however, escaped him, to some extent, in spite of himself, and the pious poet's indignation too soon completed his unfinished picture with a sermon :

[1] Boswell, *The Life of Dr Johnson*, Conversation of July 5th, 1763.

" O thou, resort and mart of all the earth,
    Chequered with all complexions of mankind,
    And spotted with all crimes; in which I see
    Much that I love, and more that I admire,
    And all that I abhor ; thou freckled fair,
    That pleases and yet shocks me, I can laugh
    And I can weep, can hope, and can despond,
    Feel wrath and pity, when I think on thee !
    Ten righteous would have saved a city once,
    And thou hast many righteous.—Well for thee
    That salt preserves thee ; more corrupted else,
    And therefore more obnoxious at this hour,
    Than Sodom in her day had power to be,
    For whom God heard his Abraham plead in vain." [1]

Here, as in other cases, the moral quickly ruined the
picturesque effect. Left almost untouched, therefore, by
Cowper, this magnificent theme was appropriated by
Wordsworth. The future poet of the lakes was really
the first, if not to feel, at any rate to attempt to render in
verse worthy of the theme, and without satirical de-
sign, the grandeur of London and the intensity of its
life. Strange as this fact appears at first sight, it is less
surprising when we reflect that the requisite striking
impression could only be felt by a man fresh from the
world outside of London, capable of new and vivid sensations, and sufficiently open in mind and independent of
classical authorities to venture on a frank description of his
novel impressions. This was the new departure taken by
Wordsworth. The man who is usually regarded as
imbued with rustic prejudices was able to understand the
strange and powerful attraction of the capital, and deemed
it worthy of poetic treatment.

He has told us how marvellous an idea of London was
conjured up by childish imagination in a remote corner of
England, with the aid of romance and narrative. He recalled a time in his own life when the conception he had
formed of London, in his foolish simplicity, surpassed all the
pictures of airy palaces and enchanted gardens invented by
poets, and all the accounts given by historians of Rome,

[1] *The Task*, iii. 835-848.

Cairo, Babylon, or Persepolis. Among his school-fellows there was a little cripple, who happened to be summoned to London, and was the envy and admiration of all the boys when he set out. On his return, after a short absence, Wordsworth examined his bearing and appearance with curiosity, and felt some disappointment at not finding more alteration in his features after his visit to the fairy city. He put a hundred questions to him, but was disconcerted at the little traveller's commonplace answers:

> Every word he uttered, on my ears
> Fell flatter than a cagèd parrot's note,
> That answers unexpectedly awry,
> And mocks the prompter's listening.

It seemed strange to Wordsworth that his school-fellow should not wear some sort of halo on his return from the great city, where, of course, mitred prelates and lords clad in ermine moved before the spectator in endless succession, and King and Lord Mayor passed by in all their glory. One thing in particular astonished him, accustomed as he was to the narrow limits of a small town : that men could live as next-door neighbours, and remain at the same time strangers to one another, without even knowing each other's names.[1]

Once already, since that distant period, Wordsworth had had the opportunity of comparing his dream with the reality. He had taken advantage of the first moment of freedom permitted him at Cambridge to visit London, and his memory retained an ever-present recollection of the day when he threaded the long labyrinth of suburban villages, and entered the mighty city for the first time :

> On the roof
> Of an itinerant vehicle I sate,
> With vulgar men about me, trivial forms
> Of houses, pavement, streets, of men and things, —
> Mean shapes on every side : but, at the instant,
> When to myself it fairly might be said,

[1] *The Prelude*, vii. 77-119. He owed this to Fielding. *Joseph Andrews*, i. ch. vi.

The threshold now is overpast,   . . .
.   .   .   .
A weight of ages did at once descend
Upon my heart.[1]

This impression had been but of the briefest duration,
and Wordsworth's stay on that occasion had been too
short to satisfy his curiosity.   It had merely served to
banish his childish illusions, and to convince him that the
great town's mysterious charm could only reveal itself
after a prolonged residence.   Hitherto he had merely
taken a casual survey of the city ; now, however, he resolved to penetrate its hidden meaning.   He sought of
London, as he walked its streets with his attention on the
alert, sensations analogous to those he had experienced at
every step among his mountains.   His chief recollections
of the four months of leisure which he devoted to a study
of the town are collected in his autobiographical poem.

Nevertheless, it is probable that when, in the seventh
book of *The Prelude*, written in 1804, Wordsworth spoke
of his visit to London in 1791, he made use of some facts
which were observed at another and later opportunity.
It is equally probable that he employed with advantage the
lively and subtle impressions of Charles Lamb, who became
his friend during the interval.   His correspondence with
Lamb, which began in 1800, turns more than once upon
the comparative merits of town and country.   Lamb took
a delight in upholding the glories of his favourite city
against the divine nature extolled in Wordsworth's solemn
strains.   He lavished on the busy spots where the London
thoroughfares met all the grateful blessings which Wordsworth poured forth upon his northern lakes and mountains.
The streets of the city, its sounds, its humblest inhabitants,
its beggars and children of the gutter,[2] stirred in him
emotion no less keen than that which the limpid streams
and simple-minded shepherds of Westmoreland aroused
in Wordsworth.   It is impossible to say precisely where
Lamb's serious mood ends and his jesting humour begins,

[1] *The Prelude*, viii. 540-560.
[2] See, especially, *The Londoner* (1810), and *The Decay of Beggars* (1822).

but it is certain that he was passionately attached to London, where his whole life was spent. From a hundred passages in his essays and correspondence we may select the following letter to Wordsworth, written on the 30th January 1801, as an example of the half-jesting, half-earnest tone of this controversy. Wordsworth had invited Lamb to visit him at Grasmere, in Westmoreland, and the latter replied :

"I ought before this to have replied to your very kind invitation into Cumberland. With you and your sister I could gang anywhere ; but I am afraid whether I shall ever be able to afford so desperate a journey. Separate from the pleasure of your company, I don't now care if I never see a mountain in my life. I have passed all my days in London, until I have formed as many and intense local attachments as any of you mountaineers can have done with dead nature. The lighted shops of the Strand and Fleet Street, the innumerable trades, tradesmen, and customers, coaches, waggons, playhouses ; all the bustle and wickedness round about Covent Garden ; the watchmen, drunken scenes, rattles ;—life awake, if you awake, at all hours of the night ; the impossibility of being dull in Fleet Street ; the crowds, the very dirt and mud, the sun shining upon houses and pavements, the print-shops, the old book-stalls, parsons cheapening books, coffeehouses, steams of soups from kitchens, the pantomimes—London itself a pantomime and a masquerade—all these things work themselves into my mind, and feed me without a power of satiating me. The wonder of these sights impels me into night-walks about her crowded streets, and I often shed tears in the motley Strand from fulness of joy at so much life. All these emotions must be strange to you ; so are your rural emotions to me. . . .

. . . Have I not enough without your mountains ? I do not envy you. I should pity you did I not know that the mind will make friends of anything. . . . So fading upon me, from disuse, have been the beauties of Nature, as they have been confidently called ; so ever fresh, and green, and warm are all the inventions of men, and assemblies of men in this great city."

It must be admitted that Wordsworth's poetry does not
attain the lyricism and intense feeling of Lamb's prose,
where enthusiasm is enlivened, without being chilled, by
irony. We, who for a century have been accustomed
to descriptions marked by acute insight, find something
altogether too ready and commonplace about the lines in
which Wordsworth enumerates all the details of London's
changing pageant. They are wanting in that which
constitutes the charm of the humorist, and is the source of
Wordsworth's own power in his pictures of rustic life;
a love of the things he describes. He may not have
detested towns as Cowper did, or Lamartine, who hated
them " as the plants of the south hate the damp obscurity
of a prison "; [1] but he certainly was not altogether happy in
towns, and considered them from the point of view, not of
a citizen, but of a provincial who is by turns dazzled and
deceived, charmed and scandalized. Though he did not
acknowledge it, he was astonished to find the splendours
he had trusted to behold, so few and far between. " Oftentimes, in spite of strongest disappointment," he was pleased
merely

> Through courteous self-submission, as a tax
> Paid to the object by prescriptive right. [2]

Independent also, as he was, of any society but his own,
he nevertheless suffered at times from the protracted
solitude of his life in London, and never entirely forgave
the city for it. He contrasted his painful loneliness
among the crowd with the sweet solitude of the country,
and with village life, in which each knows and is known
by all the rest. When he took up his permanent abode in
the lake district, he anticipated any who might be inclined
to reproach him for shunning human society, by replying
that London is the place where true solitude is to be
found:

> He truly is alone,
> He of the multitude whose eyes are doomed
> To hold a vacant commerce day by day
> With objects wanting life, repelling love;

---

[1] *Nouvelles Confidences*, book i. ch. xli.　　[2] *The Prelude*, vii. 144-149.

He in the vast metropolis immured,
Where pity shrinks from unremitting calls,
Where numbers overwhelm humanity,
And neighbourhood serves rather to divide
Than to unite.   What sighs more deep than his,
Whose nobler will hath long been sacrificed ;
Who must inhabit, under a black sky,
 A City where, if indifference to disgust
Yield not, to scorn, or sorrow, living men
Are ofttimes to their fellow-men no more
Than to the forest hermit are the leaves
That hang aloft in myriads—nay, far less,
For they protect his walk from sun and shower,
Swell his devotion with their voice in storms,
And whisper while the stars twinkle among them
His lullaby.[1]

There is in this passage something of the ill-feeling of a
man who has found in London no outlet for his affections
and no food for any faculty save curiosity.

III

We shall not follow Wordsworth in his walks about
London ; whether, from the very centre of the " monstrous
ant-hill," he watches the " endless stream of men and
moving things " as it flows past him, and amuses himself
by observing the odd and varied features of the cosmopolitan crowd ; or escapes from the tumult, " as from an
enemy," into some side street " still as a sheltered place
when winds blow loud " ; whether he makes his way into
inner courts " gloomy as coffins," or into dark and narrow
alleys,

> Thrilled by some female vendor's scream, belike
> The very shrillest of all London cries ;

whether he lingers in the " privileged regions and inviolate " of the Temple, where, among their still and silent
groups of trees, the law students enjoy a perfect quiet

The Recluse, 613-632 (written in 1800).

within two paces of the hubbub of Fleet Street, or seeks the broader avenues of the suburbs frequented by loungers in search of purer air and less scanty verdure.[1]

Doubtless his description of the streets of London contains happy touches. The lively manner in which it is presented gives a foretaste of certain chapters from Dickens, though not of their humour. But why dwell on Wordsworth's sketch when we possess the finished pictures of the great novelist? Too often, moreover, Wordsworth draws up a mere catalogue of the sights and sounds of the capital. It is evident that the objects he describes have not remained long enough in his mind, and have left behind them only a faint impression, at times even none but that of their names.

Nor is it Wordsworth whom we must take as our guide before entering the art-galleries and play-houses, particularly when Lamb freely offers himself. Although the theatre, as Wordsworth tells us, was then his " dear delight," there is less to charm in the impressions of his twenty-second year than in his simple recollections of boyish ecstasy, when, from time to time, some strolling players who visited Hawkshead, turned a rude barn into a pompous scene. " Then," says Wordsworth,

> if I perchance
> Caught on a summer evening through a chink
> In the old wall, an unexpected glimpse
> Of daylight, the bare thought of where I was
> Gladdened me more than if I had been led
> Into a dazzling cavern of romance,
> Crowded with Genii busy among works
> Not to be looked at by the common sun.

In his early manhood Wordsworth's susceptible heart retained something of this sensibility to keen enjoyment, so that he would shed tears as he watched one of the wretched sentimental dramas then in fashion. But while his heart was captivated, his imagination was neither impressed nor exalted. The storm of passion " passed not beyond the suburbs of the mind." What was needed

---

[1] *The Prelude*, vii. 149-229.

to awaken his imagination was the impersonation of one of Shakespeare's heroines by an actress like Mrs Siddons, at that time "in the fulness of her power"; then he recognised the living forms of the shadowy visions he had seen,

> When, having closed the mighty Shakespeare's page,
> I mused, and thought, and felt, in solitude.[1]

The law-courts, and Parliament itself, produced on him at this period merely an impression similar to that created by the theatre. His heart beat quickly when one of those, whose names had been familiar to him as household words from childhood, rose to address the House of Lords—a Bedford, a Gloucester, a Salisbury! At first he was astonished at the inexhaustible copiousness of these orators.

> Words follow words, sense seems to follow sense :
> What memory and what logic !

But the flow of words at last grew tedious even to his young and indulgent ears. The epoch was nevertheless one of the most splendid in the history of English parliamentary oratory. Wordsworth had the opportunity of witnessing in the House of Commons one of the oratorical passages of arms which took place between Fox, the champion of the French Revolution, and Burke, from the outset its furious antagonist, whose *Reflexions* had appeared in the preceding year. It was on the 6th of May 1791, during Wordsworth's residence in London, that the two great men had their historic quarrel in the presence of the whole House. Up to that time, in spite of the divergence of their opinions, they had remained friends. Wordsworth afterwards did more, in many respects, than anyone else to popularize Burke's political and social theories through the medium of poetry, and to magnify customs and institutions which were already objects of veneration, not to mention certain ancient abuses as well ; but he was at that time still under the spell of the Federation festivals, and had a leaning towards the doctrines of the opposite party. No doubt he was one of the

[1] *The Prelude*, vii. 399-485.

insubordinate crowd which murmured at the orator's invectives "against all systems built on abstract rights," and grew impatient of his repeated panegyrics on venerable Laws, on custom, and on loyalty. Nevertheless from that time forth his mind retained a deep impression of Burke.

> I see him,—old, but vigorous in age,—
> Stand like an oak whose stag-horn branches start
> Out of its leafy brow, the more to awe
> The younger brethren of the grove.

And, in his speeches, there were memorable moments,

> When Wisdom, like the Goddess from Jove's brain,
> Broke forth in armour of resplendent words,
> Startling the Synod. Could a youth, and one
> In ancient story versed, whose breast had heaved
> Under the weight of classic eloquence,
> Sit, see, and hear, unthankful, uninspired ? [1]

The political debates with which the halls of Parliament were ringing were carried on among the outside public by the "Society of friends of the Revolution," and Wordsworth detected their echo even in the church. These digressions, which warmed the sermons to something above their customary frigidity, were by no means displeasing to him. It was not the daring thoughts of the famous preachers that provoked his ridicule, but their affected diction, a fault already severely criticised by Cowper. The satiric vein in Wordsworth is of rare occurrence and of brief duration—he never had either the power or the desire to handle irony with effect, yet he has launched some keen shafts of sarcasm against the fashionable preachers of that day.

> There have I seen a comely bachelor,
> Fresh from a toilette of two hours, ascend
> His rostrum, with seraphic glance look up,
> And, in a tone elaborately low
> Beginning, lead his voice through many a maze
> A minuet course ; and, winding up his mouth,
> From time to time, into an orifice

[1] *The Prelude*, vii. 512-543.

Most delicate, a lurking eyelet, small,
And only not invisible, again
Open it out, diffusing thence a smile
Of rapt irradiation, exquisite.
Meanwhile the Evangelists, Isaiah, Job,
Moses, and he who penned, the other day,
The Death of Abel, Shakespeare, and the Bard
Whose genius spangled o'er a gloomy theme
With fancies thick as his inspiring stars,
And Ossian (doubt not—'tis the naked truth)
Summoned from streamy Morven—each and all
Would, in their turns, lend ornaments and flowers
To entwine the crook of eloquence that helped
This pretty Shepherd, pride of all the plains,
To rule and guide his captivated flock.[1]

IV

But the force and the novelty of Wordsworth's impressions of London reside not in these rapid observations, whatever of interest they may possess, but rather in the lines wherein he glorifies London as a great and mysterious being which influences the spectator with a power resembling, if not equivalent to, that of sea or mountain. Though often revolted by the scenes of vice displayed before him, and sickened by the coarseness and brutality characteristic of the great popular festivals, such as the fair of St Bartholomew, he was never insensible to the mighty forces revealed in these brutal aspects of the

vast metropolis,
Fount of my country's destiny and the world's ;
That great emporium, chronicle at once
And burial-place of passions, and their home
Imperial, their chief living residence.[2]

But he felt its grandeur most of all in hours of peace and solitude. He loved to wander through the streets when the city was wrapped in slumber, and to enjoy

[1] *The Prelude*, vii. 551-572   [2] *Ibid.*, viii. 593-7.

> the peace
> That comes with night; the deep solemnity
> Of nature's intermediate hours of rest,
> When the great tide of human life stands still;
> The business of the day to come, unborn,
> Of that gone by, locked up, as in the grave;
> The blended calmness of the heavens and earth,
> Moonlight and stars, and empty streets, and sounds
> Unfrequent as in deserts.[1]

At a later period, in 1802, he was to receive a similar but more joyous impression when, as he crossed Westminster Bridge in a coach, he saw the sleeping city transfigured by the dawn.

> Earth has not anything to show more fair:
> Dull would he be of soul who could pass by
> A sight so touching in its majesty:
> This City now doth, like a garment, wear
> The beauty of the morning; silent, bare,
> Ships, towers, domes, theatres, and temples lie
> Open unto the fields, and to the sky;
> All bright and glittering in the smokeless air.
> Never did sun more beautifully steep
> In his first splendour, valley, rock, or hill;
> Ne'er saw I, never felt, a calm so deep!
> The river glideth at his own sweet will:
> Dear God! the very houses seem asleep;
> And all that mighty heart is lying still! [2]

Not only can London clothe itself at certain moments with beauty equal to that of nature, but like nature it can induce in him who contemplates it a state of reverie, or even of ecstasy.

> As the black storm upon the mountain-top
> Sets off the sunbeam in the valley, so
> That huge fermenting mass of human-kind
> Serves as a solemn background, or relief,
> To single forms and objects,

which thus acquire more " liveliness and power " than they possess in reality.

[1] *The Prelude*, vii. 649-661.   [2] *Sonnet composed on Westminster Bridge.*

" How oft," says Wordsworth,

> amid those overflowing streets,
> Have I gone forward with the crowd, and said
> Unto myself, " The face of every one
> That passes by me is a mystery ! "
> Thus have I looked, nor ceased to look, oppressed
> By thoughts of what and whither, when and how,
> Until the shapes before my eyes became
> A second-sight procession, such as glides
> Over still mountains, or appears in dreams ;
> And once, far-travelled in such mood, beyond
> The reach of common indication, lost
> Amid the moving pageant I was smitten
> Abruptly, with the view (a sight not rare)
> Of a blind Beggar, who, with upright face,
> Stood, propped against a wall, upon his chest
> Wearing a written paper, to explain
> His story, whence he came, and who he was.
> Caught by the spectacle my mind turned round
> As with the might of waters ; an apt type
> This label seemed of the utmost we can know,
> Both of ourselves and of the universe ;
> And, on the shape of that unmoving man,
> His steadfast face and sightless eyes, I gazed,
> As if admonished from another world.[1]

The flaunting vanity and sumptuous extravagance of London served also to throw into relief the simple touches of courage or affection, the acts of heroism or of modest kindness which Lamb, and afterwards Dickens, loved to point out among the humblest inhabitants of the great city. With all its simplicity, with all its bareness, is there not something touching in the following little scene casually observed by Wordsworth ? A workman was

> sitting in an open square
> Upon a corner-stone of that low wall
> Wherein were fixed the iron pales that fenced
> A spacious grass-plot ; there, in silence, sate
> This One Man, with a sickly babe outstretched
> Upon his knee, whom he had thither brought
> For sunshine, and to breathe the fresher air.

[1] *The Prelude*, vii. 618-649.

Of those who passed, and me who looked at him,
He took no heed ; but in his brawny arms
(The Artificer was to the elbow bare,
And from his work this moment had been stolen)
He held the child, and, bending over it,
As if he were afraid both of the sun
And of the air, which he had come to seek,
Eyed the poor babe with love unutterable.[1]

This slight sketch of a street-scene is the only one which the poet has unearthed from the remote depths of his earliest recollections of London. Others, numerous enough, were afterwards added by degrees, and developed into curious poems. As his senses ceased to be dazzled by the bustle and uproar, and as the idea of bringing into relief the lesson of happiness contained in every spectacle he witnessed became more and more deeply rooted in his mind, he learned better how to detach the most insignificant scenes from their surroundings, and to give them a value of their own. He would take a delight in watching the ready gaiety of the common people. Wandering one evening on the right bank of the Thames with Charles Lamb, Wordsworth was the first to draw the " idolatrous Londoner's " attention to a joyous scene then being enacted on the platform of one of the floating mills which, in that day, used to line the banks of the river. A band is playing upon the quay, and straightway the miller and two women leave their work, and begin to dance merrily :—

> In sight of the spires,
> All alive with the fires
> Of the sun going down to his rest,
> In the broad open eye of the solitary sky,
> They dance,—there are three, as jocund as free,
> While they dance on the calm river's breast.
>
> Man and Maidens wheel,
> They themselves make the reel,
> And their music's a prey which they seize ;
> It plays not for them,—what matter ? 'tis theirs ;
> And if they had care, it has scattered their cares
> While they dance, crying, " Long as ye please ! "

[1] *The Prelude*, vii. 601-617.

> They dance not for me,
> Yet mine is their glee!
> Thus pleasure is spread through the earth
> In stray gifts to be claimed by whoever shall find;
> Thus a rich loving-kindness, redundantly kind,
> Moves all nature to gladness and mirth.
>
> The showers of the spring
> Rouse the birds, and they sing;
> If the wind do but stir for his proper delight,
> Each leaf, that and this, his neighbour will kiss;
> Each wave, one and t'other, speeds after his brother;
> They are happy, for that is their right! [1]

Wordsworth was again impressed by the feelings which music, however poor in quality, will excite in the least refined among the populace, when he observed the ecstatic faces which surrounded a wandering fiddler in Oxford Street—" an Orpheus," to judge by the miracles he worked. Sadness and remorse, and all business occupations, are for the moment forgotten.

> As the Moon brightens round her the clouds of the night,
> So He, where he stands, is a centre of light;
> It gleams on the face, there, of dusky browed Jack,
> And the pale-visaged Baker's, with basket on back.
>
> That errand-bound 'Prentice was passing in haste—
> What matter! he's caught—and his time runs to waste;
> The Newsman is stopped, though he stops on the fret;
> And the half-breathless Lamplighter—he's in the net!
>
> The Porter sits down on the weight which he bore;
> The Lass with her barrow wheels hither her store;—
> If a thief could be here he might pilfer at ease;
> She sees the Musician, 'tis all that she sees!
> .   .   .   .   .   .
> That tall Man, a giant in bulk and in height,
> Not an inch of his body is free from delight;
> Can he keep himself still, if he would? oh, not he!
> The music stirs in him like wind through a tree.
> .   .   .   .   .   .

---

[1] *Stray Pleasures* (1806).

Now, coaches and chariots! roar on like a stream;
Here are twenty souls happy as souls in a dream:
They are deaf to your murmurs—they care not for you,
Nor what ye are flying, nor what ye pursue! [1]

Sometimes, however, the crowd, which gathers thus in expectation of enjoyment, disperses unsatisfied and disappointed. So it fares with the people who collect around a telescope pointed to the sky in Leicester Square. The night is well chosen, for it is clear.

Calm, though impatient, is the crowd; each stands ready with the fee,
And envies him that's looking;—what an insight it must be!

But something is at fault. Is it the instrument, or the eyes of the spectators, or the heavens?

Is nothing of that radiant pomp so good as we have here?
Or gives a thing but small delight that never can be dear?
The silver moon with all her vales, and hills of mightiest fame,
Does she betray us when they're seen? or are they but a name?

Or is it rather that Conceit rapacious is and strong,
And bounty never yields so much but it seems to do her wrong?
Or is it that, when human Souls a journey long have had
And are returned into themselves, they cannot but be sad?

Or must we be constrained to think that these Spectators rude,
Poor in estate, of manners base, men of the multitude,
Have souls which never yet have risen, and therefore prostrate lie?
No, no, this cannot be;—men thirst for power and majesty!

Does, then, a deep and earnest thought the blissful mind employ
Of him who gazes, or has gazed? a grave and steady joy,
That doth reject all show of pride, admits no outward sign,
Because not of this noisy world, but silent and divine!

Whatever be the cause, 'tis sure that they who pry and pore
Seem to meet with little gain, seem less happy than before:
One after One they take their turn, nor have I one espied
That doth not slackly go away, as if dissatisfied. [2]

---

[1] *Power of Music* (1806). Here Wordsworth had been anticipated, and perhaps inspired, by Sir John Davies, *Epigram* 38, *In Philonem* and by Vincent Bourne in his Latin Poem on *The Ballad-Singer*.
[2] *Star-gazers* (1806).

It may occasion some surprise that these analyses of impressions felt by townspeople should be met with in Wordsworth's work. On the other hand, there was one sentiment which rightly fell within the province of the future " high priest of nature," who took much pleasure in observing and depicting it. This was the sentiment of affection for the country as persisting even among all the vanity and excitement of town life. Cowper had already pointed out that love of nature, " born with all," which neither luxury, nor city crowds, nor business can entirely destroy. He had instanced, in proof of it,

> The villas with which London stands begirt,
> Like a swarth Indian with his belt of beads.

He had drawn attention to the rich citizen's affection for his sterile garden where nothing thrives, a dismal well where a few sprigs of nightshade or valerian are all that will grow; and to the affection of the poor man for the crazy boxes suspended overhead which he crowds with flowers and waters every day.[1]

What Wordsworth in later days delighted especially to remark was the survival of a love for the country in those who have been born there, but whose lot has made them exiles in the great city. He speaks of a poor servant-maid's emotion, when she hears the song of a thrush in the silence of morning, as she passes the corner of Wood Street.

> 'Tis a note of enchantment; what ails her ? She sees
> A mountain ascending, a vision of trees;
> Bright volumes of vapour through Lothbury glide,
> And a river flows on through the vale of Cheapside.

> Green pastures she views in the midst of the dale,
> Down which she so often has tripped with her pail;
> And a single small cottage, a nest like a dove's,
> The one only dwelling on earth that she loves.

[1] *The Task*, iv. 731-780.

She looks, and her heart is in heaven : but they fade,
The mist and the river, the hill and the shade :
The stream will not flow, and the hill will not rise,
And the colours have all passed away from her eyes! [1]

Then there is the old farmer of Tilsbury Vale, who, through bad management, has lost his property, and having cheated his creditors has been compelled to hide himself in London.   Among the pale townsfolk he has preserved the bloom of health acquired in his early life among the fields, but he feels himself a stranger in the town ; he watches the clouds as attentively as if he had ten reapers at work in the Strand.   A passing waggon loaded with hay has an irresistible attraction for him ; he cannot help handling and smelling the withered grass. In his leisure time he is always trying to get into contact with country life, and whenever he has a moment to spare makes his way to Smithfield—but " his heart· all the while is in Tilsbury Vale." [2]

To escape the necessity of giving Wordsworth's various impressions of London in detached fragments, we have had to anticipate the future, and to connect with the lines which arose out of his stay in 1791 those which were inspired by visits paid in after years.   But our narrative of the poet's life, if we leave out of account the moral reflexions due to a later period, will not be rendered erroneous by this unavoidable confusion.   The main outlines of what thenceforth constituted his mental representation of London, and during his later life successively took on the bright or sombre tints of the various phases of his thought, became graven on his mind during his first residence in the city, when he had no other object than to play the part of a spectator, and to enjoy to the full the pleasure of merely existing and observing.   To this period of his life we possess a clue, valuable because it is contemporary, which testifies, in spite of its brevity, to the veracity of *The Prelude*.   On the 17th June 1791, Wordsworth wrote to one of his Cambridge friends : " I quitted London about three weeks ago, where my time passed in

---

[1] *The Reverie of poor Susan* (1800?).   See page 143, note 1.
[2] *The Farmer of Tilsbury Vale* (1803).

a strange manner, sometimes whirled about by the vortex
of its *strenua inertia*, and sometimes thrown by the eddy
into a corner of the stream. Think not, however, that
I had not many pleasant hours."[1] It is true that this
impression, so happy in the main, was to become tainted
with bitterness in the crucial period through which
Wordsworth was to pass. During the early days of
his moral convalescence, in his transport of gratitude
to nature, a sort of semi-misanthropy led him to be severe,
to the point of injustice, against towns, and, even in 1800,
his resentment found vent in *The Recluse*. After that
time the balance of his affections, which had been threatened with destruction, was restored. With the assistance
of Lamb's discerning raillery, Wordsworth gradually came
to understand the narrowness of his excessive indignation.
Throughout the whole of the seventh book of *The Prelude*,
and the poems on London written in 1806, there are
indications of this reversion to his original impression.

Upon the whole, that impression had been favourable.
Though he congratulated himself upon having been nothing
more than a passing guest in London, he did not close his
mind to the teachings, he listened to the lessons, of the
mighty city. London, among his teachers, came next to
Nature; yet was she a "grave Teacher, a stern Pre-
ceptress!" Wearisome at first to the eye, her ceaselessly
shifting scenery assumed at last a sort of stability and
harmony beneath his attentive gaze. In the infinite
multitude of objects, paltry in themselves, he did not
lose sight of the grandeur of the aggregate, for his was
the mind that has

> among least things
> An under-sense of greatest; sees the parts
> As parts, but with a feeling of the whole.

This breadth of vision he owed to his early education,
to his daily contact with sublime objects. Thus, even
in London, he says, " the Spirit of Nature was upon me."

> The soul of Beauty and enduring Life
> Vouchsafed her inspiration, and diffused,

[1] Letter to Mathews, 17th June 1791. Knight, *Life of Wordsworth*, i. p. 58.

Through meagre lines and colours, and the press
Of self-destroying, transitory things,
Composure, and ennobling Harmony.[1]

V

Although the winter Wordsworth had spent in London
had not been without its pleasures, he could not have
made his home there without discomfort, especially when
summer had arrived.   At Cambridge he had acquired the
habit of making an annual migration to the country.   Towards the end of May, 1791, his friend Jones, with whom
he had visited Switzerland, sent him a very seasonable
invitation to Wales, where Jones lived in a village in the
valley of the Clwyd.   Wordsworth willingly quitted the
town, with less regret for its luxury and artistic pleasures
" than for the humble book-stalls in the streets, exposed
to eye and hand where'er he turned." [2]   He stayed some
weeks with Jones at Plas-yn-llan, and afterwards made a
tour with him on foot through the north of the princi-
pality.   The picturesque scenery of this region rivals that
of the lake district, and has also the advantage of more
glorious   associations,   half   historical,   half   legendary.
Wordsworth saw thus " the sea-sunsets which give such
splendour to the vale of Clwyd, Snowdon, the chair of
Idris, . . . Menai and her druids, the Alpine steeps of the
Conway, and the still more interesting windings of the
wizard stream of the Dee." [3]   He made the ascent of
Snowdon, a rival peak to Skiddaw and Helvellyn.   This
ascent is the only part of the expedition which he has
celebrated in verse, although at one time he had the idea
of singing the praises of Wales as he had sung those of
the Lakes and of the Alps.   He singled out this experience from among his recollections, on account of its sublime symbolic significance, and because it seemed to him a
fresh revelation of the power of the imaginative faculty.

---

[1] *The Prelude*, vii. 721-770.   [2] *Ibid.*, ix. 30-33.
[3] Dedication of the *Descriptive Sketches* (1793)

In one of those excursions (may they ne'er
Fade from remembrance!) through the Northern tracts
Of Cambria ranging with a youthful friend,
I left Bethgelert's huts at couching-time,
And westward took my way, to see the sun
Rise, from the top of Snowdon.   To the door
Of a rude cottage at the mountain's base
We came, and roused the shepherd who attends
The adventurous stranger's steps, a trusty guide;
Then, cheered by short refreshment, sallied forth.

It was a close, warm, breezeless summer night,
Wan, dull, and glaring, with a dripping fog
Low-hung and thick that covered all the sky;
But, undiscouraged, we began to climb
The mountain-side.   The mist soon girt us round,
And, after ordinary travellers' talk
With our conductor, pensively we sank
Each into commerce with his private thoughts:
Thus did we breast the ascent, and by myself
Was nothing either seen or heard that checked
Those musings or diverted, save that once
The shepherd's lurcher, who, among the crags,
Had to his joy unearthed a hedgehog, teased
His coiled-up prey with barkings turbulent.
This small adventure, for even such it seemed
In that wild place and at the dead of night,
Being over and forgotten, on we wound
In silence as before.   With forehead bent
Earthward, as if in opposition set
Against an enemy, I panted up
With eager pace, and no less eager thoughts.
Thus might we wear a midnight hour away,
Ascending at loose distance each from each,
And I, as chanced, the foremost of the band;
When at my feet the ground appeared to brighten,
And with a step or two seemed brighter still;
Nor was time given to ask or learn the cause,
For instantly a light upon the turf
Fell like a flash, and lo! as I looked up,
The Moon hung naked in a firmament
Of azure without cloud, and at my feet
Rested a silent sea of hoary mist.

A hundred hills their dusky backs upheaved
All over this still ocean ; and beyond,
Far, far beyond, the solid vapours stretched,
In headlands, tongues, and promontory shapes,
Into the main Atlantic, that appeared
To dwindle, and give up his majesty,
Usurped upon far as the sight could reach.
Not so the ethereal vault ; encroachment none
Was there, nor loss ; only the inferior stars
Had disappeared, or shed a fainter light
In the clear presence of the full-orbed Moon,
Who, from her sovereign elevation, gazed
Upon the billowy ocean, as it lay
All meek and silent, save that through a rift—
Not distant from the shore whereon we stood,
A fixed, abysmal, gloomy, breathing-place—
Mounted the roar of waters, torrents, streams
Innumerable, roaring with one voice !
Heard over earth and sea, and, in that hour,
For so it seemed, felt by the starry heavens.[1]

What at first is a simple " vision, given to spirits of the
night, and three chance human wanderers," becomes, when
it has vanished, and can only be seen as reflected in calm
thought, a type of the acts and aspirations of a majestic
intellect,

> the emblem of a mind
> That feeds upon infinity, that broods
> Over the dark abyss, intent to hear
> Its voices issuing forth to silent light
> In one continuous stream ; a mind sustained
> By recognitions of transcendent power,
> In sense conducting to ideal form,
> In soul of more than mortal privilege.

In the flash of light which, without in any way altering its
substance, had so suddenly transfigured the cheerless
landscape, and had, as it were, laid bare the joyous and
beautiful soul concealed behind a veil of gloom, Wordsworth recognised the magic power of that creative imagination which can thus glorify " the whole compass of the

[1] *The Prelude*, xiv. 1-63.

universe," and "build up greatest things from least suggestions." In this transference of supremacy from earth to heavens, from ocean to mists, from stars to moon, from silence to tumult, from darkness to light, he saw a striking analogy to that glorious faculty of lofty minds, who also

> from their native selves can send ab oa l
> Kindred mutations.[1]

Haunted by this image, Wordsworth made use of it again in a modified form when he wrote the *Excursion*.[2] Apparently it was the last majestic conception appropriated by his mind before he forsook nature in order to plunge into society, and exchanged for the time being the life of calm contemplation for that of tumult and excitement.

Meanwhile Wordsworth's guardians became more and more dissatisfied as the months passed by and he made no choice of a career. He had almost reached the end of his resources. According to a calculation made by his sister on the 7th December 1791, he possessed about £1000, less the expense of his education.[3] This sum must have been considerably reduced by the three costly years he had passed at Cambridge, the journeys he had made during his vacations, and his residence in London. One hope, it is true, was left: the Lonsdale debt seemed always on the point of being discharged. Dorothy hoped that it would be paid within a year;[4] and this hope, however illusory, was doubtless not without its effect upon the young man's behaviour. At an age when hope is so easily changed into certainty, this vague expectation of easier circumstances was calculated to paralyse Wordsworth's resolution, already so inclined to hesitate between professions which were repugnant to him. Idle, and half ashamed of his idleness, he went to Cambridge in the middle of the Long Vacation of 1791, and established himself there, near the libraries, in the month of September. But his natural inclinations soon got the better of this studious humour.

---

[1] *The Prelude*, xiv. 63-130.   [2] Book iv. 1061-1081.
[3] Letter written December 7, 1791. Knight, *Life of Wordsworth*, i. p. 52.
[4] Letter written May 23, 1791. Knight, *Life of Wordsworth*, i. p. 52

He announced that he intended to learn French and Spanish, in order to qualify himself to act as tutor to some young man of means in his continental travels, and determined to spend a year in France. If he did not succeed in this he would return to England, and study the Oriental languages, in accordance with his uncle Cookson's advice.   Such was the excuse beneath which he concealed the two-fold desire of continuing his roving life and of revisiting the country which had already charmed him by its cheerful gaiety, and was beginning to inspire him with its revolutionary zeal.

CHAPTER II

Residence in France

I

WORDSWORTH reached Paris towards the end of November 1791, but without any intention of settling there. He had fixed on Orleans as his place of residence, in the hope that by separating himself more completely from his countrymen he would learn French more quickly. But he could not resist the temptation of making a halt in Paris on his way.

> Through Paris lay my readiest course, and there
> Sojourning a few days, I visited
> In haste, each spot of old or recent fame,
> The latter chiefly ; from the field of Mars
> Down to the suburbs of St Antony,
> And from Mont Martre southward to the Dome
> Of Geneviève. In both her clamorous Halls
> The National Synod and the Jacobins,
> I saw the Revolutionary Power
> Toss like a ship at anchor, rocked by storms ;
> The Arcades I traversed, in the Palace huge
> Of Orleans ; coasted round and round the line
> Of Tavern, Brothel, Gaming-house, and Shop,
> Great rendezvous of worst and best, the walk
> Of all who had a purpose or had not
> I stared and listened, with a stranger's ears,
> To Hawkers and Haranguers, hubbub wild !
> And hissing Factionists with ardent eyes,
> In knots, or pairs, or single. Not a look
> Hope takes, or Doubt or Fear is forced to wear,
> But seemed there present ; and I scanned them all,
> Watched every gesture uncontrollable,
> Of anger, and vexation, and despite,
> All side by side, and struggling face to face,
> With gaiety and dissolute idleness.
>   Where silent zephyrs sported with the dust
> Of the Bastille, I sate in the open sun,

And from the rubbish gathered up a stone,
And pocketed the relic, in the guise
Of an enthusiast ; yet, in honest truth,
I looked for something that I could not find,
Affecting more emotion than I felt ;
For 'tis most certain, that these various sights,
However potent their first shock, with me
Appeared to recompense the traveller's pains
Less than the painted Magdalene of Le Brun,
A beauty exquisitely wrought, with hair
Dishevelled, gleaming eyes, and rueful cheek
Pale and bedropped with overflowing tears.[1]

During his first weeks at Orleans he was more alive to
local and national characteristics, and to the difficulties of
a half-known language, than to the mighty convulsions
then drawing on apace.

There, by novelties in speech,
Domestic manners, customs, gestures, looks,
And all the attire of ordinary life,
Attention was engrossed ; and, thus amused,
I stood, 'mid those concussions, unconcerned,
Tranquil almost, and careless as a flower
Glassed in a greenhouse, or a parlour shrub
That spreads its leaves in unmolested peace,
While every bush and tree, the country through,
Is shaking to the roots : indifference this
Which may seem strange : but I was unprepared
With needful knowledge, had abruptly passed
Into a theatre, whose stage was filled
And busy with an action far advanced.
Like others, I had skimmed, and sometimes read
With care, the master-pamphlets of the day ;
Nor wanted such half-insight as grew wild
Upon that meagre soil, helped out by talk
And public news ; but having never seen
A chronicle that might suffice to show
Whence the main organs of the public power

---

[1] *The Prelude*, ix. 42-81. This picture, which was at that time in the Carmelite convent, was one of the "sights" of the day. Religious music was played for the benefit of those who came to view it. A year earlier Halem, the German, had felt himself thrilled with emotion before the same picture. See *Paris in* 1790, by A. Chuquet (1896).

Had sprung, their transmigrations, when and how
Accomplished, giving thus unto events
A form and body ; all things were to me
Loose and disjointed, and the affections left
Without a vital interest.   At that time,
Moreover, the first storm was overblown,
And the strong hand of outward violence
Locked up in quiet.   For myself, I fear
Now, in connection with so great a theme,
To speak (as I must be compelled to do)
Of one so unimportant ; night by night
Did I frequent the formal haunts of men,
Whom, in the city, privilege of birth
Sequestered from the rest, societies
Polished in arts, and in punctilio versed ;
Whence, and from deeper causes, all discourse
Of good and evil of the time was shunned
With scrupulous care ; but these restrictions soon
Proved tedious, and I gradually withdrew
Into a noisier world, and thus ere long
Became a patriot ; and my heart was all
Given to the people, and my love was theirs.[1]

This inward revolution was accomplished not at Orleans,
but at Blois,[2] whither he betook himself early in the spring
of 1792, and where he found that "noisier world" which
harmonized better with his youth than the discreet and
formal assemblies of Orleans.   His new associates were
French officers.   Four companies of the first battalion of
the regiment of Bassigny, renamed the 32nd Infantry,
had been drafted to Blois, in the preceding year, from
Tours, where the regiment was in garrison.   It was the
officers 'of this detachment with whom Wordsworth became intimate.   The majority of them were hostile to the
new ideas.   Their colonel, Pierre-Marie de Suffren,
Marquis de Saint-Tropez, and brother of the famous
bailli de Suffren, had recently been arrested by the patriots
of Tours when on the point of joining the fugitive king,

---

[1] *The Prelude*, ix. 81-125.
[2] It may have been that Wordsworth found too many of his countrymen
even at Orleans, and went to Blois to escape them.   This was the reason,
at any rate, which impelled Jekyll to make the same change in 1775.
Correspondence of Mr Joseph Jekyll (Algernon Bourke, 1894).

and had been compelled to resign his commission. The officers of Bassigny, when called upon to take the new military oath of obedience to the National Assembly, had not submitted to this formality, if we may depend upon the testimony of Wordsworth, without a mental reservation, or without a tremor of rage.

> Some of these wore swords
> That had been seasoned in the wars, and all
> Were men well-born; the chivalry of France.
> In age and temper differing, they had yet
> One spirit ruling in each heart; alike
> (Save only one, hereafter to be named)
> Were bent upon undoing what was done:
> This was their rest and only hope; therewith
> No fear had they of bad becoming worse,
> For worst to them was come; nor would have stirred,
> Or deemed it worth a moment's thought to stir,
> In anything, save only as the act
> Looked thitherward.   One, reckoning by years,
> Was in the prime of manhood, and erewhile
> He had sate lord in many tender hearts;
> Though heedless of such honours now, and changed:
> His temper was quite mastered by the times,
> And they had blighted him, had eaten away
> The beauty of his person, doing wrong
> Alike to body and to mind: his port,
> Which once had been erect and open, now
> Was stooping and contracted, and a face,
> Endowed by Nature with her fairest gifts
> Of symmetry and light and bloom, expressed,
> As much as any that was ever seen,
> A ravage out of season, made by thoughts
> Unhealthy and vexatious.   With the hour,
> That from the press of Paris duly brought
> Its freight of public news, the fever came,
> A punctual visitant, to shake this man,
> Disarmed his voice and fanned his yellow cheek
> Into a thousand colours; while he read,
> Or mused, his sword was haunted by his touch
> Continually, like an uneasy place
> In his own body.   'Twas in truth an hour
> Of universal ferment; mildest men

Were agitated; and commotions, strife
Of passions and opinions, filled the walls
Of peaceful houses with unquiet sounds.
The soil of common life, was, at that time,
Too hot to tread upon.   Oft said I then,
And not then only, "What a mockery this
Of history, the past and that to come!
Now do I feel how all men are deceived,
Reading of nations and their works, in faith,
Faith given to vanity and emptiness;
Oh! laughter for the page that would reflect
To future times the face of what now is!"
The land all swarmed with passion, like a plain
Devoured by locusts,—Carra, Gorsas,—add
A hundred other names, forgotten now,
Nor to be heard of more; yet, they were powers,
Like earthquakes, shocks repeated day by day,
And felt through every nook of town and field.

Such was the state of things.   Meanwhile the chief
Of my associates stood prepared for flight
To augment the band of emigrants in arms
Upon the borders of the Rhine, and leagued
With foreign foes mustered for instant war.
This was their undisguised intent, and they
Were waiting with the whole of their desires
The moment to depart.
                         An Englishman,
Born in a land whose very name appeared
To license some unruliness of mind;
A stranger, with youth's further privilege,
And the indulgence that a half-learnt speech
Wins from the courteous; I, who had been else
Shunned and not tolerated, freely lived
With these defenders of the Crown, and talked,
And heard their notions; nor did they disdain
The wish to bring me over to their cause.

But though untaught by thinking or by books
To reason well of polity or law,
And nice distinctions, then on every tongue,
Of natural rights and civil; and to acts
Of nations and their passing interests,

(If with unworldly ends and aims compared)
Almost indifferent, even the historian's tale
Prizing but little otherwise than I prized
Tales of the poets, as it made the heart
Beat high, and filled the fancy with fair forms,
Old heroes and their sufferings and their deeds;
Yet in the regal sceptre, and the pomp
Of orders and degrees, I nothing found
Then, or had ever, even in crudest youth,
That dazzled me, but rather what I mourned
And ill could brook, beholding that the best
Ruled not, and feeling that they ought to rule.

For, born in a poor district, and which yet
Retaineth more of ancient homeliness,
Than any other nook of English ground,
It was my fortune scarcely to have seen,
Through the whole tenour of my school-day time,
The face of one, who, whether boy or man,
Was vested with attention or respect
Through claims of wealth or blood; nor was it least
Of many benefits, in later years
Derived from academic institutes
And rules, that they held something up to view
Of a Republic, where all stood thus far
Upon equal ground; that we were brothers all
In honour, as in one community,
Scholars and gentlemen; where, furthermore,
Distinction open lay to all that came,
And wealth and titles were in less esteem
Than talents, worth, and prosperous industry.
Add unto this, subservience from the first
To presences of God's mysterious power
Made manifest in Nature's sovereignty,
And fellowship with venerable books,
To sanction the proud workings of the soul,
And mountain liberty. It could not be
But that one tutored thus should look with awe
Upon the faculties of man, receive
Gladly the highest promises, and hail,
As best, the government of equal rights
And individual worth. And hence, O Friend!
If at the first great outbreak I rejoiced

Less than might well befit my youth, the cause
In part lay here, that unto me the events
Seemed nothing out of nature's certain course,
A gift that was come rather late than soon.
No wonder, then, if advocates like these,
Inflamed by passion, blind with prejudice,
And stung with injury, at this riper day,
Were impotent to make my hopes put on
The shape of theirs, my understanding bend
In honour to their honour: zeal, which yet
Had slumbered, now in opposition burst
Forth like a Polar summer: every word
They uttered was a dart, by counterwinds
Blown back upon themselves; their reason seemed
Confusion-stricken by a higher power
Than human understanding, their discourse
Maimed, spiritless; and, in their weakness strong,
I triumphed.[1]

Thus the early events of the war, which were so disastrous and so humiliating for the French arms, raised the hopes of the officers of Bassigny, but brought the keenest disappointment to Wordsworth. While at Mons the troops of Biron dispersed with cries of treason when there was no enemy before them; two thousand men commanded by General Dillon, in obedience to a similar panic, or possibly to the same watch-word, fell back upon Lille at the sight of a few Austrian regiments, and there murdered their general. On 17th May Wordsworth wrote from Blois to one of his Cambridge friends:

" The horrors excited by the relation of the events consequent upon the commencement of hostilities is general. Not but that there are some men who feel a gloomy satisfaction from a measure which seemed to put the patriot army out of a possibility of success. An ignominious flight, the massacre of their general, a dance performed with savage joy round his burning body, the murder of six prisoners, are events which would have arrested the attention of the reader of the annals of Morocco." In the same letter he expresses the fear that the patriots will be

[1] *The Prelude*, ix. 125-262.

completely routed. "Suppose that the German army is
at the gates of Paris, what will be the consequence? It
will be impossible for it to make any material alterations in
the constitution; impossible to reinstate the clergy in its
ancient guilty splendour; impossible to restore an existence to the noblesse similar to that it before enjoyed;
impossible to add much to the authority of the king. Yet
there are in France some millions—I speak without
exaggeration—who expect that this will take place." [1]

Wordsworth's fears gave way to confidence and enthusiasm when he watched battalions of volunteers marching past him, all impatient to avenge these early humilia-
tions. Many of these bands were levied in the south-west,
and passed through Blois, where a departmental battalion
was also in course of formation. Among volunteer forces
like these, acts of pillage and plunder were certain to
occur, and in determining the details of those committed
by many of these troops, some historians have shown
a tendency to lose sight of the real magnanimity and true
beauty of the whole movement. It may therefore be of
service to learn the impression which this spectacle
produced upon a foreigner. It will be seen that Wordsworth is in thorough agreement with the "legend," and
readers will conclude therefrom that upon the whole the
legendary is perhaps more trustworthy than the historical
version.

> Meantime, day by day, the roads
> Were crowded with the bravest youth of France,
> And all the promptest of her spirits, linked
> In gallant soldiership, and posting on
> To meet the war upon her frontier bounds.
> Yet at this very moment [2] do tears start
> Into mine eyes: I do not say I weep—
> I wept not then,—but tears have dimmed my sight,
> In memory of the farewells of that time,
> Domestic severings, female fortitude
> At dearest separation, patriot love

[1] Letter to Mathews, 17th May 1792. Knight, *Life of Wordsworth*, i.
p. 64.
[2] In 1804.

And self-devotion, and terrestrial hope,
Encouraged with a martyr's confidence ;
Even files of strangers merely seen but once,
And for a moment, men from far with sound
Of music, martial tunes, and banners spread,
Entering the city, here and there a face,
Or person singled out among the rest,
Yet still a stranger and beloved as such ;
Even by these passing spectacles my heart
Was oftentimes uplifted, and they seemed
Arguments sent from Heaven to prove the cause
Good, pure, which no one could stand up against,
Who was not lost, abandoned, selfish, proud,
Mean, miserable, wilfully depraved,
Hater perverse of equity and truth.[1]

These are the feelings of a patriot. Wordsworth was no longer an amazed or indifferent spectator of the drama of the revolution ; he had chosen a side, and was now a proselyte. This was due to an intimacy he had formed with a man who had taught him to understand and to love the Revolution—namely, Michel Beaupuy, who at that time was merely a captain in the little garrison of Blois.[2]

II

Born at Mussidan in 1755, Beaupuy belonged to the lesser nobility of Périgord. From the commencement of the Revolution his whole family had been remarkable for its liberal spirit. In 1789 there were five brothers of the name. Nicolas, the eldest, became a member of the Legislative Assembly, and on the expiration of his term of office displayed excellent judgment in bringing the new *régime* into working order in his native town, which he preserved from the excesses of the Terror. The youngest, who had entered holy orders, hastened to take the oath of allegiance to the Constitution. The three others fell a few years later, fighting in the service of new France.

[1] *The Prelude*, ix. 262-287.
[2] For further details concerning Beaupuy, see *Le Général Michel Beaupuy*, by Georges Bussière and Emile Legouis (Paris, 1891).

Employed since 1771 as a private soldier, Michel Beaupuy had travelled with his regiment from one garrison to another throughout the whole of France, and had found in the course of this wandering life opportunities of studying the wrongs, the needs, and the undefined aspirations of his country.   Accordingly, when, provided with the proxy of his widowed mother, he took part in the election of the States-general, he hinted to the nobles of Périgord that the sacrifice of their time-honoured privileges was essential to the welfare of the country. When the elections were over he rejoined his regiment, of which he was made a captain in September 1791.   But his attitude of resolute adherence to the principle of reform was regarded by those of noble rank among his brother officers as an act of treason to the common cause.   They accused him of contracting degrading associations, and gave him the cold shoulder.   Wordsworth, who made his acquaintance at this time, was surprised at the ostracism to which he was subjected, and discerned in the despised captain a hero and a man of true wisdom.

> Among that band of Officers was one,
> Already hinted at, of other mould—
> A patriot, thence rejected by the rest,
> And with an oriental loathing spurned,
> As of a different caste.   A meeker man
> Than this lived never, nor a more benign,
> Meek though enthusiastic.   Injuries
> Made *him* more gracious, and his nature then
> Did breathe its sweetness out most sensibly,
> As aromatic flowers on Alpine turf,
> When foot had crushed them.   He through the events
> Of that great change wandered in perfect faith,
> As through a book, an old romance, or tale
> Of Fairy, or some dream of actions wrought
> Behind the summer clouds.   By birth he ranked
> With the most noble, but unto the poor
> Among mankind he was in service bound,
> As by some tie invisible, oaths professed
> To a religious order.   Man he loved
> As man; and, to the mean and the obscure,
> And all the homely in their homely works,

Transferred a courtesy which had no air
Of condescension ; but did rather seem
A passion and a gallantry, like that
Which he, a soldier, in his idler day
Had paid to woman : somewhat vain he was,
Or seemed so, yet it was not vanity,
But fondness, and a kind of radiant joy
Diffused around him, while he was intent
On works of love or freedom, or revolved
Complacently the progress of a cause,
Whereof he was a part : yet this was meek
And placid, and took nothing from the man
That was delightful.[1]

Beaupuy was near the close of his thirty-seventh year ;
Wordsworth was only twenty-two. In the friendship
which was speedily formed between them, there was a
genuine deference on the poet's part. Beaupuy, moreover,
was not his superior in years alone ; he was a man rich in the
knowledge of philosophers and political writers with whose
teachings Wordsworth was little acquainted. "Philosophy" was the passion of his family. He and his brothers
were less proud of their titles than of their ancestor
Montaigne, from whom they were descended on the female
side. The house at Mussidan in which they were born contained a huge library, where not one of the great authors of
the eighteenth century was missing, and the folios of the
Encyclopædia towered above the rest. In an address to
the assembly of the three orders of Périgord, on the 31st
July 1789, Lamarque, the future member of the Convention, had sounded the praises not only of Michel Beaupuy
but also of "his three brothers, philosophers as well
as warriors," and of his mother "who, like the Spartan
matrons, combined devotion to her country with the
virtues of her sex."[2] With such an education and training, Beaupuy was well qualified to instruct Wordsworth in
those principles of which the young man lamented his own
ignorance. Slighted by his comrades, the captain found it
delightful to lay bare his mind before one who listened

---

[1] *The Prelude*, ix. 288-321.   [2] *Le Général Michel Beaupuy*, pp. 20-21.

with such attention to his ideas and dreams. For nearly three months the two men were inseparable.

In order to understand Beaupuy's influence over Wordsworth, we must retrace our steps, and consider, from the evidence Wordsworth himself affords, what place humanity had, up to that time, occupied in his thoughts. In childhood he had regarded man merely as a part of the pageant of nature. The shepherds of his mountains, changed and magnified by their natural surroundings, had loomed before him like apparitions.

> A rambling schoolboy, thus
> I felt [man's] presence in his own domain,
> As of a lord and master, or a power,
> Or genius, under Nature, under God,
> Presiding; and severest solitude
> Had more commanding looks when he was there.
> When up the lonely brooks on rainy days
> Angling I went, or trod the trackless hills
> By mists bewildered, suddenly mine eyes
> Have glanced upon him distant a few steps,
> In size a giant, stalking through thick fog,
> His sheep like Greenland bears; or, as he stepped
> Beyond the boundary line of some hill-shadow
> His form hath flashed upon me, glorified
> By the deep radiance of the setting sun;
> Or him have I descried in distant sky,
> A solitary object and sublime,
> Above all height! like an aerial cross
> Stationed alone upon a spiry rock
> Of the Chartreuse, for worship.[1]

What a happy result of an optical phenomenon! All unknown to himself, Wordsworth was led by these means to a reverence for human nature. He congratulates himself not only on having had better examples of life around him in his childhood than most children have, but also that in this manner he saw man as purified by distance. He rejoices that he was not brought too early into contact with the ugliness of crowded life, that he did not too soon become acquainted with the irony and the

[1] *The Prelude*, viii. 256-275.

:ontemptuous laughter which arise at the sight of its
deformities, and, by lowering our conception of humanity,
pursue the mind desirous of devoting itself to the human
race, even "into the temple and the temple's heart."[1]

At Cambridge he was for the first time brought face
to face with the fevered passions, the personal fads and
idiosyncrasies, which eclipse "the impersonated thought,
the idea, or abstraction of the kind." There, too, he
found himself in close neighbourhood with vice: '

> I trembled,—thought, at times, of human life
> With an indefinite terror and dismay,
> Such as the storms and angry elements
> Had bred in me ; but gloomier far, a dim
> Analogy to uproar and misrule,
> Disquiet, danger, and obscurity.[2]

Conscious, however, of his own ignorance, he reassured
himself with the thought " that, by acting well, and understanding," he would " learn to love the end of life."[3]

In London, the vastness of the town, the splendour of
its memorials, and the solitary life he led enabled him to
recover that comprehensive idea of mankind as a unity,
which at Cambridge had become resolved into a con-
fused mass of disconnected details. Then he understood
that the human nature to which he was conscious of
belonging

> Was not a punctual presence, but a spirit
> Diffused through time and space, with aid derived
> Of evidence from monuments, erect,
> Prostrate, or leaning towards their common rest
> In earth, the widely scattered wreck sublime
> Of vanished nations.[4]

Amidst the London crowds he felt " the unity of man ";
he perceived

> One spirit over ignorance and vice
> Predominant in good and evil hearts ;

[1] *The Prelude*, viii. 293-340.
[3] *Ibid.*, viii. 528-530.
[2] *Ibid.*, viii. 513-519.
[4] *Ibid.*, viii. 608-619.

> One sense for moral judgments, as one eye
> For the sun's light.[1]

Thus Wordsworth had early acquired, and had persistently maintained, a lofty idea of man and of his earthly destiny. Nevertheless, man's place in his heart was subordinate to that occupied by Nature;

> a passion, she,
> A rapture often, and immediate love
> Ever at hand; he, only a delight
> Occasional, an accidental grace,
> His hour being not yet come.

Nor was it to come until Wordsworth had seen "two-and-twenty summers," that is to say, until he had made the acquaintance of Beaupuy.[2]   Wordsworth loved man with the imagination, Beaupuy with the heart.   Wordsworth had a feeling for the poetical aspect of the past, and for the beauty of nature.   Beaupuy was too much absorbed by his religion of humanity to shed any tears over things which were old and passing away, or to go into raptures over a landscape.   The contrast between the two minds has been acutely observed by the poet.

They would set off alone to walk beside the Loire, "innocent yet of civil slaughter," or in the forests of Blois, of Russy, of Boulogne, and of Marchenoir,—

> wide forests of continuous shade,
> Lofty and over-arched, with open space
> Beneath the trees, clear footing many a mile.[3]

Their talk was usually of

> the end
> Of civil government, and its wisest forms;
> Of ancient loyalty, and chartered rights,
> Custom and habit, novelty and change;
> Of self-respect, and virtue in the few
> For patrimonial honour set apart,
> And ignorance in the labouring multitude.

---

[1] *The Prelude*, viii. 667-674.   [2] *Ibid.*, viii. 340-357.
[3] *Ibid.*, ix. 431-437.

Their guide was Montesquieu; inspired by him, Beaupuy was " to all intolerance indisposed," and Wordsworth,

> who, at that time, was scarcely dipped
> Into the turmoil, bore a sounder judgment
> Than later days allowed ;

he was not yet led astray by the fierceness of the struggle, nor blinded by the interests of the moment.[1]

Nevertheless, though they were not " obstinate to find error without excuse upon the side " of those who strove against them, their chief delight was in picturing to themselves the miseries

> Of royal courts, and that voluptuous life
> Unfeeling, where the man who is of soul
> The meanest thrives the most ; where dignity,
> True personal dignity, abideth not ;
> A light, and cruel, and vain world cut off
> From the natural inlets of just sentiment,
> From lowly sympathy and chastening truth :
> Where good and evil interchange their names.[2]

Following Rousseau, they took especial delight also in glorifying " man and his noble nature." They shared the faith of their age in the infinite perfectibility of the human race, a subject which at that very time was occupying the thoughts of Condorcet and of Godwin. Man's blind desires would impel him to break his bondage ; his higher faculties, " capable of clear truth," would enable him to build liberty on firm foundations. " Social life, through knowledge spreading and imperishable," would thereby be rendered

> As just in regulation, and as pure
> As individual in the wise and good.

In support of these daring visions they invoked the testimony of ancient history,—at that time held in such high honour,—and

---

[1] *The Prelude*, ix. 321-340.   [2] *Ibid.*, ix. 340-354.

> thought of each bright spot,
> That would be found in all recorded time,
> Of truth preserved and error passed away ;
> Of single spirits that catch the flame from Heaven,
> And how the multitudes of men will feed
> And fan each other.

Since their enthusiasm had no object so narrow as the deliverance of a single nation, and since they had imbibed from their age that universal love of mankind which, in spite of its vague and fragile nature, remains nevertheless one of the brightest features of the eighteenth century, they remembered with joy how sects have been

> Triumphant over every obstacle
> Of custom, language, country, love, or hate ;

how " scattered tribes have made one body, spreading wide as clouds in heaven." They did not need to look to the past for a confirmation of their hopes ; " we found "

> A living confirmation of the whole
> Before us, in a people from the depth
> Of shameful imbecility uprisen,
> Fresh as the morning star. Elate we looked
> Upon their virtues ; saw, in rudest men,
> Self-sacrifice the firmest ; generous love,
> And continence of mind, and sense of right,
> Uppermost in the midst of fiercest strife.[1]

Such were the sentiments of Beaupuy, and from the outset they were echoed by Wordsworth. But if a pause occurred in the conversation, imagination soon wafted the poet far from the land of reality. His thoughts fled to other days

> When o'er those interwoven roots, moss-clad,
> And smooth as marble or a waveless sea,

[1] *The Prelude*, ix. 364-390.

Some Hermit, from his cell forth-strayed, might pace
In sylvan meditation undisturbed.

If he heard the distant hoof-beats of an unseen horse ringing on the hard soil, it was the flying palfrey of Erminia or
Angelica, the mounted heroines of Tasso and Ariosto. A
sudden burst of music, or the din of boisterous merriment
seemed to come

from haunt
Of Satyrs in some viewless glade, with dance
Rejoicing o'er a female in the midst,
A mortal beauty, their unhappy thrall.
The width of those huge forests, unto me
A novel scene, did often in this way
Master my fancy while I wandered on
With that revered companion.[1]

At times the young Englishman's piety, before all things,
let it be remembered, of a poetical character, broke
through his new revolutionary fervour, which, though
doubtless sincere, was as yet not deeply felt.

And sometimes—
When to a convent in a meadow green,
By a brook-side, we came, a roofless pile,
And not by reverential touch of Time
Dismantled, but by violence abrupt—
In spite of those heart-bracing colloquies,
In spite of real fervour, and of that
Less genuine and wrought up within myself—
I could not but bewail a wrong so harsh.
And for the Matin-bell to sound no more
Grieved, and the twilight taper, and the cross
High on the topmost pinnacle, a sign
(How welcome to the weary traveller's eyes)
Of hospitality and peaceful rest.[2]

This romantic sympathy with the past, so weak in the
best among the revolutionists, so inveterate in the hearts
of Englishmen, was one of the points on which Wordsworth was still at variance with Beaupuy. When, in the
course of their walks, they obtained a view of one of the
old castles which are the glory of that district, Blois,

[1] *The Prelude*, ix. 437-465. [2] *Ibid.*, ix. 465-479.

Chambord, Montrichard, Chaumont, Romorantin, and many others, the sight would create very different impressions on the minds of the two friends. The thought of the vices and excesses which had been proudly flaunted in these palaces filled Beaupuy with passionate indignation.

> Imagination, potent to inflame
> At times with virtuous wrath and noble scorn,
> Did often also mitigate the force
> Of civic prejudice, the bigotry,
> So call it, of a youthful patriot's mind ;
> And on these spots with many gleams I looked
> Of chivalrous delight.[1]

But, in compensation for this, his English instincts made it easy for Wordsworth to understand the advantages that would accrue from certain reforms which Beaupuy desired to see permanently secured to his country. A faith in the suppression of *lettres de cachet*, and secret condemnations, was " enough to animate the mind that ever turned a thought to human welfare." Beaupuy, moreover, perceived that his friend was more easily to be captivated through his imagination than by argument, and occasionally introduced some moving tale of passion to illustrate the iniquities of the past. Wordsworth heard with emotion the " true " story of *Vaudracour and Julia*, which proved

> to what low depth had struck the roots,
> How widely spread the boughs, of that old tree
> Which, as a deadly mischief, and a foul
> And black dishonour, France was weary of.

Vaudracour, a youth of noble rank in Auvergne, fell in love with a girl of low station, and determined to marry her, but a sealed order, which his father obtained from the king, prevented him from carrying out his intention. He was thrown into prison, and only obtained his liberty by taking an oath to renounce his mistress. Could he find the courage to keep such an oath ? The lovers met once more, but were again torn asunder with violence. Julia became a mother, and was thrust into a convent. The child was left to the care of Vaudracour, who withdrew to

---

[1] *The Prelude*, ix. 479-501.

a lodge in the depths of a forest, with no other companion
than the infant, which shortly fell ill and died.

> Nor could the voice of Freedom, which through France
> Full speedily resounded, public hope,
> Or personal memory of his own worst wrongs,
> Rouse him ; but hidden in those gloomy shades,
> His days he wasted,—an imbecile mind.[1]

Beaupuy was not contented with telling Wordsworth
stories of the evils which existed under the old *régime,*
but, better still, made him lay his finger on the wounds
which it had inflicted, and pointed out the remedies to
which his own vows and efforts were directed.

> We chanced
> One day to meet a hunger-bitten girl,
> Who crept along fitting her languid gait
> Unto a heifer's motion, by a cord
> Tied to her arm, and picking thus from the lane
> Its sustenance, while the girl with pallid hands
> Was busy knitting in a heartless mood
> Of solitude, and at the sight my friend
> In agitation said, "'Tis against *that*
> That we are fighting," I with him believed
> That a benignant spirit was abroad
> Which might not be withstood, that poverty
> Abject as this would in a little time
> Be found no more, that we should see the earth
> Unthwarted in her wish to recompense
> The meek, the lowly, patient child of toil,
> All institutes for ever blotted out
> That legalised exclusion, empty pomp
> Abolished, sensual state and cruel power,

---

[1] *The Prelude,* ix. 547-585. In *The Prelude,* ix. 548, Wordsworth states
clearly that this tale was narrated to him by Beaupuy. Finding it too long
for *The Prelude,* he published it separately in 1820 under the title of *Vaudracour and Julia.* In a note dictated near the close of his life he contradicts the
statement he had made in *The Prelude.* He had the story, he says, "from
the mouth of a French lady, who had been an eye-and-ear-witness of all
that was done and said." "Many long years after," he adds, "I was told
that *Dupligne* was then a monk in the convent of La Trappe." It appears,
therefore, that the real name of the unfortunate hero was Dupligne. As to
the contradiction between the statement in *The Prelude* and the note which
was added so much later, we shall naturally place confidence in Wordsworth's memory at thirty-five rather than at sixty-five.

> Whether by edict of the one ar few ;
> And finally, as sum and crown of all,
> Should see the people having a strong hand
> In framing their own laws ; whence better days
> To all mankind.[1]

Possibly this commonplace incident, with the phrase "*'Tis against that that we are fighting,*" which assuredly was uttered with the noble fire of passion, did more than all the rest to complete Wordsworth's conversion. With him, as with Beaupuy, the heart was henceforth enlisted in the revolutionary cause, as well as the mind. He had found a religion—that of pity and love for the wretched, combined with the hope of improving their condition. The remainder of the structure built up by the reasonings of Beaupuy was but fragile, and lasted in fact merely for a time. The only part of it to endure throughout every other change was the interest in the poor, on which it was founded. Though he afterwards became a thoroughgoing Conservative, in this sense Wordsworth could say to the end that there was still a good deal of the *socialist* and *chartist* in him.

One by one the young Englishman's last defences had given way before the fervent preaching of Beaupuy. Wordsworth became bound to him with the deferential attachment of a disciple. Passionately in love with devotion and sacrifice, Beaupuy in Wordsworth's eyes was the ideal at once of a warrior and of a citizen, and remained for him the type of the soldier-philosopher. The thought

---

[1] *The Prelude,* ix. 509-532. In 1792 he expressed the same thought as follows in the singular style of his early pieces :—

> No more, along thy vales and viny groves,
> Whole hamlets disappearing as he moves,
> With cheeks o'erspread by smiles of baleful glow,
> On his pale horse shall fell Consumption go.

Seventeen years earlier Jekyll had been similarly impressed by the destitution prevalent in the neighbourhood of Blois. "The peasants of this part of France," he wrote, "are miserably poor. The girls who herd the cows are always at work with their distaffs, and the cap is always clean and perhaps laced, while the feet are without shoes and stockings."—*Letters of Joseph Jekyll,* op. cit.

This interesting parallel has been pointed out by Mr Thomas Hutchinson in the *Academy* of March 17th, 1894.

that Beaupuy would shed his blood for his ideals of peace
and happiness heightened the attraction of his eloquence.
Addressing Coleridge, with whom, at a later period, he
frequently conversed on philosophy, Wordsworth exclaimed :—

> Oh, sweet it is, in academic groves,
> Or such retirement, Friend! as we have known
> In the green dales beside our Rotha's stream,
> Greta, or Derwent, or some nameless rill,
> To ruminate, with interchange of talk,
> On rational liberty, and hope in man,
> Justice and peace.   But far more sweet such toil—
> Toil, say I, for it leads to thoughts abstruse,
> If nature then be standing on the brink
> Of some great trial, and we hear the voice
> Of one devoted,—one whom circumstance
> Hath called upon to embody his deep sense
> In action, give it outwardly a shape,
> And that of benediction, to the world.
> Then doubt is not, and truth is more than truth,—
> A hope it is, and a desire ; a creed
> Of zeal, by an authority Divine
> Sanctioned, of danger, difficulty, or death.
> Such conversation, under Attic shades,
> Did Dion hold with Plato ; ripened thus
> For a deliverer's glorious task,—and such
> He, on that ministry already bound,
> Held with Eudemus and Timonides,
> Surrounded by adventurers in arms,
> When those two vessels with their daring freight,
> For the Sicilian Tyrant's overthrow,
> Sailed from Zacynthus,—philosophic war,
> Led by Philosophers.   With harder fate,
> Though like ambition, such was he, O Friend !
> Of whom I speak.   So BEAUPUY (let the name
> Stand near the worthiest of Antiquity)
> Fashioned his life ; and many a long discourse,
> With like persuasion honoured, we maintained :
> He, on his part, accoutred for the worst,
> He perished fighting, in supreme command,
> Upon the borders of the unhappy Loire,
> For liberty, against deluded men,

His fellow country-men ; and yet most blessed
In this, that he the fate of later times
Lived not to see, nor what we now behold,
Who have as ardent hearts as he had then.[1]

On the 27th July 1792, Beaupuy parted from Wordsworth for active service with his regiment on the Rhine.
The two friends never met again. The war which speedily
broke out between France and England soon prevented
them even from hearing of each other. Wordsworth was
wrongly informed when he supposed that Beaupuy had
perished in Vendée, where, it is true, he was dangerously
wounded. His career was of longer duration than
Wordsworth imagined. But the latter was not mistaken
in his estimate of the high qualities possessed by the
captain of Blois. It has been found possible to piece
together his whole life as a soldier, yet no traits but
those of heroism, earnest proselytism, humanity and
unchanging sincerity have been revealed. Whether at
Mayence, where he was one of the most active among
the noble defenders of the beleaguered city ; in Vendée,
where he contributed no less than Kleber and Marceau
to destroy the great army of that province, where, also,
he was, perhaps, the first who determined to make a
trial of clemency and pardon combined with good faith ;
on the Rhine under Pichegru and Moreau, down to the
battle of the Elz on the 19th November 1796 in which
he was killed, throughout he remained worthy of the
panegyric written in memory of him by the English
poet. Brave to rashness, modest to self-effacement, it
is his most distinctive characteristic that in the face of
the severest trials he preserved unimpaired that faith in
a better future, and that kindness of heart, which inspired him in the beginning. He was one of the true
knights-errant of the Revolution. In his last hour he
might have repeated the declaration recorded, less
than a year after he had parted from Wordsworth, in
his journal of the siege of Mayence : "I have zealously

[1] *The Prelude*, ix. 390-430. This passage was written shortly after the
coronation of Napoleon.

kept my oath of apostleship on every occasion that has presented itself." [1]

Wordsworth, on whom, as we have just seen, this mission of persuasion had been so successfully exercised, did not remain long at Blois after the departure of his friend. He was still there when the king was deposed after the memorable 10th August, but he returned immediately afterwards to Orleans, where he remained during the September massacres. [2] Those " lamentable " crimes did not chill his enthusiasm ; almost before they had ceased, Wordsworth was ready to believe that such horrors were for ever at an end ;

> Ephemeral monsters, to be seen but once !
> Things that could only show themselves and die. [3]

The great events which marked the close of the same month filled his heart with hope. The patriots stood their ground bravely under the cannonade of Valmy, and the Prussians fled before their " anticipated quarry."

> The State, as if to stamp the final seal
> On her security, and to the world
> Show what she was, a high and fearless soul,
> Exulting in defiance, or heart-stung
> By sharp resentment, or belike to taunt
> With spiteful gratitude the baffled League,
> That had stirred up her slackening faculties
> To a new transition, when the King was crushed,
> Spared not the empty throne, and in proud haste
> Assumed the body and venerable name
> Of a Republic. [4]

The sound of that one word was truly intoxicating in Wordsworth's ear. Left alone on the banks of the Loire, he completed his *Descriptive Sketches*, which afford evidence, still more striking than any contained in *The Prelude*, of the metamorphosis which was then taking place within him. The tone of this poem, which at first represents him as overwhelmed with despair, changes

---

[1] *Le Général Beaupuy*, op. cit., p. 86.
[2] *Autobiographical Memoranda*, op. cit.
[3] *The Prelude*, x. 41-47.
[4] *Ibid.*, x. 31-41.

towards its close. The whole face of nature, in which, but a short while ago, he found the reflection of his own sadness, seems to smile. It has been transformed by the advent of Liberty. France, that fair favoured region which his soul was to "love, till Life had broke her golden bowl,"[1] shone with new glory on the day when she ceased to be a monarchy and became a republic.

> Yes, as I roam'd where Loiret's waters glide
> Thro' rustling aspens heard from side to side,
> When from October clouds a milder light
> Fell, where the blue flood rippled into white,
> Methought from every cot the watchful bird
> Crowed with ear-piercing power till then unheard ;
> Each clacking mill, that broke the murmuring streams,
> Rock'd the charm'd thought in more delightful dreams ;
> Chasing those long long dreams the falling leaf
> Awoke a fainter pang of moral grief ;
> The measured echo of the distant flail
> Winded in sweeter cadence down the vale ;
> A more majestic tide the water roll'd
> And glowed the sun-gilt groves in richer gold.[2]

What though the war of liberty should spread fire and sword throughout the land !

> Lo ! from th' innocuous flames, a lovely birth !
> With its own Virtues springs another earth :
> Nature, as in her prime, her virgin reign
> Begins, and Love and Truth compose her train.[3]

Now that he is familiar with the language, and has himself become a Frenchman in heart and spirit,[4] he is impatient for another sight of Paris, the scene of so many events on which the destinies of all France have hung.

---

[1] *Descriptive Sketches*, 740-1.   [2] *Ibid.*, 760-773.
[3] *Ibid.*, 782-785.
[4] In *The Excursion*, the Solitary, who at the time of the Revolution had never quitted England, is made to say
> What, though in my veins
> There flowed no Gallic blood, nor had I breathed
> The air of France, not less than Gallic zeal
> Kindled and burnt among the sapless twigs
> Of my exhausted heart.   (*The Excursion*, iii. 741-5.)

III

In the month of October, on a still " day, as beautiful as e'er was given to soothe regret, though deepening what it soothed," he paused by the side of the Loire to bid a long farewell to all its

> rich domains, vineyard and tilth,
> Green meadow-ground, and many-coloured woods;

and then, leaving the quiet scene behind him, turned his face towards the turbulent metropolis.[1]

The sight of Paris very soon brought back his restless agitation. He began to range the streets with an ardour previously unfelt; he passed by the prison of the Temple, where the unhappy king was confined with his wife and children; saw the Tuileries, "lately stormed with roar of cannon by a furious host"; and crossed the empty square of the Carrousel, "where so late had lain the dead, upon the dying heaped."

> I gazed
> On this and other spots, as doth a man
> Upon a volume whose contents he knows
> Are memorable, but from him locked up,
> Being written in a tongue he cannot read,
> So that he questions the mute leaves with pain,
> And half upbraids their silence. But that night
> I felt most deeply in what world I was,
> What ground I trod on, and what air I breathed.
> High was my room and lonely, near the roof
> Of a large mansion or hotel, a lodge
> That would have pleased me in more quiet times;
> Nor was it wholly without pleasure then.
> With unextinguished taper I kept watch,
> Reading at intervals; the fear gone by
> Pressed on me almost like a fear to come.
> I thought of those September massacres,
> Divided from me by one little month,
> Saw them and touched: the rest was conjured up
> From tragic fictions or true history,
> Remembrances and dim admonishments.

[1] *The Prelude,* x. 1-11.

The horse is taught his manage, and no star
Of wildest course but treads back his own steps;
For the spent hurricane the air provides
As fierce a successor; the tide retreats
But to return out of its hiding-place
In the great deep; all things have second birth;
The earthquake is not satisfied at once;
And in this way I wrought upon myself,
Until I seemed to hear a voice that cried,
To the whole city, "sleep no more." The trance
Fled with the voice to which it had given birth;
But vainly comments of a calmer mind
Promised soft peace and sweet forgetfulness.
The place, all hushed and silent as it was,
Appeared unfit for the repose of night,
Defenceless as a wood where tigers roam.[1]

The Prelude records in detail only one other recollection
of the ten weeks over which Wordsworth's stay in Paris
at that time extended. As he passed through the still
sleeping streets one morning on his way to the Palais-
Royal, there rose above the discordant clamour which
fell on his ears when he entered the Arcades the shrill
cry of newspaper-vendors bawling: "Denunciation of
the Crimes of Maximilian Robespierre!" And a hand
as prompt as the voice held out to him the speech which
Louvet had pronounced the day before against the delegate
from Arras, accusing him of aiming at the dictatorship,
and of having organised the September massacres. Wordsworth was impressed by Louvet's boldness in coming
forward alone to oppose the powerful Robespierre; but
the desertion of Louvet by the other members of the
Convention, and "the inglorious issue of that charge,"
which turned to the advantage of the accused, filled him
with mistrust and gloom. It grieved him to see

> That Heaven's best aid is wasted upon men
> Who to themselves are false.[2]

These symptoms of a lack of moral fibre in the representatives of the nation filled him with concern.

---

[1] *The Prelude*, x. 49-93.   [2] *Ibid.*, x. 94-120.

Seeing with my proper eyes
That Liberty, and Life, and Death would soon
To the remotest corners of the land
Lie in the arbitrement of those who ruled
The capital City ; what was struggled for,
And by what combatants victory must be won ;
The indecision on their part whose aim
Seemed best, and the straightforward path of those
Who in attack or in defence were strong
Through their impiety—my inmost soul
Was agitated ; yea, I could almost
Have prayed that throughout earth upon all men,
By patient exercise of reason made
Worthy of liberty, all spirits filled
With zeal expanding in Truth's holy light,
The gift of tongues might fall, and power arrive
From the four quarters of the winds to do
For France, what without help she could not do,
A work of honour.[1]

With him the only question was whether the Revolution would be completed by pure means, for he was as far from any doubt as to its ultimate success " as angels are from guilt." His was no slothful dejection. He sought remedies for the evils he saw.

An insignificant stranger and obscure,
And one, moreover, little graced with power
Of eloquence even in my native speech
And all unfit for tumult or intrigue,
Yet would I at this time with willing heart
Have undertaken for a cause so great
Service however dangerous.

He reflected that the destiny of man had always hung upon a few individuals ;

that there was,
Transcendent to all local patrimony,
One nature, as there is one sun in heaven ;
That objects, even as they are great, thereby
Do come within the reach of humblest eyes.

[1] *The Prelude*, x. 123-142.

It was his conviction that a spirit of steadfast hope, early trained to noble aspirations and always faithful to itself,

> Is for Society's unreasoning herd
> A domineering instinct, serves at once
> For way and guide, a fluent receptacle
> That gathers up each petty straggling rill
> And vein of water, glad to be rolled on
> In safe obedience.

He held that a mind which relies upon self-restraint, on prudence, and on simplicity, is rarely baffled in its aims or betrayed by others. And he reflected, lastly, that even if the perilous enterprise should end in death and defeat, he who had defied them at the bidding of conscience would meet the reward of its approbation.

On the other hand he remembered the common-places of the schools on the weakness of tyrants and the instability of their dominion, and, like Charlotte Corday shortly afterwards, called to mind Harmodius and Aristogiton, the deliverers of Athens from the despotism of Hipparchus. The tyrant fallen, everything once more became simple. He had no doubt that a man of genius could clear a passage for a just and stable government, as did the legislators of old, in the teeth of desperate opposition from enemies without, and in spite of the ignorance of a people misled by false teaching and invested with power before it had attained maturity.[1]

Still brooding over these noble schemes he returned to England in December 1792, forced, as he said at a later period, by the gracious providence of Heaven, though at the time he lamented the necessity. Had it not been for lack of money, which was the probable cause of his departure, he would doubtless have associated with the Girondists, who soon fell victims to the Mountain. "I," he says,

> Doubtless, I should have then made common cause
> With some who perished; haply perished too,
> A poor mistaken and bewildered offering,—
> Should to the breast of Nature have gone back,
> With all my resolutions, all my hopes,
> A Poet only to myself, to men
> Useless.[2]

[1] *The Prelude*, x. 142-221.   [2] *Ibid.*, x. 221-236.

CHAPTER III

Wordsworth as a Republican in England

I

WORDSWORTH returned to England a "patriot of the world." Anxious to follow from a near standpoint the great drama in which he had been prevented from taking an active part, he chose to remain in London in preference to the country. Nature had surrendered the first place in his thoughts to Humanity. Poetry was, for the time, laid aside. It is true that on his return he published the *Evening Walk* and the *Descriptive Sketches*, but his principal object in doing so was to prove to his friends and relations that, although he had gained but little credit at Cambridge, he nevertheless "could do something."[1] Moreover, the former of these poems had been composed at an earlier period; while the latter, written on the banks of the Loire, concluded, as we have seen, with a tribute in praise of France, the country to which he vows lifelong affection, and with fervent hopes that the irresistible waves of Freedom may sweep away for ever those presumptuous tyrants who cry, "Thus far and no farther." In poetry, however, there was not sufficient scope for the expression of the new ideas which he had brought from beyond the Channel. His soul was full of ardour, his brain of theories. Since in Paris he had been unable to throw himself into the thick of the conflict, he was impatient to take up arms in England on behalf of progress. London itself had lately been the scene of a humanitarian campaign, conducted by Clarkson and Wilberforce against the slave-trade. Although their first effort in Parliament, in April 1791, had proved a failure, they had not lost heart,

---

[1] Letter to Mathews. Knight, *Life of Wordsworth*, i. p. 91.

and were preparing to renew the struggle. It might be supposed that this reform would have attracted Wordsworth's passionate sympathy, but on the contrary he was almost indifferent to it, and was but little distressed at its unfortunate issue. To him it seemed to be a mere matter of detail on which it was useless to dwell. He had returned with the conviction

> That, if France prospered, good men would not long
> Pay fruitless worship to humanity,
> And this most rotten branch of human shame,
> Object, so seemed it, of superfluous pains,
> Would fall together with its parent tree.[1]

But England, as he now saw it, presented a disheartening spectacle. It was very different from the country he had quitted. At the time of his departure, near the end of 1791, England, though already divided in opinion, might be considered, as a whole, favourably disposed to the French Revolution. Its attitude was doubtless no longer so unanimously sympathetic as at first. Doubtless an eloquent voice had been raised within the walls of Parliament, and in the press, to warn the English nation that it could not lend countenance to the new legislators of France without being false to its own nature and its true sentiments. But great as was the celebrity of Burke's *Reflexions* (1790), the sensation they made seemed at first to be overwhelmed by the numerous and vehement rejoinders of his opponents. Fox and Sheridan replied to him in Parliament. Mackintosh, then a young man, acquired a sudden reputation by attempting to refute the *Reflexions* in his *Vindiciae Galliae* (1791). Whilst Mackintosh expressed the sympathies of the Liberal Whigs for the constitutional monarchy of England, Thomas Paine prepared the English radicals to receive without alarm, and even with feelings of envy, the news that a republic had arisen in France. And between applause from the one party and cries of horror from the other, Paine's *Rights of Man*[2] attained a notoriety which rivalled that of Burke's *Reflexions*.

[1] *The Prelude*, x. 244-262.
[2] The first part of *The Rights of Man* appeared in 1791, the second in 1792.

The partisans of the French Revolution did not all confine themselves to a theoretical sympathy. Many proposed that England should follow the example of France. The tendencies to reform which had appeared after the American war became bolder and more vigorous. Reformsocieties increased in number and importance, and began to concentrate, instead of diffusing, their efforts. The object of the *London Corresponding Society*, founded early in 1792 by the shoemaker Thomas Hardy, was to unite the whole forces of liberalism scattered throughout Great Britain. Its first demand was to be for electoral reform, as a necessary preliminary to all others, and it would be supported by newspapers, pamphlets, petitions and public meetings. The claim of the majority of these societies was for nothing less than universal suffrage.[1]

Up to that time the government had remained neutral, or, at any rate, whatever its mistrust of the reformers, had not resorted to persecution. The body of the nation, always slow to rouse itself, had not declared openly for one side or the other, and indeed was not to be set in motion without some more powerful stimulus than political doctrine, such as threats of war, an appeal to the patriotic war-spirit, or else the evident danger of a social upheaval on English soil. Nevertheless the reform party had had an opportunity, in the summer of 1791, of observing the feeling of ill-will which the lower classes entertained for them. The only riot which had as yet broken out had occurred in Birmingham, where, at the cry, "For Church and King," the homes and chapels of the dissenters had been sacked. Priestley the scientist had difficulty in escaping with his life. He was the most eminent of the dissenters, and belonged to the sect of Unitarians or Christian Rationalists, who made themselves remarkable by their revolutionary zeal. But this solitary outbreak had not seemed conclusive. The radicals, who belonged chiefly to the lower middle classes, but were supported by a few young men of the literary and various

[1] For information on this society see *The Story of the English Jacobins*, by Edward Smith, London, 1881.

other liberal professions, were as yet unaware of the isolated position which they occupied in the midst of the nation, between the equally hostile factions of government and populace.

Less than a year later they were to be enlightened, when they became compromised through their own imprudence. Exasperated by the Brunswick manifesto, their several societies, in September 1792, presented addresses to the Convention congratulating it on the success of its armies. Claiming to express the feelings "of a large majority" of the English people, they denounced the neutral attitude of their government. " Britons remain neutral!" they exclaimed. " O, shame!"[1] They declared their intention of making the French Republic their pattern, and foretold the advent of a Republic in Britain. " After the example which France has given, the science of revolutions will be rendered easy, and the progress of reason will be rapid. It would not be strange if, at a period far short of what we should venture to predict, addresses of solicitation should cross the seas to a National Convention in England."[2]

Wordsworth, who was then in Paris, may have heard these addresses read, and have listened to the cordial and equally imprudent answer made by the President of the Convention to the messengers of the Constitutional Society. But only after his return could he see the effect of these proceedings. A rigorous reaction made itself promptly felt. In the same month of November, John Reeves, ex-chief-justice of Newfoundland, founded an " Association for Preserving Liberty and Property against Republicans and Levellers."[3] Parliament was specially convened, and the speech from the throne, which was read on the 13th December, affirmed that a plot existed for the destruction of the Constitution, and for the overthrow of all order and all

[1] Address of the *London Corresponding Society* to the National Convention, 27th September 1792. *English Jacobins*, p. 47.

[2] Address from the Society for Constitutional information in London, to the National convention of France, 28th November 1793. *English Jacobins*, p. 49.

[3] *English Jacobins* p. 53.

government. The same date saw the commencement
of the prosecutions against every reformer who was
accused of having uttered seditious words, and written,
or merely circulated, revolutionary pamphlets. And on
the 18th December a prosecution was instituted, and judgment passed by default, against Thomas Paine for the publication of his *Rights of Man.* The veil which had
concealed the real opinion of England from the contending
parties was finally torn away in January, 1793. For
those who were alarmed, and those who were hesitating, the execution of Louis XVI. was the signal they
had been awaiting. The whole country caught the
infection of virtuous wrath, and the English patriots
easily persuaded themselves that their hatred of France
and her friends was nothing more than a hatred of crime
and wickedness. There was, as Wordsworth says, an
" idle cry of modish lamentation which has resounded from
the Court to the cottage." [1]

The ranks of those who had at first been ardent
supporters of the Revolution had daily grown thinner,
and now became almost entirely empty. The Whigs,
who had for some time already been conscious of their
mistake, went over in a body to the government. They
recognised that Burke's prophecies had been true. The
bloodshed in France, the proclamation of the Republic,
and the agitation for universal suffrage in England, had
awakened them from their vague dreams of philanthropy.
Their sympathy with the Revolution had been mainly
due to ignorance of the deep-seated forces behind it;
to them it had appeared nothing more than the abolition
of despotism. They had regarded it as an imitation of
their own revolution, and had found in the reflection
food for their national pride. They felt flattered that
after the interval of a century a hostile people should follow
their example, and find themselves the better for doing
so. They had watched with kindly eyes the first experiments in freedom made by the French nation, just as a
sturdy adult observes with interest the first hestitating
steps of an infant. Sensible that they were greatly in

[1] *The Prose Works of W. Wordsworth,* i. p. 4.

advance of their neighbours, they expected to maintain their lead, and thought that without endangering either their interests or their principles they might allow themselves the cheap but subtle gratification of behaving with generosity. Now, convinced of their error, they seized the opportunity of withdrawal.

Few occupied a more prominent position among them, none caused a greater stir by his recantation, than Richard Watson, the Bishop of Llandaff, who, on the 15th January 1793, published a sermon, followed by an appendix, entitled " Strictures on the French Revolution and the British Constitution." Watson was the nominal occupant of the chair of theology at Cambridge, and, although he had employed a substitute since his appointment to a bishopric, was consequenpy well known to Wordsworth. The son of a Westmoreland schoolmaster, and therefore also a fellow-countryman of the poet, Watson appeared hitherto to have borne the modesty of his antecedents in mind. He had been almost the only one among the Anglican clergy to persevere in the defence " of truth and political charity."[1] He was closely attached to Fox and the Whig party.[2] His enemies called him a " levelling prelate," and " the bishop of the dissenters," but their insults only brought him honour in the eyes of his friends. The boldness of his opinions had brought upon him the enmity of the king. At first Watson had regarded the Revolution with favour, and had only begun to entertain doubts about it after the massacres in September. He had not, however, at once withdrawn from his position. Indeed, on the eve of the trial of Louis XVI., he wrote to Talleyrand, exhorting him to entreat that the king might not be tried, but should be granted the use of one of his palaces, £4000 a year, and the right to live in France provided he did not commit treason in the future.[3] Upon the execution of Louis XVI. he decided to make a public recantation. His tract aroused the indignation of Wordsworth, who considered it the work of a renegade. The

[1] *The Prose Works of W. Wordsworth*, i. p. 4.
[2] See de Quincey, *The Lake Poets*, Coleridge.
[3] *Anecdotes of the life of Richard Watson*, London, 1817, p. 268.

subject of the sermon—a somewhat commonplace disquisition upon "The wisdom and goodness of God in having made both Rich and Poor"—was in itself calculated to offend him. But it was the appendix in particular which excited his disgust. Therein Watson passed sentence upon the government which had been established in France, and pronounced upon the English constitution an enthusiastic eulogy worthy of a faithful follower of Burke. Here and there the essay betrayed the aggravating optimism of the man who has been kindly treated by fortune, and is astonished at the outcry against a state of things which he himself has found so pleasant. Watson confessed that he could not in the least understand the efforts of his contemporaries at social reform. Were not the poor admirably provided for? Was not the tax collected for them enormous? Had they not hospitals, dispensaries, and assistance of every sort?[1]

There is nothing more irritating to the man who sees an evil with his own eyes, and feels himself the suffering it causes, than this blind tranquillity, this wilful ignoring of the evil. Accordingly Wordsworth could not refrain from raising a protest. He undertook to write a reply to the Bishop of Llandaff, and signed it "A Republican";[2] but the letter was not printed. Early in 1793 it was a difficult matter to find a publisher for republican professions of faith, and Wordsworth no doubt sent it to the Anglican bishop in manuscript. It shows how far Wordsworth had assimilated the ideas, and even the turn of mind, of the French Revolutionists. It is Burke whom he attacks in the person of Watson, and it is from Rousseau or his disciples that most of his arguments are derived.

[1] *The Prose Works of W. Wordsworth*, i. p. 27.
[2] Published under the title of *An Apology for the French Revolution*, in *The Prose Works of W. Wordsworth*, i. pp. 3-23.

II

In the first place Wordsworth rebukes Watson for his sentimental lamentations on the death of Louis XVI., and on the position in which the Catholic clergy were placed. If he " had attended to the history of the French Revolution as minutely as its importance demands," he would have been convinced of the " royal martyr's " guilt. He would have approved the measures which stripped the prelates " of the rewards of their vices and their crimes," in order to preserve some thousands of poor village curés from famine. As for the bloodstains which cause him to turn in horror " even from the altar of Liberty," he ought to take the trouble to find out who is responsible for them. He ought likewise to know " that a time of revolution is not the season of true Liberty," for Liberty is too often obliged " to borrow the very arms of Despotism in order to overthrow him, and, in order to reign in peace, must establish herself by violence. She deplores such stern necessity, but the safety of the people, her supreme law, is her consolation."

It was a sorry result that Watson, who had at first shewn himself favourable to the struggle of the French nation against an arbitrary power, and had approved of their resolve no longer to obey any laws but those enacted by the will of the nation in general, should now " dictate to the world a servile adoption of the British constitution." The French had seen no security for themselves but in a Republic. Had they in adopting a republican form of government exceeded the rights to which Watson so recently acknowledged that they were entitled ? Watson's theoretical argument against a republican constitution carried but little weight. He had called it the most oppressive form of government for the mass of the people, who were thus deceived by the semblance of freedom, while they lived under the most odious kind of tyranny, that of their equals. It was unworthy of a philosopher to offer an assertion in place of a demonstration. Watson had agreed with Burke that the people should be maintained in those prepossessions which render them submissive under their slavery and attached to their bondage. Clearly he had not taken the trouble to find conclusive arguments; he was well aware that "imprisonment and the pillory, strongest of auxiliaries," were on his side. Nothing could be easier than to repel his attack against the republican form of government.

And this is what Wordsworth undertakes to do. Starting from the premise that national ills arise from the conflicting interests of rulers and those whom they govern, he chants the praises of universal suffrage. He finds the people quite worthy to exercise the sovereign power, and perfectly capable of choosing their representatives. Corrupted by centuries of tyranny, they will no doubt go to extremes at first, but the restraining influence of education will soon have its effect. Instead of throwing ridicule upon the interference of labourers and artisans in matters of government, it would be better to rejoice in the thought that the unpretending sincerity of such men will cleanse the art of governing of its treacherous subtleties and hoary Machiavelism. Besides, the executive authority will be reduced to insignificance, for the people will willingly obey laws made by themselves for themselves.

Monarchy, on the other hand, even in a modified form, is opposed to reason. To place the power in the hands of a single individual for his lifetime, and to make it hereditary in one family, is to disregard "the eternal nature of man." The office of king is too severe a trial for human virtue.

In the next place Wordsworth repels Watson's attack on the principle of equality laid down by the Constituent Assembly. He shows that the French had not aimed at absolute equality, but had merely proposed to render it as thorough as possible. Society should afford security for the possession of property, but should also prevent wealth from becoming oppressive. The legislator ought therefore to abolish that "unnatural monster," the law of primogeniture. He ought to suppress privileged corporations and monopolies. His function should be the protection of private labour and the repeal of statutes designed to reduce wages. If the poor-rate is enormous, that is because there is too much poverty on the one hand and excessive wealth on the other. Wordsworth hopes that " the class of wretches called mendicants will not much longer shock the feelings of humanity." This end can only be realized through " some wise and salutary regulations counteracting that inequality among mankind which proceeds from the present *fixed* disproportion of their possessions." He demands neither an agrarian, nor a sumptuary law, but the abolition of the law of primogeniture, of corporations and highly-paid sinecures.

In the name of equality he requires, further, that titles, ribbons, " garters, and other badges of fictitious superiority " should be done away with.[1] He will have no hereditary nobility; for, however great the services a man has rendered, a reward descending to his remotest posterity, who may perhaps prove unworthy of him, is an excessive form of compensation. He is even opposed to the granting of distinctions for life, since no one can answer for a man's future conduct. He enters a protest against degrading forms of address expressive of respect, such as " most noble, most honourable, most high, most august," &c. He has yet further grievances against the nobility; it is they who are the cause of the stigma attaching to labour, and of the honour in which not only idleness, but also racing and gambling, the vices of the unoccupied classes, are held; and it is they who do most to promote the corruption of morals and the increase of prostitution, which " deluges " the streets, and to keep up, not only the hypocrisy of social relations, but also, by their example of servile behaviour towards the king, the servility of manners. If it is contended that royalty cannot exist without the nobility, that is a very good reason for desiring a Republic.

Wordsworth concludes with an inquiry into the enthusi-

---

[1] No doubt Beaupuy had inspired him with a contempt for these distinctions—"ces crachats et ces cordons," as he calls them in his Journal of the Siege of Mayence (*Le Général Michel Beaupuy*, p. 69). Nicolas Beaupuy, the eldest brother of Michel, had been the first to lay his cross of St Louis on the table of the Legislative Assembly on the 10th August 1792. He requested that it might be converted into a medal for the first officer who should distinguish himself by a brilliant action.

astic encomium pronounced by Watson on the British constitution. According to Watson the English people enjoy the greatest amount of liberty and equality which is consistent with social order. They are obedient only to the general will of the society of which they form a part. Wordsworth answers that so long as a single Englishman is deprived of the suffrage, he is a helot in the land of his birth. He reproaches Watson with imposing on the credulity of his fellow-countrymen, when he would persuade them that they have reached perfection in matters of government; and with following the detestable example of Burke, who, as he says, with "a refinement in cruelty superior to that which in the East yokes the living to the dead, strove to persuade us that we and our posterity to the end of time were riveted to a constitution by the indissoluble compact of—a dead parchment." He is surprised that Watson should have raised his voice during the present crisis without even alluding to parliamentary reform. He congratulates him on having always had satisfactory treatment in the English courts of justice. Though he does not mention his own grievances, the reader feels that Wordsworth is thinking of the corrupt or incapable judges who had not yet compelled the Earl of Lonsdale to surrender his patrimony. He asks the bishop whether, in spite of his own good fortune, he has not at some time met with a victim of legal proceedings. Finally, Watson has endeavoured to divert public attention from the weak points of the constitution and the misdeeds of those in power. He has sought to throw dust in the nation's eyes, instead of attempting to instruct it, and has "aimed an arrow at liberty and philosophy, the eyes of the human race."

III

The letter to Watson of which we have given an account contains the most complete statement of Wordsworth's political and social ideas in his twenty-third year.

Therein, forcible arguments stand side by side with frankly expressed illusions, and from end to end the letter is inspired by a hatred of selfishness, whether individual or national. Though in respect of his ideas he is much nearer to Paine than to Mackintosh, Wordsworth nevertheless differs from the former in his sustained sobriety, his tone of almost religious fervour, and a restrained manner of expressing himself which both precludes any idea that he was seeking to raise a scandal, and indicates the puritan austerity of his temperament.

The expression of indignation, however sincere, brings satisfaction. A heated controversy in a moment of anger affords seasonable relief. But an hour had arrived when it was no longer enough to proclaim one's love for the French Republic and one's hatred for the English monarchy in the abstract. Within a few days of the publication of Watson's tract a long-dreaded event came to pass. On the 1st February 1793, war broke out between England and France, and Wordsworth saw his native country prepare fleets and armies to attack the nation which in his eyes represented progress. Which of the two sentiments, patriotism or the love of humanity, was to obtain the mastery within him? It was patriotism, in this painful struggle, that had to accept defeat.

During the eighteenth century the patriotic sentiment appeared to have declined in Europe, and to have become gradually modified even in England. In their war against prejudice on behalf of reason, philosophers had not spared this love for the land of one's birth, which offers so powerful a resistance to a cosmopolitan affection for humanity. According to them it was narrow-minded, and implied a want of reflection. Was it not due to this blind sentiment that, instead of admiring and imitating that country which occupied the first place among civilized nations, we perpetually took the side of the land in which chance had placed us without the slightest regard for absolute justice? Now, while in France the result of this doctrine had been that the great writers had lost almost all the distinctive characteristics of Frenchmen, in England it had at first caused a sort of recrudescence of patriotism.

Since it was acknowledged even by foreigners that England was the most enlightened and the most liberal country in Europe, Englishmen were so fortunate as to be able to reconcile their national instinct with the humanitarian sympathies of the age. But the expression of their patriotism had taken a philosophical form.[1] They gave a reason for it. They found the explanation of their British pride in the superiority of their institutions and customs. Thus Cowper, though but little of a philosopher, proclaims England the first among nations because she is free, and adds that she would cease to be the first if she lost her liberty.[2] As soon, therefore, as their government ceased to be wise and liberal, their minds became disturbed. The American war divided the English into two camps. Many protested against the war as unjustifiable, praised the Americans for their energetic resistance, and applauded their victory. It was the first blow to the national prejudice, which, in the breasts of many Englishmen, was worsted in its conflict with the ideas of justice and liberty. But the Americans were of British descent; the war waged against them had something the character of a civil war, and therefore the test was inconclusive. The sacrifice demanded of patriotism was not sufficient.

It was when war between France and England became imminent that a real crisis occurred in the minds of those Englishmen who looked upon the Revolution with favour. For the first time it was seen that the sentiment of the nation was not united in presence of the foreigner, and—of all foreigners—in presence of the traditional foe! The mass of the people were no doubt unconscious of this painful struggle. They had not been affected by philosophical ideas; their old antipathy was unchanged. The feelings which induced Wordsworth, when a child, to kill all the white butterflies " because they were Frenchmen,"[3] might have been ascribed to the generality of the English people. But there is something characteristic and hopeful, even in

[1] See among others Thomson's poem *Liberty* (1734-6), and *The Remonstrance of Shakespeare* (1749), by Akenside.
[2] *The Task*, v. 446-509.
[3] Dorothy Wordsworth's Journal, 1802. Knight, *Life of Wordsworth*, i. p. 300.

the spectacle of this indignant minority declaring its partiality for a neighbouring people at war with Great Britain. Hitherto religious faith had apparently been the only sentiment capable of prevailing over the spirit of patriotism. But in 1793 it was philosophical faith that triumphed over it—though, as we shall see, at the cost of the bitterest anguish.

What, then, were my emotions, when in arms
Britain put forth her freeborn strength in league,
Oh, pity and shame! with those confederate Powers!
Not in my single self alone I found,
But in the minds of all ingenuous youth,
Change and subversion from that hour. No shock
Given to my moral nature had I known
Down to that very moment; neither lapse
Nor turn of sentiment that might be named
A revolution, save at this one time;
All else was progress on the self-same path
On which, with a diversity of pace,
I had been travelling: this a stride at once
Into another region. As a light
And pliant harebell, swinging in the breeze
On some grey rock—its birthplace—so had I
Wantoned, fast rooted on the ancient tower
Of my belovèd country, wishing not
A happier fortune than to wither there:
Now was I from that pleasant station torn
And tossed about in whirlwind. I rejoiced,
Yea, afterwards—truth most painful to record!—
Exulted, in the triumph of my soul,
When Englishmen by thousands were o'erthrown,
Left without glory on the field, or driven,
Brave hearts! to shameful flight.[1] It was a grief,—
Grief call it not, 'twas anything but that,—
A conflict of sensations without name,
Of which *he* only, who may love the sight
Of a village steeple, as I do, can judge,
When, in the congregation bending all

[1] The allusion here is probably to the battle of Hondschoote (6th and 8th September 1793), and to the forced embarkation of the Duke of York at Cuxhaven.

To their great Father, prayers were offered up,
Or praises for our country's victories ;
And, 'mid the simple worshippers, perchance
I only, like an uninvited guest
Whom no one owned, sate silent, shall I add,
Fed on the day of vengeance yet to come.[1]

Whom does he hold responsible for this grievous crisis, and for the suffering which it brought to others besides himself ? Neither in 1793, nor in 1804 when he wrote *The Prelude*, does he dream of laying it at the door of France. Not that her adversaries were unprovided with arguments. After the death of Louis XVI. the Convention itself, in a paroxysm of frantic rage, had provoked every kingdom that had shown indignation at his execution. It had abetted the intrigues of revolutionists in London. Though it had claimed with justice the right of every nation to manage its own affairs, the Convention had committed the blunder of interfering in those of others. And it was from the Convention that the declaration of war had come. But Wordsworth had no fault to find with it as yet. Did it not possess a faith that justified proselytism ? Were not its internal troubles some excuse for folly and rashness ? He had no ill-feelings save against the English ministers, whose action had made war inevitable. They knew no principle but that of their own immediate interests. They, and they alone, were accountable for the blood which had been shed and the despair of the English enthusiasts. And among these ministers there was one on whom, as the most powerful and conspicuous, all this vigorous hatred was concentrated, namely, William Pitt.

When the Revolution broke out, Pitt, in contrast to Burke, had preserved a correct and impassive demeanour. He was neither wrathful nor sympathetic. He does not appear to have taken the trouble to find out whether the new ideas were salutary or dangerous, and sought only to further the interests of his country. Provided that the French Revolution confined itself within the French frontier, and did not provoke imitation, he would willingly have left it to realize

---

[1] *The Prelude*, x. 263-300.

itself without a word of blame or praise. He hindered the
war to the best of his ability, and, when it had broken
out, apparently made it his chief object to prevent France
from taking Holland. His imperturbable attitude might
justly excite the admiration of diplomatists, but at a time
when the hearts of young men were glowing with generous
love for humanity, nothing created such aversion as this
national exclusiveness. The narrow and mistrustful
patriotism of Pitt seemed to them the very opposite of
the true patriotic spirit. In their eyes England's greatness
did not depend on a few yards of territory, but on the
position which their country took among progressive
nations. Thus Pitt brought upon his own head the
implacable and, upon the whole, discerning hatred of the
friends of the Revolution. A great deal was forgiven to
Burke, as much on account of the services he had formerly
rendered to Freedom, as on account of the sincerity and
depth of his conservative faith. His very vehemence was,
as it were, a tribute to the importance of the Revolution.
There was something romantic, something sentimental and
disinterested, in the crusade which he preached against the
French Republic. But Pitt appeared as the protector of the
commercial interests of England abroad, and at home as the
champion of the rich against those poorer classes whom he
treated with crushing scorn.[1] The Liberals mourned over
Burke, but Pitt they loaded with abuse. It is curious to compare two early sonnets written by Coleridge on the two men.
Burke is the dearly-loved son of Freedom, who gently
chides his errors ; Pitt a Judas Iscariot saluting his country
with the kiss of hypocrisy, and piercing her side with
bloodthirsty lance.[2] Revolutionary spirits in England at
once subscribed heartily and unanimously to the decree
whereby the Convention declared Pitt an enemy to the
human race. And when the first frenzy of their anger
had cooled, and they came to reflect upon their hatred,
they sought the justification for their attack upon him
in his character as a man. For a portrait of Pitt, not
perhaps as he actually was, but as, at any rate, he appeared

[1] Speech of Pitt, 16th May 1794.
[2] *Sonnets on Eminent Characters* (December 1794).

to his enemies, we must again turn to Coleridge.[1] Pitt
is represented as a grotesque combination of all the qualities which Coleridge despises, and all the faults which
he abhors. Trained to oratory from childhood, skilled
in the use of words, practised in the management of general
ideas, Pitt has never lived, never known affection, and
never come into contact with reality. Vanity has been
his first object, power his second. He has grown up
much as a plant reared in a hothouse, and when, at
twenty-five, he became Prime Minister, was still entirely
ignorant of his fellow-men. The French Revolution
took him unawares, and upset his stereotyped methods.
"After the declaration of war, long did he continue in
the common cant of office, in declamation about the
Scheld and Holland, and all the vulgar causes of common
contests." He has borrowed such general terms as
Atheism and Jacobinism from Burke, without in the least
understanding their deep meaning. His eloquence consists of "abstractions defined by abstractions; generalities
defined by generalities"; no concrete terms, no definite
facts, no images, not even a pointed aphorism. His
oratory produces an illusion while he is speaking, but
"not a sentence of Mr Pitt's has ever been quoted."
There never was a better example of the power which
empty phrases can wield. Similarly Wordsworth, even
in 1804, had not as yet forgiven the ministry of Pitt.

> Oh! much have they to account for, who could tear,
> By violence, at one decisive rent,
> From the best youth in England their dear pride,
> Their joy, in England; this, too, at a time
> In which worst losses easily might wear
> The best of names, when patriotic love
> Did of itself in modesty give way,
> Like the Precursor when the Deity
> Is come Whose harbinger he was; a time
> In which apostasy from ancient faith

[1] Portrait of Pitt by Coleridge (who at this date was no longer an
advocate of revolution). *The Morning Post*, 19th March 1800. This
sketch has been reprinted in *The Life of S. T. Coleridge*, by James Gillman
(London, 1838), pp. 195-207.

Seemed but conversion to a higher creed;
Withal a season dangerous and wild,
A time when sage Experience would have snatched
Flowers out of any hedge-row to compose
A chaplet in contempt of his grey locks.[1]

IV

Wordsworth is more than half disposed to regard Pitt's administration as entirely responsible for the pessimism which overshadowed men's minds at the close of the eighteenth century.   The fact is that he has generalized, and has attributed to the whole rising generation the drama which unfolded itself within his own soul after the declaration of war.   From that day forward a cloud obscured his natural cheerfulness.   At first nothing could restore it, neither travel, of which he was so fond, nor the consolations of poetry.   He set out with a friend in the summer of 1793 on a tour through the South of England, and spent a whole month "of calm and glassy days" in the delightful Isle of Wight.   At any other time his imagination would have been charmed by the beauty of this resort.   But he could not help seeing the proud fleet which had been gathered in Portsmouth harbour in order to make war on France.   Daily, at eventide, as he paced the silent shore, he heard the report of the sunset gun ring forth with warlike challenge, when the sun's disc sank down amid the tranquillity of nature. Instead of enjoying peace, the young man's mind was

---

[1] *The Prelude*, x, 300-314.   On hearing the news of Pitt's death, he writes to one of the statesman's admirers:

"Mr Pitt is also gone! by tens of thousands looked upon in like manner as a great loss.   For my own part, as probably you know, I have never been able to regard his political life with complacency.   I believe him, however, to have been as disinterested a man, and as true a lover of his country, as it was possible for so ambitious a man to be.   His first wish (though probably unknown to himself) was that his country should prosper under his administration; his next that it should prosper.   Could the order of these wishes have been reversed, Mr Pitt would have avoided many of the grievous mistakes into which, I think, he fell.'   Letter to Sir George Beaumont, 11th February 1806.   Knight, *Life of Wordsworth*, ii. p. 69.

haunted by dark visions; his heart was painfully stirred
by a sense of woes to come, and by pity for the human
race.[1] The most touching illusion of the time was its
belief that war would cease; its greatest merit that it
so abhorred war as to hope for its extinction. And what
an outburst of generous detestation, what a shudder of
noble horror, when war broke forth again, savage and
bloody as ever! None had so revelled in the hope of
universal peace as Wordsworth, none had suffered
more keenly at the bitter awakening from his dream.
He left the Isle of Wight to make a solitary expedition
on foot across the vast and desolate expanse of Salisbury
Plain, where stand the druidic remains of Stonehenge,
the Carnac of England. His imagination summoned up
barbaric ages, when Britons clothed in wolf-skins strode
to the slaughter wielding their ponderous spears with
brawny arms; and in the darkness of the night he saw
in fancy the desert lit by baleful fires of sacrifice, and
heard the groans of ill-fated victims delivered to the flames
in the gigantic frame of wicker.[2] Then his thoughts returned to the present war; he had a presentiment that
it would be long and terrible, and, comparing the sufferings of humanity in uncivilised times with those endured
by the men of his own day, perceived that there was no
less misery in the present than in the past. He conceived the idea of a poem of bloodshed and affliction,
his most sombre piece of work, entitled *Guilt and Sorrow*.[3]
He brings face to face two victims of the American War
of Independence, whom chance has led to the same spot
on Salisbury Plain. One is a sailor, who has been pressed
into the navy, and after a long period of service has at
last returned to England. Deprived, however, by fraud, of
all his earnings, he no longer has anything to bring back to
his wife and children. He has almost reached his home,
when, rendered desperate by want, he commits a murder
with the object of robbery, and after the consummation of
his crime takes refuge in flight. Henceforth he wanders
aimlessly about the country, and when he finds his wife again

---

[1] *The Prelude*, x. 315-330.   [2] *Ibid.*, xiii. 321-325.
[3] *Guilt and Sorrow, or Incidents upon Salisbury Plain*, published in 1842.

it is only to see her breathe her last in his arms, and to learn from her that she had been driven from her home on account of the murder committed (by him) near her door. Tormented by remorse, and weary of life, the murderer surrenders to justice and begs for death.

The other character, also an unfortunate wanderer, is a woman. The sailor meets her one night in a ruined chapel, where the rain has compelled her to take shelter. Touched by his pity for her she relates her story.[1] She was living in comfortable circumstances with her husband, when lack of work suddenly plunged them into distress. Her husband enlisted in the hope of earning some money, and taking her children she followed him to America. But in the war he lost his life, while fever carried off her children. The poet revels in his own indignation as he makes her describe the evils she has witnessed, compelled to

> Protract a curst existence, with the brood
> That lap (their very nourishment!) their brothers' blood.

His method of striving for peace was that of painting vividly the horrors of war:

> And groans, that rage of racking famine spoke,
> Where looks inhuman dwelt on festering heaps! . . .
> The mine's dire earthquake, and the pallid host
> Driven by the bomb's incessant thunder-stroke
> To loathsome vaults, where heart-sick anguish tossed,
> Hope died, and fear itself in agony was lost!

the assault, too, and the burning town; Murder and Rape which, by the ghastly gleam,

> Seized their joint prey, the mother and the child.

Carried on board a vessel which landed her in England, the

---

[1] This story had been sketched out in 1791. It was published separately in 1798, before the remainder of the poem, among the *Lyrical Ballads*, under the title of *The Female Vagrant*.

woman found her native country a land of exile. She no longer possessed either a home or money;

> And homeless near a thousand homes I stood,
> And near a thousand tables pined, and wanted food.

The only people to take pity on her were some vagrants—night-thieves, who taught her their trade. Her honesty quickly rebelled; she escaped from among them, preferring to live on the harvest of the hedgerows and to sleep on the ground when charity offered her neither food nor shelter.

There is no art in the manner in which this dismal narrative is told, yet it leaves on the mind a deep and painful impression. The atmosphere of gloom which pervades it arises not so much from the incidents related as from the sombre light thrown upon them. The poem embodies not only Wordsworth's mental sufferings at the time he wrote it, but also the most tragic impressions of his childhood. Except for the murder, the soldier making his way through the darkness in solitude and misery is the same whom he met one evening on his way back to Hawkshead. The thrill of horror which Wordsworth had felt as a child at sight of the gallows is here experienced by the murderer when he comes upon the grim instrument by night. And the scene amidst which these melancholy stories are told is the same Salisbury Plain which, of all the spots visited by Wordsworth, had seemed to him the most striking picture of desolation.

The poem of *Guilt and Sorrow*, faulty as it is, is one of the very few pieces in which Wordsworth has had courage to express the full depth of his sadness: a noble sadness withal, arising not from any trouble of his own, but from those of his fellow-men. A praiseworthy courage, too, must it not seem? No doubt; yet, upon the whole, such courage is easier than the caution which the poet afterwards adopted in his treatment of grief; for although sorrow no longer merely plays upon the surface of his soul, as in the still recent days when he wrote his *Descriptive Sketches*, but has already sunk deeper into his heart, it has not reached those last recesses in which his energetic hope and his vitality remain yet ingenuous and unimpaired. Hitherto Wordsworth has felt neither the need nor the obligation to palliate and soften human suffering, for he has not acquired that terrible, ever-present conception of it which, at a later time, met with such a stubborn resistance from his optimism. Like a young warrior who has as yet had no occasion to doubt of his own strength, or to prove the terrible power of his adversary, he allows evil to profit by every favourable circumstance at the outset, and appears even to surrender every advantage to it, by intentionally accumulating his heart-rending pictures of present woe.[1] Cannot his thought recruit itself at will by plunging into the glorious future of his dreams ?

Precious indeed was that prospect, for wherever he turned his glance, nowhere was there anything to console or reassure him in the present. He had taken the part of France against England ; but France, on whose victory the realization of his dearest hopes depended, was now but a vast field of carnage. The first effect of the coalition which had been formed against her, and had been joined by England, was to throw the power into the hands of the most violent party. On the 31st October 1793 the Girondists, with whom Wordsworth sympathized, had met their doom upon the scaffold. Supporters of the Revolution abroad had been plunged into mourning by the deaths of Brissot, the disciple of Rousseau, and of Mme. Roland, "Rousseau's daughter." The Reign of Terror had begun. France, thanks to the union of all her energies, good and evil alike, against the foreign foe, was no doubt driving back the invaders, who

> fared as they deserved :
> The Herculean Commonwealth had put forth her arms,
> And throttled with an infant godhead's might

---

[1] The earliest form of the poem was more tragic than that in which it has come down to us. When in his old age the poet published the revolutionary poem written in his youth, he felt, alas! that he ought to tone down the tragedy which brought it to a close, since he was no longer actuated by a desire " to expose the vices of the penal law, and the calamities of war as they affect individuals." This was Wordsworth's original description of the object of his poem. Letter to Wrangham, written late in 1795 or early in 1796. From an extract published in *The Athenæum*, 8th December 1894.

> The snakes about her cradle; that was well,
> And as it should be; yet no cure for them
> Whose souls were sick with pain of what would be
> Hereafter brought in charge against mankind.[1]

In the midst of that "domestic carnage" which "filled the whole year with feast-days,"

> amid the depth
> Of those enormities, even thinking minds
> Forgot, at seasons, whence they had their being;
> Forgot that such a sound was ever heard
> As Liberty upon earth: yet all beneath
> Her innocent authority was wrought,
> Nor could have been, without her blessèd name.[2]

Wordsworth had watched the beginnings of the Revolution from too close a standpoint, he was following its blood-stained progress with too much attention, to contemplate the Terror with a mere vague and abstracted dismay. It haunted him like a nightmare.

> Most melancholy at that time,
> Were my day-thoughts,—my nights were miserable;
> Through months, through years, long after the last beat
> Of those atrocities, the hour of sleep
> To me came rarely charged with natural gifts,
> Such ghastly visions had I of despair.[3]

In dreams he was brought to the foot of the scaffold, or into the cells of the condemned, and underwent all their alternations of hope and fear.

> Then suddenly the scene
> Changed, and the unbroken dream entangled me
> In long orations, which I strove to plead
> Before unjust tribunals,—with a voice
> Labouring, a brain confounded, and a sense,
> Death-like, of treacherous desertion, felt
> In the last place of refuge—my own soul.[4]

His one support during this crisis was his faith in the fundamental and unconquerable goodness of man's nature.

[1] *The Prelude*, x. 390-7.
[2] *Ibid.*, x. 356-381.
[3] *Ibid.*, x. 397-402.
[4] *Ibid.*, x. 409-415.

He found evidence of it even in the Terror, which every moment called forth that spirit of sacrifice of which the soul is capable ; the time was rich in " examples, in no age surpassed, of fortitude and energy and love."

> And as the desert hath green spots, the sea
> Small islands scattered amid stormy waves,
> So *that* disastrous period did not want
> Bright sprinklings of all human excellence,
> To which the silver wands of saints in Heaven
> Might point with rapturous joy.[1]

And though the frequent recurrence of monstrous crimes might rack his heart with anguish, it did not destroy his confidence in happier days to come. He saw in present misery a chastisement for the crimes of the past. The prophets of old, watching the destruction of cities whose ruin they had foretold, found consolation in their visions of purer and brighter times beyond ;

> So did a portion of that spirit fall
> On me, uplifted from the vantage-ground
> Of pity and sorrow to a state of being
> That through the time's exceeding fierceness saw
> Glimpses of retribution, terrible,
> And in the order of sublime behests.[2]

When those around him said in scorn, " Behold the harvest that we reap from popular government and equality," he saw clearly that the calamities of the times arose not from those causes, but from

> a terrific reservoir of guilt
> And ignorance filled up from age to age,
> That could no longer hold its loathsome charge,
> But burst and spread in deluge through the land.[3]

Even when the punishment was unintelligible to his reason, Wordsworth did not retract his faith. For him there was a kind of fearful poetry in the Terror. He felt

---

[1] *The Prelude*, x. 481-490.   [2] *Ibid.*, x. 437-453.
[3] *Ibid.*, x. 454-480.

"daring sympathies with power." Sometimes, like the *Solitary* of the *Excursion*, he began to have a strange liking for

> the exasperation of that Land,
> Which turned an angry beak against the down
> Of her own breast; confounded into hope
> Of disencumbering thus her fretful wings.[1]

He discerned a wild harmony in those whirlwinds of destruction which strewed the ground with death and ruin, and found that thus "worst tempests might be listened to."[2] And, as he reflected, he perceived a lesson in what had at first seemed incomprehensible. He learned that man has only himself to blame if, from the deepest affliction, he does not derive

> Honour which could not else have been, a faith,
> An elevation, and a sanctity;
> If new strength be not given nor old restored.[3]

V

Thus, during the Terror, he was supported by a kind of fierce joy and prophetic ecstasy. But however sustained by the certainty that progress will come, the soul grows faint at last when evil is protracted beyond its anticipations, and when dawn fails to whiten the horizon at the expected hour. While in his eyes the Terror was a necessary evil, he nevertheless conceived an ever-growing hatred of the Terrorists, the "Tribe so dreaded, so abhorred." For him, as for so many others, Robespierre was crime in human form, the evil genius of revolution incarnate. Wordsworth took a harsher view of him than Southey and Coleridge, who, when they heard of the mighty Jacobin's death, at once commenced a drama in which they represented him as stained indeed with crime, but nevertheless as conscious of fulfilling a divine mission by sanguinary means. Wordsworth never had so high an

---

[1] *The Excursion*, iii. 816-820.   [2] *The Prelude*, x. 463.
[3] *Ibid.*, x. 464-470.

opinion of Robespierre. The reason is that he came back from France a Girondist. He remembered passing through Arras on the day of the Federation, and his blood boiled when he compared the gay joyousness of that city in 1790 with the mourning into which it was plunged by the crime of its son, its chosen—Robespierre. Nor must we expect of Wordsworth a faithful portrait of a man known to him only by reputation. He certainly cannot have known him well, for he describes the high priest of the Supreme Being as wielding "the sceptre of the Atheist crew." His hatred, however, was none the less vigorous, and the Terrorist's protracted reign had driven him to the verge of despair, when the long eclipse came to an end and light at last reappeared.

This happened early in August 1794, when Wordsworth was in the land of his birth. He was crossing the level sands of Morecambe Bay : the sun shone brightly overhead, and all around him was gentleness and peace. The sea, far out in the distance, was at its lowest ebb. On the vast plain of sand he observed a motley crowd of vehicles and travellers, riders and men on foot, who were wading in loose procession, under the conduct of their guide, through the shallow stream which wound its way across the sand. Wordsworth paused, longing for the skill to paint such a bright and joyous spectacle, but the leader of the band, as he approached, instead of giving him an ordinary salutation, cried, "Robespierre is dead!"

> Great was my transport, deep my gratitude
> To everlasting Justice, by this fiat
> Made manifest. "Come now, ye golden times,"
> Said I forth-pouring on those open sands
> A hymn of triumph : "as the morning comes
> From out the bosom of the night, come ye :
> Thus far our trust is verified ; behold !
> They who with clumsy desperation brought
> A river of Blood, and preached that nothing else
> Could cleanse the Augean stable, by the might
> Of their own helper have been swept away ;
> Their madness stands declared and visible ;
> Elsewhere will safety now be sought, and earth

March firmly towards righteousness and peace."—
Then schemes I framed more calmly, when and how
The madding factions might be tranquillised,
And now through hardships manifold and long
The glorious renovation would proceed.
Thus interrupted by uneasy bursts
Of exultation, I pursued my way
Along that very shore which I had skimmed
In former days.[1]

VI

The golden age which Wordsworth had expected to
see established in France, when the fury of the storm had
passed, was never to come. Nothing that was done was
calculated to pave the way for it, neither the acts nor the
language of the expiring Convention, nor those of the
Directory which followed it. Yet Wordsworth was not
cast down. His trust had not been placed in the French
government, but "in the People . . . and in the virtues
which his eyes had seen."[2] When he saw the fire of
patriotism unsubdued, he could not believe that the
enthusiasm for freedom could wane.

I knew that wound external could not take
Life from the young Republic; that new foes
Would only follow, in the path of shame,
Their brethren, and her triumphs be in the end
Great, universal, irresistible.[3]

Strong in this conviction, and confirmed by the successive
victories of the republicans, he grew proud of his own
prophetic wisdom and contemptuous of the aberrations of
his countrymen. Had not Pitt imagined that the war
would be brought to a conclusion in two or three cam-
paigns, and France easily defeated.

[I] laughed with my compeers
At gravest heads, by emnity to France
Distempered, till they found, in every blast
Forced from the street-disturbing newsman's horn,

---

[1] *The Prelude*, x. 511-603.   [2] *Ibid.*, xi. 11-12.   [3] *Ibid.*, xi. 13-17.

For her great cause record or prophecy
Of utter ruin.   How might we believe
That wisdom could, in any shape, come near
Men clinging to delusions so insane?
And thus, experience proving that no few
Of our opinions had been just, we took
Like credit to ourselves where less was due,
And thought that other notions were as sound,
Yea, could not but be right, because we saw
That foolish men opposed them.[1]

But the adversaries of the Revolution had power on their side, if not wisdom.   They provoked the ridicule of the English Jacobins, but they took bitter vengeance for it.   In their hands were the government, the machinery of justice, the military force, and a perfect system of espionage.   To avoid the revolution they dreaded, ministers had had a choice of two courses; they might either have adopted the plan advocated by Fox, and have granted the reforms for which the country had been ripe even before 1789; or they might have silenced seditious spirits by force. They chose the latter course, and thereby aroused the indignation of Wordsworth, who believed it the very way to bring about in England the same ruin and destruction which had occurred in France.   During the Terror he wrote to a friend as follows:

"I disapprove of monarchical and aristocratical governments, however modified.   Hereditary distinctions, and privileged orders of every species, I think, must necessarily counteract the progress of human improvement.   Hence it follows, that I am not among the admirers of the British constitution.   I conceive that a more excellent system of civil polity might be established among us; yet in my ardour to attain the goal, I do not forget the nature of the ground where the race is to be run.   The destruction of those institutions which I condemn appears to me to be hastening on too rapidly.   I recoil from the very idea of a revolution. I am a determined enemy to every species of violence.   I see no connection, but what the obstinacy of pride and ignorance renders necessary, between justice and the sword

[1] *The Prelude*, xi. 39-51.

—between reason and bonds.[1] I deplore the miserable
condition of the French, and think that we can only be
guarded from the same scourge by the undaunted efforts
of good men. . . . I severely condemn all inflammatory
addresses to the passions of men. I know that the multitude walk in darkness. I would put into each man's
hands a lantern, to guide him; and not have him to set
out upon his journey depending for illumination on abortive
flashes of lightning, or the coruscations of transitory
meteors." [2]

His conscience thus clear of all thought of sedition,
Wordsworth was unable to restrain his wrath and contempt when he saw the harsh measures taken by the
government. Were not the ministers setting up a kind
of counter-terror, with its own suspected characters, its
own victims?

> Our Shepherds, this say merely, at that time
> Acted, or seemed at least to act, like men
> Thirsting to make the guardian crook of law
> A tool of murder; they who ruled the State,—
> Though with such awful proof before their eyes
> That he, who would sow death, reaps death, or worse,
> And can reap nothing better,—child-like longed
> To imitate, not wise enough to avoid;
> Or left (by mere timidity betrayed)
> The plain straight road, for one no better chosen
> Than if their wish had been to undermine
> Justice, and make an end of Liberty.[3]

Not only were the reforms which had been projected
previously to 1789 postponed to a later occasion, but
arbitrary measures were taken against all friends of France
and all reformers. Government and nation alike were
possessed by a complete panic. The belief in a French
and Jacobin conspiracy grew more and more widely spread,
and represented the English reformers, who, for the most

---

[1] Both the thought and the manner of expression of the sentence are
those of William Godwin, whose influence over Wordsworth is studied in the
next chapter.
[2] Letter to Mathews, not dated. Knight, *Life of Wordsworth*, i. p. 69.
[3] *The Prelude*, xi. 62-73.

part, were well-behaved and peaceable citizens, as men thirsting for blood.[1] The conservative majority pointed at them, refused to receive them, kept them out of employment, and, if they were tradesmen, took away their custom. Owners of coffee-houses and taverns no longer dared to place rooms at their disposal for meetings. Magistrates condemned them simply as reformers, without attempting to find other grounds of accusation. In Scotland sentence of transportation was pronounced against four of them, honest and worthy men,[2] and one of the judges expressed his regret that it was no longer the practice to torture those guilty of sedition. At the close of 1794 Pitt induced Parliament to suspend the Act of *Habeas Corpus*. He had the papers of the *London Corresponding Society* seized at once, and arraigned its president, Hardy, together with Horne Tooke and Thelwall, in the courts of justice.

The press was compelled to maintain a most discreet reserve. Late in 1792 Paine had been condemned for the second part of his *Rights of Man*.[3] The publishers of the *Morning Chronicle* had been tried for issuing the report of a reform society, and the "Friends of the Liberty of the Press," under the presidency of Erskine, had been powerless to obtain any alleviation of this summary method of procedure. Nevertheless, it was in June 1794, when the persecution was at its height, that Wordsworth forwarded to a friend in London the prospectus of a monthly magazine to be called *The Philanthropist*, which should be "republican, but not revolutionary."[4] The scheme fell through, but a few months later,

---

[1] See the trial of the attorney, John Frost (*The English Jacobins*, p. 165). The pillory in which Frost was to be confined was destroyed by the crowd, and the prisoner himself set at liberty. Frost, with the utmost calmness, took the arm of his friend Horne Tooke and returned to prison.

[2] From August 1793 to January 1794.

[3] The counts of the indictment are characteristic. Paine was found guilty of having denied the title of William III. and Mary to the throne; of having declared that Parliament was corrupt, and of having said that a hereditary monarchy was a tyranny. Paine, however, had done no more than hint at these opinions. *The whole proceedings on the trial of an information against Thomas Paine*, second edition, 1793. This is the official report of the trial.

[4] Knight, *Life of Wordsworth*, i. p. 92.

on the 7th November, he asked the same friend to obtain
for him a post on the staff of an Opposition Paper, "for
I cannot," he wrote, "abet, in the smallest degree, the
measures pursued by the present ministry. They are
already so deeply advanced in iniquity, that, like Macbeth,
they cannot retreat." [1] The reply was no doubt unfavourable. Unable to enter the lists in prose, Wordsworth
attempted to do so in verse, and, towards the end of
1795, a great increase of severity on the part of the
ministry drew from him a retort in some satirical lines,
which, however, were never to be published. They were
imitations of Juvenal, and were written in collaboration
with an old college friend named Wrangham. "These
specimens," says his first biographer, "exhibit poetical
vigour, combined with no little asperity and rancour, against
the abuses of the time, and the vices of the ruling powers,
and the fashionable corruptions of aristocratical society." [2]

Wordsworth abandoned this volume of poetry after
having worked at it until the spring of 1796. It was in
the same spring that Bonaparte addressed to the French
soldiers in Italy his famous exhortations to pillage. Are
we to regard this as a mere coincidence? Though
Wordsworth could not hold the Revolution and the whole
French nation responsible for the crimes of one man,

---

[1] Letter to Mathews. Knight, *Life of Wordsworth*, ii. p. 94.
[2] *Memoirs of W. Wordsworth*, by Christopher Wordsworth, vol. i. p. 95.
The following lines have been recently found in some unpublished letters of
Wordsworth. A few of these lines were published in the *Athenæum* for
8th December 1894. They consist of a diatribe against the Prince Regent, a
great lover of boxing and horse-racing.

> The nation's hope shall show the present time
> As rich in folly as the past in crime.
> Do arts like these a royal mind evince?
> Are these the studies that beseem a prince?
> Wedged in with blacklegs at a boxers' show,
> To shout with transport at a knock-down blow—
> 'Mid knots of grooms, the council of his state,
> To scheme and counter-scheme for purse and plate.
> Thy ancient honours when shalt thou resume?
> Oh shame is this, thy service' boastful plume—
> Go, modern Prince! at Henry's tomb proclaim
> Thy rival triumphs, thy Newmarket fame,
> There hang thy trophies—bid the jockey's vest,
> The whip, the cap, and spurs thy fame attest.

it seems nevertheless to have been at this time that he withdrew from all active political strife. He made no further attempt to write in the newspapers, and abjured personal satire. Some time ere this, moreover, his dreams of universal happiness, which could find no promise of fulfilment in the world of present reality, nor any safe retreat either in France or in England, had taken refuge in the free land of thought and meditation.

CHAPTER IV

Moral Crisis

I

BUT these political feelings, however violent, were after all merely the superficial disorders of Wordsworth's mind at this period of his life. The Revolution did more than ruffle its surface with these waves ; it convulsed the very depths of his thought, and almost destroyed the ground-work even of his moral being. The eleventh book of *The Prelude* gives a powerful description of the different phases of this profound disturbance. And since in that book Wordsworth has got beneath the exterior of the individual, and has succeeded in reaching the essential feelings which make up the common heart of all mankind, his biography becomes almost an inward history of his generation. To learn how, in his case, manhood was developed out of early youth, is to learn how the nineteenth century was born from the eighteenth, so different, yet with so manifest a family likeness.

At twenty years of age Wordsworth had been suddenly dazzled by the visions of approaching universal happiness which had flashed before men's eyes in 1789. When so many others, with more experience to warn them, were captivated, how should he have escaped their fascination ? The aphorisms which had been repeated for half a century, and were now accepted as axiomatic : — that nature is good, that man is born good, that liberty is a certain cure for every ill, that man is made to be happy,—were no doubtful novelties for him ; they provided a clear and simple summary of his youthful im-pressions, of which he had scarcely been conscious until now. Had not nature made its goodness manifest to him

at Hawkshead ?   Had he not a proof of the goodness of
man in the innocence and spontaneous warmth of his own
heart, in the unstudied generosity of school and college
friendships, and in the lofty virtues which classical education, by making a specious selection from among ancient
writings and the facts of ancient history, represents as
of natural and universal growth ?

> I had approached, like other youths, the shield
> Of human nature from the golden side,
> And would have fought, even to the death, to attest
> The quality of the metal which I saw.[1]

As to the possibility of attaining happiness through freedom, was it not inevitable that at the age when vigour of
muscle and elasticity of hope are as it were a guarantee of
unlimited power, it should seem beyond dispute ?

Thus the religion of humanity had demanded no sacrifices
of Wordsworth.   It promised everything and asked for
nothing in return.   If his Christianity had been a living
faith, it would doubtless have felt uneasy concerning a
rival whose only goal was an earthly paradise and whose
only court of appeal was reason.   But Wordsworth was
then a Christian only in name, and his torpid Christianity
slept in one of the lumber-rooms of his mind.   The object
of his active worship, on the other hand, was the new
divinity of Reason, to whom, with singular felicity in its
choice of a symbol, the Convention erected an altar.   To
Reason was due all that had been won, and by Reason all
that remained to conquer must be overcome.   An idol
as well as a goddess, counting her fanatics as well as her
faithful, she seemed to preside over the glorious metamorphosis of the world.   But just as hypocrisy flourishes
most of all in an era of true piety, so the dreams which
disguise themselves under an appearance of reason impose
most easily upon public credulity in an age which believes
itself rational.   Thus, during the latter years of the
eighteenth century, more perhaps than at any other epoch,
hasty generalizations, abstractions taken for realities, conclusions rigorously deduced from false or incomplete

[1] *The Prelude*, xi. 79-82.

premises, along with genuine scientific discoveries and true
moral principles ascertained at the cost of great labour—
all passed current together in a confusion which made it
impossible to separate truth from error.

But error, even when it is not imposture, is no mere
aimless straying in that unknown which all our judgments
strive to penetrate. Our instincts and aspirations unconsciously give it a tendency. We suppose that our
reasoning is directed to the discovery of truth, when,
unknown to ourselves, it is following the bent of our
dreams. Under the influence of this delusion man tastes
the keenest joy he can ever know, since he believes in
what he wishes and finds his duty in the satisfaction of his
desires for happiness. This is how it was that Wordsworth had enjoyed the delightful illusion of obeying the
strict rules of reason, when in truth he was merely
converting his desires into realities ; an illusion so pleasing,
that twelve years later he was unable to recall it without a glow of enthusiasm at the recollection.

> O pleasant exercise of hope and joy !
> For mighty were the auxiliars which then stood
> Upon our side, us who were strong in love !
> Bliss was it in that dawn to be alive,
> But to be young was very Heaven !   O times,
> In which the meagre, stale, forbidding ways
> Of custom, law, and statute, took at once
> The attraction of a country in romance !
> When Reason seemed the most to assert her rights
> When most intent on making of herself
> A prime enchantress—to assist the work,
> Which then was going forward in her name !
> Not favoured spots alone, but the whole Earth,
> The beauty wore of promise—that which sets
> (As at some moments might not be unfelt
> Among the bowers of Paradise itself)
> The budding rose above the rose full blown.
> What temper at the prospect did not wake
> To happiness unthought of?   The inert
> Were roused, and lively natures rapt away !
> They who had fed their childhood upon dreams,
> The play-fellows of fancy, who had made

All powers of swiftness, subtilty, and strength
Their ministers,—who in lordly wise had stirred
Among the grandest objects of the sense,
And dealt with whatsoever they found there
As if they had within some lurking right
To wield it ;—they, too, who of gentle mood
Had watched all gentle motions, and to these
Had fitted their own thoughts, schemers more mild,
And in the region of their peaceful selves ;—
Now was it that *both* found, the meek and lofty
Did both find, helpers to their hearts' desire,
And stuff at hand, plastic as they could wish,—
Were called upon to exercise their skill,
Not in Utopia,—subterranean fields,—
Or some secreted island, Heaven knows where !
But in the very world, which is the world
Of all of us,—the place where, in the end,
We find our happiness, or not at all !
Why should I not confess that Earth was then
To me, what an inheritance, new-fallen,
Seems, when the first time visited, to one
Who thither comes to find in it his home ?
He walks about and looks upon the spot
With cordial transport, moulds it and remoulds,
And is half pleased with things that are amiss,
'Twill be such joy to see them disappear.[1]

These hours of fresh joyousness and unshaken confidence, when hope " laid her hand upon her object," [2]
quickly passed away. The obstacles with which the path
of reason is strewn soon forced themselves upon Wordsworth's notice. Unforeseen scourges arose on every hand,
from earth's unhealthy soil and the corrupt heart of man.
Yet his serene trust was at first scarcely overcast; he
regarded them merely as passing clouds which the sun
would shortly penetrate :

An active partisan, I thus convoked
From every object pleasant circumstance
To suit my ends ; I moved among mankind
With genial feelings still predominant ;
When erring, erring on the better part,

[1] *The Prelude*, xi. 105-152.   [2] *Ibid.*, xi. 202-203.

And in the kinder spirit ; placable,
Indulgent, as not uninformed that men
See as they have been taught—Antiquity
Gives rights to error ; and aware, no less,
That throwing off oppression must be work
As well of License as of Liberty ;
And above all—for this was more than all—
Not caring if the wind did now and then
Blow keen upon an eminence that gave
Prospect so large into futurity ;
In brief, a child of Nature, as at first,
Diffusing only those affections wider
That from the cradle had grown up with me,
And losing, in no other way than light
Is lost in light, the weak in the more strong.[1]

But the harmony which prevailed between his revolutionary ideas and his natural feelings became suddenly converted into discord. It ceased to exist on the day when " with open war Britain opposed the liberties of France." [2] This attack not only caused him bitter grief, it upset the equilibrium of his whole nature. For the first time he became aware that the elements which he had thought it possible to reconcile were radically opposed. On the day which witnessed the commencement of the struggle between England and France, his reason declared war against his heart.

This threw me first out of the pale of love ;
Soured and corrupted, upwards to the source,
My sentiments ; was not, as hitherto,
A swallowing up of lesser things in great,
But change of them into their contraries.[3]

Wordsworth's patriotism, in short, which hitherto had willingly submitted to be merged in his humanitarian faith, was now superseded by a hatred or contempt for his country.

What had been a pride,
Was now a shame ; my likings and my loves
Ran in new channels, leaving old ones dry ;

[1] *The Prelude*, xi. 153-173.　　　　[2] *Ibid.*, xi. 174-175.
[3] *Ibid.*, xi. 175-180.

> And hence a blow that, in maturer age,
> Would but have touched the judgment, struck more deep
> Into sensations near the heart.[1]

It was his reason (or what he supposed to be his reason) that obtained the victory in this conflict, but not without mutilation, and the severance of one of its bonds with joy and love.   True, it took warning from the danger it had undergone, and endeavoured to be more vigilant and circumspect, just as a driver pays more attention to his team when the rein has been broken.   It became desirous of examining itself.   This was the moment when the letter to Watson was written.   To the " wild theories " which were afloat, Wordsworth had hitherto

> lent but a careless ear, assured
> That time was ready to set all things right,
> And that the multitude, so long oppressed,
> Would be oppressed no more.[2]

But in his refutation of Watson he attempted for the first time an orderly statement of his loosely entertained ideas.

> I began
> To meditate with ardour on the rule
> And management of nations ; what it is
> And ought to be ; and strove to learn how far
> Their power or weakness, wealth or poverty,
> Their happiness or misery, depends
> Upon their laws, and fashion of the State.[3]

Little by little the close ties which bound him to France gave way in their turn.   There was not, it is true, any sudden rupture, but rather a gradual loosening of a dear embrace, accompanied by a deeply painful surprise that the eyes of one whom he had loved when her only desires seemed to be for peace and happiness should flame with fierce madness or vulgar ambition.   And as his feelings grew steadily colder, the affection he could no longer bestow on France became transferred to his own theories.

[1] *The Prelude*, xi. 183-188.   [2] *Ibid.*, xi. 188-194.
[3] *Ibid.*, xi. 98-104.

                                    But when events
Brought less encouragement, and unto these
The immediate proof of principles no more
Could be entrusted,˙while the events themselves,
Worn out in greatness, stripped of novelty,
Less occupied the mind, . . . evidence
Safer, of universal application, such
As could not be impeached, was sought elsewhere.[1]

II

Thus, the farther men seemed to him from truth and
happiness, the farther he withdrew from the real world to
bury himself in that of abstract thought, where the irony
of events could no longer exasperate by its inconsistency
with theory, nor an illogical reality confront the logical
mind with its discrepancies and incoherence. This universe,
the creation of his own thought, appeared to him at first
sight all order and all light.

This was the time, when, all things tending fast
To depravation, speculative schemes—
That promised to abstract the hopes of Man
Out of his feelings, to be fixed thenceforth
For ever in a purer element—
Found ready welcome. Tempting region *that*
For Zeal to enter and refresh herself,
Where passions had the privilege to work,
And never hear the sound of their own names.
But, speaking more in charity, the dream
Flattered the young, pleased with extremes, nor least
With that which makes our Reason's naked self
The object of its fervour. What delight!
How glorious! in self-knowledge and self-rule,
To look through all the frailties of the world,
And, with a resolute mastery shaking off
Infirmities of nature, time, and place,
Build social upon personal Liberty,
Which, to the blind restraints of general laws

The Prelude, xi. 194-205.

Superior, magisterially adopts
One guide, the light of circumstances, flashed
Upon an independent intellect.[1]

There was, however, another guide, unmentioned by Wordsworth, whom he was following even when he supposed himself most thoroughly emancipated; nay, then most of all, since it was from him that he had learnt independence. This man, who, for a brief period, had a fascination for Coleridge, and afterwards exerted a permanent influence over Shelley, was William Godwin, the intellectual master of all the young Jacobins of his country.

It was in February 1793, simultaneously with the declaration of war, that Godwin had published his *Inquiry concerning Political Justice, and its influence on general virtue and happiness.* Such was the weighty title of two weighty quarto volumes, the high price of which alone saved their author from prosecution. Pitt thought there was no danger that such a work could become popular. He had chastised Paine, but Godwin he spared.

Godwin did not write, as Paine did, for the people, but for the select and thoughtful few. He combined in one clear and rigid system all the scattered revolutionary ideas contained in the philosophical works of the period. His principal teacher was Rousseau, who had perceived two important facts—that the imperfections of governments were the only permanent source of the vices of mankind, and, what was a more profound reflection, that a government, however reformed, is almost incapable of doing good.[2] The great failing of Rousseau, in Godwin's opinion, arose from his deism and his belief in the immortality of the

---

[1] *The Prelude,* xi. 223-244. These last words are an exact poetical version of a saying of Godwin: " The true dignity of human reason is as much as we are able to go beyond them (*i.e.* general rules), to have our faculties in act upon every occasion that occurs, and to conduct ourselves accordingly." *Enquiry concerning Political Justice,* 2nd ed., i. p. 347. Wordsworth first placed these lines in Oswald's mouth, in his *Borderers* (ll. 1502-1506). Charles Lloyd, who had heard this drama read at Alfoxden, at once made use of them as a sort of text or motto for his *Edmund Oliver,* a fancy biography of Coleridge (p. 124, ed. 1798). They furnish us with a key to Wordsworth's moral crisis.

[2] *Inquiry into Political Justice,* 1st ed., vol. ii. pp. 503-504 (note).

soul. He therefore amended Rousseau by d'Holbach and Helvetius, by Hume and Hartley, and, thus confirmed in an imperturbable atheism, had arrived at the following philosophical doctrine.

In the first place, there are no innate ideas; and to believe in them in spite of Locke and Condillac is sheer fatuity. "Who is there in the present state of scientifical improvement, that will believe that this vast chain of perceptions and notions is something that we bring into the world with us, a mystical magazine, shut up in the human embryo, whose treasures are to be gradually unfolded as circumstances shall require? Who does not perceive that they are regularly generated in the mind by a series of impressions, and digested and arranged by association and reflection?"[1]

In the second place, moral freedom is a mere fiction, a popular delusion. Man has no independent will, and if language were truly philosophical, it would contain no such expressions as "*I will* exert myself . . . *I will* do this." "All these expressions imply as if man was or could be something else than what motives make him. Man is in reality a passive, and not an active being."[2]

If man has thus neither *nature* nor *freedom*, what is he? He is a pure intelligence, a simple reasoning machine. Let but his reason have free play, without interference from any external influence, and the ascertainment of truth by the individual mind, and absolute justice in the relations between man and his fellow-creatures, will be the certain result.

But the exercise of reason is fettered by political and religious institutions. The history of humanity is nothing but a history of the crimes to which these institutions have given rise—such as war, robbery, and murder, which would otherwise never have come into existence. Must we then think of reforming them? By no means, for they are naturally inimical to the free unfolding of the intellectual powers. It is the abolition of them at which we must aim. They are mighty for evil, powerless for good.

[1] *Inquiry concerning Political Justice*, 1st ed., vol. i. pp. 13-14.
[2] *Ibid.*, i. p. 310.

The one thing of true importance is education.   Since the human mind is a *tabula rasa* on which impressions and ideas become imprinted, it is education that determines whether the man shall be rational or irrational, harmful or beneficial.   Human progress depends on the pitch of perfection to which education can be brought, and on that fact we may build our hopes of the infinite perfectibility of man.   The task may be slow and difficult, but it "promises much, if it do not in reality promise everything." [1]

Education, moreover, has but a single object, and that a perfectly simple one—namely, to secure full freedom of action for the individual intelligence by removing from its path everything which hampers, deludes, or confuses it ; whether passions or sentiments, under whatsoever virtuous names disguised, or preconceived ideas, whether they pass for the maxims of wisdom or for prejudices.

It is here that the system becomes really interesting. Burke had already perceived that the whole Revolution hinged on this fixed point, and in his hatred of convulsions and his love for what was sanctified by tradition, he had boldly undertaken the defence of prejudice.   "Prejudice," he said, "is of ready application in the emergency ; it previously engages the mind in a steady course of wisdom and virtue, and does not leave the man hesitating in the moment of decision, sceptical, puzzled, and unresolved.   Prejudice renders a man's virtue his habit ; and not a series of unconnected acts.   Through just prejudice his duty becomes a part of his nature." [2]

Profound as they are, these words, unaccompanied by any admission of the defects of prejudice, appeared blasphemous to the worshippers of human reason, whom they drove to the opposite extreme.

But social "prejudices" are not the only sentiments which meet with Godwin's condemnation.   He is not content with proscribing natural affection for home or country, on the ground that it hinders the operation of justice, the only law recognised by the intelligence ; the

---

[1] *Political Justice*, 1st ed., i. p. 18.
[2] *Reflections on the Revolution in France.*   The Works of Burke, London, 1888, vol. ii. p. 359.

noxious institution of marriage, since cohabitation is a danger calculated more than any other to disturb the unruffled calm essential to the understanding; and property, which gives rise to the reprehensible "system of clemency and charity,"[1] instead of the only admissible rule of conduct, that of justice.   He goes further.   He makes an attack upon the general principles of morality, and while fully admitting that they are of service to indolent minds like ours, since they relieve us from the necessity of constantly considering how we ought to act, regards them as a lamentable and dangerous makeshift.   "The true dignity of human reason is as much as we are able to go beyond [general rules], to have our faculties in act upon every occasion that occurs, and to conduct ourselves accordingly."[2]

Man should therefore not only cease to conform to the traditional rules of morality, but should also no longer make use of a ready-made code, even of his own manufacture.   He should estimate each of his acts at the moment of performance, according to the sole law admitted by Godwin, that man should do that which tends to the greatest amount of general happiness.

The dreadful consequences of this doctrine of moral anarchy were not at first apparent to Godwin and his readers.   The impassive philosopher was genuinely convinced that all men were made in his own image, and his illusion acquired credit from the impressive sobriety of his logic.   He himself appeared to be a sage entirely free from passions, who, with truth as his only guide, and the good as his only aim, strove to reform the world from the seclusion of his study.   The prophet of individualism diffused a kind of sanctity around him.   The stoicism which he maintained himself, and advised others to imitate; the contempt he professed for vulgar pleasures, for suffering, moral or physical, for sickness and for calumny;[3] and also his superiority to all

---

[1] *Political Justice*, 1st ed., ii. p. 798.
[2] *Political Justice*, 2nd edition, i. p. 347.
[3] Godwin thus reprobates suicide: "The motive assigned for escape is eminently trivial, to avoid pain, which is a small inconvenience, or disgrace, which is an imaginary evil" (i. p. 92, 1st edition).

the narrow and trifling interests of humanity,[1] invested his system with a lofty dignity which recommended it to youthful souls in search of an ideal.   The very happiness which Godwin promised to the sage who should answer his description was of a kind which paid no regard to the appetites and coarse lusts.   It provided no satisfaction for the lower instincts, nor even for sentiments usually considered perfectly legitimate.   Human felicity would resemble the infinite serenity and omniscience of a god, and this would be the consequence of belief in *necessity*, that is to say, in unqualified determinism, a doctrine which would " make us survey all events with a placid and even temper, and approve and disapprove them without impeachment to our self-possession   He . . . who regards all things past, present, and to come as links of an indissoluble chain, will, as often as he recollects this comprehensive view, be superior to the tumult of passion ; and will reflect upon the moral concerns of mankind with the same clearness of perception, the same unalterable firmness of judgment, and the same tranquillity as we are accustomed to do upon the truths of geometry." [2]

For some years Wordsworth was one of Godwin's most fervent disciples, and must have been acquainted with his *Political Justice* from the date of its appearance.   In London he breathed a Godwinian atmosphere.   His earliest poems had just been published by Johnson, of St Paul's Churchyard, who was one of Godwin's familiar friends.   Occasionally he sat under the preaching of the dissenting minister Joseph Fawcett, a singular character who had a conscious share in the production of Godwin's *Political Justice*, and, at a later period, unconsciously assisted Wordsworth when he was writing *The Excursion*.   From him the poet derived the principal characteristics of the *Solitary*, who, after becoming intoxicated with revolutionary hopes, loses his illusions and becomes a sceptic.   In 1793, or

---

[1] " It grows out of a simple, clear and unanswerable theory of the human mind, that we first stand in need of a certain animal subsistence and shelter, and after that, that our only true felicity consists in the expansion of our intellectual powers, the knowledge of truth, and the practice of virtue " (ii. p. 833, 1st edition).

[2] *Political Justice*, i. 316

thereabouts, Fawcett was full of enthusiasm, and inculcated from the pulpit certain of the political and social ideas which he had instilled in the mind of Godwin. He was a rationalist and a republican, and adhered to the doctrines of Christianity only in so far as they coincided with his own opinions. He readily turned to Christian doctrine for arguments in defence of revolutionary ideas, or for prophecies which described the approaching glories of the golden age, or millennium. He made use of it to undermine the sentiments of friendship and patriotism ; for was not any attack on English patriotism at that time an assistance to France and her Republic ? [1] But he abandoned Christianity the moment he found himself in conflict with it, whether he desired to make a profession of determinism, or to glorify the intelligence, which he regarded as the source of virtue.[2] Not long afterwards he altogether ceased to make profession of Christianity, having already abjured it in spirit, and in 1795 gave up his ministry, thenceforth entrusting his thoughts to poetry. He had been a florid preacher, and became a declamatory poet. In his *Art of War*, which met with Wordsworth's approval,[3] and in the series of elegies in which he depicts the miseries consequent on war, there is little to praise beyond magnanimity of thought. Once only does his work approach the level of poetry, when, in his apostrophe to winter, after enumerating all its gloomy characteristics, he suddenly contradicts himself in order to hail it with gratitude as the only power in the world capable of suspending the conflicts which stain the earth with blood.[4]

At a later time Wordsworth was to judge Fawcett with severity, or at any rate to represent his life, which came to an early close in irregularity and excess, as a type of those existences which the Revolution raised aloft for the moment, only to dash them to pieces immediately after-

---

[1] Sermon xviii., Christianity vindicated as not particularly inculcating Friendship and Patriotism. "And who is my neighbour?" Luke x. 29. *Sermons delivered at the Sunday Evening Lecture, for the winter season, at the Old Jewry*, by Joseph Fawcett (vol. ii. p. 149).

[2] Conclusion of his sermon on spiritual pride, vol. i. pp. 422-425.

[3] *The Art of War*, a poem by Joseph Fawcett, London, 1795.

[4] *War Elegies*, 1801. Elegy vii., Winter.

wards. At first, however, he admired him ; and it may
have been to Fawcett that he owed his introduction to the
philosophy of Godwin, to which he surrendered himself
heart and soul as soon as he had acquired a knowledge of
it. " Throw aside your books of chemistry," said Wordsworth to a young student in the Temple, " and read
Godwin on Necessity." [1] Wordsworth himself long
remained, " even to extravagance, a Necessitarian," [2] and
Coleridge, who was at first an adherent, and afterwards
a great antagonist, of the doctrine, never knew a more
obstinate supporter of it.

Without delay Wordsworth put into practice Godwin's
main precept, that nothing should be admitted as certain
unless proved to be so by his reason. He would no
longer take anything as true on trust, nor recognise any
man as an authority. Did not experience prove that all
these philosophical systems, which fell to pieces at the
touch of fact, were vitiated by a hidden defect ? He resolved to discover the perfect system, and to rebuild the
frail work of the age on a firm basis. In this endeavour
he expected to succeed, because he had an unbounded
faith in reason, and was conscious of his own sincerity and
determination.

> Somewhat stern
> In temperament, withal a happy man,
> And therefore bold to look on painful things,
> Free likewise of the world, and thence more bold,
> I summoned my best skill, and toiled, intent
> To anatomise the frame of social life ;
> Yea, the whole body of society
> Searched to its heart.　　.　　.　　.
> Dragging all precepts, judgments, maxims, creeds,
> Like culprits to the bar ; calling the mind,
> Suspiciously, to establish in plain day
> Her titles and her honours.

The result of this quest, entered upon with enthusiasm
and in full confidence of ultimate success, was despair. He

---

[1] Hazlitt's *Spirit of the Age*, William Godwin.

[2] Letter from Coleridge to Thomas Poole, 14th January 1804. *T. Poole*, by
Mrs Sandford, ii. p. 123.

failed to get beyond the provisional doubt with which he started, and never attained the firm ground of certainty.

> Demanding formal *proof*,
> And seeking it in everything, I lost
> All feeling of conviction, and, in fine,
> Sick, wearied out with contrarieties,
> Yielded up moral questions in despair.
>   This was the crisis of that strong disease,
> This the soul's last and lowest ebb; I drooped,
> Deeming our blessèd reason of least use
> Where wanted most.

Then, transferring the feelings of a later period to the past, or, rather, explaining with a clearness which did not come until long afterwards the blank misery of the determinism which was nevertheless his own creed, Wordsworth adds:

> " The lordly attributes
> Of will and choice," I bitterly exclaimed,
> " What are they but a mockery of a Being
> Who hath in no concerns of his a test
> Of good and evil; knows not what to fear
> Or hope for, what to covet or to shun;
> And who, if those could be discerned, would yet
> Be little profited, would see, and ask,
> Where is the obligation to enforce?
> And, to acknowledged law rebellious, still,
> As selfish passion urged, would act amiss;
> The dupe of folly, or the slave of crime." [1]

III

At this point the course of *The Prelude* suddenly changes. Having shown how the moral law within him was destroyed by analysis, Wordsworth passes abruptly to the history of his restoration, which was by no means so speedily accomplished as his autobiography would lead us

[1] *The Prelude*, xi. 275-320.

to believe. Feeling that in that work he ought only to employ " guarded words," he reserved for future narration in some "dramatic tale" the truths he learnt, or thought he learnt, at that period, as well as the errors into which he fell,

> betrayed
> By present objects, and by reasonings false
> From their beginnings, inasmuch as drawn
> Out of a heart that had been turned aside
> From Nature's way by outward accidents,
> And which was thus confounded, more and more
> Misguided, and misguiding.[1]

The dramatic tale he speaks of is *The Excursion*, in which, taking the Solitary, a character whom he condemns, as his example, he makes a more profound study of that moral decomposition which was the final effect of the Revolution upon so many. No doubt the Solitary, for whom Fawcett provided the model, is not in all respects identical with Wordsworth. His life, his age, are different; Wordsworth afterwards recovered and the Solitary does not. Nevertheless, in all essential features, he is Wordsworth, suffering from a moral disease, judged by Wordsworth restored to health. The Solitary, in despair of delivering the world from the tyranny which crushes it, at first finds consolation in the thought that, through the stimulus which the Revolution has given to his mind, he will at any rate himself be free from the trammels of prejudice.

> I began to feel
> That, if the emancipation of the world
> Were missed, I should at least secure my own,
> And be in part compensated.[2]

As a pledge of his deliverance he did not scruple

> to proclaim,
> And propagate, by liberty of life,
> Those new persuasions. Not that I rejoiced,
> Or even found pleasure, in such vagrant course,
> For its own sake ; but farthest from the walk

---

[1] *The Prelude*, xi. 281-293.　　　[2] *The Excursion*, iii. 790-793.

Which I had trod in happiness and peace,
Was most inviting to a troubled mind ;
That, in a struggling and distempered world,
Saw a seductive image of herself.[1]

Wordsworth became emancipated in theory only, but it is evident that he was haunted by the idea of emancipation of the other kind. Without any moral law himself, he would have been greatly at a loss if called upon to vindicate the temperate line of conduct from which he does not appear to have swerved. At that time he certainly had a clearer perception of the causes of error, and even of crime, than of those which lead to innocence and virtue. Between 1795 and 1797 he produced only two works ; one a short essay in prose, " illustrative of that constitution and those tendencies of human nature which make the apparently *motiveless* actions of bad men intelligible to careful observers," [2] the other, to which this essay was introductory, his tragedy of *The Borderers*. It spite of its imperfection this piece is interesting as showing the matters with which the author's mind was preoccupied, and as sounding, with no less psychological boldness than lack of dramatic skill, the blackest depths of villany.

Strange indeed was the destiny of this tragedy ! For some time Wordsworth's friends regarded *The Borderers* as his *magnum opus*. On first hearing it read, Coleridge exclaimed," His drama is absolutely wonderful. . . There are in the piece those *profound* truths of the human heart, which I find three or four times in the *Robbers* of Schiller, and often in Shakespere, but in Wordsworth there are no inequalities." [3] To-day it is never spoken of by critics except as one of the sins of Wordsworth's youth, and most of them do not even seem to think it worth reading. Mr Swinburne, who at least acknowledges its literary value, asserts that it is " unparalleled by any serious production of the human intellect for morbid and monstrous,

---

[1] *The Excursion*, iii. 797-895.
[2] *The Borderers*, prefatory note. This prose essay has been lost.
[3] Letter from Coleridge to Cottle (June 1797?). Campbell, *Life of Coleridge*, London, 1894, p. 67.

extravagance of horrible impossibility." [1]   " Il n'y a que les
poètes vertueux," he quotes, with a spice of contempt,
" pour avoir de ces idées-la."   Mr Swinburne does not
reflect that what he says of *The Borderers* might with
equal truth be said of the Terror, and that it was the
Terror, in fact, which gave birth to Wordsworth's tragedy.
It is the work of a Godwinian, who, having at first seen
only the grandeur of his master's system, is horror-struck
when he suddenly perceives its consequences. [2]   If the
admiration of Coleridge is extravagant, the reason is that
Wordsworth has succeeded in laying his finger on a tender
place in the minds of Godwinian enthusiasts, who were
still numerous in Coleridge's circle of acquaintances, though
he himself was no longer one of them.   Imagine Godwin's
argument for the necessity of extirpating all the human
feelings read in the lurid light of '93 ; conceive his
condemnation of all traditional rules of conduct interpreted by aid of the wholesale executions decreed by
the Mountain in the name of public welfare, or, in other
words, of the greatest amount of general happiness, and
The Borderers acquires a meaning ; it ceases to be a fantastic vision, and reflects a reality which it is only too
impossible to deny.

Observe that the main purpose of the tragedy, which
is the delineation of the philosophical murderer, was then
in the air.   Fiction and the drama were beginning to be
anxious as to what man would be, if he were emancipated
from all social convention, and were to summon one by
one before the tribunal of individual reason all the sentiments on which society is founded ; not only those of
obedience to parents, conformity to law, and conjugal
fidelity, but also the still more essential feelings of pity,
and respect for human life.   The arguments advanced by
one to attack the hypocrisy of institutions were employed
by another to sap the foundations of human nature.   The
vilest crime might be justified by an imperious logic.

---

[1] A. Swinburne, *Miscellanies*, London, 1886, p. 118.
[2] Closely similar is the theme of M. Paul Bourget's *Le Disciple*, a novel
which gives a better idea than anything else can do of Wordsworth's state of
mind at this time.

Hence arose the transformation of the "traitor." He became the reasoner and even the moralist of the work, and enjoyed the monopoly of both doctrine and logic. Shakespeare's monsters of villany were revived, bringing to the service of their passions a philosophy no longer rudimentary like that of Richard III., Iago, or even Edmund, but one fully and consistently worked out. Schiller had led the way with *The Robbers* in 1782, and, Franz Moor's moral nihilism had founded a school, no less than the passionate revolt of his brother Charles against society. In England, "satanic" literature sprang up and flourished long before Byron gave it the sanction of his master-pieces.[1] A villain of this new variety was sketched in 1791 by the most popular English novelist of this latest epoch of the eighteenth century. Certainly the value of Anne Radcliffe's work lies not in the depth or subtlety of the characters she has drawn, but in the novelty and picturesqueness of its setting. And for that very reason she is our best source of information on what the reader of the moment considered a faithful representation of a criminal. In *The Romance of the Forest*, the Marquis Philip de Montalt wishes to have his niece Adeline put out of the way, that he may enjoy undisputed possession of the property of which he has deprived her. La Motte's life and honour are in his hands, and the Marquis, who endeavours to persuade him to the murder, strives to weaken the scruples of his accomplice by the following arguments :

"There are certain prejudices attached to the human mind," said the Marquis, in a slow, solemn voice, " which it requires all our reasoning to keep from interfering with our happiness, certain set notions, acquired in infancy, and cherished involuntarily by age, which grow up and assume a gloss so plausible, that few minds in what is called a civilised country can afterwards overcome them. Truth is often perverted by education. While the refined European

---

[1] A rapid succession of works of this class had appeared in John Moore's *Zeluco* (1786); Robert Bage's *Man as he is*; Thomas Holcroft's *Anna St. Yves* (1792), and *Hugh Trevor* (1794-1797); Godwin's *Caleb Williams*, and Lewis's *The Monk* (1796), which were followed, a generation later, by Byron's poems, Maturin's *Melmoth*, and the early works of Bulwer Lytton.

boasts a standard of honour, and a sublimity of virtue, which often leads them from pleasure to misery, and from nature to error, the simple uninformed American follows the impulse of his heart, and obeys the inspiration of wisdom. . . . Nature, uncontaminated by false refinement . . . everywhere acts alike in the great occurrences of life.   The Indian discovers his friend to be perfidious, and he kills him; the wild Asiatic does the same; the Turk, when ambition fires or revenge provokes, gratifies his passion at the expense of life, and does not call it murder.   Even the polished Italian, directed by jealousy, or tempted by a strong circumstance of advantage, draws his stiletto, and accomplishes his purpose.   It is the first proof of a superior mind to liberate itself from prejudices of country or of education.   You are silent, La Motte; are you not of my opinion?"

"I am attentive, my Lord, to your reasoning."

"There are, I repeat it," said the Marquis, "people of minds so weak, as to shrink from acts they have been accustomed to hold wrong, however advantageous. *They never suffer themselves to be guided by circumstances, but fix for life upon a certain standard, from which they will, on no acccount, depart.*   Self-preservation is the great law of nature; when a reptile hurts us, or an animal of prey threatens us, we think no farther but endeavour to annihilate it.   When my life, or what may be essential to my life, requires the sacrifice of another, or even if some passion, wholly unconquerable, requires it, I should be a mad-man to hesitate." [1]

The character of the Marquis de Montalt faintly foreshadows that of Oswald, the traitor of *The Borderers.* They are alike in their contempt for every sort of "prejudice," that is to say, in ordinary language, for all the feelings which go to make up human nature.   They admit no settled moral law, and claim the right of deciding for themselves, without any intermediary, what they ought to do.   Both of them justify murder as a sign and proof of the moral independence of the murderer.

Once virtuous, Oswald has fallen a victim to a plot, and slain an innocent man in the belief that he was punishing a

[1] *The Romance of the Forest*, bk. iii. ch. iv.

guilty one.   At first almost overwhelmed by the violence
of his remorse, he has succeeded in overcoming it, and has
gained liberty of soul in the struggle.   Formerly he was
obedient to stupid rules :

> we subsist
> In slavery ; all is slavery ; we receive
> Laws, but we ask not whence those laws have come ;
> We need an inward sting to goad us on.[1]

Since committing his crime, instead of sinking beneath
humanity he has risen above it.

> When from these forms I turned to contemplate
> The World's opinions and her usages,
> I seemed a being who had passed alone
> Into a region of futurity,
> Whose natural element was freedom.[2]

He had learned " that every possible shape of action might
lead to good "[3] ; " that things will work to ends the slaves
o' the world do never dream of."[4]   Henceforth his ethical
code is that of Godwin, as summed up in the following lines :

> They who would be just must seek the rule
> By diving for it into their own bosoms.
> To-day you have thrown off a tyranny
> That lives but in the torpid acquiescence
> Of our emasculated souls, the tyranny
> Of the world's masters, with the musty rules
> By which they uphold their craft from age to age :
> You have obeyed the only law that sense
> Submits to recognise ; the immediate law,
> From the clear light of circumstances, flashed
> Upon an independent Intellect.[5]

Proud of his superior reason, Oswald has nothing but
contempt for opinion.   From the day when he discarded
false shame and spurious popularity, " twin sisters both of
Ignorance," has he not found life stretched before him

---

[1] *The Borderers*, ll. 1866-1869.   The lines are numbered in Dowden's edition.
[2] *Ibid.*, ll. 1825-1829.   [3] *Ibid.*, l. 1790.
[4] *Ibid.*, ll. 945-947.   [5] *Ibid.*, ll. 1496-1506.

" smooth as some broad way cleared for a monarch's progress ? " [1]   The enmity of men, on the other hand, is the infallible sign of greatness.

> We are praised, only as men in us
> Do recognise some image of themselves,
> An abject counterpart of what they are,
> Or the empty thing that they would wish to be.
> I felt that merit has no surer test
> Than obloquy ; that, if we wish to serve
> The world in substance, not deceive by show,
> We must become obnoxious to its hate,
> Or fear disguised in simulated scorn. [2]

It is madness to concern oneself with the opinion

> of the world's presumptuous judges,
> Who damn where they can neither see nor feel
> With a hard-hearted ignorance. [3]

Envy is the essence of weakness :

> Join twenty tapers of unequal height
> And light them joined, and you will see the less
> How 'twill burn down the taller ; and they all
> Shall prey upon the tallest.

Doubtless there is a risk that he who defies the prejudices of his fellow-men may be driven from among them and compelled to walk in solitude.   But what of that ?   " The eagle lives in Solitude ! " [4]

And just as it has rendered Oswald indifferent to opinion, thought has gradually destroyed within him all semblance of emotion.

> Remorse—
> It cannot live with thought ; think on, think on,
> And it will die.   What ! in this universe,
> Where the least things control the greatest, where
> The faintest breath that breathes can move a world ;

---

[1] *The Borderers*, ll. 1844-1847.   [2] *Ibid.*, ll. 1833-1841.
[3] *Ibid.*, ll. 1513-1516.   [4] *Ibid.*, ll. 1522-1526.

What! feel remorse, where, if a cat had sneezed,
A leaf had fallen, the thing had never been
Whose very shadow gnaws us to the vitals.[1]

Nor does pity fare any better under the assault of his reasoning. Godwin's repudiation of violent measures is due to an arbitrary inconsistency. Is not general utility the only criterion of the worth of actions ?

Benevolence, that has not heart to use
The wholesome ministry of pain and evil,
Becomes at last weak and contemptible.[2]

This is how the more logical disciple addresses his master :

A whipping to the moralists who preach
That misery is a sacred thing; for me,
I know no cheaper engine to degrade a man,
Nor any half so sure.[3]

We kill a worn-out horse, and who but women
Sigh at the deed? Hew down a withered tree,
And none look grave but dotards.[4]

The wiles of woman,
And craft of age, seducing reason, first
Made weakness a protection, and obscured
The moral shapes of things.[5]

Such, for Oswald, are the maxims of judicious conduct. He has derived them from Godwin's philosophy. Not that this philosophy has made him the criminal that he is; nevertheless it has given him a pride in crime, and, if not the zeal, at least the arguments and the eloquence with which proselytes are made. The post-revolutionary Iago is armed with logic and philosophy against adversaries or victims who have no defence against him but their candour. Doubtless he only partially succeeds in destroying his own conscience by his reasoning. He fails to stifle his remorse, and is but half convinced of the truth of his own formulas.

[1] *The Borderers*, ll. 1570-1577. [2] *Ibid.*, ll. 618-620.
[3] *Ibid.*, ll. 1169-1172. [4] *Ibid.*, ll. 937-939.
[5] *Ibid.*, ll. 1090-1093.

Personal interest, ambition, the need of causing an innocent man to fall, that he himself may have a companion in crime, are his prime motives. But his half-faith in the maxims he propounds is sufficient to give him the appearance of one who thinks intelligently and acts with resolution. Now Oswald the *Montagnard* is surrounded by weak and virtuous *Girondins*. The *Borderers*, the kindly-disposed free-booters into whose midst he has wormed his way, have no other object than good, but they rely on their reason to distinguish it from what is bad. They obey no established law, and therein lies the danger. Oswald proves to Marmaduke, the open-hearted chief of the band, that on his own authority, and without listening to the promptings of pity, he ought to kill an old man whom Oswald represents as a criminal. Marmaduke can do no more than fall a prey to his wiles, curse the man who has given him such fatal counsel, and suffer the dire pangs of remorse. His only exclamations are those of a man groping in the darkness, unable either to see or to understand. He is crushed by his unbearable load of ignorance.

> O wretched Human-kind! Until the mystery
> Of all this world is solved, well may we envy
> The worm, that, underneath a stone whose weight
> Would crush the lion's paw with mortal anguish,
> Doth lodge, and feed, and coil, and sleep, in safety.[1]

Wordsworth, no less than Marmaduke, was at that time unable to find any answer to Oswald's cynical philosophy. He might abominate it; he could not refute it. Before the depths of depravity, now for the first time revealed, his spirit shuddered, powerless. He no longer attributed evil to Society alone, in the sense in which he understood the word in his poem on Salisbury Plain. In that work the murderer was a good man.

> Never on earth was gentler creature seen;
> He'd not have robbed the raven of its food.[2]

---

[1] *The Borderers*, ll. 1805-1810.   [2] *Guilt and Sorrow*, stanza lxviii.

"An evil world, and that world's hard law," [1] were alone responsible for his trangression. Since that time Wordsworth had thought deeply. He had perceived that the causes of crime were less simple than he had supposed, that its sources were far more difficult to exhaust. Evil was inherent in man's limited and imperfect nature. Not only was it intrenched, beyond the reach of every attempt at reform, within the most secret recesses of the human heart; it could also enlist the services of the intellect. And it was this unscrupulous antagonist to which the weak and wavering forces which make for goodness were opposed.

Wordsworth, who had once desired to contend against evil, now said, with Marmaduke,

> we look
> But at the surfaces of things; we hear
> Of towns in flames, fields ravaged, young and old
> Driven out in troops to want and nakedness;
> Then grasp our swords and *rush upon a cure*
> *That flatters us, because it asks not thought* :
> The deeper malady is better hid;
> The world is poisoned at the heart.[2]

Having, like Marmaduke, studied the wisest philosophies, and analysed every sentiment of the heart, this is now "the corner-stone" of his philosophy:

> I would not give a denier for the man
> Who, on such provocation as this earth
> Yields, could not chuck his babe beneath the chin
> And send it with a fillip to its grave.[3]

It seemed that with such convictions good men must find their last refuge in pessimism, the inevitable result of high hopes deceived, and of the despair consequent on a survey of a depraved and irreclaimable race. Such a discovery would naturally cast a permanent shadow over thought. Sadness would be the necessary accompaniment of lofty intelligence united with moral excellence. And yet, at the very time when he was writing

---

[1] *Guilt and Sorrow*, stanza lvii.   [2] *The Borderers*, ll. 1039-1046.
[3] *Ibid.*, ll. 1250-1254.

The Borderers, Wordsworth was on the brink of recovery.
He was in the midst of the conditions necessary to it, all
of which were co-operating to restore his health of mind.
He became neither a René, an Obermann, nor a Manfred.
His life was not to be wasted in idle regret ; it was not to
evaporate in contempt or pity for human effort, nor in
sneering at believers and enthusiasts.

> Depressed, bewildered thus, I did not walk
> With scoffers, seeking light and gay revenge
> From indiscriminate laughter, nor sate down
> In reconcilement with an utter waste
> Of intellect; such sloth I could not brook,
> (Too well I loved, in that my spring of life,
> Pains-taking thoughts, and truth, their dear reward).[1]

His whole life was to be devoted to the recovery of
his early lightness of heart. The instinct of an invalid
seeking a cure had already led him to take the most useful
precautions, and directed him to the surest remedies. He
found satisfaction for the need of abstract reasoning, which
long habit had engendered in him, in turning his mind to
mathematics, the science " enthroned where . . . space and
time . . . find no admission," [2] beyond the regions disturbed
by human will and power. He purged himself of his pessimism after the manner of Goethe, by giving utterance to it
in *The Borderers*. And further, with the aid of a favourable combination of circumstances, he had managed to
secure that independent life of which he had dreamed, far
from the city, where he might have suffered a dangerous
relapse, in the country atmosphere in which alone he could
breathe, and with the companionship of the being he loved
best in the world, his sister Dorothy. With such protection and support, slowly but surely he recovered what
he had lost, a moral equilibrium as perfect as any man,
or, to say the least, any poet, has ever enjoyed.

---

[1] *The Prelude*, xi. 321-327.   [2] *Ibid.*, xi. 330.

BOOK III

The Stages of Recovery

CHAPTER I

Dorothy Wordsworth

ALTHOUGH circumstances finally conspired to raise Wordsworth from his dejection, at first they tended for some time to depress him. During the three years which followed his return to England, from the end of 1792 to the end of 1795, his life had been an unhappy one. Trouble from other sources came to supplement that engendered by the course of his thought. His repeated refusals to enter the bondage of a regular profession had soon brought upon him the worse thraldom of poverty. The slender remnant of his patrimony was quickly exhausted, and on several occasions the day had seemed very near when he would be obliged to surrender his liberty whether he wished it or no. Although he restricted his desires that they might the more easily be satisfied, and laid down at this time the plan of the frugal and independent life he was afterwards to lead, he could no more carry out this programme without possessing money or earning it, than he could realize a dream of wealth and ambition. In return for what they considered his inexcusable idleness, his uncles and guardians left him to himself. They also regarded him with suspicion on account of the doubtless irrepressible vehemence of his republican opinions.[1] Was not one of them, Dr Cookson, a clergyman of the Church of England ? Wordsworth therefore conceived the idea of leading a secluded life quite apart from his hostile family, and beyond the pale of a society with which he had no sympathy ; a life to be shared by the sister who cherished the same dream as him-

---

[1] Letter of Dorothy Wordsworth written in 1793. She speaks of the prejudices "of my two uncles against my dear William," and says "the subject is an unpleasant one." Knight, *Life of Wordsworth*, i. p. 82.

self, and was prepared to sacrifice every other affection to the brother she loved beyond anything else.

Very small and unpretending was this cottage of his dreams, "sole wish, sole object" of his way,[1] in which he and his sister were to spend their "golden days" in tranquillity. It was too much, however, to expect as yet, and while they delighted in a prospect which in the distance was bright with hope, they sighed over the "dark and broad . . . gulph of time between."

Meanwhile they were unable even to meet. Since the Christmas of 1790, Wordsworth had not been allowed to visit Forncett Rectory, where Dorothy was living with the Cooksons. His example was considered dangerous, and precautions were taken to keep him separated from his sister and brothers. Homeless, lonely, and dispirited, he could discern no prospect of comfort but in a return to the wandering life he loved. But the charm of such a life depends on its being deliberately chosen, and for Wordsworth at this time it was rather a compulsory escape from worse troubles than a light-hearted pursuit of new pleasures. He wandered about rather than travelled. Yet even to satisfy this restless passion, he had to accept conditions to which a proud heart could not accommodate itself without some loss of dignity. Unable to journey at his own expense, he was obliged to act as travelling companion to an old Hawkshead schoolfellow, William Calvert, the son of a steward of the Duke of Norfolk. Calvert had become an admirer of Wordsworth, and offered to bear all the expenses of the journey in exchange for his society. Though this delicate offer was made by a friend, it was impossible that Wordsworth should feel as easy journeying to the Isle of Wight in Calvert's carriage, as when travelling on foot with a purse furnished, however slenderly, with his own cash, during his Swiss tour with Jones.[2] Others, it is true, have managed to exist under such conditions without compunction. Coleridge, for example, open-handed and communistic in spirit, found

[1] *Evening Walk*, l. 416.
[2] Wordsworth had recently expressed this sentiment, in his dedication of the *Descriptive Sketches* to Jones

little difficulty in bearing a weight of loans and obligations after he had squandered his own money. But Wordsworth, whose disposition was economical, was incapable, even when most indignant at the unequal distribution of wealth, of that contempt for money which despises even the money of other people. Nevertheless, after his tour with Calvert, which was quickly interrupted, we find him staying now with Jones in Wales, now here or there in the north, under the necessity of accepting the successive offers of hospitality made by those who were fond of him.

A delightful interval, however, occurred in the midst of his wanderings. He managed to see his sister once more, and to spend some weeks in her society early in 1794. The lot of the two orphans, who were separated from each other, had excited the compassion of a friend of their mother's, under whose roof at Halifax their meeting took place. Thence they traversed the Lake District together on foot, and spent a month at Windybrow, a small farmhouse near Keswick, placed at their disposal by Calvert. Here they amused themselves with housekeeping, and endeavoured to calculate how much the simplest possible country life would cost them. "Our breakfast and supper," writes Dorothy, "are of milk, and our dinner chiefly of potatoes, and we drink no tea."[1] Yet how much bitterness was mingled with this childlike glee! Writing to a friend to inform him that he has just met his sister again, Wordsworth says, "What is to become of me I know not."[2] The greater their delight in seeing one another again, the more distressing was the prospect of approaching and inevitable separation. It was in these days that the young fellow, stimulated by remorse for his inactivity, thought of earning a livelihood by writing in an opposition newspaper. Rendered needless, however, by the occurrence of an opportune event, these half-hearted efforts to obtain regular work were soon permanently abandoned. While Wordsworth was taking one step after another without very much zeal, Raisley

---

[1] Letter from Dorothy Wordsworth. Knight, *Life of Wordsworth*, i. p. 91.
[2] Letter to Matthews, 17th February 1794. Knight, *Life of Wordsworth*, i. p. 88.

Calvert, the brother of his late travelling companion, was dying of consumption at Windybrow. Convinced that Wordsworth, who acted as his nurse, had talents which nothing but poverty and anxiety prevented him from giving to the world, Calvert informed him some time before his death that he intended to leave him a legacy. Calvert died in January 1795, and left him in fact a sum of £900. Hesitating no longer, Wordsworth then resolved to realize his dream, and adding his sister's slender resources to this modest fortune of his own, he established himself with her at Racedown in the autumn of 1795.

II

Racedown is situated in the south of Dorsetshire, in a hollow among hills cultivated to their summits or covered with gorse and broom, and opening here and there to allow glimpses of the sea at a furlong's distance. A stream flowing on the farther side of a field marked the boundary of the warm and luxuriant county of Devon, but on the Dorsetshire side of it the soil was less fertile and more sandy, the trees more battered by winds from the Channel. The peasants were wretchedly poor; their cottages shapeless structures of wood and clay, "not at all beyond what might be expected in savage life."[1] The farm house occupied by Wordsworth was a large three-storied building of red brick, destitute of beauty. Scarcely a trace of the locality is to be found in Wordsworth's poetry, and what little he says of it gives one the impression of a rugged and dreary region. It was here that he watched poor Margaret ply her monotonous handicraft, drawing out the hemp which she had wound around her waist like a belt, and spinning it as she walked backwards before the door of her cottage, which grew more dilapidated every year.[2] Here, too, Goody Blake shivered in her wretched cabin, through

[1] Letter of Dorothy Wordsworth, 30th November 1795. Knight, *Life of Wordsworth*, i. p. 108.
[2] *The Excursion*, i. 858-860.

the open door of which the poet caught a glimpse of its interior :

> On a hill's northern side she dwelt,
> Where from sea-blasts the hawthorns lean,
> And hoary dews are slow to melt.[1]

To tell the truth, he did not reside at Racedown from choice. He had settled there from motives of economy, being allowed to occupy it without rent, on condition that the owner might spend a few weeks there from time to time. Wordsworth's biographers, moreover, are wrong in representing him as cured immediately he had established himself at Racedown. It was here, on the contrary, that his moral crisis reached its most acute stage. His thoughts were still engrossed by humanity. During the two years over which his residence at Racedown extended, he was more occupied with social evils and man's instinctive depravity, than with the beauty of sunsets or the charm of flowers, and did little more than add some touches to *Guilt and Sorrow*, write some personal satires which he never published, compose the tragedy of *The Borderers*, and outline the distressing narrative of *The Ruined Cottage*.

Though he had settled in the country, he did not straightway return to nature. Doubtless she had never cast him off. In the hours of his deepest affliction he had never lost his sensibility to the charm of spring-time. Even " when the spirit of evil reached its height," Nature maintained for him " a secret happiness." The woods had never ceased to fulfil their ministry for him,

> To interpose the covert of [their] shades,
> Even as a sleep, between the heart of man
> And outward troubles, between man himself,
> Not seldom, and his own uneasy heart.[2]

But there is a great difference between this passive acceptance of a benefit almost entirely physical, and that loving and joyous contemplation which demands the service of the entire being, body and soul, mind and heart. At this

---

[1] *Goody Blake and Harry Gill.* [2] *The Prelude*, xii. 24-27.

time, moreover, he regarded his love of Nature as a weakness which ought not to be indulged, lest his reason should be seduced from its stern supremacy.   He was like Marmaduke, who, descrying through a crevice "a star twinkling above his head,"[1] was for a moment withheld by the heavenly apparition from committing the intended rational murder, but after reflection exclaimed,

> O Fool!
> To let a creed, built in the heart of things,
> Dissolve before a twinkling atom![2]

That he might again become the poet of nature it was necessary first of all that his imagination should be healed of that strange disease which, at a later time, he never mentioned without a kind of remorse.   Abuse of analysis had not only parched and wasted his intelligence, it had distorted his power of poetic vision.

> The visible Universe
> Fell under the dominion of a taste
> Less spiritual, with microscopic view
> Was scanned, as I had scanned the moral world.[3]

He no longer saw it as it needs to be seen ; his attitude towards it was now judicial or critical :

> even in pleasure pleased
> Unworthily, disliking here, and there
> Liking ; by rules of mimic art transferred
> To things above all art ; but more,—for this,
> Although a strong infection of the age,
> Was never much my habit—giving way
> To a comparison of scene with scene,
> Bent overmuch on superficial things,
> Pampering myself with meagre novelties
> Of colour and proportion ; to the moods
> Of time and season, to the moral power,
> The affections and the spirit of the place,
> Insensible.[4]

He was a slave to the tyranny of "the bodily eye, in every stage of life the most despotic of our senses,"[5]

[1] *The Borderers*, 988-9.
[2] *Ibid.*, 1218-1220.
[3] *The Prelude*, xii. 88-93.
[4] *Ibid.*, xii. 109-121.
[5] *Ibid.*, xii.:128-129.

whereas Nature, in protest against this absolute dominion, summons " all the senses each to counteract the other, and themselves." Thus, vivid as they were, the delights he then derived from a country life were not profound.

> I roamed from hill to hill, from rock to rock,
> Still craving combinations of new forms,
> New pleasure, wider empire for the sight,
> Proud of her own endowments, and rejoiced
> To lay the inner faculties asleep.[1]

Very different had been his enjoyment of Nature before he left his native hills.

> I loved whate'er I saw : nor lightly loved,
> But most intensely ; never dreamt of aught
> More grand, more fair, more exquisitely framed
> Than those few nooks to which my happy feet
> Were limited.   I had not at that time
> Lived long enough, nor in the least survived
> The first diviner influence of this world,
> As it appears to unaccustomed eyes.
> I felt, observed, and pondered ; did not judge,
> Yea, never thought of judging ; with the gift
> Of all this glory filled and satisfied.[2]

Like his sister's friend, the maiden seen near Penrith and loved at first sight, he was not then perplexed by " rules prescribed by passive taste, or barren intermeddling subtleties." His eye was not the tyrant of his heart. " Whate'er the scene presented to [his] view, that was the best." [3]   And after his Alpine wanderings he was still the same.   It was later that degradation came, the effect

> Of custom that prepares a partial scale
> In which the little oft outweighs the great,

and also of a more passionate epoch, the tumult of which made " the milder minstrelsies of rural scenes inaudible."

But this hour of Wordsworth's life derives its interest, not from the spot in which he dwelt, for he did not see it

---

[1] *The Prelude*, xii. 143-147.   [2] *Ibid.*, xii. 174-190.
[3] *Ibid.*, xii. 151-160.

with " the poet's eye," but from the presence of one whose
example aided him to recover the gift of poetic vision;
from the companionship of his sister, who, from that time
forth, wielded over him an influence at once gentle and
stimulating, caressing and irresistible.

III

Life had treated Dorothy less harshly since the days
when she used to lament the austerity of her grand-parents
in the little mercer's shop at Penrith. To her great satisfaction, her uncle, the reverend Mr Cookson, had taken
her away with him towards the close of 1788, when she
was seventeen years old, and since then she had lived at
Forncett Rectory, near Norwich, happy in the cultivation of
her garden, and in keeping a little school for the children
of the neighbourhood. Her holidays were those which
one or other of her brothers spent with her. Her joys,
" above all joys," had been the rare visits of William, one of
which occurred in 1790 at Christmas time, when the student
passed his vacation at Forncett. Their recreations had
been of the simplest kind. The winter was mild, and
every morning and evening, for two hours at a time,
the sister had walked up and down the gravelled walks of
the garden, leaning on her brother's arm. But William's
warm affection and frank outpouring of his thoughts and
feelings made these walks so delightful to her that the
mere recollection of them induced her to repeat them during
the ensuing winters, by herself, in the icy north wind.
And two years and a half later she still spoke of them
to a friend as the most precious hours she could remember.[1] The idea of perpetuating these brief moments
of serene and perfect happiness had at once arisen
simultaneously in the hearts of both brother and sister.
Aided by her natural tastes, this idea enabled Dorothy
to resist the fascinations of a life which was not without
its periods of worldly gaiety. In his capacity as canon

[1] Letters of 23rd May 1791, Knight, *Life of Wordsworth*, i. p. 53, and
16th June 1793, p. 86.

of Windsor, Mr Cookson took her with him to spend some months at the English Versailles. In the summer of 1792, when her brother was in the first heat of his revolutionary zeal at Blois, she enjoyed the high honour of meeting the royal family every evening on the terrace, and "admired the king in his conversation with her uncle and aunt, and his interest (and that of the Princesses) in the children of her uncle and aunt." During this visit she led quite a worldly life, was taken for drives along roads traversed by sumptuous equipages, witnessed horse-races and several times went to balls.[1] The life, however, was not such as to please her long. She remained shy and unsociable, and never acquired the elegant and restrained manners of lofty society. Immediately after her return from Windsor, we find her haunted by the dream of a cottage in which she might live with William. Passionately attached to her brothers, she had from the first, with unerring instinct, detected his superiority. It was he, of them all, whom she admired and preferred. From the letters which she wrote at this period to a friend of her childhood we may gain a knowledge of her exalted affection, which he, on his part, reciprocated. They reveal also, in the absence of any other evidence, the half-feminine tenderness that was concealed under the somewhat Roman severity of bearing which the young man had adopted in his character as a republican. Speaking of Christopher, her youngest brother, Dorothy compared him to William as follows :

"His disposition is of the same caste as William's, and his inclinations have taken the same turn, but he is much more likely to make his fortune. He is not so warm as William, but has a most affectionate heart. His abilities, though not so great perhaps as his brother's, may be of more use to him ; as he has not fixed his mind upon any particular species of reading or conceived an aversion to any. . . . William has a great attachment to poetry ; so indeed has Kit, but William particularly." [2]

---

[1] Letter written by Dorothy Wordsworth, 16th Oct. 1792, Knight, *Life of Wordsworth*, i. p. 67.

[2] Letter of 16th June 1791, Knight, *Life of Wordsworth*, i. p. 57.

Pursuing the parallel between the brilliant schoolboy and the youthful genius she displays remarkable foresight as to the destiny of each. In another letter she returns to her comparison :

" Christopher," she says, " is like William. He has the same traits in his character, but less highly touched. . . . He is steady and sincere in his attachments. William has both these virtues in an eminent degree ; and a sort of violence of affection, if I may so term it, which demonstrates itself every moment of the day, when the objects of his affection are present with him, in a thousand almost imperceptible attentions to their wishes, in a sort of restless watchfulness which I know not how to describe, a tenderness that never sleeps, and at the same time such a delicacy of manners as I have observed in few men." [1]

" I cannot describe," she says elsewhere, " his attentions to me. There was no pleasure which he would not have given up with joy for half-an-hour's conversation with me." [2]

She was constantly possessed by the fixed idea of living with her brother, an idea fraught at once with charm and with bitterness. Unconsciously she always came back to it in her letters. In fancy she lived through joyful meetings which could never be realized, and visions rose before her of their future happiness in winter days :

" When I think of winter, I hasten to furnish our little parlour. I close the shutters, set out the tea-table, brighten the fire. When our refreshment is ended, I produce our work, and William brings his book to our table, and contributes at once to our instruction and amusement ; and at intervals we lay aside the book, and each hazard our observations upon what has been read, without the fear of ridicule or censure." [3]

For spring-time she had other dreams : " I have strolled into a neighbouring meadow, where I am enjoying the melody of birds, and the busy sounds of a fine summer's evening. But oh ! how imperfect is my pleasure whilst I am alone ! Why are you not seated with me ? and my dear

[1] Letter of 16th Feb. 1793, Knight, *Life of Wordsworth*, i. p. 79-80.
[2] Letter of 16th June, 1793, *Ibid.*, i. p. 86.
[3] Letter of 16th Feb. 1793, *Ibid.*, i. p. 80.

William, why is he not here also ? I could almost fancy that
I see you both near me. I hear *you* point out a spot, where
if we could erect a little cottage and call it our own we
should be the happiest of human beings. I see my brother
fixed with the idea of leading his sister to such a retreat.
Our parlour is in a moment furnished, our garden is
adorned by magic ; the roses and honeysuckles spring at
our command ; the wood behind the house lifts its head
and furnishes us with a winter's shelter and a summer's
noon-day shade. . . . You must forgive me for talking so
much of him ; my affection hurries me on, and makes me
forget that you cannot be so much interested in the subject
as I am. You do not know him ; you do not know how
amiable he is. Perhaps you reply, ' But I know how
blinded you are.' Well, my dearest, I plead guilty at
once ; I *must* be blind ; he cannot be so pleasing as my
fondness makes him. I am willing to allow that half the
virtues with which I fancy him endowed are the creation
of my love ; but surely I may be excused ! He was never
tired of comforting his sister ; he never left her in anger ;
he always met her with joy ; he preferred her society to
every other pleasure ;—or rather, when we were so happy
as to be within each other's reach, he had no pleasure when
we were compelled to be divided. Do not then expect
too much from this brother of whom I have delighted so
to talk to you. In the first place you must be with him
more than once before he will be perfectly easy in conversation. In the second place, his person is not in his favour
—at least I should think not ; but I soon ceased to discover
this—nay, I almost thought that the opinion which I had
formed was erroneous. He is, however, certainly rather
plain ; though otherwise has an extremely thoughtful
countenance, but when he speaks it is often lighted up by
a smile which I think very pleasing. But enough, he is
my brother ; why should I describe him ? I shall be
launching again into panegyric." [1]

Elsewhere she took one of those vows of affection so often
made and so often broken by many a young heart. In her
case, however, it was a sincere and accurate prediction.

[1] Letter written in June 1793, Myers, *Wordsworth*, p. 25-27.

" I am as heretical as yourself in my opinions concerning love and friendship. I am very sure that love will never bind me closer to any human being than friendship binds me to you my earliest friends, and to William my earliest and my dearest male friend." [1]

No less fervent was the brother's expression of affection for his sister.

" How much do I wish that each emotion of pleasure or pain that visits your heart should excite a similar pleasure or a similar pain within me, by that sympathy that will almost identify us when we have stolen to our little cottage. . . . I will write to my uncle, and tell him that I cannot think of going anywhere before I have been with you.   Whatever answer he gives me, I certainly will make a point of once more mingling my transports with yours. Alas ! my dear sister, how soon must this happiness expire ; yet there are moments worth ages." [2]

And somewhat later he exclaimed, " Oh, my dear, dear sister ! with what transport shall I again meet you ! with what rapture shall I again wear out the day in your sight ! . . . I see you in a moment running, or rather flying, to my arms." [3]

These brief extracts from their letters indicate better than anything else the passionate and tenacious affection by which brother and sister were united.   But the reasons for the influence which Dorothy exerted upon Wordsworth's poetry must be sought elsewhere.   In order to understand them we must have a knowledge of the rare faculties with which she was endowed.   And on this point we have an abundance of evidence, provided by observers no less acute than well-informed, and also, not only by Wordsworth himself but, better still, by the journals of her life and travels which Miss Wordsworth kept on different occasions.

" She is a woman indeed ! " cried Coleridge after his first meeting with her.   " In mind I mean, and heart ; for her person is such that if you expected to see a pretty

[1] Letter 16th June 1793, Knight, *Life of Wordsworth,* i. p. 86.
[2] Letter written in 1793, Myers, *Wordsworth,* p. 27.
[3] *Ibid.*

woman, you would think her rather ordinary; if you expected to see an ordinary woman, you would think her pretty! but her manners are simple, ardent, impressive. In every motion her most innocent soul outbeams so brightly, that who saw would say—

> Guilt was a thing impossible with her.

Her information various. Her eye watchful in minutest observation of Nature; and her taste a perfect electrometer. It bends, protrudes and draws in at subtlest beauties and most recondite faults."[1]

But a more complete and discerning portrait of her is that drawn by de Quincey. Though he did not make Dorothy Wordsworth's acquaintance until 1808, twelve years after she came to Racedown, he is so penetrative and thorough, he has so clear a perception of essential characteristics, of permanent moral and physical qualities, that there is no need to modify his description in order to make it applicable to Dorothy as she was at Racedown. After describing her as small and slender, with the complexion of a gipsy, de Quincey adds:

"Her eyes were not soft . . . nor were they fierce and bold; but they were wild and startling, and hurried in their motion. Her manner was warm and even ardent; her sensibility seemed constitutionally deep; and some subtle fire of impassioned intellect apparently burned within her, which, being alternately pushed forward into a conspicuous expression by the irrepressible instincts of her temperament, and then immediately checked, in obedience to the decorum of her sex and age, and her maidenly condition, gave to her whole demeanour, and to her conversation, an air of embarrassment and even of self-conflict, that was almost distressing to witness. Even her very utterance and enunciation often suffered in point of clearness

---

[1] Letter written in June 1797. Knight, *Life of Wordsworth*, i. p. 112-113. In drawing Dorothy's portrait Coleridge uses almost word for word the lines which he had just employed to describe Joan of Arc:

> And in each motion her most innocent soul
> Beamed forth so brightly, that who saw would say
> Guilt was a thing impossible in her.

> (*Destiny of Nations*, ll. 164-6.)

and steadiness, from the agitation of her excessive organic sensibility. At times the self-counteraction and self-baffling of her feelings caused her even to stammer. . . . The greatest deduction from Miss Wordsworth's attractions . . . was the glancing quickness of her motions, and other circumstances in her deportment (such as her stooping attitude when walking), which gave an ungraceful, and even an unsexual character to her appearance when out-of-doors. She did not cultivate the graces which preside over the person and its carriage. But, on the other hand, she was a person of very remarkable endowments intellectually ; and, in addition to the other great services which she rendered to her brother, this I may mention, as greater than all the rest, and it was one which equally operated to the advantage of every casual companion in a walk, viz., the exceeding sympathy, always ready and always profound, by which she made all that one could tell her, all that one could describe, all that one could quote from a foreign author, reverberate, as it were, *à plusieurs reprises* to one's own feelings, by the manifest impression it made upon *hers.* The pulses of light are not more quick and inevitable in their flow and undulation, than were the answering and echoing movements of her sympathizing attention. Her knowledge of literature was irregular, and thoroughly unsystematic. She was content to be ignorant of many things ; but what she knew and had really mastered lay where it could not be disturbed—in the temple of her own most fervid heart." [1]

De Quincey's subtle analysis shows clearly how intense and distinct a personality was that of Wordsworth's sister. Dorothy was something more than a companion whose affection is merely soothing. She had a measure of genius peculiar to herself, at once active and alluring. She was not content with a mere passive admiration of her brother. With all her faith in him, the greatness which her wishes as well as her fancy anticipated for him was of a particular kind. Very early she decided in her own heart that he would be a poet, and made up her mind also as to the sort of poet he would be. In 1790, during the few

[1] De Quincey, *The Lake Poets*, William Wordsworth.

weeks which they spent together in excursions around
Penrith, she had detected a strong resemblance between
her brother and Edwin, the *Minstrel* of Beattie.[1] The
comparison was an apt one; Edwin is in truth a faint but
accurate portrait of the author of *The Prelude*. To his
sister Wordsworth appeared just such another " strange
and wayward wight" as Edwin.[2] Like the young shepherd
whom nature from his infancy fashioned as a poet, Wordsworth spent his days in ranging the forest or wandering
beside the stream, shunning companions of his own age,
seeking by preference the torrent and the precipice, yet
not indifferent to milder scenes. Slightly altered, how
thoroughly the following stanza from *The Minstrel* becomes
applicable to Wordsworth :

> And yet poor Edwin was no vulgar boy;
> Deep thought oft seem'd to fix his infant eye.
> Dainties he heeded not, nor gaude, nor toy,
> Save one short pipe of rudest minstrelsy.
> Silent when glad ; affectionate, though shy ;
> And now his look was most demurely sad,
> And now he laughed aloud, yet none knew why.
> The neighbours stared and sigh'd, yet bless'd the lad :
> Some deem'd him wondrous wise, some thought him mad.[3]

These and many other points of resemblance between
Edwin and William seemed to the girl a sure token of the
latter's vocation. He would be the great poet of Nature
which it had not been in Edwin's (*i. e.*, Beattie's) power to
become. Besides, was she not the depositary of his poetic
secrets ? Was it not in her society that he had begun his first
poem, the *Evening Walk*, and had he not dedicated it to
her ? She had also in her possession other pieces of his
composition; but these, with the exception of " a little
sonnet" which she sent under the seal of secrecy to a friend
of her childhood, have been lost. She was not so far
blinded by admiration that she could not perceive the faults
of these youthful efforts. As soon as the *Evening Walk* and
the *Descriptive Sketches* were printed, she read and re-read

---

[1] Letter written in June, 1793. Knight, *Life of Wordsworth*, i. pp. 82-83.
[2] *The Minstrel*, i. st. xxii.   [3] *Ibid.*, i. st. xvi.

them with infinite care and minute attention, pointing out their real defects of style, their obscurity, and their misuse of uncommon or newly-invented words, analysing each line, and preparing, with the assistance of her younger brother Christopher, a bulky criticism intended for William's perusal. At the same time she was deeply sensible of the beauties which as yet were for the most part merely well-meant attempts. With unerring precision she pointed out the young man's peculiar gift. "The scenes which he describes have been viewed with a poet's eye, and are pourtrayed with a poet's pencil, and the poems contain many passages exquisitely beautiful." [1]

Every step, therefore, which her brother had since taken outside the path of poetry had filled her with anxiety, and with fears lest he should miss his way. She was either unwilling or unable to follow him in his political and philosophical investigations. It was her presence, more than anything else, which tended to divert the young disciple of Godwin in the hours of his sickness, and to lead him back to the object of his early worship. And how warm was Wordsworth's gratitude when he was able to recognise the full value of this favour ! "Then it was," he exclaims, after describing his despair,

> Then it was,
> Thanks to the bounteous Giver of all good !—
> That the belovèd Sister in whose sight
> Those days were passed, now speaking in a voice
> Of sudden admonition—like a brook
> That did but *cross* a lonely road, and now
> Is seen, heard, felt, and caught at every turn,
> Companion never lost through many a league—
> Maintained for me a saving intercourse
> With my true self; for, though bedimmed and changed
> Much, as it seemed, I was no further changed
> Than as a clouded and a waning moon :
> She whispered still that brightness would return,
> She, in the midst of all, preserved me still
> A Poet, made me seek beneath that name,
> And that alone, my office upon earth. [2]

[1] Letter of 16th February 1793, Knight, *Life of Wordsworth*, i. p. 81.
[2] *The Prelude*, xi. 333-348.

Nor was she satisfied with reminding him of his vocation ; she called his attention afresh to innumerable clear but hidden springs of poetry, which he had either forgotten or despised. She softened a certain austerity there was in him, and taught him to appreciate nature's " charms minute that win their way into the heart by stealth." [1]

> . . . To the very going out of youth
> I too exclusively esteemed *that* love,
> And sought *that* beauty, which, as Milton sings,
> Hath terror in it. Thou didst soften down
> This over-sternness ; but for thee, dear Friend !
> My soul, too reckless of mild grace, had stood
> In her original self too confident,
> Retained too long a countenance severe ;
> A rock with torrents roaring, with the clouds
> Familiar, and a favourite of the stars :
> But thou didst plant its crevices with flowers,
> Hang it with shrubs that twinkle in the breeze,
> And teach the little birds to build their nests
> And warble in its chambers. [2]

IV

Let us observe the working of this charm on Wordsworth's new life. The muffled clamour of the outside world only reaches the secluded farm-house at Racedown after long delay. Letters are delivered there but once a week. The excitement caused by successive shocks of public tidings, and maintained by heated arguments, gradually subsides from want of fuel. Faint inclinations for work, and the long periods of discouragement which succeed them, are replaced by regular employment. Wordsworth passes the greater part of the day in reading and writing. He has found the house well stocked with books. His solitary study doubtless brings him again face to face with the insoluble problems suggested by Godwin's philosophy, but there is no longer any reason to fear that the despondency engendered by futile analysis

---

[1] *The Prelude*, xiv. 241-242.   [2] *Ibid.*, xiv. 243-256.

will take entire possession of him. His being is penetrated by the wholesome and beneficent breath of the fresh air around him, which, unknown to himself, makes its way to the diseased foundations of his thought. His life is steeped in nature. The very necessities of his slender establishment divert him from too intense meditation. A part of his time is devoted to gardening, in which he prides himself on being proficient. Sometimes, like Goody Blake, he sets forth to warm himself by the exercise of gathering the sticks with which the gale has strewn the road. But the life he leads with his sister is so simple and frugal that from their very poverty they have long hours of leisure. Almost all their meals consist of vegetables;[1] eggs and milk are a luxury, and years will pass before their table is regularly supplied with meat. They are too poor to purchase material comforts, to which, indeed, they are indifferent. Free, moreover, from all social constraint, and without connections in the neighbourhood, they have every minute of the day to themselves. After making allowance for the time devoted to work, much remains to be spent in walking and sauntering. They take a two hours' stroll every morning, and now and then make long expeditions on foot. Many a time they must have traversed more than forty miles in the day. When Wordsworth wishes to go out, Dorothy is always ready to accompany him. She has the buoyant vigour of the first day of spring, and resembles a stream in April, "fresh and clear, . . . delighting in its strength," here "running with a young man's speed," and further on leaping to the foot of a rock in a cascade which sends forth "sallies of glad sound."[2] Nothing keeps her within doors; neither rain, nor storm, nor darkness. "Let the moon," exclaims Wordsworth,

[1] Writing from Racedown to a friend who has promised to send him a copy of Juvenal's Satires, Wordsworth says, "The copy of the poem you will contrive to frank, else ten to one I shall not be able to release it from the post-office. I have lately been living upon air and the essence of carrots, cabbages, turnips, and other esculent vegetables, not excluding parsley,—the produce of my garden." Extract from an unpublished letter to Wrangham. *The Athenæum, 8th* December 1894.

[2] *Poems on the naming of places.* "It was an April morning."

> Shine on thee in thy solitary walk
> And let the misty mountain-winds be free
> To blow against thee.[1]

At a sign from her brother she puts on her "woodland dress"[2] and sets forth. To such an extent did she carry the practice of taking long walks that her health was finally undermined by it; decay of both bodily and mental powers came prematurely upon her, and she lapsed into a premature old age[3] very different from that age of sober pleasures predicted for her by her brother, when her mind should be "a mansion for all lovely forms," her memory "as a dwelling-place for all sweet sounds and harmonies."[4]

Once in the open air with his sister, the young man can no longer apply himself to abstract thought. In her he finds again the ready wonder of his own youth; in her he beholds what he himself was once.

> In thy voice I catch
> The language of my former heart, and read
> My former pleasures in the shooting lights
> Of thy wild eyes.[5]

Her feelings find vent in cries of delight before each fresh view, each flower, each bird. Her eyes detect the most delicate tints of foliage, the faintest outline of the cloud. Her journals must be read if we are to understand the significance of these open-air walks and strolls, and their fertility for her brother's poems. In truth these walks, together with the schoolboy's observations, were the source of whatever is best in those poems—of all their essential features of beauty. That we possess no Racedown journal is of little consequence; those kept at Alfoxden and Grasmere, and during the Scotch tour, lay bare before

---

[1] *Tintern Abbey*, ll. 134-137.
[2] *To my Sister*.
[3] Such, at least, was Wordsworth's opinion as expressed to Harriet Martineau in 1845. *Harriet Martineau's Autobiography*, 3 vols., 1877, vol. I. p. 238.
[4] *Tintern Abbey*, ll. 137-142.   [5] *Ibid.*, ll. 116-119.

us not only the days with which they deal, but all other days as well, in fact the whole life of brother and sister. Here, accordingly, we must depart from strict chronology. If we desire to speak of the seed-germs we must not wait until the blossom has appeared in the form of those writings with which we are acquainted.

We will take the Alfoxden journal,[1] choosing it, not on account of its superiority—it is the shortest and most rudimentary of all—but because it is the first in point of time. The journal is only in existence for the winter months of 1798, and does not describe the delights experienced on first acquaintance, but rather expresses the feelings inspired by a six months' knowledge of the district, when daily walks have rendered it familiar. It is nevertheless a record of impressions as fresh, and of pleasures as keen, as those Dorothy Wordsworth must have felt when she and her brother took possession of Alfoxden. The treasures displayed before her seemed indeed to grow daily richer and more manifold than she had at first supposed them to be. How numerous were the wonderful or merely graceful sights which she noticed during the much abused season of winter, before it gave place to a backward but delightful spring! Here are a few prospects observed by her from the crest of the hills which overlooked their home. Many would have failed to derive such a variety of sensations from distant travel.

"*23rd January.*—The sound of the sea distinctly heard on the tops of the hills, which we could never hear in summer. We attribute this partly to the bareness of the trees, but chiefly to the absence of the singing of birds, the hum of insects, that noiseless noise which lives in the summer air. The villages marked out by beautiful beds of smoke. The turf fading into the mountain road.

"*3rd February.*—Walked . . . over the hills. The sea at first obscured by vapour; that vapour afterwards slid in one mighty mass along the sea-shore; the islands and one point of land clear beyond it. The distant country (which was purple in the clear dull air), overhung by straggling clouds that sailed over it, appeared like the

---

[1] Knight, *Life of Wordsworth*, i. ch. ix

darker clouds, which are often seen at a great distance apparently motionless, while the nearer ones pass quickly over them, driven by the lower winds. I never saw such a union of earth, sky, and sea. The clouds beneath our feet spread themselves to the water, and the clouds of the sky almost joined them.

"*26th February.*—Walked to the top of a high hill to see a fortification. Again sat down to feed upon the prospect; a magnificent scene, curiously spread out for even minute inspection, though so extensive that the mind is afraid to calculate its bounds. A winter prospect shows every cottage, every farm, and the forms of distant trees such as in summer have no distinguishing mark."

The woods around Alfoxden presented still greater variety. On the evening of the 27th January, though she mentions it as an "uninteresting" evening, "the moon burst through the invisible veil which enveloped her, the shadows of the oaks blackened, and their lines became more strongly marked. The withered leaves were coloured with a deeper yellow, a brighter gloss spotted the hollies."

Five days later they are driven by the wind to seek shelter in the same wood, the same, and yet how different.

"The trees almost roared, and the ground seemed in motion with the multitudes of dancing leaves, which made a rustling sound distinct from that of the trees."

On the 14th February she sat down in a thick part of the wood. "The near trees still, even to their topmost boughs, but a perpetual motion in those that skirt the wood. The breeze rose gently; its path distinctly marked till it came to the very spot where we were."

On the 2nd April, in a scene which many would have considered precisely similar, she distinguishes fresh details.

"A very high wind. . . . The half of the wood perfectly still, while the wind was making a loud noise behind us. The still trees only bowed their heads, as if listening to the wind. The hollies in the thick wood unshaken by the blast; only, when it came with a greater force, shaken by the rain drops falling from the bare oaks above."

A few weeks earlier, on the 17th February, the wood had undergone a transformation. A deep snow covered the ground.

"The sun shone bright and clear. A deep stillness in the thickest part of the wood, undisturbed, except by the occasional dropping of the snow from the holly boughs; no other sound but that of the water, and the slender notes of a redbreast, which sang at intervals on the outskirts of the southern side of the wood. There the bright green moss was bare at the roots of the trees, and the little birds were upon it. The whole appearance of the wood was enchanting; and each tree, taken singly, was beautiful. The branches of the hollies pendent with their white burden, but still showing their bright red berries, and their glossy green leaves. The bare branches of the oaks thickened by the snow."

The journal is in fact a ceaseless stream of minute observations, of delicate distinctions scarcely perceptible to the ordinary eye. Near the waterfall Dorothy notices how the green of adders-tongue and fern is set off by the gloom of the low, damp dell. She remarks that these plants are "in perpetual motion from the current of the air," whereas in summer they are "only moved by the drippings of the rocks." She is surprised that the sea should make a loud noise, as if disturbed, when the wind is silent. The trunks of the oaks planted on the highest ridge of a round hill "show in the light like the columns of a ruin." She notices that the trees on the outskirts of the wood, "being exposed more directly to the action of the sea breeze, [are] stripped of the network of their upper boughs, which are stiff and erect like black skeletons."

So truly are these observations the main events of her day that she mentions almost nothing else. One would think that the contemplation of nature had been the sole object of a life which, strangely empty and monotonous as it appears, was in reality as full and as varied as life can be. One whose senses are dull or cloyed may traverse the whole world, and find it but a tedious repetition of

the same scenes—water, plain, wood and mountain—always
these and nothing more. Watchful eyes and attentive
ears, on the other hand, can perceive an infinite variety of
sounds and images in the smallest corner of the universe.
Within a radius of four or five miles around their dwelling
Wordsworth and his sister saw the same objects almost every
day, and yet it seems as if an ever changing, ever beautiful
scene had unfolded itself before their gaze. A hundred
times they must have passed over the road from Alfoxden
to Stowey, and nevertheless a hundred times they found it
different. One evening when the sky grew suddenly
clearer after a violent storm, and Venus and then Jupiter
shone forth amid the clouds, their path was suddenly
transformed into a fairy-scene. "The hawthorn hedges
black and pointed, glittering with millions of diamond
drops. The hollies shining with broader patches of
light. The road to the village of Holford glittered like
another stream." [1]   A hundred times too they plunged
into the coombe; a hundred times they climbed the hill
or wandered along the shore, yet never did they pass
again over the same track without bringing home with
them some entirely fresh image to correct or complete
countless images perceived before.

And we should attempt in vain to distinguish the share
which each had in these observations of Nature. On every
page of Dorothy's journals we find touches of description
which gave rise to Wordsworth's best lines. At times,
also, certain of his verses which are in her mind awaken
the sensation in her, and suggest the terms in which she
describes it. Most commonly of all it is impossible to tell
which was the one to observe and feel, which was the
first to find the metaphor or phrase.

Nevertheless it was these observations which constituted
Wordsworth's poetical store-house. Though rarely a
purely descriptive poet, he always makes nature the
background of his subject when it is not the immediate
object of his enthusiastic strains. Yet it is perhaps impossible to convict him of a single error, of employing
any conceit which is contrary to truth, or of introducing

[1] 31st January 1798.

any image for the sake of mere embellishment. His descriptions may, in exceptional instances, be rendered obscure from their very insight, odd from their very novelty. By those who, from inattention to the external world, have but little acquaintance with it and but little desire to know it except as interpreted by the traditional language of imagery, they will be neither understood nor appreciated. But for observers inspired by curiosity and enthusiasm they will possess, on the contrary, an inestimable value. Such readers need have no fear that in Wordsworth they will meet with the contradictions commonly inflicted by reality on approximate pictures which are more brilliant than precise.

And therein lies the poet's real and incontestable merit. His ideas, though always sincere and thoughtful, and not seldom profound, may repel us by the mysticism which obscures them. The characters in his poems will strike many readers as rudimentary and devoid of interest. The poems themselves may aggravate us by the absence both of skill and spirit displayed in their composition. But, at every instant, striking and entirely original pieces of imagery remind us that the poet never erred in those minute and loving descriptions of Nature's wonders, whether great or small, which he accomplished without any assistance from his predecessors. And to the maiden who saw with, and sometimes for, the poet, yet left to him the glory of immortalizing the image which she had discovered as soon as, or earlier than, he, a large share of our admiration may justly be accorded.

V

While, in the arms of Nature, Wordsworth was recovering his early capacity for delight and admiration, no longer criticizing her, no longer improving upon her on the authority of arbitrary laws of taste, he was also regaining, though more slowly, his power of seeing and loving humanity as it is. With its existing types Godwin had made him disgusted and unfamiliar. From him Words-

worth had learnt that "nothing can be more unreasonable
than to argue from men as we now find them, to men as
they may hereafter be made." [1]   The faithful disciple had
contemplated Godwin's passionless sage, that perfect satire
upon the human race, with admiration, and had hoped

> that future times would surely see
> The man to come parted, as by a gulph,
> From him who had been. [2]

He had quarrelled with history, with the present, and
even with imaginative literature, because the best virtues of
the heroes he had met or read of

> were not free from taint
> Of something false or weak, that could not stand
> The open eye of Reason. [3]

Thus he had become " a bigot to a new idolatry." [4]   " I,"
he says,

> Like a cowled monk who hath forsworn the world,
> Zealously laboured to cut off my heart
> From all the sources of her former strength ;
> And as, by simple waving of a wand,
> The wizard instantaneously dissolves
> Palace or grove, even so could I unsoul
> As readily by syllogistic words
> Those mysteries of being which have made,
> And shall continue evermore to make,
> Of the whole human race one brotherhood. [5]

It was observation of nature which first taught him how
vain and ill-founded were these hopes of sudden and
universal change.   Nature is in fact, a Power

> That is the visible quality and shape
> And image of right reason ; that matures
> Her processes by steadfast laws ; gives birth
> To no impatient or fallacious hopes,
> No heat of passson or excessive zeal,
> No vain conceits ; provokes to no quick turns

---

[1] *Political Justice*, 1st ed., ii. p. 494.   [2] *The Prelude*, xii, 58-60.
[3] *Ibid.*, xii. 64-67.   [4] *Ibid.*, xii. 77.
[5] *Ibid.*, xii. 78-87.

> Of self-applauding intellect ; but trains
> To meekness, and exalts by humble faith ;
> Holds up before the mind intoxicate
> With present objects, and the busy dance
> Of things that pass away, a temperate show
> Of objects that endure ; and by this course
> Disposes her, when over-fondly set
> On throwing off incumbrances, to seek
> In man, and in the frame of social life,
> Whate'er there is desirable and good
> Of kindred permanence, unchanged in form
> And function, or, through strict vicissitude
> Of life and death, revolving.[1]

As the phantom of ideal man faded from Wordsworth's sight, man as he is attracted more and more of his interest. It was on him, after all, and not on any abstract being, that hopes of a better future would have to be built. The very error into which theorists and economists had fallen was that of reasoning about human beings as if they were lifeless ciphers. In order to recover his lost faith in humanity, Wordsworth resolved to examine the intelligence and the virtue of the class which is at once the simplest and the most numerous, of the unassuming beings who " hold a silent station in this beauteous world," of those who live

> By bodily toil, labour exceeding far
> Their due proportion, under all the weight
> Of that injustice which upon ourselves
> Ourselves entail.[2]

If in these he could detect the essential virtues, his returning confidence would be justified. He would have proved that " the social pile " rested on a solid basis.[3]

He turned his attention therefore to those around him, to the peasants who dwelt in the neighbourhood, availing himself more especially of his walks, and loving to

> Converse with men, where if we meet a face
> We almost meet a friend, on naked heaths

---

[1] *The Prelude*, xiii. 20-39.   [2] *Ibid.*, xiii. 96-100.   [3] *Ibid.*, xiii. 94.

> With long long ways before, by cottage bench,
> Or well-spring where the weary traveller rests.[1]

" The lonely roads," he says,

> Were open schools in which I daily read
> With most delight the passions of mankind,
> Whether by words, looks, sighs, or tears, revealed.[2]

Godwin had taught him to believe that virtue was dependent on the intelligence, which can itself be exercised only
on knowledge already acquired. He had said that " in
order to choose the greatest possible good " one " must be
deeply acquainted with the nature of man, its general
features and its varieties." [3] He had asserted that " virtue
cannot exist in an eminent degree, unaccompanied by an
extensive survey of causes and their consequences." [4] He
had sneered at Tertullian for saying " that the most
ignorant peasant under the Christian dispensation possessed
more real knowledge than the wisest of the ancient philosophers," and had shown the absurdity of pretending that
an " honest ploughman " could be " as virtuous as Cato." [5]

Thus it was a pleasant surprise to his disciple when he
discovered evidence of sound judgment and characteristics
of true uprightness in the poor and despised. He delighted
to see

> into the depth of human souls,
> Souls that appear to have no depth at all
> To careless eyes.[6]

He was led to recognise

> How little those formalities, to which
> With overweening trust alone we give
> The name of Education, have to do
> With real feeling and just sense.[7]

He heard

> From mouths of men obscure and lowly, truths
> Replete with honour, sounds in unison
> With loftiest promises of good and fair.[8]

[1] *The Prelude*, xiii. 137-141.   [2] *Ibid.*, xiii. 162-165.
[3] *Political Justice*, 1st ed., i. p. 232-233.   [4] *Ibid.*, 1st ed., i. p. 232.
[5] *Ibid.*, 1st ed., i. p. 254.   [6] *The Prelude*, xiii. 166-168.
[7] *Ibid.*, xiii. 169-172.   [8] *Ibid.*, xiii. 182-185.

He perceived that abstract philosophers, in order to make themselves better understood, or else because they did not know any better, had levelled down " the truth to certain general notions," had set forth only the outward marks whereby society has parted man from man, and had neglected " the universal heart." Enlightened by his own observations he now saw men as they are within themselves :

> How oft high service is performed within,
> When all the external man is rude in show,—
> Not like a temple rich with pomp and gold,
> But a mere mountain-chapel, that protects
> Its simple worshippers from sun and shower.[2]

For him a thought incidentally expressed by Gray in his *Elegy* was now to acquire deep meaning, and to become one of his ruling ideas. He too would sing the unknown heroes of the hamlet, especially the " mute inglorious " Miltons, exactly as he found them in his walks. He would not be satisfied with merely asserting their existence. He would choose the principal characters of his poems from among these

> men for contemplation framed,
> Shy, and unpractised in the strife of phrase ;
> Meek men, whose very souls perhaps would sink
> Beneath them, summoned to such intercourse :
> Theirs is the language of the heavens, the power,
> The thought, the image, and the silent joy :
> Words are but under-agents in their souls." [3]

To certain of these lowly ones, however, neither self-confidence nor the gift of speech was denied. What was Robert Burns, the wonderful Scotch poet, who died on the 24th July 1796, but a peasant ? Inspired by his example and his own faith, when, at a later time, Wordsworth came to write his most ambitious poem, he chose a pedlar for its hero, and endowed him with a loftier reason—one more animated by feeling, and deriving from imagination a wider range, than that of the learned sceptic with whom he argues, or even than that of the Anglican

---

[1] *The Prelude*, xiii. 212-220.   [2] *Ibid.*, xiii. 227-231.
[3] *Ibid.*, xiii. 267-273.

minister whose eloquence pales before the pedlar's. He began, however, in a less ambitious manner, contenting himself with recording in his verses the signs of moral worth among the lowly, and the words of wisdom which they spoke in ignorance. Many a homely ballad which he devoted to these subjects can only be understood by taking account of the state of mind in which it was written. A hint of unconscious sagacity from a child or ignorant peasant, a trifling but instinctive action which baffles reason or succeeds where it fails, were amply sufficient to excite the wonder of the poet, who for a period had lived apart from men, who had considered feeling in man as a sign of inferiority, and had regarded all who have had no logical training, and to whom science is a sealed book, as worthy of pity or contempt. One who has read the judgment pronounced by Godwin upon gratitude, the " sentiment, which would lead [us] to prefer one man to another, from some other consideration than that of his superior usefulness or worth,"[1] will be surprised to find his feelings stirred by grateful words ; and his astonishment will be the greater, his emotion the stronger, if the gratitude expressed is out of all reasonable proportion to the service rendered. Hence the poem on Simon Lee, formerly huntsman to the squire of Alfoxden.

---

[1] *Political Justice*, 1st ed., i. p. 84. Though the chief object of this chapter is to illustrate Wordsworth's reaction against Godwin, it may not be useless to add that this reaction did not extend to every part of Godwin's system and ideas. As late as 1798, in the first edition of the *Lyrical Ballads*, Wordsworth inserted a thoroughly Godwinian poem *The Convict*, in which the philosopher's favourite idea for the reformation of the penal laws was dramatised. Godwin proposed *colonisation* (*i.e.*, transportation) as a substitute for the gallows, adding that " colonists are men for whom we ought to feel no sentiments but those of kindness and compassion." Wordsworth echoed the thought in his last stanza :

> At thy name though compassion her nature resign,
> Though in virtue's proud mouth thy report be a stain,
> My care, if the arm of the mighty were mine,
> Would plant thee where yet thou might'st blossom again.

Moreover, Coleridge's *Dungeon*, in the same collection, is little more than a beautiful verse-translation of Caleb Williams' reflections in his prison. (*Caleb Williams*, ch. xxiii.). There is some analogy between the robbers in *Caleb Williams* (ch. xxviii.), who describe their occupation as "a profession of justice," and Wordsworth's *Borderers*. The timely assistance given by the former to Caleb bears a resemblance also to that bestowed by the kind-hearted thieves upon the " Female Vagrant."

In those days nothing could weary Simon, but now the poor old man is bent and twisted with age, his legs are lean, his ankles swollen. One day the poet saw him attempting to uproot a tree stump. The mattock trembled in his hand, and his arm was so feeble that he might have laboured there in vain for ever.

> " You're overtasked, good Simon Lee,
>   Give me your tool," to him I said ;
> And at the word right gladly he
>   Received my proffered aid.
> I struck, and with a single blow
>   The tangled root I severed,
> At which the poor old Man so long
>   And vainly had endeavoured
>
> The tears into his eyes were brought,
>   And thanks and praises seemed to run
> So fast out of his heart, I thought
>   They never would have done.
> —I've heard of hearts unkind, kind deeds
>   With coldness still returning ;
> Alas ! the gratitude of men
>   Hath oftener left me mourning.[1]

The man who holds with Godwin that property is the cause of every vice and the source of all the misery of the poor is naturally astonished to find that this so-called evil, the offspring of human institutions, is a vigorous instinct closely interwoven with the noblest feelings. The peasant is the very last person for whom property is an abstraction. It represents familiar and dearly-loved fields, a hereditary cottage, and flocks every animal of which has its own name. This fact had been forgotten by Wordsworth, who learnt it, as if for the first time, from a shepherd whom he met near the village of Holford.[2]

A sturdy man, in the prime of life, he was alone on the high road, weeping. In his arms he bore a lamb, the last of his flock, which he was obliged to sell through poverty. Yet his grief was due not to poverty, but to regret for

---

[1] " Simon Lee" (*Lyrical Ballads*, 1798).
[2] "The last of the flock" (*Lyrical Ballads*, 1798).

the fine flock of which he had been so proud, which he
had got together himself, and had then seen melt away like
snow, as one by one he was forced to sell them. He had
six children, and the parish refused him assistance because
he possessed sheep of his own. He had been obliged to
sell one first of all.

> [I] bought my little children bread,
> And they were healthy with their food;
> For me—it never did me good.

And when one had gone the others followed;

> It was a vein that never stopped—
> Like blood-drops from my heart they dropped . . .
> To wicked deeds I was inclined,
> And wicked fancies crossed my mind
> And every man I chanced to see,
> I thought he knew some ill of me. . . .
> And oft was moved to flee from home.

> Sir! 'twas a precious flock to me,
> As dear as my own children be;
> For daily with my growing store
> I loved my children more and more.
> Alas! it was an evil time;
> God cursed me in my sore distress;
> I prayed, yet every day I thought
> I loved my children less.

To one who had believed with Godwin that charity
was the evil consequence of a social order which ought to
be regulated by justice alone, it was truly delightful to
be an actual witness of charitable deeds, and to notice how
they illuminated the countenance of the doer. "Observe,"
said Godwin, "the pauper fawning with abject vileness
upon his rich benefactor, and speechless with sensations
of gratitude for having received that which he ought to
have claimed with an erect mien, and with a consciousness
that his claim was irresistible."[1] And Wordsworth remembered the old beggars whom he had seen in his boyhood as they pursued their regular round in the neighbour-

[1] *Political Justice*, 1st ed., ii. p. 800.

hood of Hawkshead.   Others of their class came and went
at Racedown.   He compares the feelings to which their
existence really gives rise with those condemned by the
philosopher.[1]   He commends charity in those who exercise
it.   He watches one of his neighbours as every week,

> Duly as Friday comes, though pressed herself
> By her own wants, she from her store of meal
> Takes one unsparing handful for the scrip
> Of this old Mendicant, and, from her door
> Returning with exhilarated heart,
> Sits by her fire, and builds her hope in heaven.

He extolled charity on the ground of its moral value for
the recipient, and reproached the statesmen who would confine the destitute in houses " misnamed of Industry " with
seeking to deprive the needy of their purest pleasure, the
obscure feeling that they are benefiting him who gives.

It would be an easy matter to follow up this subject,
and to show how, by observation of the poor, Wordsworth
restores one by one the feelings of which ideal man has
been stripped by Godwin.   For the very reason that
Godwin has endeavoured to make all the feelings subservient to the intelligence, and has asserted that the only
justification for affection lies in its subordination to the law
of general utility, Wordsworth is struck by the pathos of
unreasoning affection, whether manifested by the insane, or
bestowed on an object devoid of reason, and consequently,
in either case, useless.   He takes a delight in describing a
crazy mother's fondness for her child, her alternate thrills
of joy and fits of madness.[2]   Again, he depicts the love of
Betty, the peasant-woman, for her idiot boy, her admiration
of him in spite of his affliction, the pride with which she
hears and tells to others his least phrase which contains a
glimmering of sense, and the happiness with which the
poor idiot's existence fills her life.[3]

Association with children was destined to contribute no
less to the poet's instruction than his intercourse with the
poor.   Like almost all young people he had lived apart

---

[1] *The Old Cumberland Beggar.*
[2] *The mad mother* or " Her eyes are wild " (*Lyrical Ballads*, 1798.)
[3] *The idiot boy*, (*Ibid.*)

from children, enjoying converse with them when opportunity offered, but indifferent to their thoughts and never dreaming that anything fresh could be read on a blank page where wisdom had as yet had no time to engrave many of its maxims. It was therefore a great surprise to him to find them not amenable to logic, tenacious of ideas for which no origin could be assigned, provided with their own peculiar convictions, and possessed of a natural substratum which eluded analysis. Some years had passed already since he had met the curly-haired little girl, eight years old, with her beauty and her wild and rustic air, who, in answer to all his questions as to the number of her brothers and sisters, had replied, " We are seven," although two of the seven were sleeping a few paces distant beneath the grass of the cemetry. She could point out their grave, and loved to play near it, or to sit there singing to them as she knitted her stockings, yet nothing had induced her to relinquish the idea that they were still seven, in her obstinate ignorance of death.[1] Though the poet's conversation with the child had occurred some time before,[2] not until now did it acquire for him any meaning or instructiveness.

Hitherto, Wordsworth had had but transitory glimpses of the soul of childhood, but since settling at Racedown he had enjoyed the opportunity of making it his daily study. He and his sister had brought with them a three-year-old child, the son of a London barrister, in order to increase their slender resources by maintaining him. His education occupied but little of their time. It was very simple for that "age of systems," and would no doubt have been approved by Rousseau. "We teach him nothing at present," wrote Dorothy, "but what he learns from the evidence of his senses."[3] In return, however, with his "insatiable curiosity," his questions and his artless ways, the child afforded them " perpetual entertainment." He did more; he helped also to complete

---

[1] "We are seven" (*Lyrical Ballads*, 1798).
[2] In 1793, on the banks of the Wye.
[3] Letter written by Dorothy Wordsworth (1795 or 1796), Knight, *Life of Wordsworth* i. p. 109.

the poet's education. One of the most prosaic but not the least curious of Wordsworth's poems arose out of an artless falsehood told by his ward. To one who had learnt from Godwin that lying is opposed to human nature, and would never have existed but for the indirect compulsion of societies and religions, it must have been a revelation to hear a child tell a bold and harmless lie, without any apparent motive and uninfluenced by interest or fear. Hence the poet's *Anecdote for fathers, Showing how the practice of Lying may be taught*.[1] Wordsworth and his little pupil (now five years old) were walking near Lyswin Farm, on the banks of the Wye. In the previous spring they had strolled along the shore of the Bristol Channel at Kilve, near Alfoxden. The poet enquires which of the two delightful spots the child prefers. "At Kilve I'd rather be," the little one answers, "than here at Lyswin Farm." Five times he is urged to say why, but remains silent. At last, raising his eyes, he sees just in front of him a gilded weather-cock, glittering in the sunlight on the roof of the farm-house, and making up his mind replies, "At Kilve there was no weather-cock, and that's the reason why." At the answer a sudden light seems to dawn upon the poet ; he cannot find words to express the gratitude he feels towards his little companion.

> O dearest, dearest boy ! my heart
> For better lore would seldom yearn,
> Could I but teach the hundredth part
> Of what from thee I learn.

Many readers will be tempted to say with Landor : "If the lad told a lie, why praise him so ? And if he spoke the obvious truth, what has he taught the father ? The 'hundredth part' of the lore communicated by the child to the parent may content him : but whoever is contented

---

[1] Anecdote for fathers (*Lyrical Ballads*, 1798). Mr Thomas Hutchinson has kindly suggested to me that the poet here purposely altered the names, substituting Lyswin for Alfoxden and Kilve for Racedown. But the realistic character of the poem is beyond doubt.

with a hundredfold more than all they both together have given us, cannot be very ambitious of becoming a senior wrangler." [1] But Landor makes no allowance for the fact that the discovery of the mysterious origin and devious ways of falsehood must have been a revelation to one who had dreamed of a day when universal truth should reign in naked simplicity.

VI

Nevertheless, it must be admitted that his extreme susceptibility to feelings of wonder at the instincts and emotions which he had re-discovered in man was not without its dangers for Wordsworth's poetry. A reproach that was often and justly made against him was that he attributed to certain expressions or incidents more emotion than other people could reasonably associate with them. It is in fact difficult at times to experience the same deep impression as the poet, unless one has passed, as he did, through a real crisis of abstract thought. Like a convalescent whom the simplest actions of life—getting up, eating, walking, breathing the free air—fill with an infinitely tender emotion, he felt a joy which must appear almost childish to minds that have escaped his disease. Solitude, or the exclusive companionship of those who are too closely connected with us and too ready to humour such simple distractions and easy ecstasies, is not, in such cases, without its perils for our mental vigour. Thus, by living alone with Dorothy, Wordsworth would have been in danger of unduly prolonging that condition in which excessive susceptibility to insignificant things is accompanied by a certain general enervation of thought. The circumstances which led him to see things in detail were multiplied through the agency of his sister. More sprightly than her brother, more quick to form acquaintanceships, to chat, and to question comers and goers, she

[1] *Imaginary Conversations.* Southey and Porson (2nd conversation). The works of W. S. Landor, in 2 vols. London, 1846, vol. i. p. 68.

was frequently his medium of communication with the travellers they met upon the high road.

>   At a time
> When Nature, destined to remain so long
> Foremost in my affections, had fallen back
> Into a second place, pleased to become
> A handmaid to a nobler than herself,
> When every day brought with it some new sense
> Of exquisite regard for common things,
> And all the earth was budding with these gifts
> Of more refined humanity, thy breath,
> Dear Sister! was a kind of gentler spring
> That went before my steps.[1]

Dorothy, who had remained a true child, and had preserved the artlessness as well as the freshness of childhood, was passionately interested in the most insignificant words and actions.   And this ever-watchful interest made her a bad judge of the interest of the public.

"God forbid," wrote one who had the best opportunity of observing the collaboration of brother and sister, "that your sister should ever cease to use her own eyes and heart, and only her own, in order to know how a poem *ought* to affect mankind; but we must learn to see it with the eyes of others in order to guess luckily how it will affect them.   I do wish her to learn this; but then I would have her learn to entertain neither warm hopes nor confident expectations, concerning events dependent on minds and hearts below the distinct ken of her sympathies."[2]

There was still another reason which rendered Dorothy a partial critic of her brother's poetry.   The brother and sister became so thoroughly identified, and were so entirely in sympathy with one another, that the two formed together but a single being.   Dorothy's approbation, the mere echo of his own, was too often to take the place in Wordsworth's mind of distinct and independent testimony.

And, lastly, Wordsworth's genius ran the risk of being

[1] *The Prelude*, xiv. 256-266.
[2] Letter from Coleridge to Wordsworth in 1808, Knight, *Life of Wordsworth*, II. p. 104.

frittered away on a multitude of short poems and trivial
ballads, of which one may venture to say that he already
composed too many, since some of them are so meagre in
subject, and so lacking in beauty of form, as to justify the
saying of Landor that Wordsworth often gives us the
protoplasm of poetry in place of poetry itself. He does
not hesitate to relate in verse how the rascally Andrew
Jones appropriated a penny thrown by a passing horseman
to a crippled beggar.[1] He takes eight stanzas to tell us
that a couple of little boys, whose mother he has just met,
interrupt their play to beg of him, representing themselves
as orphans ; and that when he accompanies his refusal with
a reproof, they resume their games without the slightest
confusion at seeing their lie detected.[2] He even seeks to
commemorate in verse the bitter tears of a little girl whose
cloak has been caught in the wheel of a carriage and torn
to rags.[3] Truly childish is the morality of which he con-
descends to lisp on another occasion, when he reproaches
a redbreast for chasing a butterfly, wonders what can induce so gentle a bird to seek to injure an insect as beautiful
as itself, and fails to find the palpable reply. At times,
also, in poems the real beauties of which preserve them
from entire condemnation, he intentionally reproduces,
word for word, a conversation he has listened to, making
no effort either to raise its phrases to the level of poetry
by means of a rigorous selection and close condensation, or
to relieve them by a touch of humour. Now, with all
their difference in merit, ranging from pure poetry to mere
prosaic statement of fact which poetic rhythm rather em-
barrasses than adorns, Dorothy was capable of liking
every one of these minor poems in its entirety, because she
knew that each had had its origin in a genuine emotion.
She derived even more pleasure from these little pictures
and simple narratives, some of which she had herself
suggested, and almost all of which she had watched in the

[1] "Andrew Jones" (*Lyrical Ballads,* 1800).
[2] *The Beggars* (written in 1802).
[3] *Alice Fell, or Poverty.* This poem was written in 1802, and follows the
story as told to Wordsworth and set down with scrupulous accuracy in
Dorothy Wordsworth's Journal (16th Feb. 1802). First published in 1807,
the text of the poem was considerably altered in subsequent editions.

making, than from the more ambitious poems wherein
Wordsworth severed himself from her, and followed his
own line of thought beyond her reach. Dorothy was all
sensibility, with little or no need of thought. One requires
senses of marvellous delicacy to write journals such as
hers, but scarcely any reasoning power. In her society
Wordsworth might be cured of Godwin, but he would
also endanger his chances of ever arriving at a comprehensive philosophy of his own. He might refute the arguments of his master one by one, yet never perhaps succeed
in grasping the fundamental defect of his system. His
impressions would remain incoherent, without any common
bond of unity. Not only so, but they would probably
linger obscurely in his mind while he nevertheless failed to
understand their full meaning or to attain sufficient clearness of view to give expression to them, for want of that
illumination which a great general conception can throw
over isolated facts.

Several of the observations we have mentioned were
made at Racedown, or even earlier, but the poems which
sprang from them were not written until afterwards. The
good fortune which had thrown Wordsworth into his
sister's society, just when he needed rescuing from a
melancholy philosophy, provided him also with a friend
who was able to accompany or even to precede him in the
path of speculation, at the very time when he required a
new philosophical creed. This friend, who always, and
from the first, protested against Wordsworth's tendency
to write a multitude of poems like *Alice Fell*, was possessed
of precisely those qualifications in which Dorothy was
lacking; breadth of view, a disposition to systematize, and
penetration as deep in the sphere of thought as was
Dorothy's in that of feeling. Wordsworth's intimacy with
Coleridge was as opportune as it was beneficial. Coleridge
is the only person besides Dorothy by whom Wordsworth
has admitted that he was deeply influenced. He has said
that his intellect had contracted an important debt to him,
and that the influence of Coleridge had penetrated to his
" heart of hearts." [1] He called Coleridge the most wonder-

---

[1] *The Prelude*, xiv. 281.

ful man he had ever known, " wonderful for the originality
of his mind, and the power he possessed of throwing out
in profusion grand central truths from which might be
evolved the most comprehensive systems." [1] It was Coleridge who provided, or rather assisted him to find,
the only thing still needful to make him the poet he finally
became, namely, a philosophy.

[1] A conversation held by Wordsworth in 1834, reported by Percival Graves.
Knight, *Life of Wordsworth*, iii. p. 235.

CHAPTER II

Coleridge

I

While Wordsworth was courting the peace of solitary meditation at Racedown, the advanced party in that quarter of the country was making a considerable stir over two youthful advocates of revolution, who were attempting to rouse the population of Bristol, the capital of the west, by their poems and lectures. These young men, who protested boldly against the war, the ministry, and the established church and social order, were Robert Southey and Samuel Taylor Coleridge. Their stormy reputation, the enthusiasm of their followers, by whom they were regarded as apostles, and the indignation of the tories, who looked on them as dangerous jacobins, quickly attracted the attention and sympathy of Wordsworth. He met these " two extraordinary youths "[1] for the first time at Bristol, in the autumn of 1795. And though Southey's departure for Portugal soon interrupted his intercourse with the one, it was then that he laid the foundations of a friendship with Coleridge which proved one of the closest and most fruitful which have ever existed between poets.[2]

[1] Extract from a letter written by Wordsworth to Mathews, quoted by Gillman, *Life of Coleridge*, p. 74.

[2] Much discussion has taken place as to the exact date of Wordsworth's first meeting with Coleridge. It lies between September and the 14th November 1795. In a note to his *Lines written at Shurton Bars* in September 1795 Coleridge mentions an instance where he has borrowed from the *Evening Walk*. In a copy of his *Poems* (edition of 1797) he has added in his own hand-writing at the same place, "This note was written before I had ever seen M. Wordsworth, *atque utinam opera ejus tantum noveram.*" (*Coleridge's Poetical Works ed.* Campbell, 1893, p. 577). On the other hand, in a letter which Wordsworth sent to his friend Wrangham, along with

In respect of birth, character, and early circumstances, Coleridge was almost the antithesis of Wordsworth. Two years and a half younger, and born in the county of Devon, he was an Englishman of the south, while Wordsworth was an Englishman of the north. One had sprung from "the English Italy," the other almost belonged to Scotland. Most of the real or imaginary characteristics by which every nation loves to distinguish the inhabitants of its remotest borders were strongly exemplified in them. The opposite types of Fleming and Marseillais, of Norman and Gascon, have their equivalents on the English side of the Channel. Wordsworth was stern and unyielding, obstinate and incapable of effusion. He had neither suppleness nor flexibility, and was inclined to hide the warmth of his feelings under an air of cold reserve, and to husband his gifts from a natural tendency to intellectual economy. Coleridge, to no less an extent, was unreserved, quick to catch enthusiasm, and captivating from the very first; but, as a set-off against this, he was weak in character, liable to sudden discouragement, and, though capable of flashes of impetuous ardour, without the power of continuous effort. His works were seldom completed, and were often of an inferior order. He was a wonderful talker, and in the domain of thought was generous to the point of ignoring the distinction between mine and thine; he artlessly appropriated the ideas of others as if they were a treasure common to all, and oftener still poured out his own for the benefit of his friends, and even of his casual acquaintances, without stint, regret, or jealousy. In fact, the mere surplus of his studies, his meditations, and his dreams provided intellectual nourishment for almost a whole generation.

From his father, whom he compared to Fielding's "Parson Adams," he inherited an eccentric disposition and a strange tendency to absence of mind, as well as a certain pleasing

some satirical lines, on the 20th November 1795, Wordsworth mentions two of these lines as having been given him "by Southey, a friend of Coleridge." (Unpublished Letters of Wordsworth and Coleridge, *Athenæum*, 8th December 1894). Writing to Thelwall in May 1796, Coleridge speaks of Wordsworth as "a very dear friend." About the same date he sent Lamb the manuscript of Wordsworth's *Guilt and Sorrow*.

pedantry. His oddity displayed itself in his childhood, if he really ever had a childhood. He never played, and very early manifested a preference for thought, and the acquisition of new impressions, over physical activity. Thus he was a conspicuous example of the youthful prodigy. Sent to school at Christ's Hospital in London, where he was cut off from his friends and restrained by no counteracting influence, he gave himself up, at ten years of age, to his inclination for intellectual pursuits.

Situated in the heart of the metropolis, surrounded by tall, dark houses, and opening not upon meadows but upon a street dotted with busy wayfarers, the venerable yet depressing abode where Coleridge languished bore as little resemblance as possible to the country grammar-school at Hawkshead. Struck by the contrast between his own school-life and that of Coleridge, Wordsworth might well say that they had been " nursed and reared as if in several elements." [1] Far from the region of his birth, and looking back upon it with regret ; separated, like a deserted child, from his kindred, Coleridge passed dismally from boyhood to youth in a school where he was ill-fed and subjected to a rigorous discipline. Ever afterwards one of his masters remained for him the type of brutality, and, even in his old age, often returned to thrash him in his dreams. His only pleasure was in study and reading, and in the abstraction which transported him beyond the harsh realities of actual life. His favourite authors were the philosophers, and among these he preferred the most mystical and abstruse. At seventeen he was a Neo-platonist, and used to unfold, for the benefit of his fellow pupils, " in . . . deep and sweet intonations the mysteries of Jamblichus or Plotinus." [2] Therein he found a sort of sedative for his melancholy, and in maturer years, during hours of despair, he had recourse to it again, just as he made use of opium to relieve his physical sufferings.

This picture of Coleridge's boyhood, though drawn principally from data furnished by himself, is very likely

[1] *The Prelude*, vi. 254-255.
[2] *Christ's Hospital five and thirty years ago.* Charles Lamb, *Essays of Elia.*

somewhat darker than the reality. Here, however, it is of little consequence to know just how far the shadows are too heavy. What is important, and, at the same time, certain, is that this was Coleridge's impression of his early years at the time when he became intimate with Wordsworth, and the description which he gave of them to his friend. When they came to describe the dissimilar characteristics of their early life, a feeling for artistic contrast led the two young men to exaggerate certain of these characteristics; Wordsworth those of joyous tendency, and Coleridge those which made for gloom. *The Prelude,* which originated in part from these conversations, clearly betrays in many passages how the thought of each was influenced by this parallelism and contrast.

From the day when Coleridge left school for Cambridge the difference apparently was on the wane. To judge from appearances alone, it would even seem that his mind thenceforward followed the same course as Wordsworth's. Like Wordsworth, Coleridge was at once a republican, a poet, and a philosopher. Like him he was an ardent supporter of the French Revolution, became highly indignant at the war, and contended both in verse and in prose against an evil and tyrannous world. Like him he was for a time the admirer of Godwin. " Thy voice," he said, in a sonnet, addressed to the philosopher,

> in Passion's stormy day,
> When wild I roam'd the bleak Heath of Distress,
> Bade the bright form of Justice meet my way—
> And told me that her name was Happiness.[1]

And like him, when he became conscious of the vanity of the struggle, he contemplated withdrawing from a society he abhorred, in which generous and independent souls could find no place.

Yet beneath these surface resemblances, how deep and lasting were the differences ! Whereas Wordsworth had kept the two active functions of his being quite separate, and had merely surrendered his thought to his fantastic schemes, Coleridge had made them the guides also of

---

[1] Sonnet to William Godwin, 10th January 1795.

his actions. His life had no settled plan, but drifted at the mercy of impulse. His conduct was a continual and perplexing extemporization; his actions appeared to be dictated entirely by caprice. At school, one fine morning, he determined to become a shoemaker's apprentice. In his Cambridge days, at the very time when he was inveighing against the war and the army, he suddenly enlisted in the dragoons, for reasons not clearly understood, but probably in consequence of the remorse following upon excess. And shortly afterwards, while Wordsworth, in order to preserve his liberty, was forming the simple project, so soon to be realized, of making his home in an English village with his sister, Coleridge, in company with a few young republicans, was devising the ambitious scheme of a society of philosophers, or, as it was called, a *Pantisocracy*, a kind of phalanstery to be established on the free banks of the Susquehanna. The only result of this grand scheme was a thoughtless marriage, entered into with a view to colonization, and in order to comply with the laws of the Pantisocracy. Somewhat humbled by this failure, Coleridge settled, early in 1797, at Stowey, on a little farm, where, although absolutely ignorant of agriculture, he proposed to support his family by growing wheat and vegetables, and by earning some money during the evenings from his literary labours. These schemes, however, perished almost as soon as they came into existence; conceived in an hour of exaltation, they were abandoned the next day as impracticable. This wild career, with its shocks, collisions, and headlong falls, bears little resemblance to Wordsworth's slow but steady progress. Both had forsaken the ordinary high-road, but Wordsworth only had previously chosen the path he intended to follow in preference to it, fully conscious whither it would lead him, and no less determined to pursue it to the end.

II

By reason of the obvious incoherence of his life, and the spectacle of his ambitious programmes of works which were never written, full justice has not been done to the unity of Coleridge's thought. Throughout his whole work, in spite of all appearances, he was merely seeking, finding, and then incessantly repeating, a single thought. From the first he had attempted to do what he afterwards strove to accomplish with ever clearer and clearer consciousness : to fuse together religion and philosophy, and to consolidate them once more in their ancient union. In spite of the boldness, and even the violence, of the opinions he promulgated, Coleridge had remained deeply religious. For this reason his ideas, whether political or social, even when they were in harmony with those of Wordsworth, sounded a very different note. It was not in France and under the influence of philosophy that he became a partisan of the Revolution, but at Cambridge, under the guidance of the dissenting sect of the Unitarians, the most eminent of whom was Priestley. This man, who in England was looked upon as a dangerous free-thinker, had astonished learned men in Paris by his unshaken faith in revelation. A chemist who had remained a Christian seemed to them an anomaly. Renounce as he might the doctrines of original sin, redemption, and the divinity of Christ, for him the Bible remained none the less the book of truth. He freely claimed the right to use individual reason to interpret it, but he never dreamed of employing reason to attack it. For him the French Revolution was a fulfilment of prophecy, the arrival of the promised millennium. It was by this same spirit of religious and humanitarian enthusiasm that Coleridge was animated.

When he formed his intimacy with Wordsworth, Coleridge was doubtless not as yet in full possession of his mystic philosophy. At that time he was hesitating between various doctrines. From Priestley he had gone over to Godwin, but broke away from him in the spring of 1796, having come to regard "his Principles as vicious, and his book as a Pandar to Sensuality." [1] He stated that he was "preparing an examination" of Godwin's pretentious system. This, however, did not put an end to his uncertainty. The names by which his sons were christened afford evidence of his blind search. A son born to him in

[1] *The Watchman*, No. 5.

September 1796 he named Hartley, after the physician and philosopher who propounded the theory of the mechanical association of ideas. Another son, born on the 16th May 1798, was called by the name of Berkeley, the idealist. During the interval Coleridge had been the fervent admirer of Spinoza, and in the early days of their friendship spoke enthusiastically to Wordsworth of Spinoza's formulas concerning God-Nature. Even at this period, however, Coleridge had become partial to certain notions which he had acquired in the course of his very varied and extensive reading, and though they did not as yet constitute a complete system, they had nevertheless produced in him the state of mind necessary to the reception of mysticism. A most fruitful branch of this reading had been his study of the Neo-platonists of the Alexandrian school, who had fascinated him in his school-days and had revealed to him the infinite power of ecstasy, of intuition, and of divine love. No less precious to him was the knowledge of such theosophists as Jacob Boehme, George Fox, and Swedenborg. The writings of these *illuminati*, from which Saint Martin in France and Schelling in Germany were then drawing their inspiration, prevented Coleridge's "mind from being imprisoned within the outline of any single dogmatic system."

"They contributed," he says, "to keep alive the heart in the head; gave me an indistinct, yet stirring and working presentiment, that all the products of the mere reflective faculty partook of death, and were as the rattling twigs and sprays in winter, into which a sap was yet to be propelled, from some root to which I had not penetrated, if they were to afford my soul either food or shelter. If they were too often a moving cloud of smoke to me by day, yet they were always a pillar of fire throughout the night, during my wanderings through the wilderness of doubt, and enabled me to skirt without crossing the sandy deserts of utter unbelief." [1]

Thus early awakened, Coleridge's distrust of "the products of the pure faculty of reflexion," though at first vague and ill-founded, developed under the influence of

[1] *Biographia Literaria*, ch. ix.

Kant into a strong and coherent doctrine. His acquaintance with the writings of " the illustrious sage of Königsberg " began during his travels in Germany towards the close of 1798, and he continued to study them during the years immediately following. In 1801, or thereabouts, having obtained a thorough grasp of his principles, he hailed Kant as the master he had long sought, and sought hitherto in vain. He joyfully appropriated those ideas in the system of the German philosopher which were in harmony with his own tendencies to mysticism. He was delighted to find the limits of the understanding fixed by an " adamantine chain of logic," and conscience reinstated as the guardian of the moral law. Kant's system was the very basis of the doctrine which he made it his mission to teach his countrymen, and on which he strove to reconstruct the religion of the Church of England.

Ideas of this kind and a mind of this nature were entirely new to Wordsworth. How striking is the contrast between Coleridge and those who had been Wordsworth's friends hitherto! For Beaupuy religion was the enemy of liberty and progress, nor was it otherwise regarded by William Mathews, who, since Wordsworth's return to England, had been his most intimate friend and most regular correspondent.

Mathews, whom Wordsworth had known at Cambridge, was the son of a London bookseller, a strict calvinist, whose house was the meeting-place of a company of low-class fanatics. Personally sincere, he allowed himself to be plundered by his fellow-believers. The rigid hypocrisy which reigned in the father's house so disgusted his children that William, the eldest, retained in consequence a lifelong horror of superstition and fanaticism. The second, Charles, left his home to go upon the stage, and became one of the best comic actors of his generation. William Mathews, a great worker, with a knowledge of six languages and a passion for mathematics, was destined for holy orders, but, like Wordsworth, refused to take them, and preferred to lead a precarious life in London as law-student and journalist. Compelled by poverty to leave the country, he went to seek his fortune in Tobago, where he died a few months later, in 1801. Wordsworth's biographers have said nothing of this friend, and it may be well to reproduce here a letter, most characteristic in sentiment, which, shortly before his death, Mathews wrote to his brother. In his remote island home he has no thought but that of warning the actor's wife against " superstition and religious bigotry."

" The whole history of mankind is but a relation of the fatal and mischievous effects of this diabolical tyrant, who has uniformly preyed upon the enlightened few that have dared to lift up their heads against the oppressor of their afflicted brethren, and has gnawed the very vitals of social existence.   There is no part of the globe that is not even now groaning beneath her baneful pressure ; and, whatever form she assumes, she still arrogates to herself the claim of infallibility, and her votaries, of whatever sect they may be, damn by wholesale all the rest of the world.

" A freedom from superstition is the first blessing we can enjoy. Religion in some shape seems necessary to political existence. The wise man laughs at the follies of the vulgar, and in the pure contemplation of a benevolent Author of all Beings, finds that happiness which others in vain look for amid the load of trumpery and ceremonies with which they think the Creator is gratified.   If He can be gratified by any exertion of feeble mortals, it must be when they imitate his perfection by mutual benevolence and kindness." [1]

Though we possess nothing else written by Mathews, we may form from this letter some idea of the conversations and the correspondence he maintained with Wordsworth.   Mathews and Wordsworth attacked religion in the name of reason.   Coleridge, though in a state of indecision, was already beginning to assail the understanding in the name of religion.   If here and there Coleridge still inveighs against superstition, elsewhere he retracts and already does homage to it.   He starts a newspaper with the motto : *Knowledge is Power*, but he begins an address to those whom he hopes to gain as subscribers with the words, " I am far from convinced that a Christian is permitted to read either newspapers or any other works

---

[1] Letter of the 5th June 1801.   *Memoirs of Charles Mathews, comedian,* by Mrs Mathews, 4 vols., 1839, i. pp. 321-322.

of merely political or temporary interest."[1] If the passion for disinterested speculation, in which, happily, he never lost his faith, led him, in conversation, to avow the most irreverent opinions, his poetry, which contains all that was best in him, expresses nothing but fervent piety.

Wordsworth was naturally one of the first to receive the new truths from the lips of Coleridge, as he gradually discovered them. These at first were but flashes of eloquence, whence a few ideas stood out in strong relief and sank into the depths of Wordsworth's mind, although they did not adapt themselves to its atmosphere without undergoing some modification.

The first meetings of the two men were characteristic. Each brought the best work he had yet produced. Wordsworth read his *Guilt and Sorrow ;* Coleridge his *Religious Musings.*[2]

These *Musings* were a hymn to God, whose name is Love. Every man, through love, can attain, as Christ did, to a measure of divinity in his death ; can annihilate himself in the bosom of God, his identity, who is the all in all, "Nature's essence, mind, and energy." [3]

> Tis the sublime of man,
> Our noontide majesty, to know ourselves
> Parts and proportions of one wondrous whole !
> This fraternizes man.[4]

At the thought that God alone exists, evil being but a transient appearance, every fear vanishes. He who knows this loves all creation, "and blesses it, and calls it very good." [5] All terror springs from superstition. The priest hides God. It is the priest who incites and bestows his benediction on the despicable princes leagued against France in the name of Jesus, the man of love. But priests and princes alike are themselves the unconscious agents of an unknown good. Everything, even vice and crime, serves to build up the Good. It is man's desire for luxury, his greed and ambition, that have enabled him to rise above his primitive savagery; it is the sensual wants that have

---

[1] *Biographia Literaria*, ch. x.
[2] *Religious Musings*, a desultory poem written on the Christmas Eve of 1794.
[3] *Religious Musings*, l. 48. [4] *Ibid.*, ll. 126-129. [5] *Ibid.*, ll. 112-113.

"unsensualized the mind,"[1] and accustomed it to take
pleasure in its own activity. Transformed through the
agency of Religion, the evil passions become the energetic
auxiliaries of virtue. Then come the Bards and Philosophers, bringing Science, and Liberty, the daughter of
Science. And last of all, the multitude of the wretched
finds its way towards the light, which hitherto none have
seen but the flower of the human race. The millennium
is at hand; yet not on earth, but only in a world of pure
intelligence, will man attain to happiness. Earthly life is
but a vision, and that vision is but the shadow of truth.

Let us supplement this outburst of mystical rejoicing by
some earlier verses, expressive of a sort of poetic pantheism.
In the *Eolian Harp*, for example, Coleridge described how
a lute, which had been placed in a window of the cottage
where he spent the first months of his wedded life, vibrated
in response to every wind. Even so, it seemed to him, the
universe was one harmony; for him it would have been
impossible

> Not to love all things in a world so filled;
> When the breeze warbles, and the mute still air
> Is Music slumbering on her instrument. . . . .[2]
> And what if all of animated Nature
> Be but organic harps diversely framed,
> That tremble into thought, as o'er them sweeps,
> Plastic and vast, one intellectual breeze,
> At once the soul of each and God of all?[3]

No sooner had Coleridge asked himself the question than,
in the same poem, he repelled this invasion of human pride,
and returned to humble faith and reverential adoration of
the Incomprehensible. Wordsworth, at a later period, took
up his friend's idea and made it his own.

But in his *Destiny of Nations* Coleridge approached more
nearly to the ideas which afterwards became his settled
convictions. The poem begins with a Platonic image:

> All that meets the bodily sense I deem
> Symbolical, one mighty alphabet
> For infant minds; and we in this low world

[1] *Religious Musings*, ll. 209-210.
[2] *The Eolian Harp*, 1795, ll. 30-33.　　　[3] *Ibid.*, ll. 49-53.

> Placed with our backs to bright reality,
> That we may learn with young unwounded ken
> The substance from its shadow.[1]

The substance of all things is God, or infinite Love by love alone perceived; hence Coleridge expresses contempt for those who seek truth by means of reasoning alone:

> But some there are who deem themselves most free
> When they within this gross and visible sphere
> Chain down the winged thought, scoffing ascent,
> Proud in the meanness : and themselves they cheat
> With noisy emptiness of learned phrase,
> Their subtle fluids, impacts, essences,
> Self-working tools, uncaused effects, and all
> Those blind omniscients, those almighty slaves,
> Untenanting creation of its God.[2]

He felt drawn, on the contrary, to Imagination, by philosophers regarded with suspicion; and to Superstition, the object of their contempt.

> Fancy is the power
> That first unsensualizes the dark mind,
> Giving it new delights; and bids it swell
> With wild activity; and peopling air,
> By obscure fears of beings invisible,
> Emancipates it from the grosser thrall
> Of the present impulse, teaching self-control,
> Till Superstition, with unconscious hand
> Seat Reason on her throne.[3]

Love as the law of the world, God as the soul of the universe, intuition preferred to analysis and reasoning for the discovery of truth, visible things considered as symbols of reality, all beings, including animals and flowers, regarded as " Monads of the infinite Mind "—these, for Wordsworth, were all new and wonderful conceptions. The gloomy pupil of Christ's Hospital furnished the joyous Hawkshead schoolboy with the foundations on which he was afterwards to build his optimism and his natural religion; or, rather, he put into his head the idea of a mighty synthesis. Windy as were the imaginings of Coleridge, by

---

[1] *The Destiny of Nations*, ll. 18-22. [2] *Ibid.*, 26-34. [3] *Ibid.*, 79-87.

reason of their novelty and breadth they made a deep impression on one who at this time was "at least a semi-atheist,"[1] and had never attempted such far-reaching explorations.

Above everything else in the *Religious Musings*, Wordsworth delighted in the vision, widely as it differed from his own, of the earth as regenerated by the return of pure Faith and meek Piety victorious over atheism, and in the description of the daily joys of those who are in constant communion with heaven. Man will then enjoy

> such delights
> As float to earth, permitted visitants!
> When on some solemn jubilee of Saints
> The sapphire-blazing gates of Paradise
> Are thrown wide open, and thence voyage forth
> Detachments wild of seraph-warbled airs,
> And odours snatched from beds of amaranth,
> And they, that from the chrystal river of life
> Spring up on freshen'd wing, ambrosial gales!
> The favor'd good man in his lonely walk
> Perceives them, and his silent spirit drinks
> Strange bliss which he shall recognize in heaven.[2]

He admired also the following description of the end of the world, when it is received into the bosom of Christ.

> O Years! the blest pre-eminence of Saints!
> Sweeping before the rapt prophetic gaze
> Bright as what glories of the jasper throne
> Stream from the gorgeous and face-veiling plumes
> Of Spirits adoring! Ye, blest years! must end,
> And all beyond is darkness! Heights most strange!
> Whence Fancy falls, fluttering her idle wing.
> For who of woman born may paint the hour,
> Whence seiz'd in his mid course the Sun shall wane
> Making noon ghastly! who of woman born
> May image in his wildly working thought,

[1] A letter from Coleridge to Thelwall, 13th May 1796, says: "A very dear friend of mine who is, in my opinion, the best poet of the age (I will send you his poem when published), thinks that the lines from 364 to 375 and from 403 to 428 the best in the volume—indeed, worth all the rest. And this man is a republican, and, at least, a semi-atheist." The lines quoted below from the original edition of 1796 are those here alluded to.

[2] *Religious Musings*, ll. 364-375. *Poems on Various Subjects*, 1796.

How the black-visag'd, red-eyed Fiend outstretcht
Beneath th' unsteady feet of Nature groans
In feverish slumbers—destin'd then to wake,
When fiery whirlwinds thunder his dread name
And Angels shout, Destruction! How his arm,
The mighty Spirit lifting high in air,
Shall swear by Him, the ever-living One,
Time is no more!
                Believe thou, O my soul,
Life is a vision shadowy of Truth,
And vice, and anguish, and the wormy grave,
Shapes of a dream! The veiling clouds retire,
And lo! the Throne of the redeeming God
Forth flashing unimaginable day
Wraps in one blaze earth, heaven, and deepest hell.[1]

By the breath of these passionate effusions Wordsworth
was wafted beyond the confines of earth. Though they
did not at once exercise upon him any apparent influence,
little by little they led him to widen the range of his
thought, and to direct towards the mystery beyond the
meditation which had as yet had no object but the present
hour and the sensible world.

III

But at first, perhaps, Coleridge exerted more influence
through the admiration he felt than through that which he
aroused. The event of chief interest in his first interview
with Wordsworth was the enthusiastic welcome which he
gave to his rival's poem. He had already formed a lofty
conception of his visitor's talent, having been one of the
first to read the *Descriptive Sketches*, and perhaps the only
one in whom their perusal raised the suspicion that a great
and original genius had emerged above the horizon. As he
listened to Wordsworth's impassioned recitation of *Guilt
and Sorrow*, this suspicion became a certainty. An analysis
of the poem has already been given, but in order to understand the origin and the nature of Coleridge's enthusiasm,
we must here quote the most remarkable passage it contains.

---

[1] *Religious Musings*, ll. 403-428. *Ibid.*

The advance made by Wordsworth in two years is marvellous. There is no more obscurity, "no mark of strained thought or forced diction, no crowd or turbulence of imagery."[1] The Spenserian stanza replaces the couplet as better suited to description. And, looking at it from another point of view, man no longer appears as an intruder in nature. He is the centre of objects, which are only presented to the reader as refracted by his mind. The commencement of the poem, describing a walk taken at night by the discharged soldier whom poverty has driven into crime, is as follows:

I

A TRAVELLER on the skirt of Sarum's Plain
Pursued his vagrant way, with feet half bare;
Stooping his gait, but not as if to gain
Help from the staff he bore; for mien and air
Were hardy, though his cheek seemed worn with care
Both of the time to come, and time long fled:
Down fell in straggling locks his thin grey hair;
A coat he wore of military red
But faded, and stuck o'er with many a patch and shred.

II

While thus he journeyed, step by step led on,
He saw and passed a stately inn, full sure
That welcome in such house for him was none.
No board inscribed the needy to allure
Hung there, no bush proclaimed to old and poor
And desolate, "Here you will find a friend!"
The pendant grapes glittered above the door;—
On he must pace, perchance till night descend,
Where'er the dreary roads their bare white lines extend.

III

The gathering clouds grew red with stormy fire,
In streaks diverging wide and mounting high;
That inn he long had passed; the distant spire,

[1] *Biographia Literaria*, ch. vi. I purposely quote the judgment of Coleridge, lest it should be supposed that, since *Guilt and Sorrow* did not appear until 1842, the superiority of this poem over the earlier ones is due to modifications introduced at a later period. If Wordsworth did make any such alterations, they must have been few and unimportant, except towards the close of the poem, which he changed for moral reasons. It should also be noted that the enthusiasm of Coleridge was aroused not by the narrative of the *female vagrant*, but by that of the *murderer*. *Biographia Literaria, ibid.*

Which oft as he looked back had fixed his eye,
Was lost, though still he looked, in the blank sky.
Perplexed and comfortless he gazed around,
And scarce could any trace of man descry,
Save cornfields stretched and stretching without bound;
But where the sower dwelt was nowhere to be found.

IV

No tree was there, no meadow's pleasant green,
No brook to wet his lip or soothe his ear;
Long files of corn-stacks here and there were seen,
But not one dwelling-place his heart to cheer.
Some labourer, thought he, may perchance be near;
And so he sent a feeble shout—in vain;
No voice made answer, he could only hear
Winds rustling over plots of unripe grain,
Or whistling thro' thin grass along the unfurrowed plain.

V

Long had he fancied each successive slope
Concealed some cottage, whither he might turn
And rest; but now along heaven's darkening cope
The crows rushed by in eddies, homeward borne.
Thus warned he sought some shepherd's spreading thorn
Or hovel from the storm to shield his head,
But sought in vain; for now, all wild, forlorn,
And vacant, a huge waste around him spread;
The wet cold ground, he feared, must be his only bed.

. . . .

IX

From that day forth no place to him could be
So lonely, but that thence might come a pang
Brought from without to inward misery.
Now, as he plodded on, with sullen clang
A sound of chains along the desert rang;
He looked, and saw upon a gibbet high
A human body that in irons swang,
Uplifted by the tempest whirling by;
And, hovering, round it often did a raven fly.

X

It was a spectacle which none might view,
In spot so savage, but with shuddering pain;
Nor only did for him at once renew
All he had feared from man, but roused a train

Of the mind's phantoms, horrible as vain.
The stones, as if to cover him from day,
Rolled at his back along the living plain ;
He fell, and without sense or motion lay ;
But, when the trance was gone, feebly pursued his way.

XI

As one whose brain habitual frenzy fires
Owes to the fit in which his soul hath tossed
Profounder quiet, when the fit retires,
Even so the dire phantasma which had crossed
His sense, in sudden vacancy quite lost,
Left his mind still as a deep evening stream.
Nor, if accosted now, in thought engrossed,
Moody, or inly troubled, would he seem
To traveller who might talk of any casual theme.

XII

Hurtle the clouds in deeper darkness piled,
Gone is the raven timely rest to seek ;
He seemed the only creature in the wild
On whom the elements their rage might wreak ;
Save that the bustard, of those regions bleak
Shy tenant, seeing by the uncertain light
A man there wandering, gave a mournful shriek,
And half upon the ground, with strange affright,
Forced hard against the wind a thick unwieldy flight.

XIII

All, all was cheerless to the horizon's bound ;
The weary eye—which, wheresoe'er it strays,
Marks nothing but the red sun's setting round,
Or on the earth strange lines, in former days
Left by gigantic arms—at length surveys
What seems an antique castle spreading wide ;
Hoary and naked are its walls, and raise
Their brow sublime : in shelter there to bide
He turned, while rain poured down smoking on every side.

XIV

Pile of Stone-henge ! so proud to hint yet keep
Thy secrets, thou that lov'st to stand and hear
The Plain resounding to the whirlwind's sweep,
Inmate of lonesome Nature's endless year ;
Even if thou saw'st the giant wicker rear
For sacrifice its throngs of living men,

Before thy face did ever wretch appear,
Who in his heart had groaned with deadlier pain
Than he who, tempest-driven, thy shelter now would gain?

xv

Within that fabric of mysterious form
Winds met in conflict, each by turns supreme ;
And, from the perilous ground dislodged, through storm
And rain he wildered on, no moon to stream
From gulf of parting clouds one friendly beam,
Nor any friendly sound his footsteps led
Once did the lightning's faint disastrous gleam
Disclose a naked guide-post's double head
Sight which, tho' lost at once, a gleam of pleasure shed.

xvi

No swinging sign-board creaked from cottage elm
To stay his steps with faintness overcome ;
'Twas dark and void as ocean's watery realm
Roaring with storms beneath night's starless gloom ;
No gipsy cower'd o'er fire of furze or broom ;
No labourer watched his red kiln glaring bright,
Nor taper glimmered dim from sick man's room ;
Along the waste no line of mournful light
From lamp of lonely toll-gate streamed athwart the night.

.   .   .   .

There were two characteristics in his friend's genius
which particularly impressed Coleridge, and enabled him to
discover the nature of true poetry, namely, Wordsworth's
exactness in observing the scenes he described, and his
faculty for transforming, without distorting, reality by
suffusing it with the light, now joyous, now sombre,
reflected by the feelings. He was himself, he believed,
devoid of these supreme gifts. What was wanting to
him, or, rather, had been wanting to him during his ten
years' residence in London and at Cambridge—what he had
lost too early and found too late, was Nature. Wordsworth
took a delight in exposing the ill effects of this enforced
deprivation upon his friend's imagination. Instead of being
fed, like his, upon realities and actual impressions, the
imagination of Coleridge had had to perform its functions
without matter to operate on, and nourished only by vague
visions of remote and little known objects, obscured by
distance or distorted by time. Wordsworth, in his boy-

hood, could let his eyes roam over the lake of Esthwaite,
but what was there for Coleridge to do?

> Of rivers, fields,
> And groves I speak to thee, my Friend! to thee,
> Who, yet a liveried schoolboy, in the depths
> Of the huge city, on the leaded roof
> Of that wide edifice, thy school and home,
> Wert used to lie and gaze upon the clouds
> Moving in heaven; or, of that pleasure tired,
> To shut thine eyes, and by internal light
> See trees, and meadows, and thy native stream,
> Far distant, thus beheld from year to year
> Of a long exile.[1]

"Debarred from Nature's living images," his mind was
"compelled to be a life unto herself,"[2]

> in endless dreams
> Of sickliness, disjoining, joining, things
> Without the light of knowledge.[3]

It is true that at twenty years of age Coleridge once more
steeped himself in nature, but it was then too late for him
to collect the store of precise images and minute observations which Wordsworth had possessed from childhood
upwards, and had enriched almost daily by some newly-
minted piece of gold. Here and there, indeed, his subtle
perception caught delicate shades of colour, of which
Wordsworth himself might have envied him the discovery,
but these were too rare to form complete pictures, and
could only be used to supply imaginary scenes with the
element of truth necessary to complete their effect. He
always remained to some extent a slave to his dreaming
faculty. In 1796, and possibly earlier, he had contracted
the habit of taking opium, which increased his tendency to
hallucination. There was a suggestion of somnambulism in
his wandering manner of going about the country. He "was
not," said Wordsworth, "under the influence of external objects. He had extraordinary powers of summoning up an
image, or series of images, in his own mind."[4] From this

---

[1] *The Prelude*, vi. 263-273.　　　　　　　[2] *Ibid.*, vi. 301-302.
[3] *Ibid.*, viii. 433. An imitation of Milton's *Paradise Lost*, v. 103.
[4] *Mrs Davy's Recollections*, 11th July 1844. *Prose Works*, iii. p. 442.

time forward it was impossible for him to become a faithful painter of nature, such as Wordsworth was and always remained. The reality about him too easily gave place to the world of fancy.

His perception of the master quality in Wordsworth was perhaps all the clearer because that quality was lacking in himself. He mentions in his memoirs what it was that struck him in reading *Guilt and Sorrow* :

" It was the union of deep feeling with profound thought ; the fine balance of truth in observing, with the imaginative faculty in modifying, the objects observed ; and, above all, the original gift of spreading the tone, the atmosphere, and with it the depth and height of the ideal world, around forms, incidents, and situations of which, for the common view, custom had bedimmed all the lustre, had dried up the sparkle and the dew-drops." [1]

And *The Prelude* shows how delighted Wordsworth, on his side, was, when he witnessed the admiration of Coleridge, and ascertained its cause.

> Thou, O Friend !
> Pleased with some unpremeditated strains
> That served those wanderings [2] to beguile, hast said
> That then and there my mind had exercised
> Upon the vulgar forms of present things,
> The actual world of our familiar days,
> Yet higher power ; had caught from them a tone,
> An image, and a character, by books
> Not hitherto reflected. Call we this
> A partial judgment—and yet why ? for *then*
> We were as strangers ; and I may not speak
> Thus wrongfully of verse, however rude,
> Which on thy young imagination, trained
> In the great City, broke like light from far. [3]

Their mutual footing was determined from the outset of their friendship. Coleridge declared that it was Wordsworth who was the great poet, and founded his opinion upon his friend's imagination. He at once set to work to define that imagination, [4] and it is easy to picture him, with

---

[1] *Biographia Literaria*, ch. iv.　　[2] On Salisbury Plain.
[3] *The Prelude*, xiii. 352-365.　　[4] *Biographia Literaria*, ch. vi.

his learning, eloquence and animation, proving to his easily persuaded friend the presence of the divinity within his breast. Nothing is more curious than the simplicity with which Wordsworth accepted the recognition of his superior genius, nor more admirable than the self-denying anxiety of Coleridge to undeceive his own admirers, and to make them bow down like himself before the great man he had discovered.

When he made Wordsworth's acquaintance, Coleridge was regarded by his circle of associates at Bristol, and was still looked upon by his school and college friends, as the young man of genius for whom everybody predicts a glorious future. His schoolfellow, Charles Lamb, considered his *Religious Musings* " the noblest poem in the language next after the *Paradise Lost ;* and even that was not made the vehicle of such grand truths." [1] He entreated him to write an epic poem, to compose a work which would bring him imperishable fame, and " make the age to come " his own. [2] Cottle, the bookseller, was dazzled by him, and gave proof of his enthusiasm by paying him a high price for his poems, which had a very poor sale. Thomas Poole, the rich tanner and farmer of Nether Stowey, offered him a house in order to keep him close at hand. Charles Lloyd the poet, the son of a wealthy banker, lodged in the cottage of Coleridge in order to enjoy his society. Thomas Wedgwood, the son of the famous maker of pottery, offered to settle £150 a year on him so that he might devote himself exclusively to poetry and philosophy. How many others, too, then and since, have felt his fascination !

And in what manner did Coleridge respond to this unanimous enthusiasm ? By loudly repeating, wherever he went, that the praises lavished on him were really due to Wordsworth. On the 13th May 1796 he spoke of him to the democrat Thelwall as " the best poet of the age." In June 1797 he writes to Cottle : " I speak with heartfelt sincerity, and, I think, unblinded judgment, when I tell you that I feel myself a little man by his side." A month later he wrote to Southey : " Wordsworth is a very

[1] Letter from Lamb to Coleridge, 5th and 6th January 1797.
[2] Letter from Lamb to Coleridge, 10th January 1797.

great man, the only man to whom *at all times* and *in all modes of excellence* I feel myself inferior, the only one, I mean, whom I have yet met with."[1] To the Wedgwoods, who hesitated to believe in Wordsworth's genius, he replied: "He strides on so far before you that he dwindles in the distance."[2] Nor were these mere cries of admiration uttered in a moment of astonishment; his enthusiasm steadily increased during several years, and passed successfully through the ordeal of the closest intimacy. Four years after the first interview between the poets, Thomas Poole reproached him with excessive reverence for Wordsworth, and Coleridge replied that it had been to him a most delicious sensation to be the first who estimated the new Milton at his true worth.[3]

He told Sir Humphry Davy that he would rather have written Wordsworth's *Ruth* and *Lucy* than a million such poems as *Christabel*,[4] and with a just conviction of his own disinterestedness, added: "But why do I calumniate my own spirit by saying I would rather? God knows it is as delightful to me that they are written." To Charles Lamb, who could not altogether admire the second edition of the *Lyrical Ballads*, in which all the additional pieces were by Wordsworth, he sent a reprimand containing a formal summons to bow the knee, assuring Lamb that if "the works of a man of true genius such as Wordsworth undoubtedly was" did not please him at first sight, he ought to suspect the fault to lie in himself and not in them.[5] In a letter to William Godwin he speaks of Wordsworth as one "the latchet of whose shoe I am unworthy to unloose," and writing again to Godwin on the 25th March 1801, he says: "If I die, and the booksellers will give you anything for my life, be sure to say: 'Wordsworth descended on him like the Γνῶθι σεαυτόν from heaven, by showing to him what true poetry was, he made him know that he himself was no Poet.'"

---

[1] *Letters of S. T. Coleridge* (1895), i. p. 224.
[2] W. Hazlitt, *My first acquaintance with poets*.
[3] Letter from Coleridge to Poole, March 1800.
[4] Letter from Coleridge to Sir Humphry Davy, 9th October 1800.
[5] Letter from Charles Lamb to Thomas Manning, 15th February 1801 (published only in Canon Ainger's edition.).

On every hand Coleridge was prepared to wage war
against the incredulous on behalf of his friend's glory and
at the expense of his own.   But from the very first he
gave him a surer and more flattering proof of his admiration than any praises ; he imitated him forthwith.

A passage in *Guilt and Sorrow* describes a cart standing
in the keen air of morning near a stream which crosses a
pebbly road.   Within the cart lay

> A pale-faced Woman, in disease far gone . . .
> Bed under her lean body there was none,
> Though even to die near one she most had loved
> She could not of herself those wasted limbs have moved.

She is carried to an inn near at hand.

> From her bare straw the Woman half upraised
> Her bony visage—gaunt and deadly wan ;
> No pity asking, on the group she gazed
> With a dim eye, distracted and amazed ;
> Then sank upon her straw with feeble moan.
> Fervently cried the housewife—" God be praised,
> I have a house that I can call my own ;
> Nor shall she perish there, untended and alone ! "

But the good woman's cares are useless.   The wretched
creature's strength fails when her story is told, and she
dies almost immediately.[1]

Now Coleridge, who had contributed about a hundred
philosophical lines, mystical effusions, some of which we have
quoted,[2] to Southey's epic on *Joan of Arc*, concluded them,
somewhat oddly, with a distressing scene from family life
inspired by the above passage from *Guilt and Sorrow*.   He
intended to publish these lines separately, under the title
of *Visions of the Maid of Orleans*, their object being to show
how Joan had become conscious of her mission.   Coleridge
therefore represents her as witnessing another such melancholy scene as that described by Wordsworth.   Prompted by
her guardian angel, Joan has left her home before daylight
on a winter's morning, alone.   By the side of the high road
she finds a deserted cart.   One of the horses is dead, frozen;

---

[1] *Guilt and Sorrow*, st. xl.-xliii.
[2] Separately published by Coleridge under the title *Destiny of Nations*.

the other two are stiff with cold. She calls, and a feeble voice replies from beneath the tilt which covers the waggon, the voice of a poor wretch, with frost-bitten limbs, who creeps painfully towards her. Inside the cart are the motionless forms of his wife and children, frozen to death. With great difficulty Joan brings the vehicle to her own home. She tends the miserable survivor, but in vain; ere long he joins his wife and little ones in death. Yet he does not breathe his last until he has told his story. The village where he dwelt has been taken and burnt by the enemy, and he has fled with his family, only to find himself powerless to shelter them against the frosty night-air. And it is under the influence of the emotion caused by this scene, and by the story she has heard, that Joan has the first vision of her destiny.[1]

IV

Since Coleridge admired Wordsworth so far as to imitate him, what could Wordsworth do better than imitate himself, or rather persevere in writing poetry of the description which had procured him such a disciple ? Assured of his ability to illumine the humblest themes, he chose a subject still more simple, and much more uneventful, than that of *Guilt and Sorrow*, and began to write *The Ruined Cottage*, a poem which, at a later time, formed the first book of *The Excursion*.

This story does not deal with scenes of crime and horror, yet it is not on that account less painfully impressive than the earlier poem. It is again a picture of the unseen evils caused by war; one of those cases of wrecked happiness and unheeded ruin for which it is responsible. As afterwards overlaid with optimistic reflexions, the story loses the poignant effect due to unity, and thereby also something of its artistic value.[2] But it is possible to disencumber it

---

[1] *Destiny of Nations*, ll. 172-245.
[2] A comparison of *The Ruined Cottage* with *The Borderers*, which was written at the same time, will suffice to show that the optimistic reflexions of the Pedlar were added later. Besides, the tone of the narrative is too gloomy for these reflexions, which are made by the same man who tells the

of these excrescences, beneath which, if we disregard the modifications of style to which it must have been subjected, it is easy to discover the original form of one of the finest and most powerful works which Wordsworth ever wrote.

THE RUINED COTTAGE.[1]

'TWAS summer, and the sun had mounted high . . .
Across a bare wide Common I was toiling
With languid feet that by the slippery ground
Were baffled ; nor could my weak arm disperse
The hosts of insects gathering round my face,
And ever with me as I paced along.

Upon that open moorland stood a grove,
The wished-for Port to which my steps were bound.
Thither I came, and there, amid the gloom
Spread by a brotherhood of lofty elms,
Appeared a roofless Hut ; four naked walls
That stared upon each other !—I looked round,
And to my wish and to my hope espied
Him whom I sought ; a Man of reverend age,

story. From the prefatory note to *The Excursion*, moreover, we know what part of the poem was written first, and that part is the most distressing (*Excursion*, i. ll. 871-916). Another and very different proof may also be given. Wordsworth says in a letter written on the 11th March 1798 that he has composed 706 lines of *The Recluse*. Three days earlier Coleridge wrote that Wordsworth had composed " near twelve hundred lines of blank verse, superior, I hesitate not to aver, to anything in our language which in any way resembles it." The five hundred lines which represent the difference constitute *The Ruined Cottage*, " without " the reflexions. And to make certain that Coleridge was really referring to *The Ruined Cottage* when he wrote these words, it is sufficient to compare this letter with one he wrote to Lady Beaumont on the 3rd April 1815 : " *The Ruined Cottage*, which I have ever thought the finest poem in our language, comparing it with any of the same or similar length."

As to the date when it was composed (stated by Wordsworth in the prefatory note to *The Excursion* to have been between 1795 and 1798), it is fixed by the fact that the poem was read to Coleridge in June, and to Lamb in July, 1797. Writing to thank Wordsworth for *The Excursion*, Lamb said : " My having known the story of Margaret (at the beginning), a very old acquaintance, even as long back as when I first saw you at Stowey, did not make her appearance less fresh " (Letter of the 9th August 1814).

[1] *The Excursion*. i. I quote from the text of the first edition (1814). The modifications afterwards introduced into that portion of the first book which is here reproduced are few and unimportant.

But stout and hale, for travel unimpaired.
There was he seen upon the cottage-bench,
Recumbent in the shade, as if asleep;
An iron-pointed staff lay at his side.

.   .   .   .   .   .

His eyes as if in drowsiness half shut,
The shadows of the breezy elms above
Dappling his face.   He had not heard my steps
As I approached; and near him did I stand
Unnoticed in the shade, some minutes' space.
At length I hailed him, seeing that his hat
Was moist with water-drops, as if the brim
Had newly scooped a running stream.   He rose,
And ere the pleasant greeting that ensued
Was ended, " 'Tis," said I, " a burning day :
My lips are parched with thirst, but you, I guess,
Have somewhere found relief."   He, at the word,
Pointing towards a sweet-briar, bade me climb
The fence hard by where that aspiring shrub
Looked out upon the road.   It was a plot
Of garden ground run wild, its matted weeds
Marked with the steps of those, whom, as they passed,
The gooseberry trees that shot in long lank slips,·
Or currants, hanging from their leafless stems,
In scanty strings, had tempted to o'erleap
The broken wall.   I looked around, and there,
Where two tall hedge-rows of thick alder boughs
Joined in a cold damp nook, espied a well
Shrouded with willow-flowers and plumy fern.
My thirst I slaked, and, from the cheerless spot
Withdrawing, straightway to the shade returned
Where sate the old Man on the cottage-bench;
And, while, beside him, with uncovered head,
I yet was standing, freely to respire,
And cool my temples in the fanning air,
Thus did he speak.   " I see around me here
Things which you cannot see: we die, my Friend,
Nor we alone, but that which each man loved
And prized in his peculiar nook of earth
Dies with him, or is changed; and very soon
Even of the good is no memorial left.
. . .   Beside yon spring I stood,
And eyed its waters till we seemed to feel

One sadness, they and I.   For them a bond
Of brotherhood is broken : time has been
When, every day, the touch of human hand
Dislodged the natural sleep that binds them up
In mortal stillness ; and they ministered
To human comfort.   As I stooped to drink,
Upon the slimy foot-stone I espied
The useless fragment of a wooden bowl,
Green with the moss of years, a pensive sight
That moved my heart !—recalling former days
When I could never pass that road but She
Who lived within these walls at my approach
A daughter's welcome gave me, and I loved her
As my own child.   Oh, Sir ! the good die first,
And they whose hearts are dry as summer dust
Burn to the socket.   Many a passenger
Hath blessed poor Margaret for her gentle looks,
When she upheld the cool refreshment drawn
From that forsaken spring ; and no one came
But he was welcome ; no one went away
But that it seemed she loved him.   She is dead,
The light extinguished of her lonely hut,
The hut itself abandoned to decay,
And she forgotten in the quiet grave.

   " I speak," continued he, " of One whose stock
Of virtues bloomed beneath this lowly roof.
She was a Woman of a steady mind,
Tender and deep in her excess of love ;
Not speaking much, pleased rather with the joy
Of her own thoughts : by some especial care
Her temper had been framed, as if to make
A Being, who by adding love to peace
Might live on earth a life of happiness.
Her wedded Partner lacked not on his side
The humble worth that satisfied her heart :
Frugal, affectionate, sober, and withal
Keenly industrious.   She with pride would tell
That he was often seated at his loom,
In summer, ere the mower was abroad
Among the dewy grass,—in early spring,
Ere the last star had vanished.—They who passed
At evening, from behind the garden fence

Might hear his busy spade, which he would ply,
After his daily work, until the light
Had failed, and every leaf and flower were lost
In the dark hedges.   So their days were spent
In peace and comfort ; and a pretty boy
Was their best hope, next to the God in heaven

" Not twenty years ago, but you I think
Can scarcely bear it now in mind, there came
Two blighting seasons, when the fields were left
With half a harvest.   It pleased Heaven to add
A worse affliction in the plague of war :
This happy Land was stricken to the heart !
A Wanderer then among the cottages,
I, with my freight of winter raiment, saw
The hardships of that season : many rich
Sank down, as in a dream, among the poor
And of the poor did many cease to be,
And their place knew them not.   Meanwhile, abridged
Of daily comforts, gladly reconciled
To numerous self-denials, Margaret
Went struggling on through those calamitous years
With cheerful hope, but ere the second autumn,
Her life's true Helpmate on a sick-bed lay,
Smitten with perilous fever.   In disease
He lingered long ; and, when his strength returned,
He found the little he had stored, to meet
The hour of accident or crippling age,
Was all consumed.   Two children had they now,
One newly born.   As I have said, it was
A time of trouble ; shoals of artisans
Were from their daily labour turn'd adrift
To seek their bread from public charity,
They, and their wives and children—happier far
Could they have lived as do the little birds
That peck along the hedges or the Kite
That makes his dwelling on the mountain Rocks !

" A sad reverse it was for him who long
Had filled with plenty, and possessed in peace,
This lonely Cottage.   At his door he stood,
And whistled many a snatch of merry tunes
That had no mirth in them ; or with his knife

Carved uncouth figures on the heads of sticks—
Then, not less idly, sought, through every nook
In house or garden, any casual work
Of use or ornament; and with a strange,
Amusing, yet uneasy, novelty,
He blended, where he might, the various tasks
Of summer, autumn, winter, and of spring.
But this endured not; his good humour soon
Became a weight in which no pleasure was:
And poverty brought on a petted mood
And a sore temper: day by day he drooped,
And he would leave his work—and to the town
Without an errand, would direct his steps,
Or wander here and there among the fields.
One while he would speak lightly of his babes,
And with a cruel tongue: at other times
He tossed them with a false unnatural joy:
And 'twas a rueful thing to see the looks
Of the poor innocent children. 'Every smile,'
Said Margaret to me, here beneath these trees,
'Made my heart bleed.'"

.   .   .   .   .   .

            "While thus it fared with them,
To whom this cottage, till those hapless years,
Had been a blessèd home, it was my chance
To travel in a country far remote.
And glad I was, when, halting by yon gate
That leads from the green lane, once more I saw
Those lofty elm-trees.   Long I did not rest:
With many pleasant thoughts I cheer'd my way
O'er the flat Common.—Having reached the door
I knock'd,—and when I entered with the hope
Of usual greeting, Margaret looked at me
A little while; then turned her head away
Speechless,—and, sitting down upon a chair,
Wept bitterly.   I wist not what to do,
Or how to speak to her.   Poor Wretch! at last
She rose from off her seat, and then,—O Sir!
I cannot *tell* how she pronounced my name:—
With fervent love, and with a face of grief
Unutterably helpless, and a look
That seemed to cling upon me, she enquired
If I had seen her husband.   As she spake

A strange surprise and fear came to my heart,
Nor had I power to answer ere she told
That he had disappeared—not two months gone.
He left his house : two wretched days had pass'd,
And on the third, as wistfully she raised
Her head from off her pillow, to look forth,
Like one in trouble, for returning light,
Within her chamber-casement she espied
A folded paper, lying as if placed
To meet her waking eyes.   This tremblingly
She opened—found no writing, but therein
Pieces of money carefully enclosed,
Silver and gold.   'I shuddered at the sight,'
Said Maragaret, 'for I knew it was his hand
Which placed it there ; and ere that day was ended,
That long anxious day ! I learned from One
Sent hither by my husband to impart
The heavy news, that he had joined a troop
Of soldiers, going to a distant land.
—He left me thus—he could not gather heart
To take a farewell of me ; for he feared
That I should follow with my babes, and sink
Beneath the misery of that wandering life.'

"This tale did Margaret tell with many tears :
And, when she ended, I had little power
To give her comfort, and was glad to take
Such words of hope from her own mouth as served
To cheer us both.   But long we had not talked
Ere we built up a pile of better thoughts,
And with a brighter eye she looked around
As if she had been shedding tears of joy.
We parted.—'Twas the time of early spring ;
I left her busy with her garden tools ;
And well remember, o'er that fence she looked,
And, while I paced along the foot-way path,
Called out, and sent a blessing after me,
With tender cheerfulness, and with a voice
That seemed the very sound of happy thoughts.

"I roved o'er many a hill and many a dale,
With my accustomed load ; in heat and cold,
Through many a wood and many an open ground,
In sunshine and in shade, in wet and fair,

Drooping or blithe of heart, as might befall;
My best companions now the driving winds,
And now the 'trotting brooks' and whispering trees,
And now the music of my own sad steps,
With many a short-lived thought that passed between,
And disappeared.

         I journeyed back this way,
Towards the wane of Summer; when the wheat
Was yellow; and the soft and bladed grass,
Springing afresh, had o'er the hay-field spread
Its tender verdure. At the door arrived,
I found that she was absent. In the shade,
Where now we sit, I waited her return.
Her cottage, then a cheerful object, wore
Its customary look,—only, I thought
The honeysuckle, crowding round the porch,
Hung down in heavier tufts; and that bright weed,
The yellow stone-crop, suffered to take root
Along the window's edge, profusely grew
Blinding the lower panes   I turned aside,
And strolled into her garden. It appeared
To lag behind the season, and had lost
Its pride of neatness. From the border lines
Composed of daisy and resplendent thrift,
Flowers straggling forth had on those paths encroached
Which they were used to deck: carnations, once
Prized for surpassing beauty, and no less
For the peculiar pains they had required,
Declined their languid heads—without support.
The cumbrous bind-weed, with its wreaths and bells,
Had twined about her two small rows of peas,
And dragged them to the earth.

         Ere this an hour
Was wasted.—Back I turned my restless steps,
And, as I walked before the door, it chanced
A stranger passed; and, guessing whom I sought,
He said that she was used to ramble far.—
The sun was sinking in the west; and now
I sate with sad impatience. From within
Her solitary infant cried aloud;
Then, like a blast that dies away self-stilled,
The voice was silent. From the bench I rose;
But neither could divert nor soothe my thoughts.

The spot, though fair, was very desolate—
The longer I remained, more desolate :
And, looking round, I saw the corner stones,
Till then unnotic'd, on either side the door
With dull red stains discoloured, and stuck o'er
With tufts and hairs of wool, as if the sheep,
That feed upon the Common, thither came
Familiarly, and found a couching-place
Even at her threshold.   Deeper shadows fell
From these tall elms ; the cottage-clock struck eight ;—
I turned, and saw her distant a few steps.
Her face was pale and thin—her figure, too,
Was changed.   As she unlocked the door, she said,
'It grieves me you have waited here so long,
But, in good truth, I've wandered much of late ;
And, sometimes—to my shame I speak—have need
Of my best prayers to bring me back again.'
While on the board she spread our evening meal,
She told me—interrupting not the work
Which gave employment to her listless hands—
That she had parted with her elder child ;
To a kind master on a distant farm
Now happily apprenticed.—'I perceive
You look at me, and you have cause ; to-day
I have been travelling far ; and many days
About the fields I wander, knowing this
Only, that what I seek I cannot find ;
And so I waste my time : for I am changed ;
And to myself,' said she, 'have done much wrong
And to this helpless infant.   I have slept
Weeping, and weeping I have waked ; my tears
Have flowed as if my body were not such
As others are ; and I could never die.
But I am now in mind and in my heart
More easy ; and I hope,' said she, 'that heaven
Will give me patience to endure the things
Which I behold at home.'

.   .   .   .   .

                     It would have grieved
Your very soul to see her : evermore
Her eyelids drooped, her eyes were downward cast ;
And, when she at her table gave me food,
She did not look at me.   Her voice was low,

Her body was subdued.   In every act
Pertaining to her house-affairs, appeared
The careless stillness of a thinking mind
Self-occupied ; to which all outward things
Are like an idle matter.   Still she sighed,
But yet no motion of the breast was seen,
No heaving of the heart.   While by the fire
We sate together, sighs came on my ear,
I knew not how, and hardly whence they came.

" Ere my departure, to her care I gave,
For her son's use, some tokens of regard,
Which with a look of welcome she received ;
And I exhorted her to have her trust
In God's good love, and seek his help by prayer.
I took my staff, and, when I kissed her babe,
The tears stood in her eyes.   I left her then
With the best hope and comfort I could give :
She thanked me for my wish ;—but for my hope
Methought she did not thank me.
                                             I returned,
And took my rounds along this road again
Ere on its sunny bank the primrose flower
Peeped forth, to give an earnest of the Spring.
I found her sad and drooping : she had learned
No tidings of her husband ; if he lived,
She knew not that he lived ; if he were dead,
She knew not he was dead.   She seemed the same
In person and appearance ; but her house
Bespake a sleepy hand of negligence ;
The floor was neither dry nor neat, the hearth
Was comfortless, and her small lot of books,
Which, in the cottage-window, heretofore
Had been piled up against the corner panes
In seemly order, now, with straggling leaves
Lay scattered here and there, open or shut,
As they had chanced to fall.   Her infant Babe
Had from its mother caught the trick of grief,
And sighed among its playthings.   Once again
I turned towards the garden gate, and saw,
More plainly still, that poverty and grief
Were now come nearer to her : weeds defaced
The hardened soil, and knots of withered grass :

No ridges there appeared of clear black mould,
No winter greenness; of her herbs and flowers,
It seemed the better part were gnawed away
Or trampled into earth; a chain of straw,
Which had been twined about the slender stem
Of a young apple-tree, lay at its root;
The bark was nibbled round by truant sheep.
—Margaret stood near, her infant in her arms,
And, noting that my eye was on the tree,
She said, 'I fear it will be dead and gone
Ere Robert come again.'   Towards the House
We turned together, silent, till she asked
If I had any hope:—but for her babe
And for her little orphan boy, she said,
She had no wish to live, that she must die
Of sorrow.   Yet I saw the idle loom
Still in its place; his Sunday garments hung
Upon the self-same nail; his very staff
Stood undisturbed behind the door.
                              And when,
In bleak December, I retraced this way,
She told me that her little babe was dead,
And she was left alone.   She now, released
From her maternal cares, had taken up
The employment common through these wilds, and gained,
By spinning hemp, a pittance for herself;
And for this end had hired a neighbour's boy
To give her needful help.   That very time
Most willingly she put her work aside,
And walked with me along the miry road,
Heedless how far; and, in such piteous sort
That any heart had ached to hear her, begged
That, wheresoe'er I went, I still would ask
For him whom she had lost.   We parted then—
Our final parting; for from that time forth
Did many seasons pass ere I returned
Into this tract again.
                        Nine tedious years;
From their first separation, nine long years,
She lingered in unquiet widowhood;
A Wife and Widow.   Needs must it have been
A sore heart-wasting!   I have heard, my Friend,
That in yon arbour oftentimes she sate

Alone, through half the vacant sabbath day;
And, if a dog passed by, she still would quit
The shade, and look abroad.   On this old bench
For hours she sate; and evermore her eye
Was busy in the distance, shaping things
That made her heart beat quick.   You see that path,
Now faint,—the grass has crept o'er its grey line;
There, to and fro, she paced through many a day
Of the warm summer, from a belt of hemp
That girt her waist, spinning the long-drawn thread
With backward steps.   Yet ever as there passed
A man whose garments showed the soldier's red,
Or crippled mendicant in soldier's garb,
The little child who sate to turn the wheel
Ceased from his task; and she with faltering voice
Made many a fond enquiry; and when they,
Whose presence gave no comfort, were gone by,
Her heart was still more sad.   And by yon gate,
That bars the traveller's road, she often stood,
And when a stranger horseman came, the latch
Would lift, and in his face look wistfully:
Most happy, if, from aught discovered there
Of tender feeling, she might dare repeat
The same sad question.   Meanwhile her poor Hut
Sank to decay; for he was gone, whose hand,
At the first nipping of October frost,
Closed up each chink, and with fresh bands of straw
Chequered the green-grown thatch.   And so she lived
Through the long winter, reckless and alone;
Until her house by frost, and thaw, and rain,
Was sapped; and while she slept, the nightly damps
Did chill her breast; and in the stormy day
Her tattered clothes were ruffled by the wind,
Even at the side of her own fire.   Yet still
She loved this wretched spot, nor would for worlds
Have parted hence; and still that length of road,
And this rude bench, one torturing hope endeared,
Fast rooted at her heart: and here, my Friend,—
In sickness she remained; and here she died;
Last human tenant of these ruined walls ! "

Such is the poem which Wordsworth composed after his
early interviews with Coleridge, when he had been stimu-

lated by the admiration of the young Neo-platonist without
having been as yet influenced by his philosophy. Between
the poems which betray the effect of his moral crisis on
the one hand, and *The Recluse* and the *Lyrical Ballads*,
which contain many traces of his weakness for systematic
thought or style, on the other, the *Ruined Cottage* occupies
a unique position, and as regards both matter and form is
in every way characteristic. It gives us the measure of
Wordsworth's genius when he had just reached maturity
and had not yet acquired a bent due to any stubborn
doctrine. The melodramatic features which were such a
blemish in *Guilt and Sorrow* have disappeared, but as yet
there is nothing of that optimism which, even in his
loftiest strains, suggests that it has been deliberately
assumed. Nor is there any introduction of minute trivi-
alities in obedience to a poetic theory. The poet here
accumulates humble details without for a moment incurring
the suspicion of employing them systematically. Matter
and form, in this instance, are completely in harmony.
Wordsworth had acquired some practice in writing blank
verse when composing *The Borderers*, and here he adopts it
instead of rhymed lines ; it seems, as it were, to be a
pledge that he has forsworn all embellishment, and trusts
solely to the moving power of the subject, and such
dignity as regular rhythm can afford. And in its touching
simplicity, its serious humility, the poem was entirely
original. English poetry provided Wordsworth with no
model which bears even a distant resemblance to it. If
anything suggested to him the idea of the poetic setting of
his story and of the harmony which arises between the
human soul, with its joys and sorrows, and the scenes
amid which they have been experienced, it must have been
the romance of *Paul et Virginie*. Is not the Pedlar who,
before the ruins of the cottage, tells Wordsworth the story
of the woman who had dwelt there in alternate happiness
and misery the younger brother of the old man from whom,
near the two ruined huts in the Isle of France, Bernardin
de Saint-Pierre, a few years earlier, had learned the sweet
idyll and heart-rending tragedy which had there unfolded

themselves ? [1] The theme is the same; Wordsworth, faithful to his realism, has merely transferred it to England, and to the only spot in which he had made observation of human nature. The enthusiasm which Coleridge had evinced, even for Wordsworth's less finished work, could not but rise to a higher pitch when he read *The Ruined Cottage*. The two poets had seen very little of each other in 1796, their rare meetings being too brief to admit of frank out-pouring of heart and perfect communion of soul. But they had carried away from their earliest interviews the pleasing and tender impression of mutual admiration, the conviction that they were destined to understand and to complete one another. Their real intimacy began in June 1797, under Wordsworth's roof, where Coleridge came to spend a few weeks. It was then that Coleridge heard *The Borderers* read, and became so infatuated with it as to imitate it in the second part of a tragedy, entitled *Osorio*, of which he had already written two acts and a half. Impressed by the character of the villain Oswald, he borrowed his pride and cynical philosophy for the traitor of his own work, a flagrant piece of imitation which begins at the very point in his tragedy where Coleridge had stopped before he became acquainted with *The Borderers*. It was during the same visit, however, that *The Ruined Cottage* was read to him, and although he did not at once conceive for this work the same passionate enthusiasm, it is clear that he gradually reached the conviction that this was Wordsworth's masterpiece, "the finest poem in our language, comparing it with any of the same or similar length." [2] Greatly, however, as he admired his friend's poetry, it was Coleridge whose influence was henceforth to infuse that poetry with new elements, whereby it would be at any rate profoundly modified if not transformed.

To sum up, Coleridge had hitherto received everything, and had apparently given nothing in exchange. Wordsworth may have been struck by his friend's mystical con-

[1] Hazlitt suspected that Wordsworth had also been influenced by the same work in his *Poems on the Naming of Places*, though Wordsworth did not admit his obligation.
[2] Letter to Lady Beaumont, 3rd April 1815.

ceptions, but as yet he had not made them his own. Less amenable to influence, less easily permeated by the ideas of others, he had been stimulated, but in no way altered, by his early intercourse with Coleridge. The time when he would himself become the recipient was at hand. For this, however, it was necessary that they should share a united life. After meeting one another on a more familiar footing at Racedown, the two young men felt that each was necessary to the other, and found it impossible any longer to live apart. On the 3rd of July the Words-worths returned the visit of Coleridge, and on the 13th took up their residence in the country-house of Alfoxden, a couple of miles from Nether Stowey, where he was living. From this time a daily intercourse was established between them, and upon each its influence was continuous and profound ; an influence not merely such as is occasioned by reading or by an interview, through the shock of two intelligences, but that of a life upon a life, and of a man upon a man. It was then that Wordsworth became really acquainted with one greater in his conversation than in his writings, of whose eloquence he himself has given a superb description. He compared it to " a majestic river, the sound or sight of whose course you caught at intervals ; which was sometimes concealed by forests, sometimes lost in sand ; then came flashing out broad and distinct ; and even when it took a turn which your eye could not follow, yet you always felt and knew that there was a connection in its parts, and that it was the same river." [1]

[1] Knight, *Life of Wordsworth*, i. p. 129.

CHAPTER III

Alfoxden

I

THE Quantock Hills, the crests of which adorn the shores of the Bristol Channel with their graceful undulations, presented scenes of joyous beauty that contrasted strongly with the dreary prospect of bare cliff at Racedown. Dorothy was charmed by her first view of this region.

" There is everything here ; sea, woods wild as fancy ever painted, brooks clear and pebbly as in Cumberland, villages so romantic ; and William and I, in a wander by ourselves, found out a sequestered waterfall in a dell formed by steep hills covered with full-grown timber trees. The woods are as fine as those at Lowther, and the country more romantic ; it has the character of the less grand parts of the neighbourhood of the lakes." [1]

No less enchanted were the tenants of Alfoxden with their new home, a large mansion situated in an extensive park well stocked with deer. The front of the house opened upon a little court planted with shrubs and roses, and was sheltered from the sun by a high hill scattered with trees and clothed with fern. " The deer dwell here," wrote Dorothy, " and sheep, so that we have a living prospect." [2] Behind, the house looked out over wide-stretching meadow lands interspersed with woods, to the sea, two miles away in the distance. But the great charm of this somewhat ordinary country lay in the varied richness of its vegetation, in its abundant heath and fern,

[1] Letter written by Dorothy Wordsworth, 4th July 1797. Knight, *Life of Wordsworth*, i. p. 114.
[2] Letter written by Dorothy Wordsworth, 14th August 1799. Knight, *Life of Wordsworth*, i. p. 115.

in the great number of its yew-trees, here of quite an imposing size, and of its hollies which deck the undergrowth of the woods with their shining foliage.

Always sensitive to the cheerful or depressing influence of a locality, Wordsworth was partly indebted to the charm of Alfoxden for his rapid progress towards happiness. Nor did he owe less to the society to which his connection with Coleridge introduced him. For years he had cultivated solitude to excess. Even to his friend he appeared " to have hurtfully segregated and isolated his being. Doubtless," said Coleridge, " his delights are more deep and sublime, but he has likewise more hours that prey on his flesh and blood."[1] And now the solitary suddenly found himself in the midst of a circle of intelligent men of varied, and in some cases of lofty, character and attainments, the neighbours or guests of Coleridge. The dream of a *Pantisocracy* had not so entirely faded as to leave no trace behind. Something of it survived in this corner of Somerset, where the haphazard grouping of ordinary society had been replaced by a grouping founded on sympathy, affection, and community of ideas.

Those who were accustomed to visit Coleridge had all been united by a common bond of revolutionary zeal, or at any rate by the same spirit of independence with respect to social conventions. All, men and youths alike, had been borne aloft on the great wave of enthusiasm, and, as it fell back, had been left on the shore, according to their vitality either exhausted and shattered, or, on the contrary, stronger and better tempered for the struggle which must follow the first rude shock. Their circle included desponding as well as buoyant spirits, and afforded Wordsworth, as an observer, a most instructive spectacle.

Among the former was George Burnett, a disconsolate Pantisocrat, whose languid countenance, already marked by opium with signs of the heavy look due to constant hallucination, seemed as if in mourning for the great scheme. The eloquence of Coleridge rekindled in him a measure of warmth and life, and he hovered about the house at

---

[1] Letter from Coleridge to Poole, 6th May 1799. *Poole and his Friends*, i. p. 299.

Nether Stowey like the mournful spirit of the past.
There is something touching in the feebleness of this
modest figure, which occupies so inconspicuous a place in
the group.   At the same time Burnett has a claim to our
interest from the useful part he afterwards took in the
romantic movement, through his *Specimens* of the English
prose-writers of the sixteenth and seventeenth centuries
who had previously been contemptuously ignored.

The melancholy disposition of Charles Lloyd was less
inoffensive, and more dangerous to his friends.   This young
man was the son of a rich Birmingham banker, and had
behaved nobly at the outset of his career.   Rejecting the
life of easy pleasure which lay open to him, he had resolved
to devote his fortune to benevolence and his intellect to
poetry and the pursuit of truth.   The better to succeed in
these objects, he had spent several months under Coleridge's
humble roof, sharing the philosopher's frugal life and
meditating and moralizing with him among the Quantock
hills.   When Wordsworth arrived he was no longer the
regular guest of Coleridge, but he still made occasional
appearances in Somerset.   His gifts of heart and intellect,
however, were then just beginning to be tainted with the
effects of organic disease.   Subject to epileptic fits, he
yielded to a morbid melancholy against which the reproaches of Coleridge were of no avail.   His philanthropy
gave way to futile lamentations on the sadness of human
life, his sensibility degenerated into a maudlin egoism.
His naturally subtle and penetrative mind, which rendered
him the psychologist of the group, was led astray by
suspicion and warped by jealousy.   A deterioration of
the active source of his faculties, which terminated in
complete insanity, had already begun.   Distorted by his
hideous complaint, his pure and lofty character became
subject to fits of irresponsible malice, which rendered him
capable of falsehood and treachery.   Though a sower of
discord, and therefore dangerous as a friend, he was
nevertheless painfully instructive during those years when
for all of them the issue between happiness and despondency hung in doubt.   An infatuated slave of melancholy,
he was well fitted to warn those who perceived the

unhealthy source and the evil effects of his dark humour. Unknown to himself, poor Lloyd contributed not a little to confirm Wordsworth in the opinion that " spontaneous wisdom is breathed by health, truth breathed by cheerfulness." [1]

At that time Charles Lamb, naturally so witty and sprightly, so full of charming mockery, was also among the dismal ones. When he met Wordsworth under Coleridge's roof, in July 1797, ten months had not elapsed since his sister had stabbed her mother in a fit of madness. With quiet heroism the young man had at once sacrificed his own prospects in life, stifled a dawning love, and decided to assume the sole responsibility for his sister by taking her under his own charge. He had himself "tasted all the grandeur and wildness of fancy" in an asylum, and may possibly have feared that he might again be visited by the malady.[2] His naturally free and joyous spirit had yielded to the weight of his affliction, and had temporarily taken refuge in serious religious thoughts. He had seen the hand of God in the blow which had fallen upon him, and had felt a sudden shame for his lawless life and the bad company he kept in London. In addition to the admiration he had felt for Coleridge ever since they were school-fellows together at Christ's Hospital, he now felt a need for the exalting influence of a friendship which raised him above his customary companions. Thus it was not the true Lamb that Wordsworth saw at this time, nor was it exactly the moral coxcomb whom Lamb himself ridiculed when, shortly afterwards, he recovered from his attack of puritanism ; it was rather a silent and sentimental youth, the "gentle-hearted Charles"[3] of whom Coleridge wrote during this visit. Lamb was now under a cloud ; for the time he had lost his originality and his pungent wit, and thus seemed to the poets a mere pale reflexion of themselves. In the young clerk of the East India Company, who wrote doleful verses in the leisure he enjoyed between office hours, or, actually, even at his office-desk, they thought they detected a soul who was the younger sister of their own, and had "pined and hungered after Nature, . . . in the

---

[1] *The Tables Turned*, 19-20.   [2] Letter to Coleridge, 9th June 1796.
[3] *This Lime-tree bower my prison*, 28 and 75.

great city pent." [1]   Lamb made no effort to undeceive them,
being similarly deceived himself.   He listened thoughtfully
to Wordsworth's pastoral poems.   It was not long, however, before he recovered his natural disposition.   Though
he continued his life of self-devotion, it was with a smiling
face, with a jest on his lips, and with roguish ways which
averted compassion.   No less quickly, too, he shook off the
countrified characteristics which Coleridge had attributed
to him.   Maliciously, yet not without sincerity, he upheld
the worship of London against the religion of nature, sympathy for swarming humanity against the passion for solitude.

This half-playful, half-serious reaction seems also to
have been provoked by a secret jealousy.   Lamb had come
to Stowey to see Coleridge, and was pained to find the first
place, and so large a place, in his friend's life taken by a
new-comer.   It irritated him to see Coleridge for ever on
his knees before Wordsworth, and urging all his own
admirers to form a prostrate rank of faithful ones with
himself at their head.   It was long, consequently, before
Lamb arrived at a sound appreciation of Wordsworth, and
longer still before he learnt to like him.   Incited by
Lloyd's treacherous insinuations, he revenged himself by
secretly laughing at the solemnity of the prescribed cult,
and at the profound faith in himself of the divinity to
whom its altars were erected.   It was only very gradually,
and with difficulty, that he came to recognise Wordsworth's genius and to pardon his eccentricities ; nor did he
ever entirely forego the solace of mocking at them.

Those we have mentioned were the disconsolate ones,
who sank beneath their affliction—real or imaginary, transient or enduring.   Very different was " citizen " John
Thelwall, the intrepid democrat, whose energy and cheerfulness had remained quite unimpaired by his recent trial
for the crime of high treason.   Lamb had but just left
when he arrived from London on foot, in order to settle
near Coleridge, and to combine the occupations of farming
and writing poetry.   Six years—the most stormy of modern
times—had passed over his head without in any way modifying his faith as a revolutionist.   The rigorous measures

---

[1] *This Lime-tree bower my prison,* 28-30.

taken by the government had obliged him to withdraw from active politics, but his opinions were still what they had been in 1790, when, on the popular platform, he supported Horne Tooke, the radical candidate for Westminster, and carried his glowing language throughout the length and breadth of England as the vehement advocate of constitutional reform. Short, thick-set, and muscular, with a head indicative of indomitable resolution, he was one of the purest and best types of the English Jacobin. "Prompt to conceive, and still prompter to execute," his merits as a man of action were due as much to the deficiencies of his mind as to his real intellectual gifts. The simplifying century had set its stamp upon him. He rigidly followed a single idea because he had but one. His logic was that of Thomas Paine, as sharp and incisive as it was limited. He had the clear precision of thought, the frankness of speech, and the fearlessness of action which are half virtues and half the outcome of ignorance of obstacles and complexities. " I think," Coleridge said of him, " he is deficient in that patience of mind which can look intensely and frequently at the same subject. He believes and disbelieves with impassioned confidence. I wish to see him doubting, and doubting." [1] His ruling passion was a hatred of prejudices, amongst which he included religion. He seldom mentioned them without some sarcastic allusion. It would seem therefore as if there were the elements of serious discord between him and Coleridge ; but this was by no means the case. As " a Necessitarian," says Coleridge, " I cannot possibly disesteem a man for his religious or anti-religious opinions— and as an *Optimist*, I feel diminish'd concern." [2] Besides, Thelwall's integrity disarmed him. " Intrepid, eloquent, and honest," he won the sincere respect of Coleridge, although they disagreed on " almost every point of religion, of morals, of politics and philosophy." [3] Thus, instead of

[1] Letter written by Coleridge to Mr Wade, 1797. *Cottle's Early Recollections*, London, 1837, i. pp. 254-255.

[2] Letter written by Coleridge to Thelwall, May 1796. Campbell, *Coleridge's Poetical Works*, p. 580.

[3] Letter written by Coleridge to Cottle, 1797. *Cottle's Early Recollections*, i. p. 254.

quarrels, the difference in their opinions merely gave rise to lively and amusing discussions. The following anecdote related by Coleridge gives the tone of their conversations.

"Thelwall thought it very unfair to influence a child's mind by inculcating any opinions before it should have come to years of discretion and be able to choose for itself. I showed him my garden and told him it was my botanical garden. 'How so?' said he, 'it is covered with weeds.' 'Oh,' I replied, '*that* is only because it has not yet come to its age of discretion and choice. The weeds, you see, have taken the liberty to grow, and I thought it unfair in me to prejudice the soil towards roses and strawberries.'"[1]

It was worth while to point out the incompatibility between these two minds, since it helps to explain the process then going on in Wordsworth's thought. He witnessed, and at times no doubt took part in, these courteous passages-of-arms. In respect of his opinions he occupied an intermediate position between the other two, with a leaning, possibly, to the side of Thelwall. A semi-atheist, though progressing by slow stages towards the mysticism of Coleridge, he saw in Thelwall a copy of himself as he had been when his faith in Godwin was at its height. And Thelwall, in spite of his " extraordinary talent," and his brief flashes of eloquence, wrung by the fiery language of a people's tribune from the most common-place ideas, contributed to alienate him still more from his former master. Wordsworth, with his more cautious spirit, could not but feel, as he heard them once more retailed, how vain and empty were some of the declamatory phrases, how brutally precipitate some of the opinions, with which the honest Jacobin was infatuated. But little acquainted with the past, and for that very reason full of a rude faith in the future, " boastful of the strength of reason," because he had " never tried it enough to know its weakness,"[2] Thelwall's defects became strongly conspicuous in discussion with a man of such wide and varied

---

[1] *Coleridge's Table Talk*, 26th July 1830.
[2] Letter from Coleridge to Mr Wade, quoted above.

reading as Coleridge. It was inevitable that Wordsworth should be led by their conversations to calculate the distance his own mind had travelled since the day, however recent, when he himself reasoned in the same manner as Thelwall.

The influences of which we have spoken were, in a manner, counteractive. The characters just described were all better qualified to warn Wordsworth of the course to be avoided than to indicate the path he ought to follow. There was one man, however, whose influence, though exerted in quite a different way, was second only to that of Coleridge in bringing him to a full comprehension of the principles which for him were to remain final.

Just as Wordsworth had only come into the neighbourhood for the sake of Coleridge's society, so Coleridge himself had sought the same retreat, six months earlier, merely in order to be within easy reach of his friend Thomas Poole. This well-to-do farmer was the fixed centre of the shifting group, and the only member of it connected with the soil of the county by family and fortune. A character in whom there was much to interest, he made a fruitful impression upon Wordsworth. In spite of his coarse exterior, his want of good breeding, his churlish manners, and the harsh and disagreeable voice in which he often told his friends unpalatable truths, Poole was an excellent example of the thoroughly developed man. Though his father was a prosperous tanner, his knowledge had been of necessity self-acquired. He had not received a classical education, and had accordingly taught himself French and Latin, almost without assistance, while following his father's profession. An enthusiastic disciple of Rousseau, and thoroughly familiar with all the circumstances of the French Revolution, his fervent desires for the success of a hostile nation placed him in an isolated position among the landowners and farmers of Somersetshire, who were unanimous in their support of the established order of things. Hence he was led, in search of sympathetic minds, to form the acquaintance of Coleridge and the *Pantisocrats*. More practical, however, than they, and some years older, he was not long deceived by their vain schemes. So long as a fine field for reform presented itself in England he had something better to do than to withdraw from the struggle, in company with his friends, in order to found an ideal colony in a distant land. And just as his love of progress had been wiser, so also it was more durable than theirs. They burnt what they had adored, but Poole was content to renounce his more visionary hopes. He waited no longer for a sudden and complete transformation of humanity, but devoted all his efforts to improving the lot and the intelligence of the peasants around him. He made experiments in new methods of wheat culture, introduced the breed of merino sheep into England, founded a benefit society for women, organized a savings bank, and started a school, in the village where he lived, on the system of Bell and Lancaster. Consequently, in spite of the discredit into which his youthful opinions had brought him, he retained a strong hold upon the peasants, and remained until his death their counsellor, friend, and recognised mediator.

But Poole was not only a practical man and a man of action. In addition to these qualities he possessed one seldom found in combination with them—that of admiration for purely intellectual ability. Though he was intimate with the most learned men and the best economists of his time, though he occupies himself an honourable place among the latter, and has been described as "a Cobbett without dogmatism, an Arthur Young with more picturesqueness,"[1] for none of them had Poole the same close affection as that which bound him to Coleridge, the most visionary and fanciful among English poets, the most abstruse among English thinkers; an affection which survived more than one disillusion and more than one justifiable coolness. His feelings towards Wordsworth were less warm, but his esteem for him was as high as his admiration was profound. Even before the poet's arrival at Alfoxden, when their intercourse had been confined to a few brief interviews, Poole declared Wordsworth to be "the greatest man he ever knew."[2] Poole himself, apart

---

[1] Miss Meteyard. *A Group of Englishmen.*
[2] Letter from Coleridge to Cottle in 1797. Campbell, *Life of Coleridge*, p. 67.

from his great merits, possessed certain gifts of character and mind calculated to interest poets in his personality and conversation. Coleridge has extolled " the originality and raciness of his intellect ; . . . the life, freshness, and practical value of his remarks and notices, truths plucked as they are growing, and delivered to you with the dew on them, the fair earnings of an observant eye, armed and kept on the watch by thought and meditation." [1] " There was something (he says elsewhere) both in his understanding and in his affections, so healthy and manly that my mind freshened in his company, and my ideas and habits of thinking acquired, day after day, more of substance and reality."

Wordsworth speaks of the kindness of heart and real sensibility which were hidden beneath Poole's rough exterior. He says that after the death of Poole a lock of grey hair was found in his writing-desk with a few words on the envelope indicating that the hair was that of an old shepherd who had been in his service for a length of years. When seeking for evidence of human goodness, the poet found many proofs of it in Poole's daily life, especially in " his conduct to his labourers and poor neighbours ; their virtues," Wordsworth says, " he carefully encouraged, and weighed their faults in the scales of charity." [2] He displayed the same forbearance in telling anecdotes of those he had known, treating their weaknesses and transgressions with tenderness, " averse to all harsh judgment," and feeling " for all men as his brothers." [3]

It is not surprising that such a man should make a deep impression on the mind of Wordsworth, who listened with attention to the stories told by Poole. One of them was the starting-point of his ballad entitled *The Idiot Boy*, a celebrated piece, although in questionable taste. Another became one of the best of his lesser poems, *The Farmer of Tilsbury Vale*. Better still, he henceforth kept the image of Poole before his mind. For him Poole became the perfect type of rustic character, the man who, more than any other, united in himself its striking features. Possibly Wordsworth committed the mistake of generalizing too

[1] *Church and State*, 2nd edition, p. 115.
[2] *The Farmer of Tilsbury Vale*, prefatory note.   [3] *Ibid.*

freely from this almost unique example. When, in one of his most beautiful pastorals, he wished to portray the shepherd proprietor of Westmoreland,[1] passionately attached to his hereditary piece of ground and his independence, full of deep and tender affection, which his blunt and uncouth manners fail to conceal, he was not merely anxious to satisfy Poole, whom he considered to be perhaps the most "competent judge" in England on the point. "I had a still further wish," he said, in writing to Poole, "that this poem should please you, because in writing it I had your character often before my eyes, and sometimes thought that I was delineating such a man as you yourself would have been under the same circumstances."[2] The comparison of course cannot be very strongly insisted on. There must always be a great difference between the Somersetshire farmer, well-informed, liberal-minded, and progressive, and the poor shepherd of Westmoreland, with his life of quiet routine. But it is sufficient that they resemble one another in the essential virtues of sturdy integrity, and intense, though restrained, sensibility. When it is added that Wordsworth, always so sparing of compliments, asserts that he wrote many parts of his principal work, *The Excursion*, in the hope of pleasing Poole, and that he asked him for "a history of [his] feelings during the perusal,"[3] one may easily form an idea of the influence which Poole exercised on his mind after a whole year of close neighbourhood.

II

In spite of their dissimilarities, all those of whom we have spoken had at this period one feeling in common in their sincere yearning after nature. If disheartened, they turned to her for consolation ; if feeble and languid, for restoration to health ; if strong and active, for an increase

---

[1] *Michael* (1800).
[2] Letter from Wordsworth to Thomas Poole, 9th April 1801. Knight, *Life of Wordsworth*, i. p. 215.
[3] Letter from Wordsworth to Poole, 13th March 1815. *Ibid.*, ii. p. 248.

of vigour or for salutary relaxation. All were poets, or believed themselves to be so; all felt themselves called to an Arcadian existence. Everything they wrote at this time, both in prose and in verse, is full of reproaches against crowded city life, and against the excessive and unhealthy toil of manufacturing centres,[1] as well as of gratitude to the sweet and healthy country, the source of infinite blessings both to body and soul. But what is above all characteristic of this moment, when their feverish pursuit of a general good has been abandoned, is a new desire to be happy themselves, a quest of a certain voluptuous torpor.

That which constitutes the moral beauty of the lives of Wordsworth and Coleridge is no doubt the fact that for them this period of blissful egoism was but a passing phase. No sooner have they discovered the path to happiness than they think sadly of those who are unacquainted with it, and begin to regard it as their life's work to lead them thither. Nevertheless it is probable (and who will blame them for doing so?) that they first loitered some hours by the way with no other thought than that of enjoying the charms which lay before them.

The most conspicuous feature in Thelwall's recollections of his visit to Nether Stowey is the democrat's joyous surprise that he can forget his political passions so easily

---

[1] *E.g.*, Thelwall's poem "On leaving the Bottoms of Gloucestershire, where the author had been entertained by several families with great hospitality, 12th August 1797":

> . . . Ah! 'tis a scene
> That wakes to social rapture. Nor, as yet,
> Towers from each peaceful dell the unwieldy pride
> Of Factory over-grown; where Opulence,
> Dispeopling the neat cottage, crowds his walls
> (Made pestilent by congregated lungs
> And lewd association) with a race
> Of infant slaves, brok'n timely to the yoke
> Of unremitting Drudgery—no more
> By relative endearment, or the voice
> Of matronly education, interspersed.
> (*Poems written chiefly in retirement*, London, 1801.)

Thelwall anticipated by more than fifteen years the famous attack made by Wordsworth in *The Excursion* (books viii. and ix.). Joseph Cottle expressed the same sentiment in his poem, *Malvern Hills* (London, 1798).

and completely in the midst of rural life and in the society of his friends. The latter hastened to show him the romantic Alfoxden glen, by which Dorothy Wordsworth had been fascinated from the first day of her acquaintance with it, and there, observing how Thelwall was impressed with the wild and charming scene before him, Coleridge said to him: "Citizen John, this is a fine place to talk treason in!"—"Nay! Citizen Samuel," replied he, "it is rather a place to make a man forget that there is any necessity for treason."[1] And in a letter to his wife Thelwall described the delightful existence led by the Stowey Academy, in which all his monetary cares and all his projects of reform were forgotten. Speaking of a ramble in the dell, he says:

"There have we—sometime sitting on a tree, sometime wading boot-top deep through the stream, and again stretched on some mossy stone or root of a decayed tree, a literary egotistical triumvirate—passed sentence on the productions and characters of the age—burst forth in poetical flights of enthusiasm, and philosophised our minds into a state of tranquillity which the leaders of nations might enjoy and the residents of cities can never know. . . . Faith, we are a most philosophical party!"[2]

This placid and voluptuous calm, this epicurism which asked for no pleasures but those which nature alone could supply, was not mere imagination on Thelwall's part. Joseph Cottle, the poet and publisher, who sometimes came down from Bristol to hear the poets read their latest verses — productions which he afterwards printed, with more satisfaction to his vanity than to his pocket—Cottle, like Thelwall, was impressed by it, and like him was captivated by its infectious charm. He had come to Stowey shortly before, and had spent delightful hours with Coleridge, Poole and Lloyd under the jasmine arbour in the garden. Seated around a mug of Taunton ale,

---

[1] *Coleridge's Table Talk*, 26th July 1830. Wordsworth relates the same anecdote, though somewhat unskilfully, and in a less vivid manner, in the prefatory note to his *Anecdote for Fathers*.

[2] Letter from John Thelwall to his wife, 18th July 1797. *Thomas Poole and his Friends*, i. p. 232.

caressed by the sun's delicious warmth and the music of the birds, the friends soon reached a state of supreme felicity.

" Every interstice of our hearts being filled with happiness, as a consequence there was no room for sorrow, exorcised as it now was, and hovering around at unapproachable distance. . . . If, at this juncture, tidings had been brought us that an irruption of the ocean had swallowed up all our dear brethren of Pekin, . . . ' poor things ' would have been our only reply, with anguish put off till the morrow." [1]

If Wordsworth was not with them on this occasion, his absence was merely accidental. Cottle describes further, with an inexhaustible flow of detail, a visit which he paid to Alfoxden shortly afterwards. He gives the meagre bill-of-fare of a repast " such as every blind and starving man in the three kingdoms would have rejoiced to behold," and portrays the gay good humour, proof against a succession of disasters, which seasoned their humble cheer.[2]

Those who were merely visitors, however, knew nothing of the most prolific and delightful hours of this truly poetic existence—those, namely, which Wordsworth, his sister, and Coleridge passed together, free not only from unwelcome intruders but also from the society of their other friends. " We are three people, but only one soul," said Coleridge, speaking of this time. Almost daily they met to ramble over the Quantock hills and dales, observing nature and talking of poetry.

They paid no attention to the suspicious looks and remarks which their movements drew from the inhabitants of the district, who could not believe in the innocence of so singular and unusual an existence as theirs. The brightness of their life becomes more conspicuous by contrast with the ill-will and ignorance around them. Coleridge's settlement at Stowey had already given rise to bitter enmity against Thomas Poole, since it was he who had induced the young orator, well known through his public attacks upon the government, to come into the neighbourhood. Gradually, however, the entire openness of the life which Coleridge led under the eyes of the

[1] *Cottle's Early Recollections*, i. pp. 275-276.   [2] *Ibid.*, i. pp. 230-234.

village people at Stowey ; the presence of his wife, who
had all the reassuring characteristics of the good housewife,
without any more unusual qualities ; the poet's frank and
unreserved nature, and his avowed adherence to the
Christian religion, had allayed suspicion. But when
Wordsworth also arrived gossip and suspicion became
more busy than ever. Everything in and about him
seemed suspicious ; his want of religion, for he never set
foot inside a church ; his life of poverty and idleness in a
great lonely house ; his sister, wild-eyed and brusque in
manner, always to be seen about the roads or upon the
hills ; the child they had brought with them from no one
knew where ; and above all Wordsworth's love of solitude,
his thoughtful preoccupation, his wanderings hither and
thither among the hills or about the shore at all hours of
the day and night, and his habit of muttering to himself
things that nobody could understand.[1] People chattered
freely. Some thought him a conjurer, others a smuggler,
for why should he gaze so obstinately at a parcel of salt
water ? " As to Coleridge," said one of the neighbours,
" there is not so much harm in *him*, for he is a whirl-brain
that talks whatever comes uppermost ; but that Wordsworth, he is the dark traitor. You never hear him say a
syllable on the subject." [2] Hence Poole, who had made
himself answerable for the tenant of Alfoxden, became
doubly the object of detraction and mischief-making.

And when Thelwall, the notorious Jacobin, came down
on a visit, the scandal was still further increased. Though
he desired nothing better than to settle near them, it was
necessary to keep so dangerous a friend at a distance, and it
was thus not from mere wantonness of heart that Coleridge
decided to reject the friendly advances of a man he
esteemed. It was, however, too late ; Thelwall's visit had
had its effect. In vain Poole sought to obtain a renewal
of the lease for one year which Wordsworth had contracted,[3] and the latter saw that he would have to quit

[1] *Thomas Poole and his Friends*, i. p. 240.
[2] *Cottle's Early Recollections*, i. p. 309, and Coleridge, *Biographia Literaria*,
ch. x.
[3] Letter from Poole to Mrs St Albyn, 16th September 1797. *Thomas
Poole and his Friends.*

Alfoxden.   Finally, the alarm of the Tories, who took
steps to inform the Government that suspicious persons
were in the Quantock country, led to their being dogged
by a spy.   In those years there was quite a mania for
detraction and secret information.   Coleridge's account of
this incident may, however, contain a seasoning of imagination.[1] The spy who, for three weeks, tracked them in all
their wanderings with truly Indian perseverance was after
all a very honest fellow, for he declared at last that the
suspected characters were as faithful subjects as any in
His Majesty's dominions.   All that he had overheard was
talk about books, about a certain *Spy nosy*, and concerning
features of the landscape.   In order to surprise Coleridge
of his secret, he one day represented himself to him as a
Jacobin, but was so dazzled by the eloquence with which
the poet attempted to bring him round to sounder political
opinions, and so thoroughly convinced of the folly and
wickedness of Jacobinism, that he felt at last ashamed that
he had professed it, even for purposes of disguise.   As a
last resource he questioned the landlord of the inn at
Stowey where he was lodging, and learned from him that
the two suspicious characters, one of whom—Coleridge—
used to wander about the country with papers—maps and
charts of the district, it was said—in his hand, were no
other than poets, and that their crime consisted in wanting
" to put Quantock and all about here in print."
Neither this surveillance nor the ill-will of the neighbours
could impair the happiness of the two poets.   Coleridge
himself, who afterwards, and somewhat tardily, took exception to the petty persecution to which he and his friend
were exposed, appears, on the contrary, to have been at
the time amused by it.   As for Wordsworth, he never
complained of it, and except for the regret he at first felt
at having to leave Alfoxden, it does not seem to have
caused him any concern.   Nor was this persecution in
itself at all likely to depress them.   Possibly, even, these
paltry annoyances, which gave the last stimulus to their
waning passion for the revolutionary cause, really brought
them more satisfaction than vexation.   The meanness and

[1] *Biographia Literaria*, ch. **x**.

injustice of our enemies are by no means a source of unmixed affliction, but rather one of ironical pleasure. They lead to comforting reflexions on the folly or wickedness of our adversaries, as well as on our own superiority. They vindicate our contempt for our opponents, justify the cause which begins to appear less reasonable, and revive our flagging ardour.

If anything still restrained Wordsworth and Coleridge from transferring all their affection from the Revolution to Nature, it was precisely this blind, spiteful and absurd behaviour on the part of those who treated them as suspicious characters. So long as their enemies remained the same, it was impossible that they should clearly understand the change that had occurred in their own minds. That which was necessary to alienate them from their first faith, or, what was better, to convince them that they could do without it, and to oblige them to seek some other end on which to fix all their hopes and joys, was the commission of some grievous and unpardonable offence by those with whom they still sympathized. This crucial test was not spared them. It occurred during the winter of 1797-1798, when Switzerland was invaded by the French.

III

When the Directory dispatched an army against Berne, and when the mountaineers of the Oberland were slaughtered while defending their independence, the reprobation which the news excited among all parties was mingled on the part of the enemies of the Revolution with ironical satisfaction, and on the part of its partisans with shame and remorse. Madame de Stael, at the spectacle of the invasion of Switzerland by the French forces, felt for the first time a sincere wish that they might be defeated; and ex-director Carnot, then in exile on the shores of the Lake of Geneva, gave vent to his indignation in a pamphlet dated the 6th floréal an VI. (27th April 1798), which was shortly afterwards translated into English. "O the iniquity of this war!" he exclaimed. "It seems as if the

object of the Directory has been to see how many victims
it could find among the poorest and the most virtuous of the
free as a sacrifice to its own fancy, to strangle liberty in its
own cradle, and to punish the crags of Helvetia for having
given it birth." [1]

To the English friends of France, the blow was
fatal. It scattered them beyond hope of rallying; rather,
indeed, it annihilated them. How could men who had
constantly sheltered themselves behind the words of
"peace" and "liberty" justify an attack made by the strong
upon the weak, by a young republic upon one so venerable,
upon the country which, rightly or wrongly, thanks chiefly
to Rousseau, had been regarded by all men as the natural
temple of the republican virtues in all their grandeur and
poetry? The internal dissensions of Switzerland, the
serious defects in its constitution, and its incongruous
mixture of the feudal and democratic elements, were little
known beyond its borders. The responsibility incurred
by those of its sons who had summoned or assisted the
foreigner was lost sight of in the guilt and perfidy of the
invader. The warlike spirit in England had lain dormant
since the commencement of hostilities, but now, at the
tidings of the invasion, it suddenly awoke. Thenceforth
the war was just and necessary in the eyes of almost the
whole nation. When, five years later, Mackintosh defended
Jean Peltier the pamphleteer against the attacks of the
First Consul, he obtained one of his finest oratorical effects
by describing the invasion of Switzerland, and recalling
"the profound impression which it made upon the English
people."

Upon Coleridge that impression was sudden and irresistible. Only twelve months earlier, in his *Ode to the Depart-
ing Year*, he had pronounced his country enslaved and on
the brink of ruin. Again, in May 1797, he had shared the
enthusiasm of Poole over the French victories, and had
looked forward with exultation to the defeat of England,
since not only Ireland, but also her own sailors, were in
revolt against her.[2] Now, however, he writes at once his

---

[1] Quoted in a note by A. Angellier, *Les Œuvres de Burns*, 1893, p. 198.
[2] Letter from Thomas Poole to Purkis, 10th May 1797. *Poole and his Friends*

Recantation or palinode, which consists of a passionate impeachment of France.[1]

After summoning clouds, waves and forests to witness that he has always adored the spirit of Liberty, he recalls his enthusiasm for France when she took an oath to be free, his shame when England joined the league of monarchs against her, his hope which not even the Terror could destroy, his delight in the victories won by the Republic in spite of the assaults of foes both within and without, and his confidence that

> conquering by her happiness alone,
> Shall France compel the nations to be free,
> Till Love and Joy look round, and call the Earth their own.

And then he beseeches Liberty to pardon his error.

> Forgive me, Freedom!   O forgive those dreams!
> I hear thy voice, I hear thy loud lament,
> From bleak Helvetia's icy cavern sent—
> I hear thy groans upon her blood-stained streams!
> Heroes, that for your peaceful country perished,
> And ye that, fleeing, spot your mountain-snows
> With bleeding wounds; forgive me, that I cherished
> One thought that ever blessed your cruel foes!
> To scatter rage, and traitorous guilt,
> Where Peace her jealous home had built;
> A patriot race to disinherit
> Of all that made their stormy wilds so dear.
>   .   .   .   .   .   .
> O France, that mockest Heaven, adulterous, blind,
> And patriot only in pernicious toils,
> Are these thy boasts, Champion of humankind?

It was inevitable that, when once he had abjured the cause of France, his hopes and affections should ere long attach themselves once more to England. At that very moment his country was threatened. After the conclusion of the peace of Campo-Formio, on the 17th October 1797, England was the only nation left under arms against France, and then it was that, either in reality or only in appearance, the Directory formed a scheme of invasion,

---

[1] *France, an Ode*, February 1798.

and entrusted an army, said to be destined for England, to the care of Bonaparte. Until the 19th May, when this force embarked for Egypt, Great Britain was menaced with invasion, and it was during this period of anxiety that Coleridge wrote his *Fears in Solitude*. This noble poem, which gave to English patriotism a loftier expression than it had hitherto attained, is a sort of general confession of the errors and crimes of the whole nation, made in a spirit of love by one of its sons.[1]

Stretched on the grass in "a small and silent dell," among the Quantock hills, he reflects on the possibility of a sudden irruption of war, which might fill his blissfu retreat with slaughter. And he recognises that the punishment would not be undeserved.

> We have offended, oh! my countrymen!
> We have offended very grievously,
> And been most tyrannous. From east to west
> A groan of accusation pierces Heaven!
> The wretched plead against us; multitudes
> Countless and vehement, the sons of God,
> Our brethren! Like a cloud that travels on
> Steamed up from Cairo's swamps of pestilence,
> Even so, my countrymen! have we gone forth
> And borne to distant tribes slavery and pangs,
> And, deadlier far, our vices, whose deep taint
> With slow perdition murders the whole man,
> His body and his soul!

At home, all the springs of the State are corrupted by gold, religion, through the scepticism of some of its ministers and the indifference of most, is dying out, and atheism flaunts itself boldly in the light of day. But the extremity of crime is reached in the selfishness of a nation, itself secure from the calamities of war, which does not hesitate to spread them throughout the world. He trusts, nevertheless, that England may still be spared for a time, that she may be victorious over an invader now more criminal than herself, and that she may return from the conflict, not elate with triumph, but in fear,

[3] *Fears in Solitude*, April 1798.

and in repentance for the wrongs with which she had stung so fierce a foe to frenzy.

But the distinctively new note of this poem is the solemn joyousness of its close; the poet's delight in the patriotism which once more inspires him, after being so long repressed in defiance of nature's law; the joy, in short, of once more reconciling the love of his country with the sense of duty.

> O native Britain! O my mother Isle!
> How shouldst thou prove aught else but dear and holy
> To me, who from thy lakes and mountain-hills,
> Thy clouds, thy quiet dales, thy rocks and seas,
> Have drunk in all my intellectual life,
> All sweet sensations, all ennobling thoughts,
> All adoration of the God in nature,
> All lovely and all honourable things,
> Whatever makes this mortal spirit feel
> The joy and greatness of its future being?
> There lives nor form nor feeling in my soul
> Unborrowed from my country. O divine
> And beauteous island! Thou hast been my sole
> And most magnificent temple, in the which
> I walk with awe, and sing my stately songs,
> Loving the God that made me!

Such was the manner in which harmony of feeling was restored in Coleridge's mind. Meanwhile, what can Wordsworth's thoughts have been? At that time he was living in so close an intimacy with Coleridge that scarcely a day passed on which they did not meet and wander among the Quantock hills, yet Wordsworth maintained a silence which, in comparison with his friend's freedom of expression, is significant. He wrote no poem, nor did he mention the subject in any letter that has come down to us. His political opinions were so carefully concealed that Coleridge appears to have had but little knowledge of them. Wordsworth avoided giving expression to them even with him. "His conversation," says Coleridge, "extended to almost all subjects, except physics and politics; with the latter he never troubled himself."[1] If Coleridge's memory did not deceive him when he wrote these words, it is clear

[1] *Biographia Literaria*, ch. x.

that he was not entirely in the confidence of one who, in *The Prelude*, speaks of the revolutionary cause as his own until the coronation of Napoleon I. It may very well be that at this period Wordsworth was unwilling to talk of daily events, because it was really only to principles that he was seriously attached, and he could trust to time for their vindication. No doubt the attack on Switzerland was a severe blow to him, especially as that country was not for him the mere abstraction that it was for Coleridge, but had been the scene of his travels, the object of his admiration, and the theme of his verse. Nevertheless he did not share the sudden reaction of Coleridge. He did not as yet pour out his wrath upon France, and even so late as 1802 he still retained an affection for her.[1] He only avowed his hostility to her when Napoleon became visible in Bonaparte, and when another journey had convinced him that the free and generous spirit of 1789 had given way to the military passion. Up to that time he had felt nothing but sorrow for France, and indignation against those who led her in the path of violence and fanned the flame of conquest. He did not lay the responsibility for the crime committed against Switzerland at the door of the whole French nation. Possibly he still trusted "in the People and in the virtues which his eyes had seen." He had long ago had to make distinctions between the factions which ruled her, and doubtless he did so still. He appears, too, to have kept up a communication with some French acquaintances, for he says in a subsequent work, "I have personal knowledge that, when the attack was made which ended in the subjugation of Switzerland, the injustice of the undertaking was grievously oppressive to many officers of the French army, and damped their exertions."[2] For the moment he abstained, not only from condemning France, but even from judging her. Yet he gave himself up more

---

[1] Wordsworth returned to France immediately the English were once more at liberty to enter it, that is to say, during the peace of Amiens, and, although he was disgusted to find the country ripe for the empire, on his return he looked back upon it from the cliffs at Dover "with many a melancholy and tender thought." Dorothy Wordsworth's Journal, 30th August 1802. Knight, *Life of Wordsworth*, i, p. 350.

[2] *Convention of Cintra*, Prose Works, i. p. 164.

completely to poetical composition, and sought in nature a more sheltered retreat from the distressing spectacle of nations in conflict.

In the seclusion of the glen to which he had introduced Coleridge and Thelwall in the preceding summer he mused on the gentle beauty of the country during the first days of spring, on the delights which it freely offers to all, and then on the evils of which man is at once the author and the victim. And it was here that he wrote his *Lines Written in Early Spring.*

> I HEARD a thousand blended notes,
> While in a grove I sate reclined,
> In that sweet mood when pleasant thoughts
> Bring sad thoughts to the mind.
>
> To her fair works did Nature link
> The human soul that through me ran ;
> And much it grieved my heart to think
> What man has made of man.
>
> Through primrose tufts, in that sweet bower,
> The periwinkle trailed its wreaths ;
> And 'tis my faith that every flower
> Enjoys the air it breathes.
>
> The birds around me hopped and played,
> Their thoughts I cannot measure :—
> But the least motion which they made,
> It seemed a thrill of pleasure.
>
> The budding twigs spread out their fan,
> To catch the breezy air ;
> And I must think, do all I can,
> That there was pleasure there.
>
> If I these thoughts may not prevent,
> If such be of my creed the plan,
> Have I not reason to lament
> What man has made of man ?

This is the only immediate complaint breathed by his poetry, and it must be admitted that even here sorrow for mankind is outweighed by joy in nature. This lamentable

war, which, a few years earlier, would have filled him with
consternation, caused him, after all, but a faint and short-
lived sorrow, followed immediately by a feeling of deliverance. He severed himself from politics at once and for a
long period. Slowly and in silence he pondered over the
patriotic poems of Coleridge, and four years later his
friend's sublime thoughts found expression in his poetry.
There they reappear — the same, yet condensed and
strengthened by their long sojourn in his mind. For the
time he decided to keep silence and to wait; and, putting
aside all thought of political revolution, devoted his whole
attention to effecting a revolution in the world of letters.

The stream of his poetry, hitherto slender and inter-
mittent, now began to gush forth in an abundant tide.
The Recluse, his great philosophical work, was projected
and commenced just at the time when Coleridge was
composing his indignant ode to France.[1] Almost all the
Lyrical Ballads were written during the spring and summer
of 1798, a spring of exceptional beauty in spite of its
backwardness, a summer so marvellous that *The Prelude*
looks back towards it as the brightest and sunniest the
author had known since his boyhood. The loss of his
last illusion concerning the revolution, instead of destroying the joyousness of his spirit, taught him that in himself
and in his comprehension of nature he possessed an inexhaustible well-spring of happiness, against which no
external disappointment could prevail. Henceforth he
was conscious of his own power to resist depression, and
of the vitality of his own joyous spirit. He knew that,
without being in any way guilty of egoism, he could keep
his soul beyond the reach of the evils around him. At
certain hours he had " so much happiness to spare," he
could not "feel a pain."[2] He could "afford to suffer
with those whom" he saw suffer,[3] and could surrender
the outworks of his soul to pity or to grief, since in its
central keep there dwelt a calm which nothing could
dispel.

[1] Letter from Wordsworth to James Losh, 11th March 1798. Knight,
Life of Wordsworth, i. p. 147.
[2] *Anecdote for Fathers*, 15-16.   [3] *Excursion*, i. 370-371.

Still a convalescent when he arrived, Wordsworth left Alfoxden cured. When he came he was engaged in putting the finishing touches to *Guilt and Sorrow*, *The Borderers*, and *The Ruined Cottage*. On his departure, a year later, after addressing to Nature his first hymn of thanksgiving, written near Tintern Abbey, he carried away with him in manuscript about a thousand lines of his great consolatory poem, *The Recluse*. His self-identity, destroyed for a time by a crisis of despair, was restored. The link which was to connect his early years with those of his maturity was happiness ; happiness formerly spontaneous, but now the result of conscious reflection ; at first mere lightness of heart, but a settled optimism at last. The years of doubt and gloom had fled, leaving behind them merely a fruitful impression, a salutary warning. Those which preceded them, on the other hand, the years of his childhood and early youth, drew near again, until for him they became the present. He recognised that in them, unknown to himself, he had lived the true life ; and if for a moment he had gone astray, he would now attempt to ascertain the direction of his first innocent footsteps, in order that he might set his feet once more upon the path which they had followed.

The delights he had known in his country life at school, delights unsurpassed by those of any paradise of the fancy, were of his own instinctive creation.   Even in the hostile atmosphere of Cambridge he had successfully preserved his happy spirit by leading a separate life of his own. Of the strong wine of revolutionary enthusiasm he had drunk even to intoxication. He had believed in the Revolution, had believed in his own reason, because both alike had at first given promise of felicity for all mankind. And it was still in search of some assurance of happiness that he turned once more to nature. At last he recognised the principle of his existence ; it was joy. The idea of *The Prelude* was springing up within him, and before many months had elapsed the first fragments of it were written.

BOOK IV

Harmony Restored

CHAPTER I

Optimism

I

WHEN we have laid bare the circumstances under which a man has reached a joyous or unhappy state of mind, nothing is more tempting than to regard them as sufficient to account for that state of gladness or unhappiness. The circumstances, in themselves commonly neutral, have assumed the hue of the feelings with which they have been suffused, so that the colour which they reflect appears actually to belong to them, or even to be created by them. The greater a mind's diffusive power, the more difficult it is to guard against this illusion. It is so easy to believe that the soul has had no darkness to penetrate when we can see no shadows around it. This is how it happens that so acute an observer as de Quincey is astonished at the good fortune which fell to the lot of Wordsworth, and does not stop to consider whether it was not propitious chiefly because Wordsworth's nature had made it so.

This error is a very common one with regard to Wordsworth, and arises from an imperfect understanding of *The Prelude*, since it is there that the poet overflows with gratitude for the manner in which his youth had been spent and the education he had received. But if we examine it closely, we see that the real theme of *The Prelude* is the wonderful way in which the man contrived to profit by circumstances in themselves either indifferent or favourable and unfavourable by turns, so as to attain to a joyous harmony of all his faculties. To convince ourselves of this it will be sufficient to recapitulate the facts of Wordsworth's early life, confining our attention to those which would ordinarily be considered of importance, and regarding them, in a manner, from the outside. Is it not true that we could easily construct quite a melancholy picture from them? Can a man be reckoned a favourite of fortune when he has lost his mother during his eighth year, and his father at sixteen; when he has been arbitrarily deprived of his inheritance, has had to endure a humiliating existence under the roof of stern and narrow-minded grandparents, and for years has been coldly treated by his relations on account of his indolence, his obstinacy, and his refusal to embark upon any of the safe careers suggested to him; when he is kept apart from the sister whom he loves beyond everything else, apparently from fear that she may become contaminated by his disobedience and his subversive opinions; when he entrusts all his dreams of happiness to the French Revolution, only to see them borne under in the tempest, and loses not only his respect and love for his native country, but all hope of progress as well; when, meanwhile, his existence is so straitened, so penurious even, and so utterly without promise for the morrow, that he is compelled to postpone indefinitely his union with his sister's friend, that maiden, chosen long ago, and now beloved, whom he knows not whether he can ever make his wife?

Again, though it has been shown how he made the events amidst which his optimism became confirmed and settled turn to his own deliverance, are not those very events such as with many others would, and with more than one of his contemporaries actually did, lead to a fresh access of despondency? How thoroughly characteristic is the fact that Wordsworth began *The Recluse* just at the time when the invasion of Switzerland was ruining the last hopes which he had staked on the behaviour of France! And yet, at that very time, what genuine causes for heart-sickness he was concealing from every eye! What a cup of bitterness he had to drain when he heard the sneers of the English Conservatives, the now triumphant enemies of the Revolution, at his own vain dreams! He was not ignorant of their sarcasm, nor did he despise it; he acknowledges that it caused him suffer-

ing. "He strove," he says, "to hide, what nought could
heal, the wounds of mortified presumption." [1]

Instead, therefore, of regarding his optimism as the
result of the circumstances of his life, it would be more
correct to see in it a vigorous reaction of his nature against
them.   And with these circumstances should be associated
the external world itself, the aspects of that nature which,
nevertheless, was to yield him so many lessons of happiness and peace of mind.[2]   It would be a mistake to regard
these causes as more than secondary.   The happiness
which henceforth seems to him to clothe the world like a
garment emanates from himself.   And this is how Wordsworth's happiness was understood by Coleridge, the man
who knew him better than anyone else.

> O William ! we receive but what we give,
> And in *our* life alone does Nature live :
> Ours is her wedding-garment, ours her shroud !
> And would we aught behold, of higher worth,
> Than that inanimate cold world, *allow'd*
> To the poor loveless ever-anxious crowd,
> Ah ! from the soul itself must issue forth,
> A light, a glory, a fair luminous cloud
> Enveloping the earth—
> And from the soul itself there must be sent
> A sweet and potent voice, of its own birth,
> Of all sweet sounds the life and element !
> O pure of heart !   Thou need'st not ask of me
> What this strong music in the soul may be ?
> What, and wherein it doth exist,
> This light, this glory, this fair luminous mist,
> This beautiful and beauty-making power.
>   Joy, virtuous William ! joy that ne'er was given,
> Save to the pure, and in their purest hour,
> Joy, William ! is the spirit and the pow'r,
> Which wedding Nature to us gives in dow'r,
>   A new Earth and new Heaven,

---

[1] *The Prelude*, xi. 215-216.

[2] Thus " the tremulous sob of the complaining owl " (*Evening Walk*, v.
443) in the edition of 1793 becomes in 1836, " the sportive outcry of the
mocking owl."   Not the owl's hooting, but the feeling of the poet, has been
altered in the interval.

Undream'd of by the sensual and the proud—
Joy is the sweet voice, Joy the luminous cloud—
  We, we ourselves rejoice !
And thence flows all that charms or ear or sight,
All melodies the echoes of that voice,
All colours a suffusion from that light.[1]

II

But if the poet's happiness is really in himself, is it possible to localize it, as it were, within him : to say precisely in what part of his being it originates and has its seat ?   Does it arise from Wordsworth's temperament, as has been suggested by more than one of the poet's critics ? Before admitting so much it may be worth while to decide exactly what we mean by temperament, a vague term if ever there was one, or, what is worse, falsely precise—a convenient label which man attaches to that in man which eludes his analysis, that unknown region in human nature where the blind tendencies inherent in body and soul are confusedly combined.

We are not here concerned with that airy disposition, which, without the slightest effort, draws towards itself spontaneously the chance delights of life, while the pains glance harmlessly from it, as if from a glossy integument. It is impossible to deny self-consciousness to Wordsworth. "Somewhat stern in temperament," [2] as he describes himself, his thoughtful nature was not one of those which can lightly forget the sorrows of the past, and easily shut their eyes to the evils which menace their near future. Nor would it be less unjust to represent him as selfishly bound up in his own happiness, and as refusing, from motives of prudence, to see, and to lay his finger upon, the distress around him.   If at any time it was thus with him, the truce was but a brief one, and it is his glory that he immediately afterwards directed his steps towards

---

[1] *Ode to Dejection*, st. iv. (*The Poetical Works of Coleridge*, edited by J. D. Campbell, p. 522).   I have substituted *William* for *Edmund*, according to the earliest MS. of the poem, sent to Sir George Beaumont on April 4th 1802 (see Knight's *Life of Wordsworth*, vol. ii. p. 86).

[2] *The Prelude*, xi. 276.

suffering in order to cure it. It was, on the contrary, because he was a happy man, he says, that he was "bold to look on painful things."[1] Few poets have more frequently made human suffering the subject of their strains than Wordsworth the optimist. He refused neither to "hear Humanity in fields and groves pipe solitary anguish," nor to brood over

> the fierce confederate storm
> Of sorrow, barricadoed evermore
> Within the walls of cities.[2]

If he believed that his earthly office was that of a comforter, it was because he felt how greatly men stood in need of consolation.

Again, if by temperament be understood physical health, this rough and ready explanation of happiness is so opposed to the briefest experience that there is no necessity to refute it. Moreover, so far as Wordsworth is concerned, the most trustworthy evidence goes to show that, though vigorous upon the whole, he by no means enjoyed the privilege of complete immunity from physical suffering. From his seventeenth year he was subject to such frequent and violent headaches, that, although at that time he earnestly desired to follow the same profession as his father and his elder brother, he was compelled to abandon the idea.[3] The same trouble followed him in his career as a poet, and was inseparable from the labour of composition, so that his sister's journals are, at times, a mere monotonous repetition of lamentations over her brother's health, and of expressions of pity for him under the severe toil by which he is almost broken down.

But we have further testimony. Coleridge considered Wordsworth as neither more nor less than a hypochondriac, who was happy, not because of his temperament, but in spite of it. In 1803, Coleridge started for a tour in Scotland with Wordsworth and Dorothy, but afterwards separated from them; and one of the reasons for this

---

[1] *The Prelude*, xi. 277.   [2] *The Recluse*, 849-853.
[3] Letter from Coleridge to Poole, 3rd October 1803. *Poole and his Friends*, ii. p. 120.

separation was, he says, the hypochondriacal disposition of Wordsworth, which rendered him an unsuitable travelling companion for one who was himself ailing. In a letter written on the 15th January 1804, Coleridge enlarges upon the subject.

"In spite," he says, "of Wordsworth's occasional fits of hypochondriacal uncomfortableness—from which, more or less, and at longer or shorter intervals, he has never been wholly free from his very childhood—in spite of this hypochondriacal graft . . . his is the happiest family I ever saw. . . . Wordsworth (he says, further on) does not excite that almost painfully profound *moral* admiration, which the sense of the exceeding difficulty of a given virtue can alone call forth . . .; but, on the other hand, he is an object to be contemplated with greater complacency, because he both deserves to be and is a happy man; and a happy man not from natural temperament, for therein lies his main obstacle, not by enjoyment of the good things of this world—for even to this day, from the first dawn of his manhood, he has purchased independence, and leisure for greatly good pursuits, by austere frugality and daily self-denials—nor yet by an accidental confluence of amiable and happy-making friends and relatives, for every one near to his heart has been placed there by choice, and after knowledge and deliberation; but he is a happy man, because he is a Philosopher, because he knows the intrinsic value of the different objects of human pursuit, and regulates his wishes in strict subordination to that knowledge; because he feels, and with a *practical* faith, the truth . . . that we can do but one thing well, and that therefore we must make a choice. He has made that choice from his early youth, has pursued, and is pursuing it; and certainly no small part of his happiness is owing to this unity of interest, and that homogeneity of character which is the natural consequence of it."[1]

[1] Letter to Richard Sharp. Knight, *Life of Wordsworth*, ii. pp. 9-11.

III

It is, in short, to the conscious action of the will and to deliberate choice that, with Coleridge, we must in great part attribute Wordsworth's happiness and optimism. He affords one of the most conclusive examples of the power of the will over the formation of ideas and the ordering of existence. Having resolved to be happy, and having arrived at a clear perception of the necessary means, Wordsworth held, with invincible tenacity, to that line of life and of thought which, in his opinion, must lead to happiness. Doubtless, in order to attain this end, he employed all his individual gifts, his rare powers of mind, his genius even, and his insight into nature ; and, to this extent, there is an incommunicable element in his method. But it is the effort, the unflinching resistance to despondency, that constitutes the great moral lesson of his life ; a lesson which, in spite of differences in individual capacity, is of general applicability. From a literary point of view, also, it is instructive, as explaining Wordsworth's isolated position amidst a murmuring and rebellious generation.

Common, apparently, to all, with Wordsworth this determination to be happy derived an extraordinary intensity from a deeply-rooted faith,—a faith so essential to his mind that it was almost more of an instinct than an acquired belief,—in the identity of happiness and truth, and of both with poetry.

At the very time when poets were priding themselves on their dejection, and making it even a condition of their art, Wordsworth lays down the principle that poets are " the happiest of all men."[1] He asserts that their superiority arises chiefly from their greater capacity for joy. It is by " the deep power of joy " that " we see into the life of things."[2] He affirms that the direct object of poetry is *pleasure*, and so far from seeing anything degrading in the fact, he regards it as " an acknowledgment of the beauty of the universe."[3] And he holds

[1] Letter written in 1802 (?). *Memoirs of Wordsworth*, i. 172.
[2] *Tintern Abbey*, ll. 48-49.   [3] Preface to *Lyrical Ballads* (1802).

that just as any other man may feel it his duty to be good, so it is his own, as a man and a poet, to be happy; a duty which is often the most difficult of all, and at times even, considering the strain of energy it demands, the most painful. In truth, this glorification of cheerfulness, or, at any rate, of peace of mind, when it is not the spontaneous overflow of a feeling of pleasure, and especially when the poet's inward spring of delight grows less vigorous and abundant with every year, demands such a tension of his whole being that the impression produced upon the thoughtful reader will sometimes be more distressing than that of an unrestrained complaint or cry of revolt. There is an ever-increasing opposition between the poet's real yet limited capacity for joy, and that optimism within him which contests every inch of the ground before it will admit that any limits exist. Hence will arise works like *The Fountain* and *Laodamia*, full of deeper and sadder pathos than the work of avowed pessimists. Hence, too, many a line in which seems concentrated whatever of sorrow may underlie optimism, such as that in which hope is spoken of as " the paramount *duty* that Heaven lays, for its own honour, on man's suffering heart." [1]

Nevertheless, Wordsworth maintained, even to the end, in spite of all the sorrow which came to his knowledge or fell to his own lot, a faith in the sovereignty of happiness. He looked upon happiness as the sign of a man's fitness for the world in which he lives, and of a harmony between his actions and the law of the universe. It is to the soul what health is to the body. Sorrow, like sickness, exists only through some temporary or lasting defect in human nature. Like sickness it may be undeserved, but like sickness again it is a mark of inferiority. The man who is a slave to dejection is entitled to pity no less than one who is physically infirm; but if he fails to shake off his yoke, it must be admitted that his " vital soul " is wanting in some essential organ, that he lacks an adequate principle of life. And to take a pride in one's wretchedness is either

[1] Sonnet, " *Here pause* " (1811).

ridiculous or profane, since it is absurd to pride oneself on a deficiency, and irreverent to believe that the universe is so odiously contrived that those who suffer are more worthy on that account than those who dwell in comfort.

If happiness is identical with truth and goodness, man's first business is to acquire it, or to develop it within himself; for whatever of mystery may attach to the origin of the feelings of man, they are all, doubtless, capable of cultivation. Neither joy nor sorrow exists unalloyed in any man; the classification of men into the happy and the unhappy is merely a misleading exaggeration due to the necessities of language. Each individual soul is no essence of pure joy or unmingled sadness, but an assemblage, as it were, of feelings, in which those of joy and those of sadness are in changing equilibrium, and the individual is happy or unhappy according as the majority is with the one class or with the other. Between the two is a throng of indeterminate feelings (including almost every emotion inspired by nature), which is subject to the direction of the will, and inclines to happiness or to sorrow according to the influence exerted by volition. On the behaviour of these neutral feelings hangs the fate of the soul, and to enlist this wavering mass on the side of happiness is, in Wordsworth's view, the duty of the presiding will. Observe that if at times he seems to employ artful methods of persuasion, or to repel these feelings by the iteration of his appeals, he has at least the excuse of aiming at the health of the mind. Others during the same period, were employing spells of a contrary nature to propagate and promote the triumph of disease. The whole age, to tell the truth, witnessed an almost uninterrupted succession of wonderfully ingenious efforts to lead men to despair, efforts which would pass our comprehension did we not know that with many this despair was but a disguised yet exquisite form of intoxication, more coveted than health.

Among numerous instances which present themselves, it will be sufficient if we take the case of one of the greatest

among Wordsworth's contemporaries, who was chiefly
responsible for the spread of melancholy in France at the
very time when Wordsworth was striving to withstand it in
England.   Is it beside the truth to say that in an epitome
of life, such as Chateaubriand's *René*, by an intentional and
artful abstraction from the various component elements of
existence, those of a gloomy tendency are carefully selected
to the exclusion of others?   What is it but a marvellous
endeavour to extract the essence of melancholy from
objects; a process whereby that essence is rendered a
hundred times more powerful to blight and canker, through
being isolated instead of diffused and blended as it is in
reality?   Collecting and condensing all our thoughts of
sorrow and fatality, it mingles them in one bitter draught.
It is inevitable that, however sincere and real in its origin,
all grief thus dealt with should be artificially rendered
more absolute and distinct, that its form should become
stronger and darker in outline.   For the purposes of art,
neutral and insignificant actions, and sensations in themselves neither pleasurable nor painful, are in *René* artistic-
ally made to contribute to the general effect of melancholy.
Nature is represented by its sombre features alone.   What
we are allowed to see is " the wandering cloud, and the
rain pattering among the foliage, autumn's sullen moan and
the rustle of withered leaves "; or, elsewhere, the crater
of " Etna with its burning depths seen in glimpses
between gusts of lurid vapour."   Two mournful impressions contain an epitome of the entire human race : " Past
and Present are a pair of incomplete statues : one, all
mutilated, unearthed from the wreck of ages; the other
still lacking its future perfection."   The only recollection
left after a survey of a great city, with its intense life and
mighty forces of activity, is that of the careless indifference
of some stonemasons lounging at the foot of the statue of
Charles I., or whistling as they trim their stones, ignorant
of the monument's very name.

After 1798 Wordsworth would certainly have considered it morally wrong to draw his reader's attention to
a subject so gloomy and so destitute of any ray of comfort.
It is true that he had himself written narratives of un-

relieved sorrow or distress. Yet observe how he now modifies *The Ruined Cottage*.[1] Too beautiful, too precious a work to be sacrificed, it cannot be published without being first disguised by extenuating and tranquillizing reflections. The poet almost passes censure upon himself for having dwelt so long on a subject which can yield nothing but sorrow. In the midst of the narrative, the pedlar who recounts it becomes ashamed of his tears, and pauses abruptly to ask

> Why should we thus with an untoward mind,
> And in the weakness of humanity,
> From natural wisdom turn our hearts away;
> To natural comfort shut our eyes and ears?

Not without regret, not without a kind of remorse, does he yield to the entreaties of his listener and resume his story. And at its conclusion, seeing his friend give way to "the impotence of grief," he feels it his duty to stem the emotion he has aroused; he would leave a more serene impression on the mind he has disturbed. Making Nature his ally, and pointing to the sad and desolate garden, with its air of mourning for those who once tended it, he says:

> My Friend! enough to sorrow you have given,
> The purposes of wisdom ask no more:
> Be wise and cheerful; and no longer read
> The forms of things with an unworthy eye.
> She sleeps in the calm earth, and peace is here.
> I well remember that those very plumes,
> Those weeds, and the high spear-grass on that wall,
> By mist and silent rain-drops silvered o'er,
> As once I passed, did to my heart convey
> So still an image of tranquillity,
> So calm and still, and looked so beautiful
> Amid the uneasy thoughts which filled my mind,
> That what we feel of sorrow and despair
> From ruin and from change, and all the grief
> The passing shows of Being leave behind,

[1] He began to alter it towards the end of December 1801. (Dorothy Wordsworth's Journal.)

Appeared an idle dream, that could not live
Where meditation was. I turned away
And walked along my road in happiness.[1]

Anxious, therefore, to make the most of the power of resistance to despondency, both in himself and in others, and believing that a wilful persistence in melancholy exhausts the springs of man's vitality, Wordsworth henceforth always cuts short a narrative at any point beyond which it can only call forth the listener's tears,[2] or else summons every form of consolation known to him in order to quench them. And if no purely human hope suggests itself whereby human suffering may be assuaged, he seeks in the external world some cheering token which may enable him once more to consolidate within his own heart and the hearts of all men the shaken foundations of happiness. So frequently is he impelled, by the constant recurrence of causes for sorrow, thus to seek encouragement, that finally he enlists the whole of nature in the service of optimism.

Whatever the thoughts which engage his attention, it is his first object, and his last, to derive from them all the enjoyment they can yield. And in his choice of enjoyments he is guided only by the varying, but always lofty, needs of his being. For the present Nature suffices him, and will continue to do so throughout the most poetical years of his life. When with sorrowful eyes he watches the fading of the splendours which have so long decked the world around him, he will turn to the moral pleasures of duty[3]; when, in the evening of life, "the fair smile which Duty wears upon its face" in its turn grows dim—when, beneath the footsteps of Duty, flowers bloom no longer and cease to shed their perfume—he will turn to religion for its consolation and its hope.[4] And though, when that time comes, the poet in him will but rarely appear, as a man he will be ever the same, steadfastly setting his face towards whatever may give him cause to restrain a sigh or to express thanksgiving.

---

[1] *The Excursion*, i., earliest text (1814). In 1845 Wordsworth introduced into this passage Christian sentiments which have completely transformed it.

[2] Observe for instance the abrupt ending of the admirable pastoral *Michael*, " There is a comfort in the strength of love."

[3] *Ode to Duty* (1805).   [4] *Ecclesiastical Sonnets* (1821).

CHAPTER II

Wordsworth's Relation to Science

I

Is it at the cost of truth that the poet has won back his happiness ? To realize his dream of becoming the poet of optimism, will it be necessary for him to dwell in a world of illusion, and thus to sacrifice the pursuit of the true ? Such is not Wordsworth's opinion. His soul is too sincere to be happy under the suspicion that he owes his happiness to a deception. His conviction, scarcely ever shaken, that in discerning harmony he is also discerning truth, is the distinguishing characteristic of his work and of his life. His cheerfulness returned, he says, simultaneously with his return to nature ; in other words, his trust was restored on the day when he forsook the premature abstraction which builds its theories of the universe and of the soul of man on insufficient and unsubstantial grounds, and placed himself once more in direct contact with facts : multiplying his slender stock of observations tenfold, and demanding of his sensations and feelings immediate and positive data with regard to questions which he had once thought to solve by the mere operation of his intellectual faculties unprovided with matter. He became an optimist on the day when he perceived reality.

If, after its indescribable wave of enthusiasm, the generation to which he belongs is overshadowed by a cloud of discouragement, the evil arises from the ignorance and presumption of the philosophers and false professors who have been its guides ; who have supposed themselves acquainted with the whole of nature after brief glimpses of some of its aspects, and have imagined themselves familiar with the whole of man as soon as they have distinguished two or three faculties of that human soul " of a thousand

faculties composed, and twice ten thousand interests."[1]
Experience has rudely contradicted them. Yet, rather
than acknowledge that his intelligence has been mistaken,
man prefers to believe that Nature—including his own
nature—is at fault. If despair is not to crush him, he must
become convinced that the science of to-day is of little
consequence, and that the truths yielded by its present
methods are dependent and not ultimate. Nature is still
almost unknown ; man must humble himself before her,
and must further ascertain whether there is not some other
means of investigation concerning her than the reasoning
power which has been so wrongfully employed.

It is quite needless to say that this enquiry was not new,
and that Wordsworth's originality does not consist in
the fact that he undertook it. His struggle against
intellectual arrogance is but an episode, and not the most
brilliant episode, of the great crusade against the " philosophers " of the eighteenth century. Wordsworth did
what had been done by several of the preceding generation
and was being followed up by many of his contemporaries.
He was but a unit among the number of those who had
regained their senses after becoming intoxicated with
reasoning, and now went about cursing the folly of the
previous night. Memory is thronged with the names of
those who had already maintained that reasoning strays
from its path, and loses its self-control, when it forsakes
its appointed realm, and that it is neither qualified nor
sufficiently developed to solve the great problems of
the soul and of the universe. In France, Bernardin de
Saint-Pierre and Saint-Martin repeated it with wearisome
iteration after Rousseau. And through the agency of
Kant and Jacobi, however different their object and their
means, the same thought penetrated the German mind to
its depths. Even in England there were others besides
Coleridge who might have inspired Wordsworth with a
contempt for reasoners. Not to mention the attacks made
upon irreligious logicians by Beattie and Cowper with their
lighter weapons, what was the whole labour of Burke but
a long and often successful assault upon the dangerous

[1] *The Excursion*, iv. 987.

errors which result from the employment of rigidly scientific methods in the management of human society, an ardent exaltation of facts in opposition to enthusiasm for abstractions, an injunction to the mind to bow before the mysterious divinity of that which *is ?*

All these charges against the discursive reason found their echo in the writings of Wordsworth. It became clear to him that science in its present form was powerless to deal with metaphysical problems. Did it not leave life everywhere out of account ? It " mis-shapes the beauteous forms of things :—we murder to dissect." [1] It substitutes "a universe of death for that which moves with light and life informed, actual, divine, and true." [2] It views all objects " in disconnection dead and spiritless." [3] It commits as it were a wholesale assassination, necessary, possibly, to its own operations, but whence it is absurd to conclude that the universe is devoid of a vital soul.

Similar errors arise when analysis is applied to the soul of man.

> Who shall parcel out
> His intellect by geometric rules,
> Split like a province into round and square ?
> Who knows the individual hour in which
> His habits were first sown, even as a seed ?
> Who that shall point as with a wand and say
> "This portion of the river of my mind
> Came from yon fountain ?" Thou, my Friend ! [4] art one
> More deeply read in thy own thoughts ; to thee
> Science appears but what in truth she is,
> Not as our glory and our absolute boast,
> But as a succedaneum, and a prop
> To our infirmity. No officious slave
> Art thou of that false secondary power
> By which we multiply distinctions, then
> Deem that our puny boundaries are things
> That we perceive, and not that we have made.
> To thee, unblinded by these formal arts,
> The unity of all hath been revealed,
> And thou wilt doubt, with me less aptly skilled

[1] *The Tables Turned* (1798), ll. 26-28.
[2] *The Excursion*, iv. 961-962.
[2] *The Prelude*, xiv. 160-162.
[4] Coleridge.

Than many are to range the faculties
In scale and order, class the cabinet
Of their sensations, and in voluble phrase
Run through the history and birth of each
As of a single independent thing.
Hard task, vain hope, to analyse the mind,
If each most obvious and particular thought,
Not in a mystical and idle sense,
But in the words of Reason deeply weighed,
Hath no beginning.[1]

Henceforth, therefore, Wordsworth has nothing but distrust or contempt for the abstract systems of knowledge which charmed him in his youth because they pretended to disclose the secrets of life. He had himself reared enough of them to know their value and to detect the fallacy beneath them.

As, by simple waving of a wand,
The wizard instantaneously dissolves
Palace or grove, even so could I unsoul
As readily by syllogistic words
[The] mysteries of being.[2]

Mere mental pastimes, there is nevertheless a danger that we may regard them as containing an accurate and complete representation of nature. It is essential that man should be convinced of their vanity.

If tired with systems, each in its degree
Substantial, and all crumbling in their turn,
Let him build systems of his own, and smile
At the fond work, demolished with a touch.[3]

These attacks are well directed. But need it be repeated that they do not constitute the ground of Wordsworth's peculiar merit? In them he speaks as the disciple of Coleridge, and fails to attain his master's level. In this part of his work we shall discover neither fresh arguments nor memorable flights of eloquence. Nevertheless, this campaign against the reasoning faculty, designed to drive it back into its own territory and to put an end to its

[1] *The Prelude*, ii. 203-232.   [2] *Ibid.*, xii. 81-85.
[3] *The Excursion*, iv. 603-606.

misuse, was essential to the poet if he was to rid himself
of a long-endured tyranny. The real struggle was taking
place within himself, and the point at issue was whether
poetry, so confined of late, was again to occupy in his
mind an ample space in which it might breathe in freedom.
And here the result of the struggle is of more importance
than the struggle itself. That result was the emancipation
of the poet's really powerful and original faculties, and,
at the same time, the transformation of the world as it
appeared to his eyes.

When, indeed, the mind has once perceived the limitations of reasoning, what a revolution takes place within!
Unless they should agree upon a kind of peaceful *con-
dominium*, the other faculties of the soul, hitherto regarded
with suspicion or contempt, are now seen in conflict for
the empty throne. Feeling and instinct, intuition and
imagination, urge their legitimate claims. Superstition,
prejudice and habit, presentiments and dreams, produce
their more equivocal credentials.

And what a metamorphosis without! Those whose
intellectual prowess so recently compelled both admiration and approval resume their natural stature and place
among the crowd. They are recognised as no less
(possibly more) incompetent than the ordinary run of
men to solve the enigma of things, and even to suspect
its existence. Every forward step which they have taken
in the field of pure thought has carried them farther
from reality. Those, on the other hand, who but yesterday were the objects of scorn, who, by reason of the
weakness of their understanding, were thrust aside as
incapable of contributing anything to the solution of
the great and obstinate problems of the mind, now occupy
the first place in the wise man's thought. Forth step
the ignorant and illiterate, whose senses, not yet distorted
by analysis, yield them immediate perceptions of the world,
whose souls have not been so "smooth-rubbed" by
the play of abstractions that neither "form, nor feeling,
great or small,"[1] can cling to them; women, whose hearts
speak so loudly and so promptly that reason cannot impose

[1] *A poet's Epitaph*, ll. 29-30.

upon them, whose real or fancied lack of logic ceases
to be a defect and becomes a token of superiority; above
all, children, still half enveloped in the mystery which
is the origin of every creature, and on that account better
able to judge concerning a universe which they view
as it were from the outside, and, still urged by the
impetus which has carried them to earth, more capable
of marching straight towards the true goal. But the
train of those restored to honour is not yet ended.
There follow those in whom all purely intellectual light
appears extinct—the crazy and the idiotic, to whom the
common people, perhaps not wrongly, attribute inspiration, and from whom even the wise may learn much,
for none can say beforehand what phrase will issue from
their lips; and since the utter impotence of so-called
rational beings is admitted, may it not be that these
will presently let fall words not less profound than
mysterious? And though human beings have now passed
by, the procession still continues. Shall the multitudes
which the philosophy of a Descartes would proscribe,
the animals which cannot reason, be set aside on account
of so insignificant a deficiency? They possess the principle of life; they possess instinct. In them divinity lives
and speaks. What might not man learn, did he but
know their language, and could he but follow their
inward reverie? Nor is even this enough. Plants also
have their joys and sorrows; they live and feel; they
speak a language which the poet should strive to understand and to interpret. The invisible elements too, and
things inanimate, have their place in the universal chorus.
Are there indeed inanimate things? Are not the things
we thus designate those whose hidden life eludes us?

> Oh; there is life that breathes not; Powers there are
> That touch each other to the quick in modes
> Which the gross world no sense hath to perceive,
> No soul to dream of.[1]

Nature as a whole has her own mighty and indefinable
voice, the sum of all these separate voices. It is this

[1] *Address to Kilchurn Castle.*

and no other, which, were it understood, would reveal the great secret.

II

This mysticism, fully or partially developed, undisguised or concealed, is met with in almost all the imaginative writers of the nineteenth century. It was always at Wordsworth's disposal when his optimism found itself in conflict with some disheartening conclusion of logic or science. Not with impunity, however, not without the survival of some of its traces, had the poet devoted years to the cultivation of his intellectual faculties. Strongly as he was opposed to the worship of reasoning, he became one of the most argumentative of poets, for the only means of confounding reasoning as yet discovered consists in reasoning it away. Nor did he become such a narrow and infatuated antagonist of science as certain sharp and ill-judged outbursts against men of learning would lead us to expect.[1] In a mind that had been for the moment mis-led by the science of the age, we may pardon these acts of retaliation against it for its delusive predictions: its promises of the complete revelation of the mysterious, the conquest of death, the transformation of human life into a god-like state of existence, and the establishment of the golden age on earth in a future so near as to be within sight, and almost within reach of an outstretched hand. Anyone who compares the moderate results achieved with the enormous promises made will not be too severe upon a few outbreaks of exasperation and even of impertinence. Moreover, though he attacked false science, Wordsworth never ceased to do honour to the true. Few poets have paid a more splendid tribute to geometry, or shown an equal admiration for that "independent world, created out of pure intelligence."[2] Regretting his neglect of it at Cambridge, he applied himself to it afresh, hoping

---

[1] *E.g.* the *vade retro* addressed to the naturalist who could " botanize upon his mother's grave." *A Poet's Epitaph* (1799).
[2] *The Prelude*, vi. 166-167.

to find in its stability a refuge from the contradictions and uncertainties of philosophy.   When his residence at Alfoxden came to an end, in September 1798, he set out for Germany, not with the intention of acquiring a knowledge of German literature, but in order to study natural history.[1]   Three years later he contemplated learning chemistry, from a desire " not to be so wholly ignorant of knowledge so exceedingly important." [2]

Nor did he lose hope that, after science had humbly returned to the study of nature, it might some day fulfil all its splendid promises.   He loved to indulge in a poet's dream of the science of the future, which, instead of holding out a prospect of happiness for the individual intelligence alone, would be at once the product and the delight of the whole being of man.   It would originate in the *sensitive intellect*, in the *intelligent heart*.   A time may come " when what is now called science shall be ready to put on, as it were, a form of flesh and blood." [3] Love will unite with reason to accomplish the glorious metamorphosis.

> Science then
> Shall be a precious visitant ; and then,
> And only then, be worthy of her name :
> For then her heart shall kindle ; her dull eye,
> Dull and inanimate, no more shall hang
> Chained to its object in brute slavery ;
> But taught with patient interest to watch
> The processes of things, and serve the cause
> Of order and distinctness, not for this
> Shall it forget that its most noble use,
> Its most illustrious province, must be found
> In furnishing clear guidance, a support
> Not treacherous, to the mind's *excursive* power.[4]

Thus penetrated with love and holy passion, man's intelligence will be truly " wedded to this goodly universe."

---

[1] Letter to James Losh, 11th March 1798.

[2] Letter from Coleridge to Thelwall, 3rd February 1801.   *Fragmentary Remains of Sir H. Davy*, p. 86.

[3] Preface to the *Lyrical Ballads* (1802).

[4] *The Excursion*, iv. 1251-1263.   These lines were written early in 1798 (see prefatory note to *The Excursion*).   Doubtless they formed part of the 706 lines of *The Recluse* which were finished on the 11th March 1798.

The poet does but chant, long before the hour arrives, "the spousal verse of this great consummation."[1]

Not only, however, does he see in imagination a vague presentment of true science, but, joining her as an auxiliary, he offers her the indispensable assistance of poetry as a means to the study of reality. He will, it is true, be an independent auxiliary, employing his own arms and his own method of warfare, but he will do battle in the same cause, the cause of truth.

Now, certain among the various and innumerable *facts* of the soul are under the control of the poet, to whom, more than to anyone else, it appertains to reveal them, and to form judgments concerning them, since he alone, perhaps, can discern them clearly. But for him, these facts would remain unknown or despised, and philosophers would continue to discourse upon abstract man, a being free from, or rather stripped of, passions. The heart of the man of flesh and blood is the poet's special province. Poetry " is the history or science of feelings."[2]

Its object is to throw light upon those operations of the soul which are not yet correctly explained. Wordsworth's poetry, at any rate, has no other object than this. His aim in writing *The Thorn* was " to exhibit some of the general laws by which superstition acts upon the mind."[3] He wrote *Goody Blake and Harry Gill* because he " wished to draw attention to the truth that the power of the human imagination is sufficient to produce such changes even in our physical nature as might almost appear miraculous. The truth is an important one ; the fact (for it is a *fact*) is a valuable illustration of it."[4] " I have said," he wrote, in the preface to the second edition of the *Lyrical Ballads* (1800), " that each of these poems has a purpose. I have also informed my Reader what this purpose will be found principally to be : namely to illustrate the manner in which our feelings and ideas are associated in a state of excitement. But speaking in less general language, it is to

[1] *The Recluse* (1800), ll. 825-830.
[2] *The Thorn*, note written in 1800.   [3] *Ibid.*
[4] From the preface to the *Lyrical Ballads*, second edition, 1800. This and the following passage were suppressed in subsequent editions, and have never been reprinted.

follow the fluxes and refluxes of the mind when agitated by the great and simple affections of our nature. This object I have endeavoured in these short essays to attain by various means ; by tracing the maternal passion through many of its more subtle windings, as in the poems of the *Idiot Boy* and the *Mad Mother ;* by accompanying the last struggles of a human being at the approach of death, cleaving in solitude to life and society, as in the poem of the *Forsaken Indian ;* by showing, as in the stanzas entitled *We are Seven*, the perplexity and obscurity which in childhood attend our notion of death, or rather our utter inability to admit that notion ; or by displaying the strength of fraternal, or to speak more philosophically, of moral attachment when early associated with the great and beautiful objects of nature, as in *The Brothers ;* or, as in the Incident of *Simon Lee*, by placing my Reader in the way of receiving from ordinary moral sensations another and more salutary impression than we are accustomed to receive from them."

Is it a poet or a psychologist who speaks thus ? Both at once, Wordsworth would say, for poetry is only the highest and at the same time the most profound form of psychology ; that which studies man's living soul, watches the birth of sensations and their conversion into acts, and detects the secret forces which determine conduct.

Poetry, it is true, cannot claim this branch of study for itself alone. And although, by reason of his peculiar gifts, the poet may be better qualified than any one else to prosecute it with success, it is nevertheless not his exclusive privilege. But in the study of man and of the world there is a vast domain, as yet unexplored, or visited only by writers such as Anne Radcliffe, in whom true imaginative observation is constantly hindered and warped by their use of vulgar means and their hankering after thrilling effects. This domain is his beyond dispute, and without a knowledge of it the science can never be brought to completeness. "The appropriate business of poetry (which, nevertheless, if genuine, is as permanent as pure science), her appropriate employment, her privilege and her *duty*, is to treat of things not as they *are*, but as they *appear ;* not as they exist in themselves, but as they *seem* to exist to the *senses*, and to the *passions*."[1]

And if it be objected that these appearances are illusory, the poet replies, in the first place, that they are undeniably *facts* of the soul, and for that reason ought to be studied. Further, their influence upon human actions cannot be called in question, and without an acquaintance with them it is folly to pretend to a knowledge of human nature, and to attempt to control men. Lastly, if closely pressed, he will tell you that this impression of reality, imperfect and changeable as it may be, is nevertheless the least inaccurate that we possess; since the passions, by casting their lights and shadows upon the world, lend it at any rate life and movement, and invest it with meaning and an object, while the man of science who looks upon it with eyes devoid alike of love and hate sees before him merely an inert mass, senseless and dead. To see, as did the earliest men, divinity, wrathful or kindly, come down to earth; to ascribe a moral significance to the motions of the heavenly bodies, like the Chaldæans; or, with the Greeks, to attribute human life and human feelings to every natural object—mind to matter[2]—is to come infinitely nearer than the learned of the present day to the central truth.

So far from being inanimate, the universe maintains, on the contrary, a perpetual dialogue with man. And the work of Wordsworth is but a transcription of the fragments he has caught, and, as he thinks, understood. The main subject of his poetry is the relation between the world and the soul.

> My voice proclaims
> How exquisitely the individual Mind
> (And the progressive powers perhaps no less
> Of the whole species) to the external World
> Is fitted :—and how exquisitely too—
> Theme this but little heard of among men—
> The external World is fitted to the Mind ;
> And the creation (by no lower name
> Can it be called) which they with blended might
> Accomplish :—this is our high argument.[3]

[1] *Essay Supplementary to the Preface of the Poems* (1815).
[2] *The Excursion*, iv.   [3] *The Recluse*, 835-844.

It is the argument of *The Prelude*, in which Wordsworth describes more fully than in his dramatic poems, and with a deeper and more acute perception of truth, all that he knew and felt of the influences exerted over each other by nature and his own mind.   Perhaps, however, the psychology peculiar to the poet may be better illustrated by the analysis of a shorter and more humble work; one which, from its strangeness, has frequently been turned into ridicule, which intentionally runs counter to poetic tradition, and makes use of details, previously regarded as merely ludicrous, with serious intent.   This is the story of *Peter Bell*, the pedlar.[1]   More precisely, it is an account of the conversion of a brutal and profligate churl, who is brought to a state of grace by the impressions made upon his senses, one fine evening, by a donkey and a landscape.

III

Peter Bell was a hawker.   For more than thirty-two years he had driven his donkeys with their load of pottery in every direction throughout England and Scotland.   His journeys took him from the cliffs of Dover to the rocky shore of Cornwall, from the Scotch Highlands to the Lincolnshire fens.   His life was spent in the free air, amid the solitude and the changing beauty of nature, in daily contact with wood or open field, mountain or sea.   But never yet had he felt the charm or the grandeur of the scenes he witnessed in the course of his wandering life.

> He roved among the vales and streams,
> In the green wood and hollow dell;
> They were his dwellings night and day,—
> But nature ne'er could find the way
> Into the heart of Peter Bell.

> In vain, through every changeful year,
> Did Nature lead him as before;
> A primrose by a river's brim
> A yellow primrose was to him,
> And it was nothing more.

[1] *Peter Bell* was written in 1798.   The following quotations are from the earliest text, published in 1819.

> Small change it made in Peter's heart
> To see his gentle panniered train
> With more than vernal pleasure feeding,
> Where'er the tender grass was leading
> Its earliest green along the lane.
>
> In vain, through water, earth, and air,
> The soul of happy sound was spread,
> When Peter on some April morn,
> Beneath the broom or budding thorn,
> Made the warm earth his lazy bed.
>
> At noon, when, by the forest's edge
> He lay beneath the branches high,
> The soft blue sky did never melt
> Into his heart ; he never felt
> The witchery of the soft blue sky!

A churlish, half-savage kind of fellow was Peter, and a profligate to boot, contracting easy matrimonial ties wherever he went, careless of the laws, for he had as many as a dozen wedded wives. His vices were no doubt the product of the towns in which he stayed here and there. But nature had as yet failed to soften his rugged soul; she appeared, on the contrary, to have rendered it still more savage in character, so that her wildest features were reflected in his countenance and imprinted even on his heart. The wilderness had fostered within him

> . . . the unshaped, half-human thoughts
> Which solitary Nature feeds
> 'Mid summer storms or winter's ice.
> .   .   .   .   .
> His face was keen as is the wind
> That cuts along the hawthorn-fence ;

his forehead all wrinkled "by knitting of his brows beneath the glaring sun."

> There was a hardness in his cheek,
> There was a hardness in his eye,
> As if the man had fixed his face,
> In many a solitary place,
> Against the wind and open sky!

But though nature had failed to instil her lessons of loving-kindness and morality into him by slow degrees, she finally succeeded by means of a sudden shock in which she combined all the potent spells at her command in order to subdue his rebellious spirit.

On a beautiful evening in November, when the full moon shone brightly upon the river Swale, Peter was travelling alone on the bank of the rapid stream.

> He trudged along through copse and brake
> He trudged along o'er hill and dale ;
> Nor for the moon cared he a tittle,
> And for the stars he cared as little,
> And for the murmuring river Swale.
>
> But, chancing to espy a path
> That promised to cut short the way ;
> As many a wiser man hath done,
> He left a trusty guide for one
> That might his steps betray.
>
> To a thick wood he soon is brought
> Where cheerily his course he weaves,
> And whistling loud may yet be heard,
> Though often buried like a bird
> Darkling, among the boughs and leaves.

But the footpath gives no sign of coming back to the road, and Peter begins to rave against his ill-luck. When the path ends abruptly in a deserted quarry, he becomes more angry still. Pressing onwards, however, among the huge, shapeless blocks of stone, with their shadows, "massy and black," he passes right through the quarry, and behold ! there lies before him a lawn of a soft and lovely hue, an exquisite green plot of earth, encompassed with rocks, beneath which flows the Swale, noiseless and unseen. He has crossed the plot of meadow, when, turning his head, he sees a solitary ass. His first impulse is to take possession of the creature to compensate himself for having come so far out of his way. But first of all he casts his eyes around him ; not a house is to be seen, not a woodman's hut, nor cottage light. He seizes the halter, leaps upon the animal's back, and belabours its sides with his heels. The ass remains motionless. Then Peter gives " a jerk that from a dungeon-floor would have pulled up an iron ring"; and still the ass makes no movement.

> Quoth Peter, leaping from his seat,
> "There is some plot against me laid ; "
> Once more the little meadow-ground
> And all the hoary cliffs around
> He cautiously surveyed.
>
> All, all is silent—rocks and woods,
> All still and silent—far and near !
> Only the Ass, with motion dull,
> Upon the pivot of his skull
> Turns round his long left ear.
>
> Thought Peter, What can mean all this?
> Some ugly witchcraft must be here !
> —Once more the Ass, with motion dull,
> Upon the pivot of his skull
> Turned round his long left ear.

Peter Bell begins to grow fearful, and then his dread turns to fury. With the skill of long practice he deals the poor creature a terrible blow with his staff; the ass staggers, and without a groan drops upon its knees, then sinks down on its side by the brink of the river, and turns towards Peter its " shining hazel eye."

> 'Twas but one mild, reproachful look,
> A look more tender than severe ;
> And straight in sorrow, not in dread,
> He turned the eye-ball in his head
> Towards the smooth river deep and clear.

Still the sapling rings upon its fleshless sides ; three times the animal groans piteously ; yet neither its moans nor its gaunt and skeleton-like appearance touch Peter Bell's cruel heart. Maddened by this passive resistance, Peter swears he will fling the ass into the river.

An impious oath confirmed the threat—
But, while upon the ground he lay
To all the echoes, south and north,
And east and west, the Ass sent forth
A loud and piteous bray !

This outcry, on the heart of Peter,
Seems like a note of joy to strike,—
Joy at the heart of Peter knocks ;
But in the echo of the rocks
Was something Peter did not like.

Whether to cheer his coward breast,
Or that he could not break the chain,
In this serene and solemn hour,
Twined round him by demoniac power,
To the blind work he turned again.

Among the rocks and winding crags ;
Among the mountains far away ;
Once more the Ass did lengthen out
More ruefully an endless shout,
The hard dry see-saw of his horrible bray !

What is there now in Peter's heart !
Or whence the might of this strange sound ?
The moon uneasy looked and dimmer,
The broad blue heavens appeared to glimmer,
And the rocks staggered all around—

From Peter's hand the sapling dropped !
Threat has he none to execute ;
" If any one should come and see
That I am here, they'll think," quoth he,
" I'm helping this poor dying brute."

He scans the Ass from limb to limb,
And Peter now uplifts his eyes ;
Steady the moon doth look and clear,
And like themselves the rocks appear,
And tranquil are the skies.

Recovering his confidence Peter Bell is about to strike
again, when he catches sight of something in the river so

startling that suddenly he seems as if turned to iron; the hair rises on his scalp, he utters a shriek and swoons away. Among the inverted images of the trees in the depths of the stream he has caught a glimpse of the body of a drowned man, the owner of the ass. Four days earlier he had fallen into the river, and the poor animal had faithfully kept guard over him ever since without a thought of grazing on the tempting herbage of the greensward. Some instinctive feeling of humanity urges Peter to draw the corpse to land. Entangling his sapling in the dead man's hair he pulls him upwards, until at last he rises from the river, head-foremost, like a ghost. The ass shows every sign of joy, and, as best he can, gives Peter to understand that he must mount upon his back. Peter's feelings have been touched and he obeys. Then begins a ride through the lonely night, not unlike that of Tam O'Shanter, though marked by no marvellous occurrences; and in the course of it a succession of sensations, commonplace enough for the most part, and all quite probable, are destined to soften Peter Bell's hard heart.

First of all there falls on his ear a doleful cry; it comes from a cavern close at hand, in the neighbourhood of which the dead man's child has lingered after seeking his father far and wide. At the call of a familiar voice the ass stops short, and Peter, not knowing whence the sound proceeds, is filled with undefined terror. He feels sure that vengeance will fall upon his head to punish him for his cruelty to the gentle creature. And already, as the ass pursues his journey, things assume an altered appearance around Peter Bell.

> The rocks that tower on either side
> Build up a wild fantastic scene;
> Temples like those among the Hindoos,
> And mosques, and spires, and abbey-windows,
> And castles all with ivy green!
>
> And while the Ass pursues his way
> Along this solitary dell,
> As pensively his steps advance,
> The mosques and spires change countenance,
> And look at Peter Bell!

Now they reach an upland

> Where, shining like the smoothest sea,
> In undisturbed immensity
> A level plain extends.

> How blank!—but whence this rustling sound
> Which, all too long, the pair hath chased!
> —A dancing leaf is close behind,
> Light plaything for the sportive wind
> Upon that solitary waste.

> When Peter spied the withered leaf,
> It yields no cure to his distress.
> "Where there is not a bush or tree,
> The very leaves they follow me—
> So huge has been my wickedness!"

A little further on, in a narrow lane, where "the white dust sleeps" upon the ground, Peter sees, here and there, as he looks behind him, a crimson stain.

> A stain—as of a drop of blood
> By moonlight made more faint and wan;
> Ha! why these sinkings of despair?
> He knows not how the blood comes there—
> And Peter is a wicked man.

> At length he spies a bleeding wound,
> Where he had struck the Ass's head;
> He sees the blood, knows what it is,—
> A glimpse of sudden joy was his,
> But then it quickly fled;

> Of him whom sudden death had seized
> He thought,—of thee, O faithful Ass!
> And once again those darting pains,
> As meteors shoot through Heaven's wide plains,
> Pass through his bosom—and repass.

In vain Peter Bell struggles against the terror and remorse which slowly take possession of him. In vain he recovers a gleam of his good humour, and even, in a spirit of defiance, exchanges a grin with his ass; the least fresh shock can startle him. And at that very moment a rumbling sound begins to roll in long and muffled murmurs beneath the road; it is caused by miners, who are blasting with gunpowder twenty fathoms underground, and Peter believes that earth is "charged to quake and yawn for his unworthy sake." Immediately afterwards he passes before a little ruined chapel, all overgrown with ivy, which seems

> To bow to some transforming power,
> And blend with the surrounding trees.

Peter Bell reflects that it was in just such a place that he married his sixth wife. He remembers the tears he has brought to the eyes of innocent girls, the deceit he has practised to lead them astray.

> But, more than all, his heart is stung
> To think of one, almost a child;
> A sweet and playful Highland girl,
> As light and beauteous as a squirrel,
> As beauteous and as wild!

She had left her mother to follow Peter Bell, and when she learned the truth about the man she loved, died of a broken heart before giving birth to the child whom she had already named Benoni, the child of sorrow.

> And now the Spirits of the Mind
> Are busy with poor Peter Bell;
> Distraction reigns in soul and sense,
> And reason drops in impotence
> From her deserted pinnacle.

> Close by a brake of flowering furze
> (Above it shivering aspens play)
> He sees an unsubstantial creature,
> His very self in form and feature,
> Not four yards from the broad highway: [1]

[1] To assure ourselves that this is an instance not of pure invention but of an attempt to present a well-established case of hallucination, *cf.* the following note, written by Coleridge on the 12th May 1805:—"I am more convinced by repeated observation that, . . . in certain states and postures of the eye, as in drowsiness, in the state of the brain and nerves after distress or agitation, . . . we see our own faces, and project them according to the distance given them by the degree of indistinctness—that this may occasion in the highest degree the Wraith (*vide* a hundred Scotch stories, but better than all, Wordsworth's most wonderful and admirable poem, *Peter Bell* . . .)" (*Anima Poetae*, edited by E. H. Coleridge, 1895, p. 146).

And stretched beneath the furze he sees
The Highland girl—it is no other;
And hears her crying as she cried,
The very moment that she died,
" My mother! oh my mother! "

The sweat streams down Peter's face, and at the same moment a voice rising from a wooded glade reaches his ear. Ringing as a hunter's horn, and re-echoed by a naked rock, the voice proceeds from a tabernacle, where a fervent Methodist is preaching to his attentive flock.

" Repent! repent! " he cries aloud,
" While yet ye may find mercy;—strive
To love the Lord with all your might;
Turn to him, seek him day and night,
And save your souls alive!

" Repent! repent! though ye have gone,
Through paths of wickedness and woe,
After the Babylonian harlot;
And though your sins be red as scarlet,
They shall be white as snow! "

Even as he passed the door, these words
Did plainly come to Peter's ears;
And they such joyful tidings were,
The joy was more than he could bear!—
He melted into tears.

Sweet tears of hope and tenderness!
And fast they fell, a plenteous shower!
His nerves, his sinews seemed to melt;
Through all his iron frame was felt
A gentle, a relaxing, power!

Each fibre of his frame was weak;
Weak all the animal within;
But, in its helplessness, grew mild
And gentle as an infant child,
An infant that has known no sin.

His heart is now opened to his own sorrows, and all that is required to heal his soul is that it should be opened

to those of others. The dead man's cottage is reached at
last, and with deep emotion Peter witnesses all the alternations of joy and despair caused by his arrival and
the tale he has to tell. The tears of the widow and her
children make him feel " what he for human kind had
never felt before."

> And now is Peter taught to feel
> That man's heart is a holy thing ;
> And Nature, through a world of death
> Breathes into him a second breath,
> More searching than the breath of spring.
>
> .   .   .   .   .   .
>
> And Peter turns his steps aside
> Into a shade of darksome trees,
> Where he sits down, he knows not how,
> With his hands pressed against his brow,
> And resting on his tremulous knees.
>
> There, self-involved, does Peter sit
> Until no sign of life he makes,
> As if his mind were sinking deep
> Through years that have been long asleep !
> The trance is passed away—he wakes ;
>
> He lifts his head—and sees the Ass
> Yet standing in the clear moonshine ;
> " When shall I be as good as thou ?
> Oh ! would, poor beast, that 1 had now
> A heart but half as good as thine ! "

His wish was gratified. The wild pedlar forsook his
crimes and follies, and, " after ten months' melancholy,
became a good and honest man."

Although, as presented, it may seem to have something
of a manufactured air, something too " Radcliffian " even,
we need not doubt that Peter Bell's conversion was regarded by its author as a contribution to the knowledge
of the soul. Wordsworth no longer scoffs at conversion
in the manner of a philosopher, nor sets it before us as
mysterious and ineffable after the fashion of a mystic. He
explains it as a normal mental phenomenon, and takes satisfaction in pointing out the parts played by the senses and

by external objects, fearlessly revealing the trivial circumstances in which it may originate.   Yet he does not consider that in doing this he is lessening or destroying its importance.   Its moral value is not to be impaired by the most searching analysis.   And Wordsworth means the reader to argue from the emotions of Peter Bell to the innumerable corresponding emotions he must have experienced himself, to the countless insignificant and gentle influences, entirely free from any consciously intellectual element, whereby his actions—and possibly not the least important nor the least virtuous of them—have been determined.   By this means his conception of human nature will be in a sense broadened.   Man's conduct, which the philosopher has endeavoured to place in an independent and isolated position, becomes intimately bound up with the events of the universe.   The whole of nature is involved in a single human action.   The blending, "the unity, of all things," becomes manifest in the soul's faintest impulse.   The false psychology gives place to the true.

But poetry cannot justify its claim to extend and to complete the science of the soul by merely exploring an unknown region of reality, it must also vindicate its favourite means of enquiry.   The imagination, which is to the poet what induction is to the scientist, must be a faithful and accurate instrument of knowledge.   This is how Wordsworth understands it.   Imagination, as he desires and indeed believes himself to possess it, has nothing in common with Pascal's "teacher of untruth"[1] or Malebranche's "mad inmate of the mind."[2]   For him it is the supreme faculty, "another name for absolute power and clearest insight, amplitude of mind, and Reason in her most exalted mood."[3]   A singular and arrogant definition!   Evidently we must no longer look to the ordinary usage of the word for the sense which Wordsworth attributes to it ; he gives it a new and revolutionary meaning.   Those who not only examine it but discern its full import will become aware that therein the poet has formulated the characteristics of his own genius.

---

[1] " la maîtresse d'erreur."   [2] " la folle du logis."
[3] *The Prelude*, xiv. 188-192

CHAPTER III

Wordsworth's Realism

I

A SIMPLE account of Wordsworth's attempts to collaborate with Coleridge during his residence at Alfoxden will prepare the reader, better than any definition or analysis could do, to apprehend the peculiar character of the poet's imagination. Coleridge, as we have seen, had already recognised and admired the predominant faculty in his friend's mind, and had endeavoured not only to define it, but even to reproduce its effects in his own work. But he was to render it much more clearly conspicuous by means of contrast. Hitherto he had merely, as he says, " fed the great river with a thousand nameless rills." Now, however, he found again the path he had for a moment lost. His own genius awoke once more to life, and became conscious of itself. Not only did he refuse to follow; he attempted in his turn to influence the course taken by Wordsworth, to lead him through a new region; and the impossibility of keeping company with Coleridge, and the discomfort of feeling his natural progress thwarted, were to Wordsworth a decisive and imperious revelation of the inevitable tendency of his own poetic genius. Wordsworth's realism asserted itself through being brought into conflict with Coleridge's preference for the fantastic.

At Alfoxden they led a common life. Their friends, their walks, their reading were the same, and the same natural scenery lay spread before each. Moreover, there was one problem in which, far more than in any other, both of them were at that time interested; for each it had the same besetting fascination. Preoccupied with the mysterious connection between body and soul, with the mutual interaction of senses and mind, they blindly sought some concrete form in which to express the result of their investigations.   The same subject presented itself to both in the effects of a curse on him who is the object of it, the transformation of the external world around one who is a prey to just remorse, or even the innocent victim of sorcery, the hallucinations of which he is consequently the subject, the madness in which they may result, and the physical decline to which this in its turn may lead.

Hitherto their minds had travelled the same path.   But no sooner was it a question of throwing this idea into poetic form than they immediately diverged, starting off in opposite directions.   Thrice they endeavoured to collaborate, and thrice were compelled to abandon the attempt.

First of all Coleridge takes up the subject, and transfers it to the obscure beginnings of history.   In an excursion to the west of Somersetshire, in Wordsworth's company, he had visited the wild Valley of Stones, " bedded among precipices overhanging the sea, with rocky caverns beneath, into which the waves dash, and where the sea-gull for ever wheels its screaming flight. On the tops of these are huge stones thrown transverse, as if an earthquake had tossed them there, and behind these is a fretwork of perpendicular rocks, something like the *Giant's Causeway*." [1]

At once Coleridge conceived the idea of making the same use of this rugged gorge as Wordsworth had made of Salisbury Plain.   He would place a murderer in this wild and desolate spot, but, instead of a poor soldier of his own day, his hero should be the first assassin, clothed in all the grandeur with which the legend invests him. And by the addition of some purely fanciful details he would transform this secluded corner of Somersetshire into a rugged solitude of a Biblical or entirely visionary character.   He and Wordsworth would write a prose-poem which should form a sequel to Gessner's *Death of Abel*, but be " far superior " to the German work.   Its title was to be *The Wanderings of Cain*. [2]

[1] William Hazlitt, *My first acquaintance with poets.*
[2] S. T. Coleridge, *The Wanderings of Cain.*

" The title and subject " says Coleridge " were suggested by myself, who likewise drew out the scheme and the contents for each of the three books or cantos of which the work was to consist, and which, the reader is to be informed, was to have been finished in one night! My partner undertook the first canto; I the second: and whichever had done first was to set about the third. Almost thirty years have passed by; yet at this moment I cannot without something more than a smile moot the question which of the two things was the more impracticable, for a mind so eminently original to compose another man's thoughts and fancies, or for a taste so austerely pure and simple to imitate the *Death of Abel?* Methinks I see his grand and noble countenance as at the moment when, having dispatched my own portion of the task at full finger-speed, I hastened to him with my manuscript— that look of humorous despondency fixed on his almost blank sheet of paper, and then its silent, mock-piteous admission of failure struggling with the sense of the exceeding ridiculousness of the whole scheme—which broke up in a laugh: and the *Ancient Mariner* was written instead." [1]

Here again Coleridge attempted to lure Wordsworth into the region of pure fancy, and again he failed. How significant are the numerous details, which the two poets have left us concerning the genesis of that famous ballad, *The Ancient Mariner!*

On the 13th November 1797, Wordsworth and Coleridge, accompanied by Dorothy, had set out at nightfall to visit the same Valley of Stones. Though they travelled on foot the trip was too expensive for their scantily-furnished purse, and it was necessary to defray the cost of the journey by a poem which would bring them five pounds from the editor of *The Monthly Magazine.* It was to be a ballad, for Coleridge was just then full of enthusiasm for Bürger's *Leonora*, which had recently been translated into English, and Wordsworth was beginning to feel drawn towards the popular ballads collected by Bishop Percy. The subject of the projected ballad was to be derived from an account given to Coleridge by a friend, of

[1] *The Wanderings of Cain*, preface.

a dream in which he had seen a phantom-ship with passengers on board.   But how was such a voyage to be described ?   Coleridge had never been at sea ; he fancied that the furrow appeared to those upon the vessel to follow it instead of streaming away from it.[1]   However, it was a question, not of a real, but of a fictitious voyage, and Coleridge found the necessary material for it in his casual readings about queer old sea-farers, long forgotten, and in the observations he had made himself on land as he watched both ships and sea from the heights of Quantock.   What Coleridge aimed at was to reproduce, through the medium as it were of his own dreams, not only the pure hallucinations which are directly conditioned by the visionary state, but also the ideas he himself had formed, either from his reading or through his own imagination, of the storm and the ice-pack, a dead calm at sea, the phenomena of phosphorescence and the terrible effects of the vertical sun of the tropics.   In order to succeed he only required to discover a form of poetical expression so exquisitely subtle in its music as to make the reader's gross logical faculty falter and vanish away, and for a moment to increase twofold his power of fantastic representation.

What share was Wordsworth to have in the composition of *The Ancient Mariner* ?   At first he adopted the plan suggested by Coleridge ; but almost at once he sought to *explain* the subject, to trace the causes and origins of the extraordinary sensations of which Coleridge wished to portray the effects alone.   The mysterious " Navigator," who had endured all the wrath of the ocean and the heavens, and of the powers of life and death, must have brought such chastisement upon himself by some crime. And Wordsworth, who had just read *Shelvocke's Voyages*, a narrative of fact, suggests the idea of the murder of an albatross during the passage round Cape Horn, to be avenged by the tutelary spirits of those regions.   Thus the moral and earthly notion of an expiation finds its way into the magic poem.   At a later time Coleridge came to regret having assented to its introduction.   The poem, he

---

[1] The first edition of *The Ancient Mariner* reads : *The furrow followed free* (l. 100).   In 1817 this was altered to, *The furrow streamed off free.*

said, "ought to have had no more moral than the 'Arabian Nights'' tale of the merchant's sitting down to eat dates by the side of a well, and throwing the shells aside, and lo ! a genie starts up, and says he *must* kill the aforesaid merchant, *because* one of the date shells had, it seems, put out the eye of the genie's son."[1]

No sooner had Wordsworth provided the idea of the expiation, and four or five lines of the ballad, than he withdrew from the undertaking. From the very first evening he felt that it was impossible for him to keep company with the airy genius of Coleridge. "Our respective manners proved so widely different that it would have been quite presumptuous in me to do anything but separate from an undertaking upon which I could only have been a clog."[2]

And though Wordsworth did not entirely refuse to admire this exquisite work when once it was completed, he nevertheless accorded it only, as it were, a regretful and unwilling admiration, which showed too plainly that he was not sensible of all its beauty. He judged it with a coldness surprising in a poet and a friend, and declared it responsible for the failure of the *Lyrical Ballads*. And when Coleridge, hearing of this accusation, wished to withdraw his *Ancient Mariner* from the second edition of the *Ballads*, Wordsworth protested against his doing so, and retained the poem, but did not refrain from conscientiously enumerating its real or supposed defects for the benefit of the reader. He discovered as many as four, and, of these, two are worth mentioning as showing the trend which Wordsworth would have given to the poem had he been its author. "First, that the principal person has no distinct character, either in his profession of Mariner, or as a human being who having been long under the controul of supernatural impressions might be supposed himself to partake of something supernatural." The other, and chief remaining fault which he finds with the poem is, "that the events, having no necessary connexion, do not produce each other."[3] In place of the work which Coleridge, notwith-

---

[1] *Table Talk*, 31st May 1830.   [2] *We are Seven*, prefatory note.
[3] Note to *Lyrical Ballads*, edition published in 1800.

standing Wordsworth's judgment, produced, the latter
would have preferred a narrative in which the mind was
never projected beyond the region of the explained, nor
carried very far from the world of reality.   And, on the
other hand, as if to indemnify himself for having, out of
deference to Wordsworth, introduced some semblance of
reasoning and of probability into *The Ancient Mariner*, it
was entirely by himself that Coleridge wrote his weird
Christabel, that true magic evocation, full of an indescribable
music, in subject mysterious, undefined, incomplete, which
not even the poet himself, it would seem, knew how to
bring to a conclusion.[1]

Meanwhile Wordsworth had also suggested a subject
for a ballad to Coleridge.[2]   The fundamental idea of it
was the same ; that of the desolation wrought by a curse
in a terror-stricken heart.   But Wordsworth brings us
back from the realm of legend and fancy to an anecdote
current in local gossip, an actual and recent event.   Its
scene is no Biblical landscape or Ocean of fable, but an
English country churchyard, where a garrulous old sexton
tells the story of three neighbouring graves, above which
a thorn is in blossom.   Edward, a young farmer, loves
Mary, the daughter of a widow of forty, who, though
still handsome, is violent in temper and capricious.   At
first the widow promised him her child's hand, but afterwards, having herself taken a fancy to the young man, she
attempts to alienate him from her daughter and to win him
for herself.   The meanness and absurdity of the proposition
are both so apparent to Edward that he bursts into a
hysterical fit of laughter, which so enrages the widow that
she falls on her knees and invokes the vengeance of
Heaven against him and against her daughter.   In spite
of this the marriage is celebrated, but the happiness of the
young couple is blasted from the outset by their mother's
curse.   All their attempts to become reconciled to her fail,
and on Ash-Wednesday, before the congregation assembled
in the church, she pronounces a fresh curse upon her
children's friend, Ellen, who had planned their union and

---

[1] Note to *Lyrical Ballads* (edition of 1800)
[2] *The Three Graves.*

helped to bring it about.   Ellen gradually becomes insane, and the life of Mary and Edward is rendered permanently unhappy.

Coleridge wrote only a part of *The Three Graves*.   His want of perseverance, of which the sketches and fragments that bestrew his work as a poet give evidence, is quite enough to account for his failure to finish this ballad. But it is also certain that the subject had no great attraction for him, and that his treatment of it was not altogether calculated to please Wordsworth, with whom the suggestion had originated.   They both thought but little of this fragmentary production afterwards, though for different reasons.

Finally Wordsworth determined that he would himself give concrete form to the idea of a curse.   He found a subject ready to his hand in a scientific work.[1]   It was a story vouched for as true, or rather a medical case, with every detail precisely and plainly stated, so that the poet could follow its different phases one by one without missing a single link of the chain.   Taking the anecdote just as it was, he made no change in it except to transfer the scene from Warwickshire, with which he was unacquainted, to the familiar county of Dorsetshire.   Such was the origin of one of the most unpretentious and therefore of the most daring among his ballads, *Goody Blake and Harry Gill*,[2] " a true story."

> Oh ! what's the matter ? what's the matter ?
> What is't that ails young Harry Gill ?
> That evermore his teeth they chatter,
> Chatter, chatter, chatter still !
> Of waistcoats Harry has no lack,
> Good duffle grey, and flannel fine ;
> He has a blanket on his back,
> And coats enough to smother nine.
>
> In March, December, and in July,
> 'Tis all the same with Harry Gill ;
> The neighbours tell, and tell you truly,
> His teeth they chatter, chatter still.

[1] *Zoonomia, or Laws of Organic Life*, by Erasmus Darwin (1794-1796)
[2] From the text of the *Lyrical Ballads*, 1798.

At night, at morning, and at noon,
'Tis all the same with Harry Gill;
Beneath the sun, beneath the moon,
His teeth they chatter, chatter still!

Young Harry was a lusty drover,
And who so stout of limb as he?
His cheeks were red as ruddy clover;
His voice was like the voice of three.
Old Goody Blake was old and poor;
Ill fed she was, and thinly clad;
And any man who passed her door
Might see how poor a hut she had.

All day she spun in her poor dwelling:
And then her three hours' work at night,
Alas! 'twas hardly worth the telling,
It would not pay for candle-light.
This woman dwelt in Dorsetshire,
Her hut was on a cold hill side,
And in that county coals are dear,
For they come far by wind and tide.

By the same fire to boil their pottage,
Two poor old Dames, as I have known,
Will often live in one small cottage;
But she, poor Woman, dwelt alone.
'Twas well enough, when summer came,
The long, warm, lightsome summer-day,
Then at her door the *canty* Dame
Would sit, as any linnet, gay.

But when the ice our streams did fetter,
Oh then how her old bones would shake!
You would have said, if you had met her,
'Twas a hard time for Goody Blake.
Her evenings then were dull and dead:
Sad case it was, as you may think,
For very cold to go to bed;
And then for cold not sleep a wink.

O joy for her! whene'er in winter
The winds at night had made a rout;
And scattered many a lusty splinter
And many a rotten bough about.

Yet never had she, well or sick,
As every man who knew her says,
A pile beforehand, wood or stick,
Enough to warm her for three days.

Now, when the frost was past enduring,
And made her poor old bones to ache,
Could any thing be more alluring
Than an old hedge to Goody Blake?
And, now and then, it must be said,
When her old bones were cold and chill,
She left her fire, or left her bed,
To seek the hedge of Harry Gill.

Now Harry he had long suspected
This trespass of old Goody Blake;
And vowed that she should be detected—
That he on her would vengeance take.
And oft from his warm fire he'd go,
And to the fields his road would take;
And there, at night, in frost and snow,
He watched to seize old Goody Blake.

And once, behind a rick of barley,
Thus looking out did Harry stand:
The moon was full and shining clearly,
And crisp with frost the stubble land.
—He hears a noise—he's all awake—
Again?—on tip-toe down the hill
He softly creeps—'tis Goody Blake;
She's at the hedge of Harry Gill!

Right glad was he when he beheld her:
Stick after stick did Goody pull:
He stood behind a bush of elder,
Till she had filled her apron full.
When with her load she turned about,
The bye-road back again to take;
He started forward, with a shout,
And sprang upon poor Goody Blake.

And fiercely by the arm he took her,
And by the arm he held her fast,
And fiercely by the arm he shook her,
And cried, " I've caught you then at last! "

Then Goody, who had nothing said,
Her bundle from her lap let fall ;
And, kneeling on the sticks, she prayed
To God that is the judge of all.

She prayed, her withered hand uprearing,
While Harry held her by the arm—
" God ! who art never out of hearing,
O may he never more be warm ! "
The cold, cold moon above her head,
Thus on her knees did Goody pray ;
Young Harry heard what she had said :
And icy cold he turned away.

He went complaining all the morrow
That he was cold and very chill :
His face was gloom, his heart was sorrow,
Alas ! that day for Harry Gill !
That day he wore a riding-coat,
But not a whit the warmer he :
Another was on Thursday brought,
And ere the Sabbath he had three.

'Twas all in vain, a useless matter,
And blankets were about him pinned ;
Yet still his jaws and teeth they clatter.
Like a loose casement in the wind.
And Harry's flesh it fell away ;
And all who see him say, 'tis plain,
That, live as long as live he may,
He never will be warm again.

No word to any man he utters,
A-bed or up, to young or old ;
But ever to himself he mutters,
" Poor Harry Gill is very cold."
A-bed or up, by night or day ;
His teeth they chatter, chatter still.
Now think, ye farmers all, I pray,
Of Goody Blake and Harry Gill !

To place so humble and so crude a ballad by the side
of such a gem as Coleridge's *Ancient Mariner* is no doubt
to present Wordsworth's poetry in the most unfavourable
and the least attractive light. But, on the other hand,

nothing can make us understand better how he longed for tangible reality, how necessary it was for him to hold, as it were, a little of his mother-earth within his fingers, and why he refused to adventure himself, without ballast, in his friend's airy skiff.

This he has acknowledged himself, in the Prologue [1] to *Peter Bell*, which was written after the various unsuccessful attempts made by Coleridge to lure him into the realm of pure fancy. This prologue, which was begun on the 20th April 1798, is a profession of faith in realism, and, at the same time, a farewell, not unmingled with irony, to their schemes for writing supernatural poems together.

The form of this whimsical prologue was occasioned by the appearance of the crescent moon. The poet has dreamed of having a little crescent-shaped boat which would carry him through the air, far away from the earth, far away from human tears and joys. And now we find him sailing aloft, no longer caring " for treasons, tumults, and for wars," and mounting among the stars. Saturn is passed, and the Pleiads, and Mercury and Jupiter. But presently he is smitten with regret. These stars,

> and all that they contain,
> What are they to that tiny grain,
> That darling speck of ours?
>
> Then back to Earth, the dear green Earth :—
> Whole ages if I here should roam,
> The world for my remarks and me
> Would not a whit the better be ;
> I've left my heart at home.
>
> And there it is, the matchless Earth !
> There spreads the famed Pacific Ocean !
> Old Andes thrusts yon craggy spear
> Through the grey clouds ; the Alps are here,
> Like waters in commotion !
>
> Yon tawny slip is Libya's sands ;
> That silver thread the River Dnieper ;
> And look, where clothed in brightest green
> Is a sweet Isle, of isles the Queen ;
> Ye fairies, from all evil keep her !

[1] Earliest text, 1869.

And see the town where I was born!
Around those happy fields we span
In boyish gambols ;—I was lost
Where I have been, but on this coast
I feel I am a man.

Never did fifty things at once
Appear so lovely, never, never ;—
How tunefully the forests ring!
To hear the earth's soft murmuring
Thus could I hang for ever!

In vain the luminous boat rallies the faint-hearted poet,
whose mortal ears are overpowered by "the music of the
spheres," and mocks him for a clumsy fellow who could
only

Creep along the dirt, and pick
His way with his good walking stick,
Just three good miles an hour!

In vain it proposes, instead of the heavens, to explore the
mysterious regions of the earth, the snows of Siberia, or
some delicious land unknown to men :

Fair is that land as evening skies,
And cool, though in the depth it lies
Of burning Africa.

In vain his bark offers to take him to the realm of Faery,
"among the lovely shades of things," or, if he desires to
visit stormier scenes, to show him, by a prompt voyage,

How earth and heaven are taught to feel
The might of magic lore.

These promises are no longer seasonable, and none of
them tempts the poet. The skiff forgets "what on the
earth is doing."

There was a time when all mankind
Did listen with a faith sincere
To tuneful tongues in mystery versed ;
Then Poets fearlessly rehearsed
The wonders of a wild career.

Go—(but the world's a sleepy world,
And 'tis, I fear, an age too late)
Take with you some ambitious Youth !
For, I myself, in very truth,
Am all unfit to be your mate.

Long have I loved what I behold,
The night that calms, the day that cheers ;
The common growth of mother-earth
Suffices me—her tears, her mirth,
Her humblest mirth and tears.

The dragon's wing, the magic ring,
I shall not covet for my dower,
If I along that lowly way
With sympathetic heart may stray,
And with a soul of power.

These given, what more need I desire
To stir, to soothe, or elevate ?
What nobler marvels than the mind
May in life's daily prospect find,
May find or there create ?

A potent wand doth Sorrow wield ;
What spell so strong as guilty Fear !
Repentance is a tender Sprite ;
If aught on earth have heavenly might,
'Tis lodged within her silent tear.

The poet has come down from the ethereal heights where for a moment he dreamed of soaring, and having once more gained a footing on firm ground, proceeds to commemorate the adventures of Peter Bell, the pedlar.

More than four hundred years before Wordsworth, the first great English poet had experienced a similar strange vision. Fresh from the reading of Dante, Chaucer dreamed that he was being carried by a mighty eagle as high as the sphere of the Galaxy, whence the whole earth " no more semed then a prikke." While he was in a mood between

admiration and fright, a characteristic dialogue took place
between the bird and the poet :

> With that this egle gan to crye :
> ' Lat be,' quod he, ' thy fantasye ;
> Wilt thou lere of sterres aught ? '
> ' Nay, certeinly,' quod I, ' right naught.'
> ' And why ? ' ' For I am now to old '
> ' Elles I wolde thee have told,'
> Quod he, ' the sterres names, lo,
> And al the hevenes signes to,
> And which they been.'   ' No fors,' quod I.

As the eagle insisted on teaching him the names and
places of all constellations made famous by mythology and
poetry,

> ' No fors,' quod I, ' hit is no nede :
> I leve as wel, so god me spede,
> Hem that wryte of this matere,
> As though I knew her places here ;
> And eek they shynen here so brighte,
> Hit shulde shenden al my sighte
> To loke on hem.' [1]

Thus did the future realistic painter of the Canterbury
Pilgrims elude the sublime wanderer through heaven and
hell.   Not the milky way, he smilingly admitted, was fit
haunt for himself, but the rutty, inn-bordered road from
the Tabard to St Thomas à Becket's shrine.

How like Chaucer is Wordsworth here—yet how different !   While Chaucer is humorously conscious of his
own limited flight, and represents himself as a tender,
fluttering sparrow in a majestic eagle's talons, Wordsworth
hints that soaring is possible only to those who, lacking
due weight of flesh and bone, are unsubstantial and void
as phantoms.   Far from envying Coleridge, Wordsworth
is inclined to attribute his friend's airy voyages to a want
of the sinews and muscles whose very burden incapacitates
man from spiritual excursions, and of those feelings which
form so many strong links to bind a man to earth.

[1] *The Hous of Fame*, Bk. ii., ll. 991-1017.

Henceforth, then, the field of poetry is definitely allotted. To the share of Coleridge fell such subjects as were supernatural, or at any rate romantic, which he was to endeavour to infuse with a human interest, and with that " semblance of truth sufficient to procure for these shadows of imagination that willing suspension of disbelief for the moment which constitutes poetic faith." [1] Wordsworth's share was to be the events of every-day life, by preference in its humblest form; the characters and incidents of his poems " were to be such as will be found in every village and its vicinity where there is a meditative and feeling mind to seek after them, or to notice them when they present themselves." [2]

Certain hints, dropped by Coleridge in an undertone, show indeed that Wordsworth's choice was to him a matter for some regret. To Hazlitt, who, when quite a young man, in the summer of 1798, came to pay him a visit, " he lamented that Wordsworth was not prone enough to believe in the traditional superstitions of the place, and that there was a something corporeal, a matter-of-factness, a clinging to the palpable, or often to the petty, in his poetry, in consequence. His genius was not a spirit that descended to him through the air; it sprung out of the ground like a flower, or unfolded itself from a green spray, on which the goldfinch sang." [3] But neither Coleridge's regret, nor anything else, induced Wordsworth ever again to turn aside from the path he had elected to follow.

II

Nothing, to all appearance, can be more opposed to the ordinary conception of imagination and poetry than this refusal to leave the ground, to take flight and soar above the low-lying regions which are the scene of man's mean and sorry existence. Wordsworth was so fully conscious of this that he took great care to repudiate on behalf of

[1] *Biographia Literaria,* ch. xiv.   [2] *Ibid.*
[3] Hazlitt, *My first acquaintance with poets.*

the word "imagination" the inaccurate and misleading senses, as he considered them, in which it is employed. Hence the famous distinction between *imagination* and *fancy*, which Coleridge, returning to it at a later time, took such pleasure in following up with the help of the German romantic school. The germ of the distinction, however, was already in existence. All that part of fiction which poetry embraces gradually came to be assigned to the term "fancy." That term denotes the caprice, or habit of wilful misrepresentation, which leads the poet to shed the light of his own feelings over beings and things quite independently of their real aspect, to people the quiet fields with signs of woe, to interpret the raven's blithe croaking as a harbinger of death, the hooting of the owl as a foreboding of evil, and the trills of the nightingale as the voice of mourning and sorrow.[1] Fancy transforms the reality of things just as it pleases, guided by no law but its own pleasure. Its only aim is to divert the mind by means of ingenious comparisons. It is "the power by which pleasure and surprise are excited by sudden varieties of situation and by accumulated imagery."[2] It is, in short, to be regarded with suspicion and held in scant respect, and Wordsworth afterwards grouped by themselves, under the heading *Poems of the Fancy*, such of his compositions as seemed to him of an inferior order.

Imagination, on the other hand, is, as nothing else is, the faculty of seeing nature. It does not seek to afford pleasure by an artificial accumulation of images, or by strange combinations of ideas. It "produces impressive effects out of simple elements."[3]

The poetic art which can command such an instrument is no mere mental recreation. It has the weight and the importance of a science; the same prudence marks its advance, its progress is as steady and as certain, the same truth is alike its aim and its result. In method it resembles a science which proceeds by observation; it demands facts, and requires them to be certain, numerous, verified, and relative to the question at issue. Of all Wordsworth's

---

[1] *A Morning Exercise.*　　[2] *The Thorn* (note to the edition of 1800).
[3] *Ibid.*

poems there is not one of which he cannot analyse the formation, not one which was not originally founded on strong evidence.   Sometimes the foundation is an incident witnessed by himself, which has found its way quite un-modified into his poetry ; sometimes it is an anecdote which was told or read to him, the authorities for which he is able to quote.   Or again he has grouped together a number of distinct and individually true incidents, reducing the part played by invention to a minimum.   After an interval of forty years he still remembers where he met this or that character, where such an image originated, the precise spot in which he experienced a certain sensation.   And the very changes which he occasionally makes in his facts are so fully explained and justified by him that they are less characteristic of the poet's privilege to invent than of the scientific process of experiment.

Far from priding himself on his clever construction of a poem, he is more apt to apologize for such a concession to art, which consists at best in making a selection from among the facts provided by nature.   It involves a sort of violation of the truth, and as such is to be regretted.   The "fable" of a poem is of little consequence ; a fact is a far better foundation.   Yet the poet should concern himself not with the singularity of the fact, but with the impres-sion it may produce.

> My gentle reader, I perceive
> How patiently you've waited,
> And I'm afraid that you expect
> Some tale will be related.
> O reader ! had you in your mind
> Such stores as silent thought can bring,
> O gentle reader ! you would find
> A tale in every thing.
> What more I have to say is short,
> I hope you'll kindly take it :
> It is no tale ; but, should you think,
> Perhaps a tale you'll make it.[1]

The art of keeping the reader breathless throughout a narrative in the hope of penetrating the secret of a compli-

[1] *Simon Lee* (*Lyrical Ballads*, 1798).

cated and mysterious intrigue, though well enough for
Anne Radcliffe, is quite inferior :

> The moving accident is not my trade ;
> To freeze the blood I have no ready arts :
> 'Tis my delight, alone in summer shade,
> To pipe a simple song for thinking hearts.[1]

It was the same contempt for artifice, the same respect
for nature, which led the poet to reform, or rather to sweep
away, " poetic diction." Thus originated that famous revolution which Wordsworth achieved through his *Lyrical
Ballads*, and of which he explained the theory in his
prefaces.

There is nothing to prevent those who look upon
poetry as an intellectual amusement from admitting its
right to a style of its own, an ornamental language independent of that spoken by men ; but the poet, with whom
truth is the first concern, will discard every adornment
which has the effect of throwing a veil before nature.
The ideal language at which he should aim is that of
passion, though he may reasonably despair of ever attaining its full force and beauty, " for his employment is in
some degree mechanical compared with the freedom and
power of real and substantial action and suffering." [2]
Away, therefore, with those anomalies in grammar or
vocabulary, and those traditional figures of speech which
doubtless originated in a direct transcription of the
language of passion, but having gradually acquired an
independent existence, have become their own justification,
and are now used by artificial poets as labels intended to
distinguish their language from that of prose. It is absurd
to pretend " to trick out or to elevate nature." [3] In his
youth Wordsworth had greatly sinned against simplicity
of style, and now he pledged himself to employ for the
future only simple words and expressions. And since he
might make mistakes if he claimed to draw the line between the simple and the artificial on his own authority,
he would acquire a vocabulary by means of observation.

---

[1] *Hart Leap Well* (1800).   [2] Preface to *Lyrical Ballads*, 1802.
[3] *Ibid.* This was the aim of Erasmus Darwin, see above, p. 136.

His style should be taken if possible from actual life, especially from the life of those with whom passion finds the most direct expression, and pays the least regard to conventional figures of speech.   He turns, therefore, to humble and rustic life, as that in which these conditions seemed to be best realized,

... because in that condition the essential passions of the heart find a better soil in which they can attain their maturity, are less under restraint, and speak a plainer and more emphatic language ; because in that condition of life our elementary feelings co-exist in a state of greater simplicity, and, consequently, may be more accurately contemplated and more forcibly communicated ; because the manners of rural life germinate from those elementary feelings, and, from the necessary character of rural occupations, are more easily comprehended, and are more durable ; and, lastly, because in that condition the passions of men are incorporated with the beautiful and permanent forms of nature.[1]

The poet would interfere only in order to make a selection from among these materials of style, and to purify them of such dross as they naturally carry with them.   And the result would be a truly " permanent and philosophical language."

In this theory, so attractive from its excessive simplicity, so thoroughly democratic, all the revolutionary and levelling dreams of Wordsworth's youth had taken refuge after their expulsion from the region of politics.   This violent reaction against the poetry of the eighteenth century is exactly what connects him most closely with that century, that which bears the clearest marks of it, and breathes most thoroughly its spirit of uncompromising simplification. The inflexibility of a theory so unfitted to adapt itself to the multiform requirements of art, the narrowness of its foundation, which, for all its apparent stability, failed to support the poet's work, the rigid principles which he infringed in half, and the best half, of the lines he wrote, are the very essence of all the hasty generalizations which he condemned so strongly everywhere else.   And it was in an evil hour that he attempted to reduce his views to

---

[1] Preface to *Lyrical Ballads*, 1800.

a system. Sometimes he purposely and conscientiously reproduces the common-places of every-day language, using as expletory phrases instead of the usual decorative expressions, such as are flat and awkward, and showing the bare wood devoid of gilding.[1]　At other times he yields to his better genius, and, breaking the fetters he has himself assumed, rises to the true dignity of poetry by interpreting the feelings of the lowly through the nobler language of a poet;[2] but in doing so he runs the risk of being reminded of his principles, and detected in self-contradiction.

Is it, however, in his servile reproduction of ordinary language that we must search for the precise origin and

---

[1] In the matter of expletory phrases Wordsworth's eccentricities, which are so many protests against the customary forms of embellishment, may be referred to one or other of two principal groups. They serve either to locate objects with the scrupulous exactitude of a surveyor, *e.g.*:

> This thorn you on your left espy;
> And to the left, *three yards beyond,*
> You see a little muddy pond
> Of water, never dry;
> I've measured it from side to side:
> *This three feet long, and two feet wide.* (*The Thorn*);

or else to substantiate his narrative by the profuse asseverations of a witness whose veracity is liable to suspicion (as is always the case with poets), *e.g.*:

> By the same fire to boil their pottage,
> Two poor old dames, *as I have known,*
> Will often live in one small cottage,
> But she, poor woman, dwelt alone. (*Goody Blake and Harry Gill.*)

> Yet never had she, well or sick,
> *As every one who knew her says,*
> A pile before-hand, wood or stick,
> Enough to warm her for three days. (*Ibid.*)

> And Harry's flesh it fell away;
> *And all who see him say 'tis plain,*
> That, live as long as live he may,
> He never will be warm again. (*Ibid.*)

[2] Mr Myers has very appropriately cited the following lines, the poetry of which is a superb protest against their author's theory (*Wordsworth*, by F. W. H. Myers, 1885). They are spoken by a peasant woman whose son had gone to sea, and had been unheard of for seven years.

> Perhaps some dungeon hears thee groan,
> Maimed, mangled by inhuman men;
> Or thou, upon a desert thrown,
> Inheritest the lion's den;
> Or hast been summoned to the deep,
> Thou, thou and all thy mates, to keep
> An incommunicable sleep. (*The affliction of Margaret*, 1804.)

the exact nature of Wordsworth's failing? Other poets, since Wordsworth's day, have imitated more scrupulously than he the simple speech of country folk, and even their dialect and peculiarities of pronunciation, without ever lapsing into prosaicism.[1] To tell the truth, a dangerous model had come between Wordsworth and nature, in the shape of popular poetry. He has himself declared that English poetry had been "absolutely redeemed" by the collection of old ballads published by Percy in 1765. "I do not think," he says, "that there is an able writer in verse of the present day who would not be proud to acknowledge his obligations to the *Reliques ;* I know that it is so with my friends; and, for myself, I am happy in this occasion to make a public avowal of my own."[2] Now of all the poems in that celebrated collection, there was one in particular which haunted Wordsworth's mind, and affords a perfect example of the style at which he aimed in his own ballads—namely, the popular tale of *The Children in the Wood*,[3] wherein two little orphans are entrusted by their dying parents to the guardianship of an uncle, who has them put to death in order to obtain possession of their property. The pathetic story is entirely unadorned by any literary graces. Half of the stanzas consist of bare statements of fact.

> The father left his little son,
>   As plainlye doth appeare,
> When he to perfect age should come,
>   Three hundred pounds a yeare.
>
> And to his little daughter Jane
>   Five hundred poundes in gold,
> To be paid downe on marriage-day,
>   Which might not be controll'd :
> But if the children chance to dye,
>   Ere they to age should come,
> Their uncle should possesse their wealth ;
>   For so the wille did run.

The expression of feeling is confined to the plainest

---

[1] See Tennyson, *The Grandmother, The Northern Farmer*, &c.
[2] Essay supplementary to the Preface.   [3] *Percy*, viii. 19.

language possible, and the emotion it arouses is indisputable, although rhyme and rhythm are perhaps insufficient to raise it many degrees above that which the same narrative would excite in the form of prose :

> Now, brother, said the dying man,
>   Look to my children deare ;
> Be good unto my boy and girl,
>   No friendes else have they here :
> To God and you I recommend
>   My children deare this daye ;
> But little while be sure we have
>   Within this world to staye.
>
> You must be father and mother both,
>   And uncle all in one ;
> God knowes what will become of them,
>   When I am dead and gone.
> With that bespake their mother deare,
>   O brother kinde, quoth shee,
> You are the man must bring our babes
>   To wealth or miserie :
>
> And if you keep them carefully,
>   Then God will you reward ;
> But if you otherwise should deal,
>   God will your deedes regard.
> With lippes as cold as any stone,
>   They kist their children small :
> God bless you both, my children deare ;
>   With that the teares did fall.

Stanzas now prosaic, now full of simple grace, follow one another throughout the poem. Here we have a common-place relation of the plot laid by the uncle in conjunction with the two ruffians, who, under the pretence of taking them to London, are to carry the children to a lonely spot and kill them; there the painful yet charming description of the children's delight when they set out :

> Away then went those pretty babes,
>   Rejoycing at that tide,
> Rejoycing with a merry minde,
>   They should on cock-horse ride.

> They prate and prattle pleasantly,
> As they rode on the waye,
> To those that should their butchers be
> And work their lives decaye.

Further on we come to a matter-of-fact account of the fight between the two robbers, one of whom relents, refuses to commit the crime, and kills his more obdurate companion. A single poignant touch relieves the colourless recital, when we are told that during the struggle in an unfrequented wood " the babes did quake for feare"! Bitterly complaining of hunger the children are led a great distance by the good robber, who finally leaves them alone, promising to return with food. Then come two wonderful verses in which popular poetry reaches its highest perfection simply by means of detail, or, in other words, of facts, without the least embellishment or inflation of style.

> These pretty babes, with hand in hand,
> Went wandering up and downe ;
> But never more could see the man
> Approaching from the towne :
> Their prettye lippes with black-berries
> Were all besmear'd and dyed,
> And when they sawe the darksome night,
> They sat them down and cryed.

> Thus wandered these poor innocents,
> Till deathe did end their grief,
> In one another's armes they dyed,
> As wanting due relief :
> No burial "this" pretty "pair"
> Of any man receives,
> Till Robin-red-breast piously
> Did cover them with leaves.

Lastly we have an account, devoid of either art or beauty, though clearly and circumstantially told, of the remorse and punishment of the guilty man.

Now not only is there, in the perfect simplicity of both the manner and the style of the two central stanzas, an inimitable charm and a world of grace and pathos, but also in the ballad as a whole, in spite of certain tame or awkward passages, there is such a harmony that any one who should venture to introduce the least modification by way of embellishment must, it would appear, be very ill-advised. Addison, to whom belongs the merit of having unearthed it somewhere or other, had derived " a most exquisite pleasure" from its perusal, and had gone so far as to express the thoroughly Wordsworthian opinion, that " only those who are endowed with a true greatness of Soul and Genius can divest themselves of the little Images of Ridicule, and admire Nature in her Simplicity and Nakedness." But Addison was assuredly in error when he asserted that there was a " despicable Simplicity in the Verse," and that the narrative was delivered " in an abject Phrase and Poorness of Expression."[1] Wordsworth was right in believing that the character of the language in this poem was an essential part of the whole powerful effect, and that since the style consisted simply of an absolutely sincere and disinterested statement of facts, and therefore derived all its value from the truth with which feelings were expressed and events described, it possessed, at any rate in places, the sure marks of imperishability.

One fact, however, of which Wordsworth makes no admission, must not be overlooked. In this, as in almost all popular poems, an unadorned style has the support of a genuine drama, we might almost venture to say a melodrama,[2] in which several scenes, by turns graceful, tender and tragic, stand out so strongly in relief, afford such a sustained emotional interest, and are so universally appreciable, that the poet could not do better than allow his narrative to speak for itself.

But the less of dramatic interest the subject of a ballad contains the more important and essential becomes the function of the poet himself. In his poem of *Lucy Gray*,[3] at any rate, Wordsworth grasped this fact. Here there is practically no drama at all; but, above and beyond the

---

[1] *The Spectator*, No. 85.
[2] The ballad was in reality founded on a drama dating back to the Renaissance: *Two Lamentable Tragedies* (1601).
[3] Written in 1799.

touching qualities which the subject itself nevertheless possesses, the poet has redeemed its inferiority by some exquisite verses thoroughly characteristic of his poetic style :

> No Mate, no comrade Lucy knew ;
> She dwelt on a wide Moor,
> —*The sweetest Thing that ever grew*
> *Beside a human door !*

> You yet may spy the Fawn at play,
> The Hare upon the Green ;
> But the sweet face of Lucy Gray
> Will never more be seen.

At her father's bidding Lucy went out to meet her mother, but was caught in a snowstorm and never came back. All night the parents explored the roads, the fields, and the hill ; and at daybreak her mother espied her footmarks. They traced them as far as the middle of the plank across the river close to their dwelling, but "further there were none."

> Yet some maintain that to this day
> She is a living Child ;
> That you may see sweet Lucy Gray
> Upon the lonesome Wild.

> O'er rough and smooth she trips along
> And never looks behind ;
> And sings a solitary song
> That whistles in the wind.

By means of a few pleasing figures,—the writer of the *Two Children* had not allowed himself a single one,—with the help, too, of the concluding legend, which carries over the slender subject into the realm of dreams, Wordsworth has here been able to contend, upon fairly equal terms, with the superiority of the popular ballad in respect of theme. But when he has neither drama nor legend to deal with, and, at the same time, sets himself to reproduce a simple emotion with as little obtrusion of himself as possible, the result is that he writes such pieces as *An Anecdote for Fathers* or *Alice Fell*.[1]

Now, in the case of poems like these, where Wordsworth intentionally chose the subject for the very reasons that it was lacking in interest and that most people would have passed it by without a moment's pause, the important thing is necessarily the poet's imagination or feeling, which has led him to consider the subject worthy of attention and to render it so for others. If, however, he merely reproduces the fact in its natural crudity, and abstains from contributing to it anything of his own, he will simply have added one more to the multitude of incidents which contain food for thought or emotion, but nevertheless pass unnotic '. It is not enough to photograph them; in other words, to present a picture, accurate indeed, but far inferior to reality. They must be raised to the level of beauty and of poetry. If we are to derive from them the same emotion as the poet, he must represent them to us as modified by his emotion. He must find out the poetic equivalent of each one of their details. *Art* must intervene, and to art we can refuse neither the right nor the duty of refining, not incidents alone, but also the language in which they are described. On no other condition can our imagination, henceforth beset by the wavering outlines of some poetic vision, and our memory haunted by the sound of lines more harmonious, phrases more pleasing or more compact than ordinary speech, strengthen our sensibility, and render it more delicate in presence of these events of every-day experience. And in practice, after all, Wordsworth has, as a rule, conceded this place to art, though not always. In his theory he makes no admission of it.[2]

---

[1] See above, p. 314 and p. 317.

[2] To be complete, an appreciation of Wordsworth's theory of poetry would involve a systematic statement of the laws poetics in general, and cannot be entered upon within the limits of this book. Almost an entire work, moreover, has already been devoted to it—a volume so admirable in its critical chapters as to be almost a standard work, and in any case greatly superior to anything which has since been written on the same subject; I mean the *Biographia Literaria* of Coleridge.

Having, however, fully recognised the extremes into which Wordsworth was led, carried away, as he was, by his tendency to systematize, and blinded also by his admiration for popular poetry, we may justly praise the utter scorn of conventional forms of embellishment and the sincere love of truth which inspired his theory of the art. It was through the lofty conception he had formed of his own calling that Wordsworth had arrived at a doctrine which Malherbe himself, scant as was his respect for the claims of the imagination, would have regarded as rigorous to excess. We can see clearly enough, too, the fundamental difference between this revolution in poetic style and that which Hugo effected, thirty years later, in France. Wordsworth has less desire to extend than to limit the vocabulary. He would have poetry use no other words than those employed in prose. Hugo would have it employ all words admissible in prose in addition to its own. The English poet, regarding words as at best but a veil which covers the naked thought, endeavours to attenuate them to the utmost possible limit. The Frenchman prostrates himself in adoration before verbal signs, " for the term is the Word, and the Word is God." Hence the difference between their faults of style ; the one tending, and purposely tending, to become more prosaic, the other, to become more pompous. The one reminds us of the Quakers who sympathized with the Revolution at its commencement, because it seemed to promise the abolition of distinctions and ornaments which in their eyes were worthless, and at the same time an increase in the importance of man's simple and essential qualities. The other, though agreed with the first upon the overthrow of a feeble and effete nobility, soon diverges from him in order to build up a new and imperial nobility out of fortunate adventurers, full-blooded and vigorous, restless and blustering, who, anxious to prove their titles by displaying them, flaunt themselves in gaudier plumes than those of the men they have dispossessed, or, finding the satisfaction of their pride in parading their plebeian origin, pass off vulgarity with haughty insolence.

And now to recapitulate. One by one Wordsworth

discards, or rather rejects with contempt, all the peculiar privileges which from time immemorial the poet has enjoyed. He denies himself the marvellous; he will have none of either fiction or fable; scarcely even will he admit the need of a subject. With a gesture he sweeps aside all the time-honoured flowers of language, though around them, like a faded perfume, lingers the faint recollection of the hour when some early observer gathered them in the open air. He declares himself the obedient interpreter of that reality which seems the absolute antithesis of poetry.

> To the solid ground
> Of nature trusts the Mind that builds for aye;
> Convinced that there, there only, she can lay
> Secure foundations.[1]

Even this, however, is too much to say. Reality itself is at times not only eccentric but even monstrous. It has its exceptions, no less perplexing than the wildest chimera which ever sprang from a fantastic brain. The poet who describes an actual shipwreck or an earthquake which really occurred can very well do without additions of his own invention. But Wordsworth renounces the extraordinary features of reality, no less than those of fiction. The mountains which occupy so large a place in his work appear in it only by accident, if I may say so—because he was born and had lived among them, and because he never describes anything but what has presented itself to his senses. They are unnecessary to his poetry, and almost inconsistent with his doctrine. The peculiar province of Wordsworth is that of the *common*. Wherever selection was possible he held it his duty to borrow nothing from those elements of the world which are marvellous or unusual.

But when he had thus thrown to the winds all the customary auxiliary resources of poetry, what was left to prove his claim to the title of poet? There remained a powerful imagination directed upon common objects, and upon the simple incidents of life. What Wordsworth saw or heard or felt was of little consequence; the important

---

[1] Sonnet, *A volant tribe of Bards.*

thing was the manner in which he saw, heard, and felt, and how he interpreted his sensations. Properly understood, every poem he wrote is an imaginative lesson of striking psychological truth. Far from concealing the transitions by means of which he had passed from the ordinary or prosaic to the imaginative or poetic state of mind, like an Alpine guide he makes us place our feet where his own have been set, and feel each step he himself has climbed. Whereas the generality of poets present us with nothing more than the result of their precious sensations, Wordsworth makes it his purpose to reveal to us the mystery of his own, to analyse them, and to distinguish the several stages of their growth,[1] that we in our turn may recognise and reproduce them within ourselves. With prudent deliberation, and without ever allowing us to lose sight of our starting-point, he raises us step by step above the gross soil of earth to an upper world, from the height of which we ask ourselves whether that matter, which all the while is lying beneath our eyes, has any existence.

[1] *The Leech Gatherer*, or *Resolution and Independence*, may be studied from this point of view. A suggestive comparison might be drawn between this poem and the well-known passage of *The Journal of the Plague Year*, wherein Defoe relates how he (or the fictitious journalist), as he was walking along the Thames at Blackwall, was confronted by a poor waterman whose resignation and faith, in the midst of the most heart-rending affliction, shamed his own feverish alarm. The theme is almost identical; the two accounts vie in simplicity of style and minuteness of detail. But Defoe (in this instance more truly artistic) had the sombre and awful background of plague-stricken London to set off his touching anecdote, while the more philosophical poet has made his story absolutely bare of dramatic interest, and wholly dependent for its effect on the wonder-working eye which saw an indifferent sight, and the imaginative ear which listened to a tale of common distress.

CHAPTER IV

The Imagination and the Senses

I

WORDSWORTH'S veneration for accurate facts and minute details is consistent with the turn of mind of the nation from which he sprang. He has his full share of that "mental materialism" which Emerson[1] considered the principal characteristic of the English mind, and detected not only in the novel-writers of the realistic school, in Swift, who "describes his fictitious persons as if for the police," in Defoe, whose habit of amassing small but precise items of information borders on prolixity, but even in the most abstract thinkers, such as the platonist Henry More, and William Browne the transcendentalist.

This forms a connecting link, either real or apparent, between Wordsworth and the poet who was both his predecessor and his contemporary, and had anticipated him in urging the claims of reality in opposition to fancy. In *The Village* Crabbe had already raised a protest against the fictitious in poetry by narrating in verse such anecdotes of human life as had come to his knowledge, and providing his characters with a background which owed nothing to invention. Nevertheless, not only is the vein of gloomy satire which runs through the work of Crabbe the exact opposite of Wordsworth's optimism, but the two poets have seen reality in entirely different lights; the contrast between which Wordsworth is most careful to bring out whenever he speaks of Crabbe.[2] While for Crabbe, reality is, as it were, a hard, impenetrable substance against which his mind beats itself, only to find the approaches to the

[1] *English Traits*, Literature.
[2] Among other instances, see the introductory note to *Lucy Gray*.

supersensible world stubbornly closed, for Wordsworth
it possesses the power of melting away, of becoming
spiritualized, until the eye of the poet obtains through it,
if not a steady view, at least a glimpse of the ideal world.
For each, reality is the object of his persistent attention ;
but, while to Crabbe it seems ever heavier, more oppressive, and more sombre, to the steadfast gaze of Wordsworth it becomes gradually lighter and more effulgent,
until it vanishes in pure light. By the one it is endured,
by the other transfigured, yet with one consent they
acknowledge it as the only legitimate object of poetry.
For although, in Wordsworth's opinion, there is no other
field for the exercise of the imagination than reality, we
are not on that account to suppose that he makes it the
slave of the real, or that he would have it inert and
passive, reflecting the aspects of the universe like a lifeless
mirror. He regards it, on the contrary, as an active, living
force, working upon nature no less than nature works upon
it, half creating the world, half perceiving it.[1] Nor does this
mean that the imagination effects an artificial transformation
of natural objects, which has no truth nor deep significance.
" Like the moisture or the polish on a pebble, genius neither
distorts nor false-colours its objects ; but on the contrary
brings out many a vein and many a tint, which escape the
eye of common observation, thus raising to the rank of
gems what had been often kicked away by the hurrying
foot of the traveller on the dusty high-road of custom." [2]
The imagination sees accurately, but because its vision
is powerful it sees what has never been seen, or
sees better and more clearly the objects which are displayed before the gaze of all men. It is indeed an
illumination proceeding from the soul,

> the gleam,
> The light that never was, on sea or land,
> The consecration, and the Poet's dream.[3]

[1] *Tintern Abbey*, l. 106 (*Lyrical Ballads*, 1798).
[2] Coleridge, *Biographia Literaria*, ch. xxii. The same image was afterwards
employed by Wordsworth in his sonnet, " Happy the feeling from the bosom
thrown " (1827).
[3] Wordsworth, *Peele Castle* (1805).

Shed abroad upon the world, this light brings forth its
beauty; a beauty which no doubt exists, though latent,
and hidden from the great majority. It is the poet's
business to render it distinct; his office "to give the
charm of novelty to things of every day, and to excite
a feeling analogous to the supernatural, by awakening
the mind's attention from the lethargy of custom, and
directing it to the loveliness and the wonders of the world
before us; an inexhaustible treasure, but for which, in
consequence of the film of familiarity and selfish solici-
tude, we have eyes, yet see not, ears that hear not, and
hearts that neither feel nor understand."[1]   A landscape
lighted by the moon, or gilded by the rays of the setting
sun, is no less *true* than the same landscape seen by the
dull light of a cloudy sky. It is the same; yet how
different—how much more beautiful, how much more
impressive! Under the influence of that celestial radiance a transformation seems to have been wrought—
nay, rather, a creation. Thus, too, may genius create;
thus, in fact, does the genius of Wordsworth create.
"In life's every-day appearances," he said,

> I seemed to gain clear sight
> Of a new world—a world, too, that was fit
> To be transmitted, and to other eyes
> Made visible; as ruled by those fixed laws
> Whence spiritual dignity originates,
> Which do both give it being and maintain
> A balance, an ennobling interchange
> Of action from without and from within;
> The excellence, pure function, and best power
> Both of the object seen, and eye that sees.[2]

II

This new world is the true one; the world revealed to
man by his immediate sensations, before they have been
disintegrated by analysis; the world of the senses, but

[1] Coleridge, *Biographia Literaria*, ch. xiv.
[2] *The Prelude*, xiii. 368-378.

of senses as yet neither perverted by reasoning nor
blunted by use. Every one of man's fundamental errors
arises from the fact that he no longer simply *feels* nature,
that he neither *sees* nor *hears* her, but that a rapid and
almost irresistible act of his intelligence causes him immediately to reason upon what he feels, hears, and sees.
Wordsworth believes himself to be a poet, because he,
for his part, beholds the earth with the eyes of the first
human being, as if he "were her first-born birth, and
none had lived before" him.[1] He is a poet-philosopher
because he has the "inevitable" eye and ear. The
senses are the only great metaphysicians; they alone,
at certain moments, can grasp the central life of the
world, the essence of truth. The highest knowledge
possible to man concerning himself and the world around
him will be attained when he places himself in the
heart of nature and occupies himself merely with ab-
sorbing the impressions of sense.

If a friend reproaches Wordsworth with spending the
day in dreaming in the open air, and with neglecting
books, "that light bequeathed to Beings else forlorn
and blind," the poet replies:

> The eye—it cannot chuse but see,
> We cannot bid the ear be still;
> Our bodies feel, where'er they be,
> Against or with our will.
>
> Nor less I deem that there are powers
> Which of themselves our minds impress,
> That we can feed this mind of ours
> In a wise passiveness.
>
> Think you, 'mid all this mighty sum
> Of things for ever speaking,
> That nothing of itself will come,
> But we must still be seeking?[2]

He questions his friend in his turn and reproaches him
with giving all his time to reading:

---

[1] *Expostulation and Reply (Lyrical Ballads, 1798)*   [2] *Ibid.*

Books! 'tis a dull and endless strife,
Come, hear the woodland linnet,
How sweet his music; on my life,
There's more of wisdom in it.

And hark! how blithe the throstle sings!
And he is no mean preacher;
Come forth into the light of things,
Let Nature be your teacher.

She has a world of ready wealth,
Our minds and hearts to bless—
Spontaneous wisdom breathed by health,
Truth breathed by chearfulness.

One impulse from a vernal wood
May teach you more of man;
Of moral evil and of good,
Than all the sages can.

Sweet is the lore which Nature brings;
Our meddling intellect
Mis-shapes the beauteous forms of things;
We murder to dissect.

Enough of science and of art;
Close up these barren leaves;
Come forth, and bring with you a heart
That watches and receives.[1]

This is "sensualism," but as far removed from sensuality, as spiritual, as possible; the sensualism of the philosopher whom at this very time Coleridge and Wordsworth admired above all others, that of Berkeley, who extolled the divine and universal language of the senses, and said that "vision is the language of the Author of Nature."

Not for its own sake does Wordsworth glorify sensation, nor for the pleasure or pain which accompanies it, but for what it reveals. Neither is it on account of the clear knowledge of detail which it supplies to the intelligence; but because each single impression, taken as a

[1] *The Tables Turned* (*Lyrical Ballads*, 1798).

whole, with all the mystery in which it is enveloped,
contains a conception of the world. Yet how difficult
it is to understand the pure, spontaneous language of the
senses! No sooner is it uttered than reason interposes to
misconstrue it under the pretence of correction and explanation. And yet, even to-day, after so many centuries
of inherited reasoning, we are not altogether unable to
discover within us some traces of the first integral sensations. Doubtless the concurrence of circumstances, of
man's outward surroundings and inward moods, are now
required before they can arise within him. There must
be something peculiar in the sensation if it is to yield,
even to a slight extent, the revelation which was originally
obtained without an effort. The soul is no longer thrown
into the visionary state by any chance sound, heard no
matter where or when. Yet in childhood, among the
fields, a strange call like the cuckoo's can give rise to it
still.

O blithe New-comer! I have heard,
I hear thee and rejoice:
O Cuckoo! shall I call thee Bird,
Or but a wandering Voice?

While I am lying on the grass
I hear thy restless shout;
From hill to hill it seems to pass
About and all about!

I hear thee babbling to the Vale
Of sunshine and of flowers,
And unto me thou bring'st a tale
Of visionary hours.

Thrice welcome, Darling of the Spring!
Even yet thou art to me
No Bird, but an invisible Thing,
A voice, a mystery.

The same whom in my Schoolboy days
I listen'd to; that Cry
Which made me look a thousand ways
In bush, and tree, and sky.

To seek thee did I often rove
Through woods and on the green ;
And thou wert still a hope, a love ;
Still longed for, never seen !

And I can listen to thee yet ;
Can lie upon the plain
And listen, till I do beget
That golden time again.

O blessèd Bird ! the earth we pace
Again appears to be
An unsubstantial, faery place ;
That is fit home for Thee ! [1]

This vanishing of the material world is for the poet a higher and more certain truth than the most ingenious philosophical edifice built up by the understanding of man. For sensation that in no way depends upon man is divine, and its teaching sacred.   But to use the senses for no other purpose than to draw up the catalogue of nature's sights and sounds, in the hope of thereby attaining to perfect knowledge, is to put them to the least valuable of their uses.   Every sensation ought to bring us, and actually does bring us, into touch, not with the object which gives it birth, but with the soul which that object conceals,—with absolute truth.   It is a dialogue between the *soul* of man and the *soul* of external things.   The senses provide the means, the object the occasion.   Higher minds are

By sensible impressions not enthralled,
But by their quickening impulse made more prompt
To hold fit converse with the spiritual world. [2]

Our belief in matter is due to reasoning.   Things gradually lose their opacity and become transparent, if our senses are sufficiently keen.   When sensation has reached its utmost intensity, there remains in the whole universe but one life, one being, one reality, of which we cannot say

[1] *The Cuckoo* (1802), first printed in 1807.
[2] *The Prelude*, xiv. 106-108.   (1802.)

whether it is an infinite development of ourselves, or an infinite in which we are absorbed.

For these unspeakable moments of life there is a name—that of " ecstasy." Ecstasy is not sensation itself, although it cannot arise without it. But the sensation must vanish in giving it birth. The glory of the soul breaks forth " when the light of sense goes out, but with a flash that has revealed the invisible world."[1] This is

> that blessed mood,
> In which the burthen of the mystery,
> In which the heavy and the weary weight
> Of all this unintelligible world,
> Is lightened :—that serene and blessed mood,
> In which the affections gently lead us on,—
> Until, the breath of this corporeal flame
> And even the motion of our human blood
> Almost suspended, we are laid asleep
> In body, and become a living soul :
> While with an eye made quiet by the power
> Of harmony, and the deep power of joy,
> We see into the life of things.[2]

But on these heights, attainable though they may be, it is doubtless impossible to abide. Their atmosphere is such as man can scarcely breathe.

> Too, too contracted are these walls of flesh,
> This vital warmth too cold, these visual orbs,
> Though inconceivably endowed, too dim
> For any passion of the soul that leads
> To ecstasy.[3]

Nevertheless, if ecstasy is of its own nature rare, brief, and incommunicable, it does not depart without leaving beneficent traces behind it. Thence springs whatever of sublimity there is in man. The poet refers the origin of the sublime within himself to the ecstasies of terror he had known as a child amid the mysterious sounds of nature :

[1] *The Prelude*, vi. 600-602. [2] *Tintern Abbey (Lyrical Ballads, 1798).*
[3] *The Excursion*, iv. 179-183.

> I would walk alone,
> Under the quiet stars, and at that time
> Have felt whate'er there is of power in sound
> To breathe an elevated mood, by form
> Or image unprofaned; and I would stand,
> If the night blackened with a coming storm,
> Beneath some rock, listening to notes that are
> The ghostly language of the ancient earth,
> Or make their dim abode in distant winds.
> Thence did I drink the visionary power;
> And deem not profitless those fleeting moods
> Of shadowy exultation: not for this,
> That they are kindred to our purer mind
> And intellectual life; but that the soul,
> Remembering *how* she felt, but what she felt
> Remembering not, retains an obscure sense
> Of possible sublimity, whereto
> With growing faculties she doth aspire,
> With faculties still growing, feeling still
> That whatsoever point they gain, they yet
> Have something to pursue.[1]

But the function of the senses is by no means limited to implanting in the human mind the idea of the sublime. They bring man into the immediate presence of divinity. The God of the pantheists, instead of being the final term of a chain of syllogisms, may become the pure product of sensation. When, in the midst of nature, the poet has freely opened his sense to every impression, he has felt at certain moments the universal life.

> I have *felt*
> A presence that disturbs me with the joy
> Of elevated thoughts; a sense sublime
> Of something far more deeply interfused,
> Whose dwelling is the light of setting suns,
> And the round ocean and the living air,
> And the blue sky, and in the mind of man:
> A motion and a spirit, that impels
> All thinking things, all objects of all thought,
> And rolls through all things.[2]

[1] *The Prelude*, ii. 302-322.
[2] *Tintern Abbey*, ll. 92-102 (*Lyrical Ballads*, 1798).

The poet no longer merely believes in God; he sees Him. For him the universe becomes, as it were, the transparent veil of divinity. The sound of the world is, in a manner, God's voice perceptible to the senses:

> I have seen
> A curious child, who dwelt upon a tract
> Of inland ground, applying to his ear
> The convolutions of a smooth-lipped shell;
> To which, in silence hushed, his very soul
> Listened intensely; and his countenance soon
> Brightened with joy; for from within were heard
> Murmurings, whereby the monitor expressed
> Mysterious union with its native sea.
> Even such a shell the universe itself
> Is to the ear of Faith; and there are times,
> I doubt not, when to you it doth impart
> Authentic tidings of invisible things;
> Of ebb and flow, and ever-during power;
> And central peace, subsisting at the heart
> Of endless agitation. Here you stand,
> Adore, and worship, when you know it not;
> Pious beyond the intention of your thought;
> Devout above the meaning of your will.
> —Yes, you have felt, and may not cease to feel.
> The estate of man would be indeed forlorn
> If false conclusions of the reasoning power
> Made the eye blind, and closed the passages
> Through which the ear converses with the heart.[1]

If God is thus the gift of the senses, it is evident that they also yield a knowledge of the good and the beautiful. Since a theodicy can be derived from them, so also can an ethic and an æsthetic.

> [I was] well pleased to recognise
> In nature and the language of the sense
> The anchor of my purest thoughts, the nurse,
> The guide, the guardian of my heart, and soul
> Of all my moral being.[2]

---

[1] *The Excursion*, iv. 1132-1155.
[2] *Tintern Abbey*, ll. 107-111 (*Lyrical Ballads*, 1798).

.   .   .   .   .
> [I knew] that Nature never did betray
> The heart that loved her; 'tis her privilege,
> Through all the years of this our life, to lead
> From joy to joy,

such is her power to "impress with quietness and beauty," and to "feed with lofty thoughts." [1]   The mind of one whose senses have been thus versed in Nature becomes "a mansion for all lovely forms"; his memory "as a dwelling-place for all sweet sounds and harmonies." [2]   By this means, in spite of the sorrows of mankind, the poet was enabled to strengthen himself in the "cheerful faith that all which we behold is full of blessings." [3]   Within himself he felt the pleasures of the senses changed in some obscure manner into virtue.   To them he owed those feelings

> Of unremembered pleasure; such, perhaps,
> As have no slight or trivial influence
> On that best portion of a good man's life,
> His little, nameless, unremembered, acts
> Of kindness and of love. [4]

> Thus deeply drinking in the soul of things,
> We shall be wise perforce   .   .   .
> .   .   .   Whate'er we see
> Or feel, shall tend to quicken and refine;
> Shall fix, in calmer seats of moral strength,
> Earthly desires; and raise, to loftier heights
> Of divine love, our intellectual soul.

Man will learn his "duties from all forms" presented to his view.   One who contemplates those natural objects alone which "excite no morbid passions, no disquietude, no vengeance, and no hatred—needs must feel the joy" of the "pure principle of love."   He will shed this love around him, and forgetting his aversion, will feel "a holy tender-

---

[1] *Tintern Abbey*, ll. 122-128 (*Lyrical Ballads*, 1798).   [2] *Ibid.*, ll. 129-132.
[3] *Ibid.*, ll. 132-133.   [4] *Ibid.*, ll. 30-35.

ness pervade his frame." Looking about him, he "seeks for good, and finds the good he seeks." [1]

Is this really the effect produced by Nature and the senses? Do they in truth convey such teaching? It is a bold challenge—that which Wordsworth hurls at those who see in Nature a force which is blind, deaf, dumb, immoral and stupid, and accuse the senses of insidious suggestions or licentious counsels. Coleridge had made trial of the same cure as Wordsworth and amidst the same scenes, and, finding himself incapable of happiness in the presence of nature, recognised that we cannot hope " from outward forms to win the passion and the life whose fountains are within." [2] We have seen that he explained the very happiness of Wordsworth as the source and not the result of his natural religion. The calm confidence, therefore, with which Wordsworth declares his faith may occasion some surprise. Nevertheless he is sincere, and, as regards the restricted side of Nature with which his poetry deals, and so far as concerns his own senses—at once so penetrative and so defective—he is even truthful.

III

Observe that the senses of which he speaks are sight and hearing. The world he praises is that of the eye and the ear, by which it is half created, half perceived. After quoting so freely from *The Prelude*, it is needless to prove by further evidence the power and intensity of these two senses in Wordsworth's case. The best poetry he wrote is formed from the impressions they yielded him. But however vigorous and acute, they were not chiefly, or not solely, enamoured of beautiful forms and harmonious sounds.

[1] *The Excursion*, iv. 1207-1274. (This passage was written in 1798.) I do not remember to have seen it noticed how strong a resemblance this fine passage bears to Akenside's *Pleasures of the Imagination* (Bk. III., ll. 568-633), a likeness that is perceptible not in the subject and ideas only, nor merely in the general sweep of the verse, but also in many particular touches and striking phrases. Coleridge, who was in youth a professed admirer of Akenside, may have been the medium of communication between the two poets.

[2] *Ode to Dejection.*

It is agreed by all those who have described Wordsworth that the expression of his eyes was that rather of the "Seer" than of the artist. Hazlitt tells us that there was a fire in his eye "as if he saw something in objects more than the outward appearance."[1] De Quincey had seen his eyes "after a long day's toil in walking, . . . assume an appearance the most solemn and spiritual that it is possible for the human eye to wear. The light which resides in them . . . seems to come from unfathomed depths."[2] So, too, Leigh Hunt: "Certainly I never beheld eyes that looked so inspired or supernatural. They were like fires half burning, half smouldering, with a sort of acrid fixture of regard. . . . One might imagine Ezekiel or Isaiah to have had such eyes."[3] Never satisfied with the pure form or colour of things, the poet's gaze, in fact, always sought to discern the soul or ideal contained within them. Did he not protest against the tyranny of the *bodily eye*, that most despotic of all the senses, which, if we yield to its appetite for physical beauty, prevents us from spiritualizing things, and delights to compare and to criticize the outward form, when the important thing is to discover the spirit within? Accordingly the poet made vigorous efforts to delay the coming of that time of visionary impotence when the eye is made subservient to the reasoning faculty.

The ear, in Wordsworth, was similarly cultivated, or, rather, uncultivated. A thousand subtle suggestions of natural sounds amply prove the pitch of acuteness to which this sense was developed in him, but its development was in no wise artistic. Doubtless other poets have, like him, been devoid of the ear for music. In Wordsworth it was entirely wanting, and he was long unable to distinguish one air from another. But his ear for poetic rhythm, even, was not trained to a high degree of perfection. He remarked that Coleridge was "a perfect epicure to sounds." He was not so himself. His earliest poems were rugged and distressing to the ear, and the beauty of the most beautiful lines of his

---

[1] *My first acquaintance with poets.*   [2] *The Lake Poets*, Wordsworth.
[3] *The autobiography of Leigh Hunt* (London, 1860), p. 249.

maturity is not strictly due to their melody. Wordsworth originated no metre of novel rhythm, no fresh notes " of linkéd sweetness long drawn out," though his was the age when Coleridge lived and Keats and Shelley sang. It was in blank verse, the form which was, in fact, best suited to his puritan severity, that he excelled—a point of resemblance between him and the Milton of those later years when the sweet singer of *Lycidas* had become the bard of *Paradise Lost*, and was half ashamed of the exquisite "jingling sound of like endings" he had loved in his youth. So far as he was able, Wordsworth endeavoured to write verse which should be beautiful by its *soul* alone.

Even in nature the sounds preferred by Wordsworth were preferred, not on account of their sweetness or their melody, but because of their meaning, their striking peculiarity, the emblem he discerned in them, or the spiritual state which they occasioned. The cuckoo's singular note or the murmur of the turtle dove were dearer and more inspiring to him than the trills of the nightingale. The raven's croak and the hoot of the owl are, of all nature's voices, those of which he has best felt and reproduced the effects.

And what of the other senses? To read his work it would appear that there were none. Yet the poet does not seem to have repressed them out of prudence,—to have controlled them upon principle. There are grounds for believing that they were naturally rudimentary with him (he himself admitted as much with regard to scent), and that they gradually became extinct from want of use; since the only powers which Wordsworth delighted to exercise were the "two sublime faculties of seeing and hearing," which alone spontaneously yielded him new and profound materials for thought. The consequence is that his poems contain practically nothing that did not come to him either through hearing or through sight, for he had too much individuality and sincerity to reproduce anything but his own impressions. His poetry is, in truth,—and we wish that there were some means of saying so with the effect not of uttering a criticism but of specifying its limitations,—as devoid of perfume and of flavour as any in existence. No poet ever decked his garden with flowers more chaste, less over-powering, less intoxicating. His favourites, beloved already not on account of their beauty, but for their rustic air or their modest appearance, such as the daisy or small celandine, have no scent. He did not breathe those " soul-dissolving odours " so dear to Shelley. Roses are seldom met with in his poetry, their fragrance scarcely once. He was but partially successful in rendering the spirit of flowers, and shows more insight in his descriptions of birds and streams, the pure objects of sight and hearing.[1]

So, too, that splendid frugality, which enabled him for years to live in independence on the most slender resources, found its mainstay in the weakness of the sensuous element in his own nature. The poet does not appear to have been more sensitive to the succulence than to the perfume of objects. Not, of course, that long descriptions of Rabelaisian banquets are necessary to betray the existence of this sense. One of the most spiritual among poets reveals it by a couple of lines,

> Ce jour s'est écoulé comme fond dans la bouche
> Un fruit délicieux sous la dent qui le touche.[2]

We should seek vainly in Wordsworth for a trace of one of these pleasures of taste. When he describes a rustic meal, the viands spread upon the white cloth are regarded as objects of beauty with which the eye alone can make acquaintance. The butter which the Solitary of *The Excursion* sets before his guests seems only meant to be looked at :

> cakes of butter curiously embossed,
> Butter that had imbibed from meadow-flowers
> A golden hue, delicate as their own
> Faintly reflected in a lingering stream.[3]

[1] On this point compare his poem *To the Daisy* or *To the Celandine* with that marvellous piece, *The Green Linnet*, or with the description of the stream in *It was an April Morning*.

[2] *Jocelyn*, first epoch, ll. 1-2.   [3] *The Excursion*, ii. 678-681.

And when the sober, water-drinking poet endeavours to enter into and to express the delights of intoxication—a weakness for which, by way of exception, he had the same indulgence as Rousseau—whether he is giving an opinion on the *Tam o' Shanter* of Burns,[1] or celebrating the adventures of Benjamin the waggoner,[2] he sees nothing in it but that glorious transformation of objects, that momentary alleviation of the burden of life, that peculiar and in its way illuminative ecstasy, which follow the sensual pleasure of the drinker.

Hence, while there is no necessity to suppose a kind of virtuous self-mutilation, a chastened sensibility which seems natural to the poet. Hence, too, something virginal in the image of nature as reflected in him. And hence a pure and healthy moral philosophy, built up from materials provided by the senses alone. The poet, it is true, cannot entirely ignore the other side of sensualism. It is true, also, that it would be unreasonable to argue from the fact that he scarcely admits this in his work to the existence of an absolutely angelic sensibility in Wordsworth as a man.[3] Notwithstanding, although a fear of sadness was the constant shadow of his optimism, which only emerged triumphant after a painful struggle, his faith in the morality of the senses remained almost unshaken. If nature is suspected of recommending sensuality, it is not in Europe—

---

[1] *A letter to a friend of Robert Burns*, 1816 (Prose Works, ii. pp. 1-19).
[2] *The Waggoner.*
[3] It may be allowed to De Quincey that Wordsworth's intellectual passions, like those of all great and original poets, were founded on a " preternatural animal sensibility." But it is difficult to follow De Quincey (who moreover contradicts himself more than once on this point) when he says that this sensibility was "diffused through *all* the animal passions (or appetites)." For a contradiction of this assertion read the account of Wordsworth's marriage in Knight, *Life of Wordsworth*, Vol. I. ch. xvi. See also the only poem in which Wordsworth attempted to describe sensual love, where, after a few fine lines, he acknowledges his incompetence. He is speaking of the first bliss of gratified passion :—

> I pass the raptures of the pair ;—such theme
> Is, by innumerable poets, touched
> In more delightful verse than skill of mine
> Could fashion ; chiefly by that darling bard
> Who told of Juliet and her Romeo.
> *Vandracour and Julia*, ll. 87-91.

except perhaps on the shores of the lake of Como—at any
rate not in England.   If anywhere it has so evil an
influence it is in some distant region of the tropics, in
Georgia for example, where the seducer of *Ruth* contracted
his licentious habits.

> The wind, the tempest roaring high,
> The tumult of a tropic sky
> Might well be dangerous food
> For him, a Youth to whom was given
> So much of earth, so much of heaven,
> And such impetuous blood.
>
> Whatever in those climes he found
> Irregular in sight or sound
> Did to his mind impart
> A kindred impulse, seem'd allied
> To his own powers, and justified
> The workings of his heart.
>
> Nor less, to feed voluptuous thought,
> The beauteous forms of nature wrought,
> Fair trees and lovely flowers;
> The breezes their own languor lent;
> The stars had feelings which they sent
> Into those magic bowers.

Still, the enervating influence of those regions is probably
exaggerated:

> Yet, in his worst pursuits I ween
> That sometimes there did intervene
> Pure hopes of high intent:
> For passions linked to forms so fair
> And stately, needs must have their share
> Of noble sentiment.[1]

With this exception, so reluctantly admitted, Nature is
moral and self-restrained.   Her happiness, the reflection of
the poet's own, is almost spiritual.   Victor Hugo's simple
quatrain, which appeals to every sense at once,

[1] *Ruth* (1799).

Parfums et clartés nous-mêmes
Nous baignons nos coeurs heureux
Dans les effluves suprêmes
Des éléments amoureux,[1]

is a more complete rendering of the physical effect of
spring than all the lines, numerous and beautiful as they
are, and often superior in accuracy of detail and solidity
of painting, in which Wordsworth has sung the praises of
that season. Observe the spiritualized and almost religious
expression which Wordsworth gives to the same mood:

It is the first mild day of March:
Each minute sweeter than before,
The redbreast sings from the tall larch
That stands beside our door.

There is a blessing in the air,
Which seems a sense of joy to yield
To the bare trees, and mountains bare,
And grass in the green field.

.   .   .   .   .

Love, now an universal birth,
From heart to heart is stealing,
From earth to man, from man to earth:
—It is the hour of feeling.

One moment now may give us more
Than fifty years of reason;
Our minds shall drink at every pore
The spirit of the season.

Some silent laws our hearts may make,
Which they shall long obey;
We for the year to come may take
Our temper from to-day.

And from the blessed power that rolls
About, below, above;
We'll frame the measure of our souls,
They shall be tuned to love.[2]

[1] Victor Hugo, *Les Contemplations*, I. livre ii., Après l'hiver.
[2] *To my Sister* (*Lyrical Ballads*, 1798).

The poet is speaking to his sister. And is it not in truth a fraternal love—the strongest and most passionate form of affection which he ever knew—that the poet feels for nature also, that he receives from her and lavishes upon her? He is no lover for whom every veil is cast aside. He never communes with her but in the chaster hours of thought and feeling; their intimacy stops short of certain subjects upon which they never touch. It is not a procreative nature of which he sings.

Neither is it the nature which destroys. And indeed since no one has seen more than a few of her innumerable aspects, how can we portray her according to the conception he had formed? He found that conception mirrored in the region where his youth had been spent, and his life was shortly to pass by, among the fair hills of Cumberland, where no avalanche nor wild animal is to be dreaded, and scenes of awful sublimity and desolate solitudes are alike unknown, where slumber lakes innocent of shipwreck, and streams which never become torrents fall in joyous cascades, where the peasant builds and cultivates without fear that his work will be overwhelmed by the lava of the volcano, or that the earth will be rent asunder beneath his feet. A beautiful nature, presenting no great dangers, impossible to regard as an enemy; sufficiently terrifying in aspect to send a shudder through the little Hawkshead schoolboy, yet not enough to overwhelm the man for whom her fiercest wrath is but a delicious incitement to his meditations.

Though formerly the nature of which he sings may have been hostile to human beings, she has since then formed alliance with them, adapting herself to their needs; and now that they are—many of them—sufficiently free from material cares to enjoy her beauty, to observe her forms and colours, and to admire the blossoms of plants which had at first attracted them only by their fruits, she spreads that beauty before them in profusion.

What a happy result of narrowness of vision! How fortunate that deficiency in the senses of the poet! He will be able to "find his wisdom in his bliss."[1] In the very

---

[1] *The kitten and the falling leaves.*

course of his diligent search for real fact, and notwithstanding his refusal to allow himself to be deluded by fancy, he will make his dwelling in a reality more delightful than illusion. Not to the land of utopia, not to the coming of the millennium, does he defer the realization of his dreams of unalloyed happiness and ideal beauty; it is within himself that he succeeds in uniting, or rather that he unites without an effort, the true with the good and both with the beautiful. Conscious of having renounced illusion in order to perceive that which is, and of having found that which is to be not only magnificent but moral, he is able to proclaim the good news to mankind in all sincerity.

Conclusion

I

DURING the latter part of his residence at Alfoxden Wordsworth arrived at a full consciousness of his moral and poetic mission. The part which he was to play was already taking definite shape before his eyes. The poet's actual lot forms a strange contrast to the lofty ambition he entertained.

At first sight nothing in his appearance gave promise of the wonderful future so eloquently predicted for him by Coleridge to every one he met.[1] Wordsworth was not handsome, as even his sister was obliged to acknowledge; his long bony face was supported by a spare body, with narrow, sloping shoulders, and ill-shaped legs meant for use, says De Quincey, rather than for ornament. There was not a particle of elegance about him; the portrait taken in 1798, which represents him as dressed in a dark frock coat with thick lappels, his neck and even his chin stiffly confined in the ponderous white cravat of the period, has all the awkwardness and the gravity of a young farmer dressed out in his best clothes. His ordinary attire was more characteristic. Hazlitt found him "in a brown fustian jacket and striped pantaloons." Possibly he was wearing the famous pair of huge, heavy shoes which Lamb, one day when they happened to be in his possession, exhibited to his London friends as provincial curiosities.[2] When he walked there was a lounging roll in his gait

[1] A certain Richard Reynall, who, through the influence of Coleridge, was predisposed to admire Wordsworth, wrote in August, 1797: "[I visited] Alfoxden, a country seat occupied by a Mr Wordsworth, of living men one of the greatest—at least, Coleridge, who has seen most of the great men of this country, says he is; and I, *who have seen Wordsworth again since*, am inclined very highly to estimate him. He has certainly physiognomical traits of genius. He has a high manly forehead, a full and comprehensive eye, a strong nose to support the superstructure, and altogether a very pleasing and striking countenance." *Illustrated London News*, 22nd April 1893. (Unpublished Letters of S. T. Coleridge.)

[2] Letter to Coleridge, 4th November 1802.

suggestive of his pedlar hero, Peter Bell. He spoke
"with a mixture of clear gushing accents in his voice, a
deep guttural intonation, and a strong tincture of the
northern burr, like the crust in wine."[1]

But he requires to be seen in repose ; his features should
be long and carefully scrutinized. Even then the poet in
him is not at once revealed. What impresses us is the
appearance of animal health, indicated by the powerful jaw
with its strong white teeth, and by the prominence and
fulness of all the parts around the mouth. Tempered at
present by a bronzed complexion set in a frame of auburn
hair, this healthy look will become more and more marked
when a ruddy and sanguine hue, destined gradually to re-
place the sunburnt tint, is thrown into relief as auburn
turns to grey.

The next thing that strikes the observer is the strength
of the will, discernible in the angular chin, and in the lips,
firmly closed in spite of the heaviness of the jaw ; whence
something of a grin, "a convulsive inclination to laughter
about the mouth, a good deal at variance with the solemn,
stately expression of the rest of the face " ;[2] and a drawn
appearance in the painfully furrowed cheeks. It resides in
the powerful and sharply-outlined Roman nose, and in the
high retreating forehead with its deep temples. Wordsworth's countenance early began to look old, and its
lines, already careworn, are indicative of suppressed
struggles, pains taken to bridle a violent and irritable
disposition, the tension of solitary thought, and the
workings of an inward fire which itself becomes visible
only when the eye, raising its heavy lids, takes on at
certain hours the strange expression described by Hazlitt,
Leigh Hunt, and De Quincey.

And predominant over all other characteristics are those
of solemn gravity, fixity of thought, honest and concentrated enthusiasm. Hazlitt's first sight of Wordsworth
reminded him of Don Quixote, and odd, irreverent even
as the comparison may seem, it is sufficiently expressive of
that almost painful tension of a single thought which was
madness in the one case and genius in the other. De

[1] Hazlitt, *My first acquaintance with poets.*   [2] *Ibid.*

Quincey detected a striking resemblance between Wordsworth at forty years of age and the stern-looking portrait of Milton painted by Faithorne a few years before the death of the great puritan and republican poet. We, too, cannot help seeing in young Wordsworth's portrait one of the purest types of that revolutionary epoch when faith in earthly happiness was held by many with all the solemnity of a religion.

Yet how few at that time saw anything in Wordsworth beyond the first outward appearance of awkwardness and vulgarity! With the exception of his sister, Coleridge, and Poole, there was perhaps not a soul about him who had thorough confidence in his powers and in his destiny. Only the closest intimacy could bring out the passionate affection hidden in his heart, the profound thoughts concealed within his mind. Fond of conversation and even talkative as he afterwards became, he was at this time scarcely beginning to acquire that readiness in connecting ideas which conversation demands. "His genius," says Coleridge, "rarely, except to me in *tête-à-tête*, breaks forth in conversational eloquence."[1] He possessed the gift, and the love, of silence.[2]

> He is retired as noontide dew,
>   Or fountain in a noon-day grove ;
> And you must love him, ere to you
>   He will seem worthy of your love.[3]

Poor, and as yet bound by neither tie nor expectation to the powerful and the fortunate, he had broken with his family, with every calling in life, with all political parties and religious creeds.[4] No road to fame and happiness remained open to him but that of poetry.

---

[1] Letter to the Rev. J. P. Estlin, May, 1798. (*Letters of S. T. Coleridge*, edited by Ernest Coleridge, i. p. 246).

[2] De Quincey, *The Lake Poets*, Wordsworth.   [3] *A Poet's Epitaph* (1799).

[4] In the letter quoted above, Coleridge wrote to the Rev. J. P. Estlin, a unitarian minister, as follows: "On one subject we are habitually silent; we found our data dissimilar, and never renewed the subject. It is his practice and almost his nature to convey all the truth he knows without any attack on what he supposes falsehood, if that falsehood be interwoven with virtues or happiness. He loves and venerates Christ and Christianity. I wish he did more, but it were wrong indeed if an incoincidence with any one of our wishes altered our respect and affection to a man of whom we are, as it were, instructed by one great Master to say that not being against us he is for us."

II

But in the realm of poetry all his high hopes, all his ambition, whether for himself or for mankind, had taken refuge.

He possessed a consciousness of having been elected to a sacred office. Everything around him was suffused with a light which emanated from himself.

> To me I feel
> That an internal brightness is vouchsafed
> That must not die, that must not pass away.
> Why does this inward lustre fondly seek,
> And gladly blend with outward fellowship ?
> Why do *they* shine around me whom I love ?
>
> . . . . . .
>
> Possessions have I that are solely mine,
> Something within which yet is shared by none,
> Not even the nearest to me and most dear,
> Something which power and effort may impart,
> I would impart it, I would spread it wide.[1]

"Divinely taught" himself, he had no right to remain silent. He had within him the genius which is "the introduction of a new element into the intellectual universe," of which "the only infallible sign is the widening the sphere of human sensibility for the delight, honour, and benefit of human nature."[2]

It was his to accomplish the highest earthly mission, that which formerly belonged to the priest, and the philosopher and the scientist had since vainly endeavoured to fulfil in his place ; namely, to tell to men the ultimate truths concerning life and the world. Or rather, it behoved him, emancipated alike from dogma and from reasoning, to make men *see* the beauty of the universe and the grandeur of the human heart—a real beauty, a true grandeur, requiring not to be invented but to be laid bare.

Never before had poetry conceived so high an opinion of itself. In the most ambitious poems of the eighteenth

---

[1] *The Recluse,* 695-710.
[2] *Essay supplementary to the Preface of the Poems.*

century it modestly represented itself as a clear and attractive medium for popularizing philosophical ideas.[1] It gloried, not in discovering truth, but in disseminating, to the best of its power, truths discovered already. Even the daring and spirited poets of the Renaissance had been far from attaining the new conception. They had prided themselves upon creating a marvellous world of beauty and of virtue, but had never supposed that the universe they had created was the same as that which their own feet had trodden. In Bacon's phrase, they had "satisfied the soul, which feels the emptiness and the vanity of the real, with shadows." [2] Milton alone had been deeply conscious that a revelation was entrusted to him. He was inspired by "that eternal Spirit, who can enrich with all utterance and knowledge, and sends out his seraphim, with the hallowed fire of his altar, to touch and purify the lips of whom he pleases." [3] He had been genuinely convinced that poetry, as he conceived it, was truer than, and independent of, science, though only upon condition that it went hand in hand with religion, and devoted itself to interpreting the sacred volumes to mankind.

Wordsworth was shaking himself free from all philosophical or religious subjection. For him the poet, using no bible but nature, was the *Seer* whose keener senses and fresher and more integral imagination make him the supreme teacher, whose office it is to render men better and happier by revealing to them their own nature and that of the universe in which they dwell. With the stubborn faith of the unrecognised prophet, Wordsworth, at a later time, described the nature of that moral revolution which he did not doubt of effecting by means of his poetry, and it was with the tones and almost in the words of Christ that he consoled one of his admirers for the disparagement to which he was himself subjected. Alluding to his poems he writes :—

" Trouble not yourself about their present reception ; of what moment is that compared with what I trust is their

---

[1] See the Preface to Pope's *Essay on Man*.
[2] *De augmentis Scientiarum*, lib. II., ch. xiii. p. 3.
[3] *The Reason of Church Government*.

destiny? To console the afflicted; to add sunshine to daylight by making the happy happier; to teach the young and the gracious of every age, to see, to think, and feel, and therefore to become more actively and securely virtuous—this is their office, which I trust they will faithfully perform long after we (that is, all that is mortal of us) are mouldered in our graves."[1]

Twenty years after these proud lines were written they received a brilliant confirmation in the impression made by the reading of Wordsworth's poems upon a young man in whom the intense and painful intellectualism of his generation was personified. John Stuart Mill passed through a mental crisis similar to that which Wordsworth had experienced, and almost at the same age. Misuse of analysis had dried up the springs of feeling within him, and though he still prosecuted the researches whereby he hoped to promote the good of humanity, he failed to derive the least satisfaction from the noble work of his intelligence. "There seemed no power in nature sufficient to begin the formation of my character anew, and create in a mind now irretrievably analytic, fresh associations of pleasure with any of the objects of human desire."[2] He was convinced that his safety lay in the cultivation of the feelings, but he did not yet understand how to cultivate them himself. The reading of Wordsworth in the autumn of 1828 was one of the important events of his life. Of Wordsworth's poems he says:

"In them I seemed to draw from a source of inward joy, of sympathetic and imaginative pleasure, which could be shared in by all human beings; which had no connexion with struggle or imperfection, but would be made richer by every improvement in the physical or social condition of mankind. From them I seemed to learn what would be the perennial sources of happiness, when all the greater evils of life shall have been removed. And I felt myself at once better and happier as I came under their influence.

---

[1] Letter to Lady Beaumont, 21st May 1807. Knight, *Life of Wordsworth*, ii. p. 88.

[2] *Autobiography*, by J. S. Mill, 1873, ch. v. (French translation by M. E. Cazelles).

. . . The result was that I gradually, but completely, emerged from my habitual depression, and was never again subject to it."

Thus, by means of his own impressions, Stuart Mill has expressed the gratitude which thousands of unknown readers, suffering in various degrees from the same complaint, have felt towards the poet. Yet for Stuart Mill, scarcely a trustworthy judge of pure poetry, Wordsworth was only " the poet of unpoetical natures." To the pleasures he owed to the happy character of the general impetus which Wordsworth gave to his mind must be added that more direct and more exquisite enjoyment which others derived from an art doubtless not free from faults, but nevertheless many a time capable of enshrining beauty in adequate verse, or even in poems of unblemished perfection.

Appendix I

A COMPARISON of the following parallel passages will show in what manner Wordsworth was indebted to Ramond de Carbonnières:—

Descriptive Sketches, ll. 372-380.

Thro' vacant worlds where Nature
    never gave
A brook to murmur or a bough to
    wave,
Which unsubstantial Phantoms
    sacred keep ;
Thro' worlds where Life and Sound,
    and Motion sleep,
Where Silence still her death-like
    reign extends,
Save when the startling cliff un-
    frequent rends :
In the deep snow the mighty ruin
    drown'd,
Mocks the dull ear of Time with
    deaf abortive sound.

Ramond, Vol. I. pp. 213-4.

" C'est une chose nouvelle et sur-
prenante pour un habitant de la
plaine, que le silence absolu qui
règne sur cette plateforme [du Saint
Gothard] : on n'entend pas le
moindre murmure; le vent qui traverse
les cieux ne rencontre point ici un
feuillage dont l'agitation bruyante
trahisse son passage ; seulement,
lorsqu'il est impétueux, il gémit
d'une manière lugubre contre les
pointes des rochers qui le divisent. . ."

Ramond, Vol. II. pp. 135-6.

" Un silence éternel règne sur
cette région isolée. Si, de loin
en loin, une lavange tombe dans
ses précipices, si un rocher roule
sur ses glaces, ce bruit sera isolé ;
. . . les tortueux labyrinthes
de ces monts, tapissés d'une neige
qui les assourdit recevront en silence
ce son que nul autre ne suivra."

Descriptive Sketches, 380-389.

—To mark a planet's pomp and
    steady light
In the least star of scarce-appearing
    night,
And neighbouring moon, that coasts
    the vast profound,
Wheel pale and silent her diminish'd
    round,

Ramond, I. p. 261.

" Du haut de notre rocher, nous
avions une de ces vues dont on ne
jouit que dans les Alpes les plus
élevées. . . . Rien de plus majes-
tueux que le ciel vu de ces hauteurs :
pendant la nuit, les étoiles sont des
étincelles brillantes dont la lumière
plus pure n'éprouve pas ce tremble-

While far and wide the icy summits
  blaze
Rejoicing in the glory of her rays;
The star of noon that glitters small
  and bright,
Shorn of his beams, insufferably
  white,
And flying fleet behind his orb to
  view
Th' interminable sea of sable blue.

ment qui les distingue ordinairement
des planètes ; la lune, notre sœur et
notre compagne dans les tourbillons
célestes, paraît plus près de nous,
quoique son diamètre soit extrême-
ment diminué ; elle repose les yeux
qui s'égarent dans l'immensité : on
voit que c'est un globe qui voyage
dans le voisinage de notre planète.
Le soleil aussi offre un spectacle
nouveau : petit et presque dépourvu
de rayons, il brille cependant d'un
éclat incroyable, et sa lumière est
d'une blancheur éblouissante ; on est
étonné de voir son disque nettement
tranché et contrastant avec l'obscur-
ité profonde d'un ciel dont le bleu
foncé semble fuir loin derrière cet
astre, et donne une idée imposante
de l'immensité dans laquelle nous
errons."

Descriptive Sketches, 390-1.

Of cloudless suns no more ye frost-
  built spires
Refract in rainbow hues the restless
  fires.

Ramond, I. p. 260.

"Les sommets épouvantables qui
bordaient cette vallée, couverts
comme elle de neiges et de glaciers,
réfléchissaient les rayons du soleil
sons toutes les nuances qui sont
entre le blanc et l'azur."

Descriptive Sketches, 392-7.

Ye dewy mists the arid rocks o'erspread
Whose slippery face derides his[1]
  deathful tread !
—To wet the peak's impracticable
  sides
He opens of his feet the sanguine
  tides,
Weak and more weak the issuing
  current eyes
Lapp'd by the panting tongue of
  thirsty skies.

Ramond, I. p. 301.

"Des orages subits mouillent les
roches et les rendent si glissantes, que
la chaussure, quelque bien ferrée
qu'elle soit, ne peut s'y cramponner ;
quelquefois la chaleur a tellement des-
séché leurs faces brulantes et les a cou-
vertes d'une poussière si mobile, que
le malheureux qui les gravit s'est vu
forcé de les humecter avec son sang
en se faisant à la plante des pieds et
aux jambes de larges coupures."

Descriptive Sketches, 474-491.

Far different life to what tradition
  hoar
Transmits of days more bless'd in
  times of yore.
Then Summer lengthen'd out his
  season bland,

Ramond, I. p. 280.

"Malgré cette prodigieuse fécondité
[des vaches en laitage], ces bons
bergers imaginent un tems où elle a
été plus considérable : la tradition
leur a, disent-ils, transmis la mémoire
d'un âge heureux où les glacières

[1] *i.e. the chamois hunter.*

And with rock-honey flow'd the happy land.
Continual fountains welling chear'd the waste,
And plants were wholesome, now of deadly taste.
Nor Winter yet his frozen stores had pil'd
Usurping where the fairest herbage smil'd;
Nor Hunger forc'd the herds from pastures bare
For scanty food the treacherous cliffs to dare.
Then the milk-thistle bad those herds demand
Three times a day the pail and welcome hand.
But human vices have provok'd the rod
Of angry Nature to avenge her God.
Thus does the father to his sons relate,
On the lone mountain top, their chang'd estate.
Still, Nature, ever just, to him imparts
Joys only given to uncorrupted hearts.

n'avaient pas encore envahi la plus belle partie de leurs Alpes ; alors les plantes maintenant vénéneuses étaient saines : les *tithymales* augmentaient de leur lait celui des vaches, et l'on pouvait les traire trois fois par jour. Les péchés des hommes, ajoutent-ils, ont attiré la malédiction du Ciel et les glaces sur leurs paturages. Ces traditions sont précieuses, dans quelque sens qu'on les considère."

Appendix II
Additions and corrections to the First Edition.

A QUARTER of a century has elapsed since this book was first published. In the meanwhile some important additions have been made to our knowledge of Wordsworth's life which closely affect the interpretation of his poetry. Here follows a list of the chief works from which new information can be gathered:

Dorothy Wordsworth's Journals, edited by W. Knight, 2 vols., 1897.
E. Yarnall, Wordsworth and the Coleridges, 1899.
Letters of the Wordsworth Family from 1787 to 1855, pub. in 1907.
Biographia Epistolaris, being the biographical supplement of Coleridge's Biographia Literaria, with additional letters, Ed. Turnbull, 2 vols., 1911.
Coleridge's letters hitherto uncollected. Ed. Prideaux. Privately printed 1913.
Letters written by Dorothy Wordsworth to Mrs Clarkson. (British Museum. Additional MSS. 36,997.)
Sir Walter Raleigh. Wordsworth, 1903 (a masterpiece).
A Beatty— { Joseph Fawcett: The Art of War—Its relation to the early Development of W. Wordsworth. (Univ. of Wisconsin Studies in Language and Literature, No. 2.)
Wordsworth and Hartley.
The Nation, 17th July 1913. New York.

O. J. Campbell. Sentimental Morality in Wordsworth's narrative
  Poetry. (Univ. of Wisconsin Studies in Language and Literature,
  No. 2, 1921.)
E. C. Knowlton. The Novelty of Wordsworth's *Michael* as a Pastoral.
  (Pub. of the Modern Language Association of America, xxviii. 4.)

But by far the most considerable contribution to the poet's biography
is the work of Professor J. M. Harper, of Princeton University:

William Wordsworth : His life, works and influence. 2 vols., John
  Murray, London, 1916.

The first volume covers the same period of Wordsworth's life that I
retraced in my study of *The Prelude.* It brings to light several facts
which, had I known them when I wrote, would have induced me to alter
or complete some of my statements.

Besides the new particulars he drew from the publication of the afore-
named journals, letters and documents, Professor Harper has increased
our knowledge of the poet's youth by personal research. During a
prolonged stay he made at Blois, he gathered much curious information
on the political societies that flourished in that city while Wordsworth
lived there, and the third chapter of B. II. of the present work has to be
supplemented by Chapters VII and VIII. of his own (also by his article on
Wordsworth at Blois, in *The Texas Review,* July 1916).

But the fact of greatest importance from a psychological point of
view, among those first made public by Prof. Harper, is beyond doubt
Wordsworth's liaison with a young French lady during his residence in
France in 1792, which resulted in the birth of a daughter.

While preparing this revised edition I thought of making further
research into that love episode and giving the results in this Appendix.
But my discoveries have been so many and have appeared to me so suggestive that I have decided to develop them into a separate publication. I
therefore confine myself to the statement of the following facts:

The French lady loved by Wordsworth was Marie Anne Léonard, dite
Vallon, born at Blois on 22nd June 1766. She belonged to a family
which for several generations had engaged in the practice of surgery.
Her father was Jean Leonard, dit Vallon, maître en chirurgie at Blois,
her mother dame Françoise Yvon.

Wordsworth made her acquaintance in the winter of 1791-2 at Orleans,
where she was probably staying with her brother Paul, "clerc de notaire"
in that town. Wordsworth's changes of residence from Orleans to Blois
and back to Orleans were conditioned, out of doubt, by those of the young
lady herself. She was twenty-five years old when he met her ; her
brother was twenty-nine.

It is not yet known whether a marriage was contemplated nor whether
the obstacle came from the poet or from the young lady's family, though
it seems more probable to ascribe the refusal to the Vallons who were out-
and-out Royalists. Wordsworth had become a determined Republican in
the summer of 1792. He was moreover nominally a Protestant, practically a free-thinker, and besides was too poor to maintain a family, either
in France or in England.

A daughter was born to them at Orleans on 15th December 1792, and
christened Anne Caroline Wordwodsth (*sic*). This curious baptismal
document was first pointed out to me by Professor Harper. She was
owned by the poet, but he had then left Orleans for Paris and was not
present at the christening. Paul Vallon stood godfather to the child.

The Vallons suffered great misfortunes under the Terror. Paul Vallon was
compromised in the pretended royalist assault against the " représentant
du peuple," Léonard Bourdon, at Orleans in March 1793, for which nine

Orleans citizens were guillotined. He himself only escaped death by flight and concealment. His sister appears to have helped him (and probably helped other suspected persons) at the peril of her own life. Dorothy tells Mrs Clarkson that Annette "from the first was a zealous Royalist, has often risked her life in defence of adherents to that cause, and she despised and detested Buonaparte" (Harper, II. p. 214). Dorothy says elsewhere that "owing to her over-generous disposition she and her daughter had to struggle through many difficulties" (*Ibid.* p. 211).

We occasionally hear of Annette (the mother) and Caroline (the daughter) in Dorothy's letters or journals. Annette kept up a correspondence with Wordsworth, but her letters did not always reach him on account of the state of war between the two countries. On 30th November 1795, Dorothy wrote to her friend Mrs Marshall (formerly Miss Pollard): "William has had a letter from France since we came here (*i.e.* Racedown). Annette mentions having despatched half-a-dozen, none of which he has received."

Several allusions to other letters from or to Annette (or "poor Annette") are found in Dorothy's Journals from 21st December 1801 to 26th March 1802. This epistolary commerce culminated in an appointment at Calais, after the peace of Amiens, where William and Dorothy spent four weeks from August 1 to August 29, with Annette and Caroline, just before William's marriage to Mary Hutchinson.

Then follows another gap in the correspondence owing to the re-awakening of the war. When Annette left Blois or Orleans to settle in Paris with her daughter is not known. But they were living in Paris, 35 rue du Paradis (quartier du Faubourg Poissonnière) when the French king was first restored, or came there as soon as the Restoration took place. Annette could now look forward to better things. She had "the promise of a place for herself or one of her family, in recompense for services performed by her for the royal cause" (Harper, II. p. 217). Caroline, who was over twenty-one in October 1814, was to be married to M. Jean Baptiste Martin Baudouin, "chef de Bureau au Mont de Piété." We read much about the project of marriage in Dorothy's letters to Mrs Clarkson (Harper, Vol. II. p. 211-8). J. B. Baudouin was the elder brother of Eustace Baudouin, a young officer, "instructeur en chef de la Compagnie Écossaise," who had visited the Wordsworths in England and was called a friend by them. The wedding was long put off on account of Napoleon's return from Elba, and also because mother and daughter wished the Wordsworths to be present.

The ceremony finally took place with great "éclat" on 20th February 1816, without the Wordsworths, but with the poet's legal authorization. Caroline was this time described as the daughter of "Williams (*sic*) Wordsworth (with the spelling duly rectified), propriétaire, demeurant à Grasner Kendan (*sic*) duché de Westermorland (*sic*) in Angleterre." It would seem from Dorothy's letters that she received some small dowry from her father.

On the 27th of December 1816, a daughter was born to the Baudouins, to whom Wordsworth was godfather by proxy, and who was given the name of Louise Marie Caroline *Dorothée*.

Some time after the wedding, Madame Vallon and the Baudouins, who seem to have lived together, removed to 47 rue Charlot, quartier du Temple, where they were visited by the poet, his wife and sister, together with their friend, Crabbe Robinson, in October 1820.

After 1820 we no longer find their names in those papers of the Wordsworth family which have been published.

Annette died in Paris on the 10th of January 1841, aged seventy-five. She is designated on the register as "Marie Anne Vallon, *dite William*."

She then lived at 11 Boulevart des Filles du Calvaire, about five minutes' walk from rue Charlot. She seems to have obtained from the Bourbon government, besides a small pension, the post she coveted in 1816 and have kept it till her death (she never became rich), for she is in her death certificate denominated an "employée."

Her daughter survived her more than twenty years, and died in Paris on the 8th of July 1862.

Wordsworth's relations to Annette and Caroline were no secret to his family nor to his intimate friends. Coleridge, Crabbe Robinson, Mrs Clarkson, Mrs Marshall, and others, knew them. Wordsworth as a man behaved honourably, never concealed the fact, nor lost sight of his responsibilities towards the child who bore his name.

As a poet he was, at least from an artistic point of view, reticent to a fault, maimed his autobiographical recollections and presented to the public a partial, incomplete, and, to a certain extent, enfeebled, image of his life and feelings. He was, of course, fully justified in refusing to tell a story the secret of which did not belong to him alone. But a more open avowal, in general terms, of his youthful passions could have harmed neither him, nor Annette, nor the reader.

The newly revealed facts constrain us to touch up several statements made in this book :

P. 14, l. 29. Wordsworth had some excellent reasons for not saying everything concerning himself.

Pp. 157-8. The melancholy that colours the *Descriptive Sketches* was not so artificial as we (following *The Prelude*) had represented it. When he wrote the poem, he was really haunted by " Crazing Care," and " Desperate Love."

As he thought of the unwedded mother, he might well feel " Conscience dogging close his bleeding way."

P. 159, l. 24. We were wrong in affirming that he had no opportunity to develop his melancholy mood while he was in France.

B. II. ch. ii. The whole chapter ought to be supplemented with the love episode. W.'s emotions at the time were surely much more complex than he depicts them in *The Prelude*. Politics did not hold the whole scene; they were probably thrown into the background by Annette.

P. 269, ll. 5-10. Instead of " the temperate line of conduct from which he does not appear to have swerved," read "from which he is now known to have swerved." Surely Wordsworth put even more of himself into the character of the Solitary than I first admitted.

P. 463. The whole page (and specially note 3) ought to be re-written. Long before I was acquainted with the Annette episode, I had come to be dissatisfied with it. I felt I had no right to go against Wordsworth's own statement and De Quincey's always penetrating (though sometimes erroneous) observations.

There *was* self-mutilation in Wordsworth's case. He willingly refrained from the picture of passionate love, not because he could not paint it, not because he was unsensualized or ignorant of the tumult of the soul, but because he *would* not tell his own experiences, and also because the affections (not the passions), and the purified senses, were the basis of his optimistic doctrine.

But there is nothing to change in the conclusion of the chapter. The Nature he celebrates is spiritualized, hence incomplete and in a sense non-existent. Yet, by prolonged omissions of her wilder effects in his poems, he seems in the end to have believed in the reality of her exclusively pure, serene, and benignant power

April 1921.

Index